★ NEW ENGLAND STUDIES ★

Edited by John Putnam Demos, David Hackett Fischer, and Robert A. Gross

EDWARD BYERS
The Nation of Nantucket

RICHARD RABINOWITZ
The Spiritual Self in Everyday Life

JOHN R. MULKERN
The Know-Nothing Party in Massachusetts

The Know-Nothing Party in Massachusetts

THE RISE AND FALL
OF A PEOPLE'S MOVEMENT

John R. Mulkern

Northeastern University Press

BOSTON

Northeastern University Press

Copyright © 1990 John R. Mulkern

Library of Congress Cataloging-in-Publication Data
Mulkern, John R.
   The Know-Nothing party in Massachusetts : the rise and fall of a
people's movement / John R. Mulkern.
      p.   cm.
   Includes bibliographical references.
   ISBN   1-55553-071-0
   1. American Party. 2. Massachusetts—Politics and government—1775–
1865. I. Title.
JK2341.A8M84   1990
324.2744'02—dc20   89-28828
                            CIP

Designed by Richard C. Bartlett and Ann Twombly

This book was composed in Bodoni Book by The Composing Room of
Michigan, Inc., in Grand Rapids, Michigan. It was printed and bound by
Hamilton Printing Company in Rensselaer, New York. The paper is
Sebago Antique, an acid-free sheet.

MANUFACTURED IN THE UNITED STATES OF AMERICA
94   93   92   91   90   5   4   3   2   1

To Rita

Contents

Acknowledgments

I AM INDEBTED to Babson College for the support it has afforded me during the many years in which I was engaged in this project. Special thanks go to the Board of Research for having funded part of the research expenses; George Recck, Director of the Computer Center, for his positive response to my many requests; student assistant Daniel Draper, for having prepared the summary results for the tables; and Beverly Balconi, Victoria Delbono, and Concetta Stumpf for having handled with uncommon patience the onerous task of typing the manuscript.

Most of the research for this book took place in the Boston Public Library; Essex Institute (Salem); Houghton and Widener Libraries (Harvard University); Massachusetts State House Library; Massachusetts State Archives; Massachusetts Historical Society; New England Deposit Library; and town and city libraries throughout Massachusetts. I want to extend my thanks to the staffs of all the libraries I visited. Winifred Collins of the Massachusetts Historical Society and Edwin Sanford of the Boston Public Library deserve special mention for their exceptional courtesy and help in locating countless items that I consulted in preparing this book.

I am particularly grateful to my colleagues Stephen Collins and James Hoopes, who read parts of the manuscript and passed on to me their insights, suggestions, and encouragement. The book has benefited from their comments. Another colleague, John McKenzie, was most generous of his time and expertise in assisting me in the task of organizing statistical data.

My principal debt is to Ronald Formisano, whose close critical analysis of the entire manuscript and suggestions for improvement provided me with a guideline for the final revision of the manuscript.

Whatever inadequacies or errors that remain are my own.

THE KNOW-NOTHING PARTY IN MASSACHUSETTS

Introduction

STUDENTS OF ANTEBELLUM politics agree that the collapse of the second American party system in the 1850s triggered the shutdown of the processes of accommodation and compromise that might have moderated sectional passions and averted the tragedy of civil war. However, they are divided on the causes of the downfall, and that is the subject of a heated, ongoing historiographical debate. Some argue that sectional and national controversies over slavery weakened the party system and ultimately brought it crashing down; others, including this writer, attribute its demise to state and local factors.

National politics does not exist in a vacuum. In fact, it may even be argued that all politics is local in the sense that diverse but interrelated elements at all levels of the multilayered federal system fuel the political dynamics of the nation. This certainly was the case in the antebellum era. The critical party battles that mortally wounded the second party system were waged not in Washington but in the states; and the ensuing processes of party dealignment and realignment took place not in the quadrennial presidential contests, but in the annual state elections held between 1852 and 1860. An accurate reading of antebellum politics must take into account the local conditions and concerns responsible for these fateful developments. For this reason, historians like Michael Holt and William Gienapp have called the states the crucial arena of antebellum politics and the proper locus for the study of party transformation in the 1850s.[1]

Massachusetts, like her sister states in the North, shared in the common experience that historians quarry in their efforts to explain the fate of the national party system. Fear of sectional conflict, antislavery sentiment, the determination to check the spread of slavery into the national territories, xenophobia and Catholic-Protestant divisions, and disillusionment with the established parties and professional politicians roiled her political waters; but the currents of the

3

public debate ran as strongly elsewhere, and the particulars were as hotly debated in other political arenas. Yet, in no other state was the collapse of the party system more sudden or so unexpected, and in no other state did the instrument of its destruction draw such strength from the multitude.

In 1854, a new political party, shrouded in secrecy and campaigning only within the confines of a network of members-only lodges, scored its greatest triumph in Massachusetts. Dubbed Know-Nothing by its detractors and American by its founders, the secret order in its first run for statewide office tallied the largest number of votes of any party to that time and swept its candidates—political unknowns, for the most part—into virtually every elective office in the state. Of the three other parties contending the election—Whig, Free-Soil, and Democratic—only the last of these survived the upheaval. Nowhere else in the nation did the American party come close to matching its landslide victory in Massachusetts, and nowhere else did it level the existing party system with a single blow. Despite this promising beginning, its reign was brief and its fall was nearly as precipitous and sudden as that of the second party system. After only three years in power, the Know-Nothings succumbed to another new party, the Republican party, and quickly disappeared.

Why was voter response in 1854 to the same influences operating in all the free states so exceptional in the Commonwealth? Why this extraordinary outpouring of support for Know-Nothingism? And why did Bay State voters suddenly abandon the American party, after having endorsed it in three consecutive elections?

The standard explanation is that the Irish had offended the Yankee Protestant majority by supporting the Fugitive Slave Law and the Kansas-Nebraska Act. Also allegedly disturbing the native-born was Irish opposition to popular local reforms. In 1851, the Free-Soilers and "Locofoco" or antimonopoly Democrats had joined forces to wrest control of the slate from the Whigs. The Free-Soil/Democratic "Coalition" launched a wave of reforms, culminating in a proposed new constitution that was placed on the ballot in the state election of 1853. Its defeat was widely ascribed to the Irish joining their votes to those of the Whigs against it. Determined to curb Irish obstructionism, the Coalitionists and anti-Nebraska men shifted en masse into the Know-Nothing order, where they took their places alongside the party's nativist recruits.[2]

Recent studies employing ecological regression estimates, however, have revealed that there was no significant Irish vote in the early 1850s.[3] It was the solid Whig vote against it that killed constitutional reform in 1853. A year later, when the Whigs contributed more votes to the Know-Nothing total than either the Democrats or Free-Soilers, it was clearly not because they were angry with the Irish for having opposed the constitution. In sum, the Coalition, far from being the engine of Know-Nothingism, was a spent political force that contributed little to the electoral success of the new party.

Among the historians who have most recently examined the rise and fall of the Know-Nothing party in Massachusetts, only Dale Baum challenges the assumption that Know-Nothingism was the successor of the Coalition and progenitor of the Republican party. Baum, however, in ascribing the eventual triumph of Republicanism in Massachusetts almost entirely to the popularity of the antislavery cause in the state, downplays the vital contribution that the American party made both to the transformation of the party system and to the forging of the Republican majority in Massachusetts.[4]

William Gienapp, on the other hand, asserts that the American and Republican parties alike owed their success to tensions arising out of mass immigration and sectional divisions.[5] But if public reaction to these forces explain the success of Know-Nothingism, why should they have exercised their greatest influence in Massachusetts? Other states experiencing the same stresses did not respond to the appeals of the secret order with anywhere near the same degree of enthusiasm. Moreover, if sectional tensions and ethnocultural conflicts had aroused public ire to such a pitch in Massachusetts as to have triggered the mass conversion to Know-Nothingism, why did the state's voters desert the American party in favor of the Republicans after it had chalked up record gains on behalf of the antislavery, prohibition, and nativist causes?

Ronald Formisano approaches the question of the unprecedented popularity of Know-Nothingism in Massachusetts from a different direction, noting that while nativism and anti-Catholicism were the lowest common denominator of the secret order, Know-Nothingism was a populist upheaval of unprecedented proportions that capitalized on the pervasive antiparty feelings at the grass-roots level to attract support from many sources. This certainly was the case; but in locating the source of Know-Nothingism in the small-town, rural-centered Coalition of the early 1850s and the Workingmen's party of the early 1830s, Formisano tends to obscure the urban, industrial focus of Massachusetts' greatest populist movement.[6]

Finally, Michael Holt has noted (as did George Haynes) that a different and greater force brought the antiparty, ethnocultural, and sectional tensions to a boil in the 1850s, and that was rapid social and economic change.[7]

It was indeed the transcendent force of modernization that accounts for the unparalleled strength of Know-Nothingism in Massachusetts. The political fallout from the pressures of modernization, however, included more than the backlash of the native-born majority against immigrants, Catholics, and the South that most historians perceive as the essence of Know-Nothingism. Explosive urban and industrial growth had thrust the Commonwealth into the forefront of the industrializing states in the antebellum period, creating, in the process, wrenching social and economic dislocations. The failure of the established parties to mount a significant response to the myriad issues and problems spawned in the matrix of modernization weakened partisan attachments and set the rank and file of the established parties on a quest for a political vehicle that would make a difference in their lives. In 1854, such a vehicle materialized in the form of an antiparty, antipolitician populist movement that promised to cleanse the statehouse of corrupt old parties and self-serving political careerists and turn the government over to the people so that they might right the wrongs that had for so long afflicted them. Among the afflictions, it is true, were the many social problems associated with mass immigration; but there were other troubling and pervasive concerns endemic to an unharnessed, rapidly expanding urban, industrial order, including the tyrannical factory system, the decline in the status of labor, the widening gulf between rich and poor, and the deteriorating quality of urban life.

Clearly, the causes of the phenomenal Know-Nothing success in Massachusetts were embedded deep within the complex of social, economic, and political conditions prevailing in the state; the results, however, were manifest. The American party, in the span of a single election, drove the state's political elites from power and transformed Massachusetts into a one-party state. Yet, three years later, it, too, was dead, having fallen victim to a new party calling itself Republican and basing its appeal on its nativist, anti-Catholic, prohibitionist, antislavery, and anti-Southern stands.[8]

The turning point in the struggle between the Know-Nothings and the Republicans as to which would survive to challenge the Democrats for control of the national government occurred in 1856. Thanks to a bargain in which the Republicans agreed not to contest the state election in return for Know-Nothing support for John C. Fremont, Know-Nothings cast a majority of the Republican votes in the presidential contest, and Fremont carried the state by a huge margin.[9] In the following year, the Republicans triumphed over the American party and quickly forged a majority at the state level.

Nevertheless, Know-Nothingism was not the progenitor of the Republican party. The American party had met defeat not because of what had happened in the presidential election but because of failures at the state level. In the formative period of its development, the American party had proclaimed itself the people's party, dedicated to serving the people's needs. That promise was its bond with the people, and it had sustained the party's momentum in its drive for control of the state government. The bond was broken, however, once a new set of political elites gained control of the party and converted it into a political organization similar to those the voters had rebelled against in 1854. Having alienated its original supporters by neglecting it populist promises and faced with an ascendant Republican party that was rapidly establishing itself as the dominant party in the North, the American party's hold on the electorate finally snapped. The party that was crushed in 1857, however, bore little resemblance to the grassroots movement of 1854, which had sprung the most amazing election triumph in the history of Massachusetts.

CHAPTER ONE

The Whig Hegemony and the Loyal Opposition

MASSACHUSETTS, whose flinty soil, limited resources, and harsh climate, according to local wits, was best suited for the production of ice and granite, led antebellum America in the rapid expansion of machine and factory production. As early as 1824, manufacturing had replaced commerce as the mainstay of the state's economy. In ensuing years, factories sprouted wherever fast water flowed. Total value of manufacturing, exclusive of farm and sea products, stood at $83 million in 1845; ten years later, it had soared to $215 million, the mark of an industrial growth rate that the Secretary of the Commonwealth proclaimed "without parallel in the history of the world."[1]

The secretary's boast was not without merit. At mid-century, Massachusetts dwarfed her sister states in the production of textiles and footwear, the nation's first- and third-ranking industries. Boot and shoe production in just three counties—Essex, Plymouth, and Worcester—accounted for more than a third of the nation's output. Lowell, known as "the Manchester of America," was home to the largest factories in the country. Lynn had emerged as the shoe capital of the world. Other industries, such as farm equipment, firearms, clothing, shipbuilding, industrial machinery and toolmaking, furniture and upholstery, metals and metal working, and the manufacture of glass, paper, and marine supplies, experienced a similar boom and in the process transformed the state into a beehive of manufacturing.[2] Superb communication and transportation networks—the product of revolutionary technological developments—made accessible the internal and external markets that production of this magnitude demanded. Ubiquitous telegraph wire transmitted messages at the speed of electricity. Oceangoing and coastal vessels hauled freight to far-flung domestic and foreign shores. Massachusetts boasted an outstanding network of railways, which local boosters hailed as without equal in North America. Over eleven hundred miles of tracks—more per square mile than in any other state—threaded their way from the depot city of Boston to every region of the Commonwealth and through linkup points to the nation beyond. Construction of these "great thoroughfares" opened up the remote interior of the state, and by tying into the railroad and canal systems of its neighbor, New York, tapped "the untold riches" of the nation's hinterland, whose agricultural bounty poured in ever-increasing measure "into the lap of Boston."[3] Outward-bound on ribbons of iron flowed the products of the state's factories and shops.

To build the telegraph lines, railroads, ships, and factories, to harness the flowing water and import the coal needed to power industrial machinery, and to expand production through technological development necessitated huge capital outlays, much of which came from the state's merchant princes, bankers, and industrialists (mainly Boston Brahmin money), some from the selling of shares in railroad and manufacturing companies, and the rest from state-backed loans.[4] Government involvement was vital to economic expansion of this magnitude, and this the business interests obtained through their special relationship with the Whig party, the dominant power in state politics.

Boston ranked second only to New York as a financial center, and Boston capital, controlling as it did the major railroads, banks, insurance companies, and manufacturing enterprises, dominated the state and much of the New England region economically. Economic power translated into political power. The medium for this translation was the Boston Associates—a consortium of Boston businessmen who controlled most of the state's major corporations. Statewide the writ of the Associates extended to public policy, thanks to the probusiness Whig party. So long as the Whigs controlled the statehouse—and they did so almost without interruption during the 1830s and 1840s—the mercantile, banking, and manufacturing interests of Boston exerted a controlling influence over legislation that affected their interests. Boston, complained a country Democrat, with "its overwhelming Whig majority, Whig money and Whig influence, has for many years . . . completely monopolized the legislation of the state." Support for the party was strongest in the cities and chief towns where modernization had made its greatest inroads and where the Brahmin-controlled daily press, pulpit, bar, and bench were enrolled in the service of the Whig party.[5] But the party also ran well in the rural hinterland, owing in part to Whig-sponsored internal improvements that had created jobs and raised property values.

Those most dependent on the new economic order for their livelihood—a dependence that cut across the socioeconomic spectrum—tended to gravitate into the Whig orbit. Political opponents ascribed this to the sinister influence of the so-called Money Power. "Wealth," Free-Soiler Henry Wilson said, "exerts a vast and commanding influence" on public affairs in the Commonwealth:

> We are a commercial and manufacturing people. . . . The men who con-
> trol the hundreds of millions of corporate and industrial wealth employed

in the immense manufacturing and mechanical interest of this State, and their agents, overseers, clerks, and master workmen who are dependent upon them for positions of influence and pecuniary value, are very apt to think that the policy of the government affects that interest, and that the laborers and mechanics dependent upon that interest should vote, not according to their own convictions, but according to their supposed interests, or the interests of their employers.[6]

There were other, more positive reasons for Whig electoral successes than critics like Wilson cared to admit, including a booming economy and the popularity of Whiggery's cheerful message that today's worker is tomorrow's capitalist. It was a promise that blurred class lines. The road to riches, or at least to a comfortable old age, lay open to all who worked hard, lived sober lives, and saved money.[7]

This concept of upward mobility sprang from the commonwealth ethos, a patrician vision of an organic society in which an overarching common interest binds together people from all walks of life into a harmonious whole. Whig governor John W. Davis, in his 1841 inaugural address, capsulized the idea for his fellow Bay Staters: "We are agriculturists, manufacturers, mechanics, navigators, fishermen, merchants, each class following its own pursuits but all united closely together by innumerable strong ties in a common interest." The common interest was economic growth, and in the Whig order of things, that necessitated a positive state that would promote expansion through government intervention in the economy on behalf of the commercial-financial-industrial complex.[8]

Whiggery's commitment to an activist state was, in a word, selective. Where private enterprise lacked the capital (or was unwilling to risk it) to underwrite costly but vital internal improvements, the Whig government rushed in with state loans. Public subsidies to railroads and other business enterprises, they explained, brought general prosperity and convenience. Those at the lower end of the socioeconomic scale, on the other hand, had to rely entirely on their own resources to improve their living standards; for as party theorists cautioned, it was not the place of government to "innovate" on behalf of labor lest such misguided philanthropy upset the natural economic balance.[9]

Implicit in the commonwealth ethos was a trickle-down theory: If the Whig stewards made governmental aid and encouragement to business their leading policy, it was to promote the well-being of society as a whole. All Bay Staters had a collective interest in a sound economy, and Massachusetts being preeminently a manufacturing state, her economic condition depended on performance in the industrial sector. So long as the manufacturing interests prosper, reasoned the exponents of the commonwealth concept, all other interests prosper. Relations between capital and labor being mutually dependent, a disruption of the natural harmony of interests, such as a labor strike, would endanger the welfare of all. A majority of voters across the socioeconomic spectrum accepted this rationale, thus ensuring the Brahmins an almost uninterrupted hold on the state government prior to mid-century.[10]

In the social and economic spheres, Whig policy reflected the party's vision of a modern, positive state juxtaposed with a stable, harmonious society. Massachusetts, as the renowned jurist Rufus Choate described it, had evolved under a succession of Whig administrations into

> the most homogeneous community that ever existed . . . a family of persons . . . clustered closely on a little area of seven thousand square miles; every man within a day's ride of every other; all occupations and interests distributed with remarkable uniformity everywhere; and no one tendency . . . to conflict with any other; town linked to county, and county to county, by "cords no man can break."[11]

In the political domain, on the other hand, the party's ideal of rule by notables was rooted in an aristocratic past. The party fathers, cognizant that in the Age of the Common Man it was not politic to approach the electorate as the party of the good, the wise, and the rich, did leaven its slates of nominees with dependable men drawn from the ranks of the humble and did dispatch working-class stump speakers on their appointed rounds; but a spirit of noblesse oblige tinged with a strain of antiparty sentiment informed the Whig concept of public office and governance. The party betrayed its patrician bias by presenting its candidates to the electorate as men of exalted character who stood above the hurly-burly of politics: The office sought them, not they the office; and government is only as good as those who hold those offices. To strike the appropriate balance between order and liberty and to maintain the harmony of interests essential to the well-being of all required a special breed of public servants—selfless stewards who answered only to the call of duty.[12]

Such paragons abounded in the Whig ranks, their stewards being men of "personal character, intellectual ability, and large statesmanship," who (unlike their opponents) kept inviolate their positions of trust "from the approach of party intrigue and political corruption." Men of "faith, integrity, and principle," they dedicated their talents to perfecting a system of government that combined "absolute security . . . with as much liberty as you can live in." To continue this happy state of affairs, the people need only retain in office the party that sought political ascendancy "not for the sake of power or patronage nor for the elevation of particular men for their own sake, but to preserve for Massachusetts her prosperity, and . . . her elevated character."[13] The aristocratic tone of the party was most pronounced in Boston, where "the very air" was pungent with Whiggery, and where "every man of consequence [was] supposed to be a Whig." Brahmin dominance extended as well to the daily press, the bar and the bench, the public lecture circuit, and the pulpit, all of which were enrolled in the service of the Whig hegemony.[14]

The Whigs liked to say that there were no fixed classes, only interests, and that their party, by striking a balance between all interests, worked for the good of the whole. It was, of course, the common good as the Whig overseers, and not necessarily the people, understood it; but so long as most voters supported Whiggery, all that the party's inner ruling circle needed to do to set the agenda for public programs was to pack its annual nominating conventions with hand-picked delegates, draw up conservative platforms and slates of party loyalists, and present them through the party press and a battery of skilled platform orators to the electorate.[15]

Whig government was pyramidical by design, reflecting Brahmin reluctance to test the Jacksonian tenet that the people should rule. The party did bend to the power of the ballot box by sponsoring mass rallies, torchlight parades, huge outdoor barbecues, and other forms of campaign hoopla designed to get out the vote; but decisions on public policy and party affairs (including convention nominations) flowed from the top downward. The proper role of the people within this hierarchical framework was to approve or disapprove these decisions on election day.

However distant the Whig concept of public life was from the democratic spirit of the times, even their opponents conceded that the Whigs produced superb leaders. Whig government, paternalistic though it was, had achieved notable successes in its conduct of state affairs during the 1830s and 1840s, outstanding among which was its contribution to the building of a vigorous, mixed economy and a booming economic growth rate. Bay State commerce during the Whig era (1834–1854) stood second only to New York's; her fisheries ranked first; and the value of her annual industrial production was more than twice that of the South's entire cotton crop. Property valuation doubled in one decade (1840–1850), from $300 million to $600 million, eliciting from the chairman of the state's valuation committee the observation that "the just valuation of her property exceeds that of any like area in the country, perhaps in Christendom."[16] Party patriarchs were justifiably proud of this record and took full credit in the name of their party for it. Whig public policies, after all, had nurtured into vigor the modern business culture that had enabled the state's manufacturing enterprises, banking and currency systems, railway and telegraphic networks, public schools, and charitable institutions to shine as beacons of progress, beckoning other states to follow.

These successes had earned Massachusetts the title of "the model Commonwealth." They helped make possible, as well, the survival of a quasi-aristocratic republic in an egalitarian age. Jobs, stability, and prospects for advancement— the hallmarks of Whig government—provided reasons enough to vote Whig. It was to the ordinary citizens that the party directed its slogan "a full dinner pail"—and they responded with their votes. The party's appeal, moreover, crossed regional as well as class lines. The Whigs believed in a mixed economy in which town and country, coast and interior, industry, trade, commerce, fishing, and agriculture exist in a state of mutual interdependence. If wealth centered in Boston, that wealth built the railroads and factories that opened up the back country to the rush of progress. If Boston was the metropolis of New England, it was the chief market for the region's farmers as well.[17] The message found a receptive audience. Throughout the era of the Whig hegemony, the party polled a strong vote in every county. Prior to 1854, for example, it was unbeatable in rural

Hampshire County in western Massachusetts and in maritime Cape Cod; and its lock grip on most of the cities and major towns of the industrial east ensured its dominance over that region.

Progress, however, had not brought harmony. Massachusetts, as that generation of Bay Staters was aware, was in the throes of "a great social revolution." Technological developments in transportation and communication and the shift away from cottage and small-shop production toward machine and factory manufacturing had ushered in disturbing changes—changes that, by widening the gulf between rich and poor, capital and labor, small town and city, and town and country, drastically altered the nature and composition of Bay State society and rendered untenable the Whig concept of a dynamic state wedded to a static society.[18]

Among the more dramatic changes was the population flow unleashed by industrialization. Manufacturing towns in the state's six most heavily industrialized counties experienced a population growth rate from 1830 to 1860 on the order of six times that of nonmanufacturing towns. Industrial employment grew rapidly, expanding 70 percent between 1845 and 1855. In that latter year, nearly a quarter of a million Bay Staters held manufacturing jobs, a greater number than those engaged in all other kinds of employment combined.[19]

Factories were the harbingers of social and economic dislocation. Time-honored social mores withered in the shade of multiplying factories, which extended their influence beyond their gates into the communities in which they were located. Social tensions and class conflict grew. Centralization in the workplace and technological innovation in the form of more demanding machines—corollaries of the drive for lower costs and higher profits—impinged with increasing severity on the lives of factory workers. Consolidation of machine production was most pronounced in the textile industry, although by no means confined to it. Huge mills, each employing hundreds of workers, displaced smaller competitors. The number of cotton and woolen spindles nearly doubled between 1840 and 1850, so that even as the number of factories declined, production soared and the demands placed on the workers intensified. Moving from city to city and manufacturing town to manufacturing town in a constant quest for jobs, this immense, roving mass of factory workers had jelled by the late 1840s into the state's largest social class—a conglomerate of displaced farmers, fishermen, mariners, artisans, working women and children, out-of-staters (drawn mainly from northern New England), and foreigners.[20] Lacking the organization needed to make their voices heard either in the workplace or in the political arena, they were vulnerable, and vulnerability opened them up to exploitation.

One consequence of the spread of modernization was that Boston capital—the catalyst of this social revolution—waxed rich and powerful. Another was a steady erosion after 1840 in working conditions and the status of labor. Out of economic necessity, industrial workers were tied to jobs that demanded much but gave little in return. The power that the owners exercised in the workplace tended to be absolute, and concern for the welfare of their employees, which was a hallmark of the old paternalistic system, receded as the drive for greater efficiency and higher profits gained momentum. Factory work meant low pay, excessive hours, harsh discipline, and deplorable working conditions on a year-round basis. Female operatives put in a seventy-five- to eighty-hour week. Factory children, who constituted a majority of the employees in some mills, worked up to seventy hours a week for a few pennies a day. And everyone labored under a contract dictated by the owners.[21]

Through it all, Whig spokesmen and other apologists heaped encomiums on the factory system as the benefactor of the workers. Preachments that factory employment in the mills spelled opportunity for the self-reliant, however, clashed with the ugly reality of factory life and failed to persuade those tens of thousands of Bay Staters who preferred instead to try their luck in the California gold fields or on the rich agricultural lands of the Midwest. Thousands of others, however, joined the rush of emigrants and foreigners to fill factory job openings, thus adding their numbers to a rising pool of cheap, tractable labor.[22] Those who were part of that pool had cause to ask whether petty tyranny in the workplace and social fragmentation and dislocation on so massive a scale were compatible with the ideal of the common good or whether in truth they marked a dangerous trend that threatened American republican ideals and standards.[23]

Another aspect of industrialization and the urban growth that accompanied it was their impact on the relations between town and country. Rural Bay Staters, ever jealous of their political influence on Beacon Hill, viewed with trepidation the demographic trends that were multiplying the number of urban seats in the General Court. Unlike the industrial workers, however, they did not lack for spokesmen, especially those with political axes to grind. R. H. Dana, Jr., a Free-Soiler who wanted to dislodge the "Cotton" Whig hold on the government, was not above blending anticity and nativist fears for that purpose. "We are in a peculiar state of things such as the world never saw from the days of Noah to the present time," he warned the state constitutional convention in 1853:

> There's a tide of immigration setting into this country and especially into the Atlantic cities, such as was never seen. It is a transient population and an alien population. It counts in the census. Now I ask whether in this state of things that is the kind of numbers to which the principle of political equality in basing political representation is to apply. I apprehend not.[24]

Dana's remarks referred to another major trend fueled by rapid industrialization: the influx during the 1840s and 1850s of thousands of Irish immigrants, driven by poverty, famine, and oppression from the Old World to seek a better life in the New. Over ten thousand arrived in the Commonwealth in 1845. Just two years later, the number entering had doubled, and by 1855, one out of every five Bay Staters was foreign-born. Immigrants and their children were in the majority in Boston, the capital city of Yankee Massachusetts, and were fanning out in apparently inexhaustible numbers to the other cities and manufacturing towns of the state. Theodore Parker, for one, grasped what had happened: Suffolk County, he observed, had in a single decade become a "New England County Cork" and Boston "the Dublin of America."[25] Mass immigration, in brief, had given birth to an alien ethnoreligious subculture whose dynamic expansion threatened to engulf the Yankee Protestant majority.

As soon as they disembarked, Irish immigrants stacked up in Boston or sought employment in the cities and growing mill towns in the Merrimack, Blackstone, and Connecticut valleys, where they "pigged" into ghetto tenements, shanties, and "Paddy Camplands." Slum conditions and poverty made more difficult the transition that the newcomers had to make in their adopted country and led to the usual social aberrations of the uprooted and maladjusted. Approximately half the inmates in the state asylums, poorhouses, and prisons were foreigners. Most of the new arrivals, however, were self-supporting, taking whatever work was available. Generally, this meant domestic work or mill jobs for the women and unskilled, manual labor for the men. Paddy labor came cheap; Irish construction gangs, for example, built the railroads at 60 cents a day per man. They also dug the canals, laid the roads, and in the main provided the muscle for the kinds of dangerous, low-paying jobs that most American workers shunned.[26]

Textile manufacturers, in particular, welcomed the new arrivals as an endless source of cheap, tractable labor. By the early 1850s, half the workers in the mills of Lowell, Fall River, and Holyoke were foreigners, and by the end of the decade, half the textile work force in southern New England was Irish. As the Irish poured in, Yankee workers left in droves, their decision triggered not so much by an inability or unwillingness to compete for place—the native-born continued to monopolize the better jobs—as by the deteriorating conditions. The flood of foreign workers accelerated the erosion of working conditions, and management's use of them as scabs no doubt stirred resentment; but in general, only the relatively few unskilled Yankee laborers and domestics had to compete directly with the newcomers for jobs. Other major industries, like boots and shoes and shipbuilding, employed few foreign workers. Lacking skills and connections in the building and maritime trades, the Irish remained mired at the bottom of the occupational strata at the close of the antebellum era.[27]

These developments in the manufacturing sector coincided with a decline in the former mainstays of the economy—agriculture, trade, and the fisheries. The railroads that had opened up the rural interior of the state had proved a mixed blessing. Easier access to urban markets and greater availability of goods and services had improved the quality of rural life. But modernization had its drawbacks as well, particularly the fact that greater involvement in the market-oriented economy opened up the state to a flood of cheaper western agricultural products. Thousands of marginal farmers, unable to meet the competition, were forced off their land. Output of grains, dairy products, wool, and livestock plunged.[28] Mass production added to the woes of rural Massachusetts. Cheap machine-made products crowded homemade goods off the shelves, dried up the major source of outside income for farm families, and presented growing numbers of them with a stark choice: migration to the state's burgeoning manufacturing towns and cities or to the West. At mid-century, Massachusetts had fewer males relative to the total work force engaged in agriculture and more in manufacturing than any other industrial state. Small-town artisans experienced the same pressures.[29]

Those who wrested their living from the sea also had to adjust to the pressures of modernization. Fishermen from North and South Shore coastal towns, long dependent for off-season employment on the manufacture of footwear—called the "sociable handicraft" because in the old days shoemakers worked in small groups in one-room shanties—found themselves gradually displaced as technological advances (for example, the introduction of the sewing machine in the early 1850s) and the spread of the central shop system accelerated consolidation and transformed bootmaking and shoemaking into a mass-production industry that shod one-third of the nation and that required a full-time work force.[30] At the same time, shipments by rail doomed the slower freight trade carried by Cape Cod coasting vessels and grounded their crews. Common seamen could still find work, but only at the going pay scale of around $18 a month. Yankee fishermen and mariners, no longer sure of off-season jobs and unwilling to work for "the wages of a foreign sailor," gave up the sea in such great numbers that by the 1850s, foreigners made up three-quarters of the hands on Bay State fishing boats and merchant ships.[31]

Demographic change, in fact, touched the lives of all Bay Staters. In 1830, virtually all were Protestants, living in a basically agrarian and maritime society. A quarter of a century later, 22 percent were foreign-born; at least four-fifths of the newcomers were Irish Catholics; the Commonwealth ranked as the nation's most densely populated and urbanized state; and eastern and central Massachusetts stood second only to Great Britain as the most heavily industrialized region in the world.[32] Bay Staters of that generation had to pay a price for so rapid and profound a metamorphosis. Population flux and the spread of the factory and machine manufacturing unhinged the old life-style with its appreciation for village neighborliness, its close family ties, and its pride in Yankee self-reliance. Emerging in its place was a new social order—urban, industrial, and pluralistic—in which the reality of mounting tensions between capital and labor, rich and poor, and native and foreigner clashed with the myth of a harmonious society. Those caught on the cutting edge of this change—in particular, the uprooted farmers and seafarers and the throngs of itinerant industrial workers—could expect little relief from a party system that hailed the industrial order as the engine of progress and cornucopia of the people.

Other industrial states experiencing similar (albeit less pervasive) growing pains in the antebellum period had softened the impact of modernization with popular, egalitarian reforms. Legislation in other states tailored to the needs and aspirations of the common man, however, had little influence on public policy in Massachusetts. Other than public education, which was generously funded because the propertied classes associated it with social stability and higher productivity, the reform impulse in Massachusetts was channeled into philanthropic causes that conformed to an evangelical concept of the moral order, in which the state took a role in reshaping the lives of those with special needs. Massachusetts, under the Whig hegemony, pioneered in providing institutions for the deaf, the dumb, the blind, and the insane and in implementing special education programs for handicapped children, humane poor laws, and prison and asylum reforms.[33] Temperance and abolitionism, too, were popular, even at the highest levels of the party, until they proved disruptive. However, measures that would have had a more direct bearing on the lives of the common people—the ten-hour workday being the outstanding example—failed passage in the General Court because the Brahmin establishment, through its instrument, the Whig party, quarantined the state from substantive changes inimical to its interests.

Thus, at mid-century, Whig Massachusetts stood fast against the egalitarian spirit of the times that had impelled other state governments to define the legal workday as ten hours; abolish all tax and property qualifications for the suffrage and public office; democratize their judiciaries either through popular election of judges or limitation of their tenure; secure the secret ballot; greatly expand the number of elective public offices; allow pluralities to elect; enact mechanics' lien laws; partially exempt homesteads and other property from legal attachment; and establish more equitable tax and legal systems. And at a time when four-fifths of the states had abolished imprisonment for debt, Massachusetts reinforced its reputation as the "Shylock of States" by jailing on the average some fifteen hundred debtors a year.[34]

From the Whig point of view, cries of "down with the money power" were out of order in a state "now in the enjoyment of one of the most beneficent Governments in the world" and where, thanks to universal public education and general prosperity, equality and liberty reigned. Yet, in a state where corporations accounted for two-thirds of the taxable wealth, the Whig government extended unrestricted loans to private businesses, a practice eschewed by all the states outside New England. It ignored, as well, the example of other states that had enacted free banking and general incorporation laws or tightened public control of railroads, insurance companies, and banks.[35] Party policy, after all, was devised by its inner council, which paid scant attention to the needs of the masses, the assumption being that people from all walks of life benefited from economic expansion. How other states responded to *vox populi*, therefore, was of little concern to the ruling elite except for its fear that egalitarian reforms might prove contagious and unleash "tyranny of the majority" at home.

To cap that potential, the Whig oligarchy rigged the electoral process. The general ticket system, for example, accorded to the party registering a citywide majority every legislative seat irrespective of the vote outcome in the wards. Whig majorities in the cities accordingly nullified Democratic ward majorities and produced a phalanx of Whig legislators from Boston and most of the other cities. Their urban power base virtually assured the Whigs a majority of seats in the General Court as well, an advantage not only because such a majority controlled the legislative process but also because the majority system—another Whig electoral contrivance—empowered the Whig-controlled General Court to decide those state elections that failed a majority.[36] Other measures, such as the $1.50 poll tax, the open ballot, which intimidated workers from voting against their employers' wishes, and the "sunset" law, which closed polls at the same time that the factories let out, were designed to winnow out potential opposition votes from the lower classes and further tighten the Whig grip on the state government.[37]

Such heavy-handed subterfuges, however, were incidental to Whig successes at the polls during the 1830s and 1840s, when most voters supported Whiggery as the party of economic progress. Well might political opponents despair when they contemplated their prospects against "so much of the wealth, of talent, of learning, so many powerful corporations and societies and associations, such a combination of influences" in the hands of "so well appointed and disciplined a party."[38]

By the late 1840s, however, prospects for the opposition were on the upswing. Sectional confrontation and the politicization of the slavery issue had created enormous strains within the party. Even more damaging was the impact of modernization on the Commonwealth's established social order. Against a backdrop of population flux, sprawling urban ghettos, and revolutionary advances in manufacturing, transportation, and communication, the Whig portrait of "a State perfectly homogeneous . . . without ranks, orders, classes; without antagonisms of interests, institutions, pursuits, or moral sentiments" was devoid of reality.[39] Ethnocultural and class divisions shouldered their way into the front ranks of public concerns. Economic growth and development had come to mean disruptions and dislocations in the lives of the ordinary people. None were so vitally affected as the industrial workers, whose straitened circumstances and subjection to the vagaries of an impersonal economic system called into question Whig paeans to harmony of interests, upward mobility, and general prosperity.

In the late 1820s and early 1830s, farm and labor organizations in a number of states, including Massachusetts, formed Workingmen's parties in an effort to advance egalitarian and populist reforms. The movement proved short-lived, falling victim to the familiar nemesis of third parties—the inability to siphon off large numbers of voters from the major parties because of constitutional roadblocks, organizational weaknesses, inexperienced leadership, ideological dogmatism, factionalism, and the infiltration of political opportunists and impractical idealists with a penchant for diversionary causes. Nevertheless, the Workingmen did leave a permanent mark on antebellum party politics: their platform demands, which included a shorter workday and better working conditions; universal public education; elimination of all property qualifications for the suffrage and public office; popular election of all public officials; abolition of imprisonment for debt; a mechanics' lien law; free banking and general incorporation laws; cheaper banking and legal fees; equitable property taxes; and revision of the state militia system, whose burden fell most heavily on young men of humble station.[40] It is a mark of the unresponsiveness of the second party system in Massachusetts that twenty years after the Workingmen had passed from the political scene, most of their demands remained unfulfilled.

Among the host of reforms that gave the Age of Jackson its tone, the one that touched the lives of most people was the shorter workday. At mid-century, the textile industry in Massachusetts alone employed nearly forty thousand people, their workday, like that of biblical times, fixed by the hours of daylight. From wake up to return home, the job exacted as many as fifteen hours a day from the life of a mill hand, the only respite from the strain of these long hours being a half-hour break for the morning meal and another thirty to forty-five minutes for dinner. Technological progress in the form of new, more demanding machines subjected workers to tighter discipline, heavier work loads, and greater stress; yet, the major manufacturers failed to match the rise in production and profits with corresponding wage increases or steps to alleviate the severe strain that speedup and excessive hours exerted on the physical and mental well-being of their workers. Those permanently employed in factory work paid a terrible price for this neglect: They lived, on the average, twenty years less than farmers.[41]

Mechanics in all the industrial states outside New England had won the ten-hour day by 1835; fifteen years later, those in the Bay State were still working from dawn to dusk. Boston alone among the major cities of the country remained without the ten-hour day in 1854, despite the fact that thirty years earlier the mechanics of Boston had staged the nation's first strike for a ten-hour day. Nationally, labor continued to make gains. In 1840, President Martin Van Buren issued an executive order granting federal workers the ten-hour day. Pressure at the state level pried from the New Hampshire legislature a ten-hour law in 1848, albeit one that carried a special contract provision that in practice forced operatives to work longer hours. In the next few years, eleven other states enacted similar statutes—but not Massachusetts.[42]

Failure of the labor movement in Massachusetts to match even these symbolic gains was directly attributable to a party system that endorsed without question the concept of industrialism and the factory as benign institutions. All of the parties turned a blind eye to the degraded condition of industrial workers, paying obeisance instead to what Carl Siracusa has labeled the myth of the respectable worker, that is, the image of the American worker as a manly, independent, upwardly mobile, prosperous fellow imbued with a get-ahead spirit. He needed no help from the state, since he was free to bargain his labor and skills in return for contract terms satisfactory to him.[43] In reality, workers seethed with discontent, and this discontent crystalized into a drive by labor against excessive hours in the workplace. Waged on a national scale, the struggle for shorter hours nevertheless centered in the Commonwealth, where the degree of industrialization, particularly in the labor-intensive textile industry, created the greatest need for redress. Nowhere else was agitation for this reform so intense, so pervasive, and so prolonged; and because the dominant Whig party's procorporation stance stiffened the resolve of the combined corporate power, nowhere else was opposition to it so formidable.[44]

By mid-century, the ten-hour crusade had become the rallying point of labor's quest for equal rights. Outwardly, the drive for the shorter workday evinced labor's determination to have a voice in matters pertaining to hours, wages, and working conditions. But behind the bread-and-butter concerns lay the realization that workers were subordinate to those who exercised control over their jobs and their workaday lives. Experience in the workshops and mills had taught workers that capital's claim that they were party to contract negotiations was false, that the harmony of class interests posited in the commonwealth concept was a myth, and that they were in fact members of an exploited class. The reality of their situation offended their republican ideals and nurtured a growing militancy in the ranks.[45]

Employers had sound reason to try to contain that militancy. Labor's demand for a ten-hour law posed a dangerous challenge to the vital interests of the industrialists, threatening at once their profits and their power to dictate unilaterally the terms of the labor contract. If labor won its struggle for the ten-hour system by united action, pressure for higher wages and improved working conditions would mount; or if the General Court were to bend to the political will of labor by enacting a statute that defined the legal workday, it would set a precedent for wholesale legislative intrusions into the affairs of corporations. Either way, the establishment of a ten-hour day would spell an end, at least temporarily, to the unchecked power that the Boston-based corporations exercised over their employees. For these reasons, the major industrialists and like-minded factory owners throughout the state acted in concert for more than half a century to thwart the attainment of the transcendent goal of industrial workers—the ten-hour day. That they were successful in their efforts exemplifies the fatal flaw in the second party system in Massachusetts: The Whig and Democratic party managers, by attempting to defuse or suppress volatile issues like prohibition, slavery, nativism, and the ten-hour day, committed their parties to a policy of status quo in a period of revolutionary change and thus fueled a growing public perception of the parties as corrupt or irrelevant.

In the struggle between employers and workers, capital enjoyed a number of advantages besides its controlling influence over the state government, not the least of which was the endless supply of surplus labor fed by rural New Englanders and, after 1845, by increasing numbers of foreigners. Collectively, the industrial workers entered the 1840s an inchoate mass with no appreciable support outside their own ranks. Not even the so-called humanitarian reformers spoke out on their behalf. To organize so transient a group into a cohesive force capable of collective action on behalf of reform had proved too formidable an undertaking for the state's fledgling trade union movement. Lacking organizational skills, easily replaceable factory workers, even when united in a labor organization, simply were no match for the power of capital. Sporadic strikes broke out in the 1830s and 1840s, but they usually failed. Given the tenuous ties to their jobs—striking workers risked both replacement by scabs and the blacklist—the wonder is not that the workers launched so few strikes but that they struck at all.[46]

During the 1840s, the steady deterioration in working conditions and the corresponding decline in the status of labor made mock of the myths of the happy worker and a virtually classless society. Workers certainly were aware of the disparity between the official line on factory life and the reality of their condition. Millwork out in the countryside had bred camaraderie among the operatives, and in the large, urban, Waltham-style factories, the harsh conditions of the job instilled a sense of solidarity. Heightening tensions between capital and labor triggered a rash of strikes beginning late in the decade, and by the early 1850s, some of the skilled workers had won the ten-hour day. For the overwhelming majority of workers, however, harsh discipline, low pay, speedup, and unconscionable hours remained the norm.[47]

It would appear at first glance that an issue like the ten-hour day was tailor-made for the Jacksonians, who billed their party as the champion of the producing classes. The chief opponents of the Whigs, they were much the stronger of the two in national politics; and because they rejected the Whig premise that a common interest united capital and labor, they were positioned at the state level to exploit growing public concerns with the multitude of problems that rapid industrialization, urbanization, and mass immigration had raised. The populist thrust of Jacksonian ideas, moreover, contrasted favorably with the patrician outlook of Brahmin Whiggery and lent itself to the task of harnessing a nascent class consciousness; and by hearkening to the democratic ethos of the times, the Democracy spelled out an ideological alternative to Whiggery's commonwealth concept.

Antimonopoly Democrats, called Locofocos, shared neither Whiggery's cheerful view of harmonious relations between the classes nor its concept of government as an agency to promote prosperity through public largess to the commercial-financial-industrial complex. As the spiritual heirs of the Workingmen of the early 1830s, the Locofocos waged rhetorical class warfare against the Whigs, lashing out at such practices as special acts of incorporation, imprisonment for debt, and the open ballot and ascribing to them an economic system in which Boston capital reigned in a spirit of monopoly to the benefit of its own interests and at the expense of the people. State subsidies, they asserted, were but part of an unholy alliance between the Whig government and the vested interests that conspired to keep closed the door of opportunity to all but the privileged few. Scant opportunity for ordinary people could be expected from a system in which special legislation and the absence of regulation made it possible for "the money power" to swallow "all the property and all the industry of the Commonwealth"; for insurance companies to swindle the public out of thousands of dollars each year; for banks to flood the state with unsecured paper currency, thus robbing labor by driving up prices; and for state-subsidized railroads to set rates at whatever the freight would bear and to operate in a manner callous to life and limb.[48]

Such abuses, according to the Democrats, were the spawn of Whiggery's subordination to the Boston plutocracy. "Why, Sir," said a Locofoco in describing the

Money Power, "here [in Boston] are our merchant princes, with their elegant and powerful bearing, our wealthy capitalists, with their all-controlling banking system and operations, our immense railroads, and manufacturing corporations; an empire—yes, sir, an EMPIRE of business men are here in the city of Boston."[49] But if the state government tolerated this empire, it could also topple it, simply by reversing its role from servant of the greedy few to defender of the people's rights. Two-term Democratic governor Marcus Morton struck this theme in both of his inaugural addresses. Man, he intoned, rather than capital, should be the primary subject of legislation. Let the banks and corporations stand or fall on their own resources.[50]

Consistent with the party's vision of the state as promoter of democratic government, protector of individual liberties, and guarantor of free enterprise were the egalitarian reforms championed by the Locofocos, such as general laws of incorporation, free banking laws, more equitable taxation, the secret ballot, and extending the ballot to most state and local appointive offices. The people need only elect the Democrats to power to rid the state of the oppression of wealth and bring to fruition the birthright of a free people—an egalitarian society.

This the electorate, with rare exception, refrained from doing. However egalitarian its tone, the Democratic campaign against the Money Power failed to persuade a majority of voters that they could better either their own condition or that of the Commonwealth by replacing the Whig positive state with one that was both negative and retrogressive. Where the Whigs acknowledged the primacy of industrialism in the economy, the Locofocos maintained the fiction that the economy of the Commonwealth rested on agriculture; and where the Whigs linked the state and private enterprise in partnership for the construction of the internal improvements that opened up the Commonwealth to the rush of progress, the Democratic party argued against such joint ventures.[51] Such a stance, while popular with hard-pressed, marginal farmers who had to compete with Midwestern produce carried into the Bay State over state-subsidized railroad lines, would militate against commercial and industrial growth. Whatever problems modernization had wrought, the stifling of progress was neither going to solve them nor attract much support.

Nor did Democratic class rhetoric rally the urban poor and working class en masse to the party. The Democracy was an establishment party. Its ideology, stripped of the fulminations against the Money Power, was as probusiness as that of the Whigs. Quick to resort to promises of reform, the party nevertheless failed to come to grips with the nature of an industrial order whose disruptive progress was wreaking havoc on the lives of ordinary people. Party sachems shared with the Whigs a vision of industrialization as the benefactor of mankind. They sat on the boards of directors of banks, railroads, and other corporations, even as they lashed out against the aristocracy of privilege. Their quarrel was not with the industrial order per se, so long as the manufacturers operated within a laissez-faire environment.[52] Democratic politicians, no less than the Whigs, left unexamined the root causes of the social ills of their times. Whatever inequities existed, they were not systemic. It was monopoly that was the root of all evil; and the root of monopoly was the Whig–Money Power conspiracy. End that linkup, and abuses like state subsidies and the establishment of pet corporations through special legislative charters would disappear.

Under Democratic guidance, the role of the government with respect to the economy would be limited to the minimal regulation needed to protect the public and keep open the door of opportunity for everyone. Private enterprise would take care of the rest. For those people who regarded corporations as citadels of unrestrained power in their own right and who would use the state to circumscribe that power or who, like the advocates of a ten-hour law, looked to government for more than regulation, the Democratic vision of limited government offered little hope. Its strictures against monopoly were pitched to the self-employed—the farmers, artisans, and entrepreneurs—who aspired to upward mobility.[53] For wage-earning industrial workers, who were experiencing a decline in status and conditions, the Democratic promise of an unfettered economic system was irrelevant.

Not even the party's call for a more egalitarian society rang true. Because the national Democratic administrations demanded conformity on policy matters from their state appendages, federal patronage and control of the state party machinery and subsidized press in Massachusetts fell into the hands of urban conservatives who, for all of their denunciations of the Boston plutocracy, were linked to the leading financial and commercial interests in the state.[54] Called "Hunker" Democrats (because they hunkered after office) or national Democrats, and led by wealthy businessman David Henshaw, *Boston Post* publisher Charles Greene, and Boston lawyer Benjamin Hallet, they were reluctant to commit their organization to the campaign for reform waged by the country Democrats. They attacked special charters as licenses for corruption and monopolistic privileges, only to line up with their Whig counterparts to vote them through. They also courted the Irish Catholic minority and espoused "doughface" or pro-Southern positions on sectional issues to the delight of their patrons in Washington but to the consternation of the average Bay State voter. Winning elections, however, was less a consideration with the Hunkers than conforming to the dictates of the national party from which they reaped the rewards of federal patronage.[55]

The willingness of the Hunkers to write the state off to the Whigs did not sit well with the country populists, who despised the urban spoilsmen as representatives of the same moneyed interests as the Whigs. Conflict over control of the party and patronage widened the gulf between the two factions. "There are Democrats in Massachusetts," the Locofocos complained, "who have done nothing else but work in aid of the Whig party; they want to keep the Democratic party conveniently small so that they and their friends may absorb all the spoils which fall to the State."[56]

Locofocoism failed to shake the Whig hold on urban easterners partly because Hunker foot-dragging on local reform and its doughface stands on national issues militated against party unity. Marcus Morton described his party as riven by "cliquism," its regional factions positioned on opposite sides of "collateral issues" such as temperance, coalition with other parties, and reorganization of the state government.[57] Probably the most significant sticking point, however, was the regional bias of the Locofoco agenda, much of which dated back to the preindustrial era. Fed by fears of economic and political domination by Boston capital, Locofocoism's appeal was strongest among the agrarians and small-towners of the interior.[58] Underlying their concerns was the knowledge that growth, both in human and economic terms, was the source of Whig strength. Where the huge, floating population of emigrants, aliens, and factory workers clustered, namely, in the cities and major towns, was precisely where the largest accumulation of property and wealth was concentrated and where the Whigs derived most of their votes. It was this juxtaposition of numbers, wealth, and power—a pattern that spokesmen for the country called "centralization"—that troubled the people of the hinterland the most, particularly so when they contemplated the social, cultural, economic, and political advantages that the process of centralization bestowed on the capital city.[59]

Boston, indeed, was the mecca of the Commonwealth. Most of New England's major corporations were headquartered there; she possessed approximately half the assessed wealth of the entire state; talented young lawyers, clergymen, and orators from all parts of the state flocked there, leaving behind them an intellectually impoverished countryside; and thirteen daily newspapers promoted her interests and helped extend her sway over the Commonwealth. In the eyes of the yeomanry, Boston's three estates—wealth, talent, and numbers—had conferred on her merchants, bankers, and industrialists a political influence far in excess of that which adhered to the city's solid Whig delegation in the General Court. The advantages of centralization were by no means confined to Boston. They had transformed all the cities and leading towns into reservoirs of wealth, growth, and power and had radiated outward to satellite towns that shared the outlook and interests—including an enthusiasm for Whiggery—of their larger neighbors. But Boston—the great metropolis of New England, the seat of the Whig hegemony, and the chief exemplar of centralization—was the focal point of rural fears and resentments.[60]

The success of the Locofocos in stirring up rural hostility to urban society and wealth proved costly to their party. It was along this divide between what Ronald Formisano has called the cosmopolitan Center and the rural Periphery that most of the party battles were fought in the era of the second party system.[61] And the Democracy consistently lost these battles.

At the economic level, rural Massachusetts spearheaded the drive against state subsidies to Boston-owned railroads, banks, and other corporations; and at the political level, it blocked reform of the state's retrogressive system of representation in the General Court, which, because it was based on towns rather than population, favored the hinterland. Even some of the country party's more progressive recommendations, such as homestead exemption and abolition of imprisonment for debt, had greater appeal for the yeomanry and small-town artisans than for the urban lower classes. Indebtedness, while not peculiar to rural Bay

Staters, fell with particular severity upon them. Farmers sometimes lost their holdings in bankruptcy proceedings.[62] Poor, transient, propertyless industrial workers were spared that calamity. And while the country Democrats' promise to exorcise special privileges and monopoly and their commitment to equal opportunity for all had a catholic appeal, they failed to match in popularity the Whig themes of jobs and growth.

Perhaps because it would violate laissez-faire doctrine, or, more likely, as Carl Siracusa has argued, because they failed to comprehend or chose to disregard the pernicious ramifications of unregulated industrialism, the Democrats did not resort to a more obvious appeal—the promise to use the power of the state for the general mitigation of the negative aspects of modernization.[63] Talk of a Money Power conspiracy was no substitute for state action against unconscionable hours, exploitation of child and female labor, a primitive work environment, and the refusal of industrialists to accord their employees a voice in setting the terms of the contract under which they labored.

The absence of an alternative party program more germane to the specific needs of urbanites in a state where at mid-century nearly three-quarters of the people lived in cities and towns with twenty-five hundred or more inhabitants helps explain the long life of the Whig political hegemony. Every fall, the voters had two choices: a Whig party that puffed itself as the party of progress and the full dinner pail, or a bifurcated Democratic party whose anticity country wing offered a program for reform of limited relevance to an industrial people and whose urban wing was manipulated by "customhouse" politicians more interested in "federal pap" than in answering the call to reform.[64] Add to this the Democratic wooing of the foreign vote and the unpopularity of the party's positions on sectional issues, and it is not surprising that the Democrats prior to mid-century won control of the legislature only once and the governorship twice.

The first Democratic gubernatorial victory occurred in 1839, when outraged voters turned out against the Whig party's "fifteen-gallon law," a piece of class legislation fathered by evangelical Whigs that aimed at closing the saloons by limiting the sale of spirituous beverages to quantities of not less than fifteen gallons. In 1842, the Democrats won again, this time over a Whig party weakened by its supportive role in the crushing of the Dorr Rebellion in neighboring Rhode Island and by defections to the abolitionist Liberty party.[65]

The Democrats also benefited from a gigantic Chartist campaign underway since 1840, which had flooded the General Court with petitions for a ten-hour law signed by thousands of workers. Corporation spokesmen and their Whig allies denounced the campaign as Democratic demagoguery; and, in fact, some Democratic politicians, cognizant that the mill owners and their overseers were Whig to the man, had expressed interest in the movement. Thus, when the Democrats assumed control of the state government in 1843, expectations ran high that legislative relief was at hand. Worker petitions in support of a ten-hour law were referred to a special joint committee, which, after examining the merits of the case, reported out a bill that defined the legal workday as ten hours. But the measure bore the imprint of the manufacturers' lobby. Attached to it was a special contract provision that allowed the imposition of longer hours under the pretext that ambitious workers would want to earn more money by working overtime. So pervasive was the influence of the corporations among both parties in the General Court that even this "humbug bill" failed to reach the floor of the house for a vote. By its inaction, the Democratic-controlled legislature nourished the distrust with which the labor movement in Massachusetts regarded both political parties.[66]

The failures of the Democracy were self-induced. Nevertheless, the Whig defeat in 1839 exposed an area of vulnerability in the majority party that the Democrats had been quick to exploit—the presence in the Whig ranks of ideological cohorts for whom cause was dearer than party. Their single-minded obsession with volatile social and moral issues like prohibition, nativism, and abolition posed a dilemma for the party's inner council: To commit the party to absolute positions on these questions would weaken its hold on the electorate, but to compromise or dodge them might trigger a bolt that would likewise damage the party. The Whig decision makers had succumbed to the pressure of the temperance crusaders in 1839, but the chastening experience resulting from its support of the fifteen-gallon law prompted the party the following year to abandon its "dries" in favor of repeal.

The party had paid a heavy price for its one-time sponsorship of a temperance law, a mistake that it never repeated. And to the relief of the Whig leadership, its fears of a bolt by the prohibitionists did not materialize. The reluctance of the "cold water" enthusiasts to boost the fortunes of the Democracy, which was awash with "wets," militated against their going it alone. Similar efforts to moderate and contain the widespread nativist and antislavery sentiments within the party, however, met with less success.

Native-born Bay Staters had long looked to the state government for relief from problems such as the rising incidence of crime, poverty, and disease that followed in the wake of mass immigration; and the state had responded to their pressure with legislation mandating a means test for all immigrants at ports of entry to screen out potential social problems. For many Americans, mass immigration had political as well as social implications. Disgruntled nativist elements in the Whig party blamed the foreign vote for the defeat of Henry Clay in 1844 and demanded action to protect the sanctity of the ballot from the foreign threat. Their party's lukewarm response prompted them to bolt to the newly formed Native American party, whose proposals to bar Roman Catholics and the foreign-born from the suffrage and public office they found more alluring than the Whig party's mild flirtations with nativism.[67]

In 1845, the Native Americans made their debut in Massachusetts electoral politics, attracting around 8 percent of the total vote, mostly from Boston and surrounding cities and towns. The inability of the party to expand on or even retain its 1845 base in the next two elections prompted them to disband their organization and rejoin the Whig party.[68] There they resumed their pressure-group tactics and bided their time for a more opportune moment to launch another America First crusade.

Difficult as it was for the Whig party to contain its nativist elements, it faced even graver internal dissension generated by the growing sectional controversy over slavery. Abolitionists in the free states, who, unlike the Garrisonians, favored taking their case to the voters, formed the Liberty party in 1839. In Massachusetts, the party got off to an unpromising start, its gubernatorial candidate garnering less than 1 percent of the total vote; but by improving its performance mainly at the expense of the Whig party in subsequent elections, it posed a more formidable threat than did the ephemeral Native American movement. Whig appeals based on moral and material progress rang false for growing numbers of antislavery party members. In 1842, the Liberty party drained off enough Whig votes to force the election into the General Court, which decided the outcome in favor of Marcus Morton.

The Democratic party, however, was also weakened by national developments and was in no position to exploit its opponents' difficulties. Bitter quarreling had erupted between proslavery Calhounites and antislavery Van Buren men over sectional matters and patronage. War with Mexico and the Wilmot Proviso widened the divisions within both parties. After 1844, the Democrats as a party ceased to be competitive. The Whigs, too, were hard hit, their party splitting into two wings—"Conscience" and "Cotton"—whose differences over the Southern question proved irreconcilable.[69]

In 1848, antislavery cadres from the free states consisting of Liberty party men, "Conscience" Whigs, and Van Buren Democrats joined forces to form the Free-Soil party. Its presidential candidate, Martin Van Buren, failed to carry a single state, but in Massachusetts, the new party placed second with 29 percent of the vote, ahead of the badly divided Democrats. Van Buren's name at the top of the Free-Soil ticket attracted many Democratic votes. The Free-Soil emphasis on free labor in the territories and its strategy of attacking the Whig hegemony and reminding workers that Van Buren as president had put federal workers on a ten-hour day also contributed to their strong showing.[70]

Not surprisingly, the party peaked in its first outing in Massachusetts, a presidential election year in which public concerns over slavery and the territories were more readily expressed at the polls. In subsequent off-year elections, when state and local issues forged to the front, the party's third-place finishes demonstrated the limitations of free soilism as a vote producer and created serious divisions in the party over policy matters. Like the older parties, the Free-Soilers embraced the concept of the industrial order as a benign instrument for human progress, but as V. O. Key has observed, "Parties do not thrive on the certainty of defeat."[71] Hence, party pragmatists, for tactical reasons, favored widening its appeal among the masses by championing popular causes like the ten-hour day. Its upper-class ideologues, however, eschewed such bread-and-butter reforms, concealing their distaste for them behind the claim that the adoption of secondary causes would divert public attention from the party's paramount purpose—to prevent the extension of slavery into the national territories.[72] Thus, the reformist impulse in the Free-Soil party, like that in the Democratic, was circumscribed by national political considerations. Adding to the woes of the Free-Soilers was the realization that they were not strong enough to win on their own. The only way they were going to exercise power was to enter into a coalition with one of the older parties in which they would have to play a subordinate role.

Failure of the loyal opposition to force the Whig oligarchy into responding to the negative aspects of urban and industrial growth helps explain why so few adjustments were forthcoming. Simply put, the Whigs could afford to disregard them so long as they kept winning. However, the fact that the electorate did not perceive either opposition party as an attractive alternative concealed a growing disillusionment with status-quo Whiggery. [73]

CHAPTER TWO

Coalition Politics
and the Constitutional Convention

THE FREE-SOIL PARTY'S impressive showing in its maiden run in Massachusetts—its 29 percent share of the total vote was topped only in Vermont—proved a turning point in the fortunes of the Whig party, for even though the results favored the Whigs, a majority of the electorate had supported their opponents. This was not the first time that had happened, but where in the past the party had always managed to recoup its losses, the defection of up to eighteen thousand Conscience Whigs to the Free-Soil party in 1848 sliced its statewide edge permanently from a majority to a plurality. The best the Whigs could look forward to in the future was to remain the top vote-getter in a tripartite system, and since the General Court decided state contests that failed a majority, winning a plurality by no means guaranteed control of the government.[1]

That fact was not lost on certain opposition leaders, who met in the aftermath of the election to discuss the possibility of the Free-Soilers and Democrats forging a united front against their common foe. Both parties took steps in their next conventions toward some sort of union, the Free-Soilers by writing Locofoco planks into their platform and the Democrats, still smarting over the South's lukewarm response to Lewis Cass's presidential bid the previous November, by embracing antislavery resolutions.[2] However, mutual suspicions and irreconcilable differences on national issues sparked bitter opposition within each party to the idea of fusion, precluding, for the time being, a formal alliance. Free-Soilers and Democrats in some towns and cities did enter joint legislative tickets in the autumnal election, but with the Whigs capturing 49.3 percent of the vote, the rebounding Democrats 28.2 percent, and the Free-Soilers slipping to the third place with 22.4 percent, the state government remained in Whig hands. Nevertheless the victors had little cause to celebrate. Thirteen cosponsored senatorial candidates and 130 of those endorsed for representative had won, demonstrating to the Democratic and Free-Soil collaborators that they had hit upon a winning formula.[3]

National developments quickened the movement toward alliance. Zachary Taylor's election, which had driven the national Democrats from power, strengthened the hand of the reform-minded Democrats in the Bay State. Passage of the Compromise of 1850, with its odious Fugitive Slave Law, badly rattled the Whig ruling class. "The Fugitive Slave Law appears to have set many of the free states in a blaze," groaned merchant-industrialist Abbott Lawrence. "Old Massachusetts it seems will not countenance the Law, and yet it is the Law of the Land." Daniel Webster's Seventh of March speech in which the Whig titan defended the law added to the Whig woes. "Our little state," Whig lawyer George Hillard reported to Robert C. Winthrop, "has been reeling and staggering under the blow dealt by Webster's speech." Hillard feared that the fugitive slave issue might so inflame public opinion as to cause the loss of the state to "a mongrel party made up of democrats and disunionists." Former Whig governor John Davis expressed similar misgivings: "If we approve of the compromise or of Mr. Webster's course, can men who are committed against both and yet otherwise Whigs vote with us?"[4]

Some antislavery political activists were convinced that the answer to that question was no. True believers themselves, these Free-Soilers expected that the course followed by the national Whig party would shock its rank and file into mass defections to the antislavery party; and to facilitate that anticipated development, they launched an ardent courtship of Whig voters.

An alarmed Whig state organization moved quickly to nip that romance in the bud. At its annual convention, it placed the party squarely in opposition to the Fugitive Slave Law. Professions of commitment to antislavery principles, however, failed to address another source of unrest: a growing perception that the Whig commitment to the interests of Boston capital acted to the detriment of the common people.[5] And it was from this quarter that the major challenge to Whig rule issued in the 1850 state election.

The architect of this challenge was Henry Wilson, who, in the wake of the Compromise and the alleged sellout of the Webster Whigs, broached the idea of a joint venture with Democratic leaders Nathaniel Banks and George Boutwell. The patronage-conscious Democrats proved ready listeners. Their party had lost the White House in 1848 and had not occupied a major state office since 1843. All three party managers—Wilson, "the Natick Cobbler"; Banks, "the Waltham Bobbin Boy"; and Boutwell, the former clerk in a country store—were self-made men who took to heart abolitionist William Jackson's observation that in the quest for political power, it did not do "to be too perpendicular for the sake of principle."[6] Besides, there were compelling reasons to put to the test Wilson's contention that although neither party alone could defeat the Whigs, together they could. Majorities in both parties agreed on most matters relating to state affairs.[7] They shared a common enemy in "the Lords of the Loom," and if successful, the partners would reap the harvest of electoral victory: control of state government, implementation of public policy, and access to the emoluments of office, not the least of which would be the allocation of state patronage.

The trio agreed on an informal arrangement "for state purposes solely" to avoid conflict within their respective parties. Both parties would retain their separate identities and their mutually exclusive positions on national affairs, and both would continue to field separate slates of candidates for statewide and national offices. But—and this was the key to the proposed coalition—the three men pledged to unite their parties behind union legislative tickets.[8] Success hinged on two expectations: (1) that cosponsored candidates would capture a majority of legislative seats, and (2) that the majority rule on elections would throw the choice of governor into the General Court. Because the Whigs no longer commanded a majority of the statewide vote, the gubernatorial choice automatically devolved upon the legislature. Thus, the party that controlled the General Court could reasonably expect to control the executive branch as well.

Together the negotiators succeeded in fashioning a new political organization— a bipartisan Coalition—with which they hoped to topple the Whig hegemony and seize control of the state government. The presence of large numbers of former Democrats in the Free-Soil party facilitated the task of rallying the rank and file of that party behind the idea of state reform. Prolabor Free-Soil politicians like James M. Stone, William S. Robinson, and J.Q.A. Griffin (all of whom were activists in the ten-hour day movement) joined Wilson in the task of convincing the ex-Locofocos in their party that the bipartisan alliance would "extend the rights and secure the interests of the people . . . [and] reward the dignity of labor." And all Free-Soilers were delighted with the prospect of striking a blow at the Cotton Whigs, whose profits they deemed soiled by slavery. On the Democratic side, Boutwell and Banks, in league with Robert Rantoul of Beverly and the flamboyant ten-hour day leader Ben Butler of Lowell, undertook the task of marshalling the rank and file of their party behind the proposed coalition by promising to use it to break the grip of Boston capital on the state government and write into law a wide-ranging reform program. Adding wings to that promise was the realization that without an alliance, the Democrats would remain an ineffectual minority.[9]

But while mobilization proceeded smoothly at the grass roots, bitter infighting erupted among Free-Soil leaders that threatened to short-circuit all arrangements. A faction of ultraconservative former Conscience Whigs, headed by Charles Francis Adams, John G. Palfrey, Richard Henry Dana, Jr., Stephen C. Phillips, and Samuel Hoar (who had begun political life as a Federalist), bitterly assailed their erstwhile ally Wilson for truckling with Democrats. For them, the Democracy—in either its state or national form—was the enemy, and any arrangement with it "would take the virtue out of our party." Besides, the question of slavery or freedom was of such transcendent importance that the antislavery party must perforce concentrate on that question alone. To incorporate other issues into the party agenda would detract from that commitment and make it possible for the Democrats to banish the slavery issue from the political arena. [10] Masked behind the argument that in a coalition secondary Locofoco considerations would overshadow the great national issue of human freedom was a callous attitude to the plight of the working class. Except on the question of slavery, these Free-Soil patricians were by their own admission ultra-Whigs "of the old school." Like the Brahmins, they shuddered at the prospects of what would ensue were the state to pass into the hands of populist reformers. [11]

They also were offended by the sort of men who led the Coalition. "The democratic party of Mass. [*sic*] has always been a low party," sniffed Richard Henry Dana, Jr. "I can hardly account for its long continued debasement. Hardly one of its public men has been a clean, pure, honorable man." Henry Wilson, in particular, offended their aristocratic sensibilities. So long as Wilson had served the antislavery cause in the capacity of a lieutenant, he had been accepted. But Wilson's vault from subordinate to leader in the Free-Soil party—he was twice nominated its gubernatorial candidate—had come at the expense of those who felt that they had given the party its "weight and character." Heightening their indignation was the conviction that Wilson was "the source from which all the attacks on what is denominated the aristocratic freesoilers have originated." Such "invidious distinction," fumed Charles Francis Adams, "has done infinite mischief and will yet do more." [12] Still another major sticking point between plebeian and patrician was their antithetical concepts of how the political game should be played. Adams's group, viewing the political scene from the lofty vantage point of the well-born, approached politics in the spirit of noblesse oblige. Their motives were pure—or so they assured themselves—and their cause righteous; and this imposed on them the duty of safeguarding the cause from the kinds of bargains and accommodations that intriguers like Wilson were seeking. "The older I grow," Adams confided to his diary, "the clearer I see the folly of temporizing politics." [13] Adams's outlook may have stemmed as much from frustration over his political isolation as from conviction. Indeed, it is possible, as some have argued, that behind the Adams clique's steadfast commitment to an antislavery party unsullied by accommodations either with other parties or with other causes lay another concern: control of the antislavery movement. [14]

Wilson, for his part, was as contemptuous of the narrow vision of his party's elites as they were furious with him for having struck a bargain with the Democracy. Unlike his ideological critics, Wilson was a study in pragmatism. He comprehended politics as the art of the possible, and to make things work, it was sometimes necessary to blur divisive issues and to resort to expediency. Indeed, he took pride in pushing clever compromises through to fruition. He also understood the significance of political power and that in a republic such power flows from the ballot box. Political victories, he wrote, were not won by adhering scrupulously to abstract ideals, however noble they might be. Witness the abolitionists: Armed with the power of truth, they watched helplessly as Texas was annexed. Something more than a beatific vision was needed to halt the march of the Slave Power into the national territories, and that something was a political

party powerful enough to check its advance. Wilson ranked votes as more powerful than words and political parties as more effective than protest meetings or
petitions. However, to limit a party to a single issue, as the Adams people
demanded, was to neuter it, for to win elections, a party must first broaden its
appeal among different voting groups.[15]

Henry Wilson was a politician of rare gifts. He was without peer in the Commonwealth as a builder and manager of political parties. The son of a penurious
farm laborer and himself a self-educated mechanic, he developed an uncanny
feel for the public pulse.[16] In his travels around the state, he cultivated the
acquaintance of local newspapermen and talked politics with townspeople in
saloons, restaurants, shops, and factories. Wilson, said an admirer in a tribute to
his indefatigability, "never goes to bed." Equally at home with men from all walks
of life and conversant with all points of view across the political spectrum, he
strove for the common ground on which to reach an agreement. It was his penchant for compromise and accommodation that drew the heaviest fire from critics.
Wilson, they carped, "had an incurable propensity to manage and to man-
oeuvre." Blue bloods of every political persuasion sneered at Wilson's lowly
origins, and almost all attacked him as a political manipulator and unprincipled
power broker. Not without reason, they castigated him for political opportunism
and for being too prone to invoke the doctrine of expediency. He was, said one,
constitutionally incapable of seeing wrong in unnatural coalitions and alliances,
even when they were "based on personal ambition and hunger for office."[17]

Wilson, in fact, did on occasion put his own ambitions ahead of considerations
of principle; but it was he, and not his detractors, who grasped the fundamental
point that while principles might rise above political parties, it was political
parties that implemented principles. He, too, longed for the collapse of the
existing party system so that an all-powerful antislavery party might rise in its
place, and he worked toward that end. Better than most, he could read election
returns, and these had demonstrated clearly enough that for the Free-Soil party of
Massachusetts to exercise political power, it must work in tandem with one of the
established parties. He was cognizant, as well, that the fate of slavery rested in
Washington and not in Boston. Hence, he wanted the Senate seat left vacant by
Daniel Webster upon his appointment as secretary of state filled by a Free-Soiler;
and in exchange for that prize, he and his supporters had dangled before the
Democrats the lure of public office and the promise of support for local reforms.[18]

In the 1850 campaign, bitter class feelings erupted on both sides. The
Brahmins took few pains to conceal their disdain for the Coalition triumvirate—
Wilson, Banks, and Boutwell. The plebeians, in turn, blasted away at the Money
Power, concentrating their heaviest fire on the textile magnates whom the Locofocos reviled as oppressors of the producing classes and whom the Free-Soilers
scored as profiteers from slave labor. But behind the noise of the campaign, the
Coalition was working quietly in the small towns of the interior, where it hoped
that its promise to reapportion legislative seats in their favor would rally support
for its bipartisan legislative tickets. The strategy paid off, for even though Whig

gubernatorial candidate George Briggs received a plurality of the votes (47.3 percent) statewide, the Coalition, thanks to the heavy preponderance of seats that it had won in the small towns, swept comfortable majorities into both houses and thus paved the way for its takeover on Beacon Hill. [19]

A jubilant Henry Wilson hailed the results as a triumph over those accustomed "to hold the reins of power, to feel they were born to rule, to look with lofty contempt upon the rest of mankind." Conservative Whigs and Free-Soilers, on the other hand, ascribed the results to deep divisions within the Whig party. The Websterites had "strained the bow too far" on the fugitive slave matter. It was "the load of Websterism" and not the alliance between Free-Soilers and Democrats that pressed the Whigs down to defeat. [20] Actually, neither interpretation accounts for the outcome. It was the Coalition's modus operandi, not the voters, that defeated the Whigs.

During the campaign, rumors had circulated that men of "quite different principles" had entered into the same fold to secure high office for themselves; and when the Coalition majority in the General Court chose Boutwell governor, Banks speaker of the house, and Wilson president of the senate, it lent credence to the charge that the principals behind the Coalition had struck a bargain "to divide the loaves and fishes of office." Under the constitution, the governor and the executive council had at their disposal a large number of state offices such as sheriffs, district attorneys, registers of probate, clerks of court, and registers of deeds. In the past, these posts went to Whig loyalists. Now it was the Coalitionists' turn to reward their friends. [21]

The trade-off in offices triggered howls of protest from the Adams camp, which likened the scramble after offices to jockeys throwing a race. "There was," said one outsider, "an undeniable aroma about the partition of the offices." [22] Even more impassioned were Whig hard-liners. Stirred into a fury by the thought of social upstarts assuming posts at the head of the government and by the prospect of legislative intrusion into the sanctuaries of the privileged, they counseled the taking of extreme countermeasures to nullify the election results. At their head was the president of the Massachusetts Bar Association, Benjamin R. Curtis, who issued an address to the people of the Commonwealth—signed by all but a handful of the Whig members of the General Court—denouncing the Coalition as a criminal conspiracy and recommending that Charles Sumner, Henry Wilson, George Boutwell, and other Coalition leaders be indicted on criminal charges. Curtis's intent was to overturn the election results, but his party's inner council, after meeting in secret session to consider the proposal, decided against such a brazen step. The demoralized Brahmins could only console themselves with the hope that "a single year of Free Soil and Loco Focoism will bring back the old Bay State to a sense of her interests and true honor." [23]

Free-Soil and Whig reactionaries were not the only ones upset by the emergence of the Coalition. Democratic party bosses Benjamin F. Hallett and Charles Greene had from the start been cool to the idea of collaboration with the enemies of the Compromise. But Hallett and Greene were willing to sublimate their reservations so long as the Coalition confined its attention to state matters. The Coalition, after all, had defeated the Whigs. Not all Hunkers thought even this turnabout a good thing. Caleb Cushing, a former Whig of high social station and a bitter opponent of both labor and abolitionism, gagged at the prospect of having the Commonwealth "shoemakerized." Thus, when the state senate, in fulfillment of the Coalition pact, voted for Charles Sumner for U.S. senator, Cushing launched a counterattack. He commanded the allegiance of a score of Democratic reactionaries in the house and joined their votes to those of the Whig representatives to block the election. The struggle dragged on through three months and twenty-six ballots, before the house by a majority of one vote awarded "the great prize of the whole arrangement" to the controversial Free-Soiler. [24]

Former Democratic governor Marcus Morton, for his own set of reasons, joined his right-wing rivals in the party in their running attacks on the Coalition. "Coalition of parties of different principles," he explained, "generally bring into power the worst materials of both parties." The present alliance was no exception to that rule. "In selfishness, greediness, and intrigue, and I may say down-right corruption," Morton fumed, "there is very little to choose between the leaders of the two parties whose united action has achieved this victory." He lashed out at these "designing men who look more to aggrandizement of themselves and their immediate friends than the welfare of any party or the promotion of any principle." Morton, who had waged a longstanding battle with the national Democrats over patronage matters, was particularly riled that "Wilson and his immediate friends . . . were making efforts to secure to the Whig Free-Soilers every office that should fall to the share of the party" to the exclusion of the "old Democrats." [25]

Most anti-Coalitionists, regardless of party, aimed their harshest criticisms at Henry Wilson, which underscores the pivotal role that "the Natick Cobbler" played in fashioning and directing the bipartisan alliance. An unrepentant Wilson brushed aside the charges of corrupt bargain, observing that those within his party who were most antagonistic to his handiwork warmly applauded the election of Sumner. [26]

The trade-off between the two parties had in fact been fair and advantageous for both. Sumner's elevation to the Senate greatly amplified the Free-Soil voice in the national government, where the real struggle over slavery was taking place. Free-Soil cooperation with the Democrats at the state level, in turn, enabled the Locofocos to break the Whig logjam, which for years had blocked efforts to reform the state along Jacksonian lines.

The 1851 legislature responded to Locofoco prodding by passing a secret ballot law; a general incorporation law for the establishment of public-related corporations like gas companies, insurance companies, and railroads; a general banking act, which required banks to post security for notes circulated as money; homestead exemption and mechanics' lien laws; and a measure to loosen Whig control of the Harvard College Corporation by empowering the General Court to elect its board of directors. The General Court also took a step in the direction of state regulation of the business community by establishing a board of banking commissioners.[27] However, the Coalition had more than reform in mind when it sponsored a reapportionment proposal to increase the number of seats held by small towns in the lower house. It was a power play designed to tighten the grip of the rural-based Coalition on the state government. Every Democratic representative in the house, Hunker and Locofoco alike, backed the measure, but it failed passage when conservative Free-Soilers combined with the Whigs to defeat it. A bill to remove the seat of government from Boston to Worcester met the same fate.[28]

Predictably, the Whigs blasted the legislature's work in its entirety, but what agitated them the most was the secret ballot law, whose aim was to prevent employers from influencing the votes of their workers.[29] Never had the temptation for employers to exercise such an influence been greater, for as pressure mounted behind the movement in behalf of a ten-hour law—the reform that posed the greatest threat to corporate interests—the urge to co-opt the votes of their employees grew apace. By mid-century, the state's ten-hour day movement, its leadership seasoned by twenty-five years of struggle, had developed a following among workers formidable enough in numbers—as evidenced by the thousands who had signed ten-hour petitions—to prompt the announcement that it was time to take their organization into the political arena and align its membership behind candidates pledged to the cause.

Faced with this challenge, the corporations and their champions in the Whig party spared no effort to sway public opinion to the righteousness of their position. Enactment of a ten-hour law would hurt business and labor alike. Production would fall, and since profit margins and wages were pegged to production, they, too, would sink; and this would trigger a flight of both capital and labor to the friendlier environs of other states, where no such pernicious law existed. It would disrupt, as well, the process whereby today's worker becomes tomorrow's capitalist, for essential to this transmutation was the worker's freedom to bargain his labor and skills to his best advantage in the job market. Factory hands assuredly were intelligent enough to negotiate their own terms uninhibited by legislative intrusion; and the more ambitious the worker, the more eager he would be to get ahead by working longer hours for more money.[30]

To proponents of the ten-hour system, the claim that factory workers were party to contract negotiations was a cruel subterfuge. Capital did not bargain with replaceable workers; it dictated terms. Either the worker signed a contract that said nothing about his rights and everything about his obligations, or he did not get the job. Equally false was the assertion that a reduction in hours would spell economic disaster. In England and in those parts of the United States where the ten-hour system was operative, it had proved a boon to both capital and labor. Production levels did not sag; profits and wages held steady; there was no capital flight; and worker morale soared. In light of this experience, it was imperative that the General Court intervene on the side of the disadvantaged workers, for it alone possessed the power (and authority) to force its creatures—the recalcitrant corporations—into conformity with a long overdue reform.[31]

The Coalition was sufficiently impressed by developments on the labor front to introduce a bill to limit the workday in corporations to ten hours, but the measure died in committee. The Coalitionists excused their failure to act on the ground that they lacked sufficient time to study the question; and both the Free-Soil and Democratic parties made amends for this lapse at their 1851 conventions by incorporating ten-hour planks into their platforms.[32]

Prospects for the Coalition's repeating its 1850 win again hinged on the fielding of bipartisan legislative tickets. Arrayed against it was a Whig party whose national branch had been afflicted by "complete political paralysis" since the Compromise of 1850. Whig luminary John W. Davis, however, discounted this handicap, counseling his party to concentrate instead on state issues and leave divisive national questions to an appropriate time, when the party could deal with them in a "manly independent way"; and this was the strategy that the party followed in the 1851 campaign.[33]

The Coalitionists were delighted to meet their opponents on this ground, presenting themselves on the hustings as champions of state reform who intended to stay the course. At the same time, they quietly canvassed the small towns of the interior, promising them an amplified voice in the General Court.

The decision by both sides to remain silent on national developments afforded the voters the opportunity to express themselves on state and local concerns, particularly so in the case of the ten-hour issue, which played a pivotal role in the election. Public agitation over the question was most pronounced in the state's manufacturing towns and cities, and nowhere more than in Lowell—the nation's top-ranking textile center. Lowell was a city whose economy was tied to cotton and whose politics was "Whig to the backbone"; yet the Coalition, which had fielded a slate of legislative candidates pledged to the ten-hour law, carried it in a stunning upset that underscored the Whig vulnerability on the issue. The city fathers—all of whom were Whigs—declared an irregularity in the returns and decreed a new election, their action prompted by their awareness that control of the General Court hinged on the results of the city's vote; for even though the Coalition had again exploited its advantage in the interior, statewide the Whigs had matched them seat for seat. Thus, whichever side gained the Lowell seats would control the General Court.[34]

Never before had the Boston-owned corporations faced so serious a challenge to their power. The Coalition, as the excitement over the ten-hour issue illustrated, had the potential of becoming what the major manufacturers never before had to face—a prolabor party capable of winning elections; and if events were to follow their normal course in Lowell, the Coalition would win. Rumors swirled through the city that the owners were threatening to fire workers who voted Coalition in the pending retrial; and the rumors were substantiated when it was revealed that Linus Child, an overseer of the Hamilton Company and a Whig party official, had posted notice that "Whoever, employed by this corporation, votes the Ben Butler Ten-Hour ticket on Monday next will be discharged." Other companies had done likewise.[35]

A high state of excitement reigned in the City of Spindles. Native son Ben

Butler, who "like an elephant in an Indian army . . . sometimes sets his foot upon friend and sometimes upon foe," threatened to torch the city. Whig gubernatorial candidate Robert C. Winthrop, a man of calmer temperament, accepted the inevitable. "I haven't a particle of confidence in the Whig calculations," he confided to a friend. "The ten-hour system will carry Lowell."[36] He was right. In the runoff election, the ten-hour ticket again prevailed, thus assuring the Coalition control of the General Court and another year in power.

The 1852 legislative session brought more reform: a law (in response to the Linus Child episode) that made it a crime to attempt to bribe or coerce voters, a compulsory school attendance law, and abolition of capital punishment for all crimes except murder. And to the delight of rural Massachusetts, the Coalition government established a board of agriculture and submitted a referendum for calling a constitutional convention to the people.[37]

On the whole, however, the momentum for reform flagged. Strong Whig opposition abetted by Caleb Cushing and his "Indomitables" blocked the passage of several bills, most notably a personal liberty bill and a proposal to grant jurors the power to determine the law as well as the facts in criminal cases.[38] But the major cause for the Coalition slowdown sprang from the failure of its two component groups, Free-Soil and Locofoco, to transcend their own parochial interests and reach a level of reform more relevant to the needs of a rapidly changing urban, industrial society. Instead, the Coalitionists wielded their newfound power in the service of their different constituents. Thus, the Locofocos, in contradistinction to their opposition to the Whig policy of subsidizing wealth-producing commercial and manufacturing enterprises, backed the establishment of the State Board of Agriculture, whose aim was to promote a declining industry. Free-Soilers, on the other hand, responded quickest to the general mix of anti-Southern, temperance, and nativist voters who supported them. And neither Democrat nor Free-Soiler paid much attention to industrial workers other than at election time, even though the shift from Whig to Coalition in industrial cities and towns had tipped the balance in their favor in the 1850 and 1851 elections.

When the General Court had convened in January 1852, it carried with it a clear mandate from the voters in mill towns to establish by law a shorter workday in Massachusetts. Both the Democratic and Free-Soil parties had incorporated the reform into their platforms, and the Coalition had carried the election, thanks to that pledge. Labor turned up the pressure on its behalf. No issue was dearer to factory workers; and with the Coalition holding majorities in both houses and a Democrat in the governor's chair, they had every reason to expect favorable action. Hopes ran high when for the first time a bona fide ten-hour bill withstood intense lobbying pressure and reached the floor of the house. The measure was crushed by a vote of 48 for and 117 against. By its failure in two successive terms to muster majorities behind ten-hour bills or to meet its promise to moderate arbitrary corporate management procedures, the Coalition drove home the point that it was a country party longer on promises to the working class than on delivery. It demonstrated, as well, that factory workers faced a bleak future if they were to continue to look to the existing parties for help. Consequently, labor adopted a new tactic. It established a nonpartisan ten-hour organization with auxiliaries located in manufacturing towns throughout the state. Its sole purpose was to secure passage of a ten-hour law by endorsing candidates pledged to vote for the measure, and its effectiveness was demonstrated by the reaction of the manufacturers, who, shortly before the 1852 election, reduced the workday in their machine shops to eleven hours.[39]

Labor was not alone in its disappointment with the Coalition. Many Democrats were also upset. What particularly miffed them was the Free-Soil decision to scrap its role as junior partner at the statehouse and press the fight for its own controversial agenda. It was the Free-Soilers, for example, who fathered the Pauper Removal Act, a nasty piece of legislation that authorized the shipment of foreign wards of the state, such as paupers and the insane, back to the old country. The measure delighted Free-Soil extremists and nativists in all parties, but it gave Democrats cause for concern. Its principal target—the Irish Catholic underclass—was a Democratic constituent group. More divisive still was the Free-Soil penchant for moral causes, which sometimes clouded their practical judgment. Free-Soil prohibitionists, for example, introduced a punitive antiliquor bill into the 1852 legislature that touched off an angry and protracted debate. Only through the skill of Democratic Speaker of the House Nathaniel Banks, who was himself a temperance man, was the bill maneuvered around legislative road-blocks to passage. It was the first temperance law placed on the books since the ill-fated 1838 Whig measure, and like its predecessor, it proved costly. In the past, the Democracy had contained the issue by asserting that the best way to advance temperance was through moral suasion rather than through legislation. Passage of the 1852 antiliquor law, however, set the Democratic "wets" and "dries" to warring among themselves.[40] Nor were the Free-Soilers spared. Democratic Coalitionists like Whiting Griswold of Franklin County lashed out at the Free-Soil ultras for having, in their zeal, pushed through a liquor law that endangered the alliance. It did not help matters when the 1852 Free-Soil convention put in nomination Horace Mann, an outspoken champion of the Maine Law.[41]

Also militating against the continuation of the Coalition was the intrusion of national politics. The Coalition had achieved its electoral successes in off-year elections, when state and local concerns predominated. But 1852 was a presidential year, one portent of which was the flare-up of the Democrats when their Free-Soil partners, in violation of their pledge to leave slavery out of state politics, introduced a personal liberty bill designed to protect fugitive slaves.[42] Benjamin Hallett, in an open letter to fellow Democrat George Boutwell, reminded the governor that the Coalition had been formed "on the sole basis of state reforms in which both parties agreed, yet the result is manifest that contrary to its professed object, it has passed out of that circle into national affinities in which the two parties cannot act together without either becoming assimilated or professing one thing and acting out another." Once the Coalition had violated the original compact to deal only with state and local matters, the *modus vivendi* between it and the national Democrats ceased. The Coalition, Hallett conceded, had done some good. It had elected a Democratic governor and enacted some worthwhile laws. On balance, however, the harm that it had done far outweighed the good. It had sent to the U.S. Senate "a talented agitator" in the person of Charles Sumner, and it had introduced an unconstitutional personal liberty bill that fanned the flames of disunion. State reform and even the defeat of the Whigs, he continued, "can be too dearly purchased by disrupting the democratic party of Massachusetts from the democratic party of the Union."[43] Only a united national Democratic party could keep whole the Union. This was the party's imperative, and this precluded any further collaboration with the Free-Soil disunionists at the state level.

Stiffening the Hunker stand was their anticipation of victory in the pending presidential election, an anticipation that gave weight to their threats to cut off patronage and persuaded a number of local Democratic committees and caucuses to withhold endorsement from proposed union legislative tickets. Conversely, Adams reminded his fellow Free-Soilers that if the Democrats were to win the presidency in November, a continuation of the alliance would be impossible without total surrender of principles.[44]

Not surprisingly, the Whigs, no longer faced with Coalition-sponsored union legislative tickets, won the election. The outcome of the presidential election also had a profound impact on state politics, compelling each of the state parties to reassess its position in light of a dramatically altered national party system. For the Democrats, the election of Franklin Pierce resuscitated the Democratic patronage machine in the Bay State and militated against the continuation of the Coalition; for the Whigs, Winfield Scott's landslide defeat—he carried only Massachusetts and three other states—bolstered the proposition that since the Whig party could no longer compete at the national level, it should stick strictly to state concerns; and for the Free-Soilers, John Hale's surprisingly weak showing—down by almost half from Martin Van Buren's 1848 total—demonstrated that political antislavery had to look elsewhere for a viable national organization.[45]

Victory over the Coalition in the 1852 state election by no means brought the Whig party respite from the pressures for reform. It still faced the challenge of a constitutional convention scheduled to open in May whose purpose, according to its Coalition sponsors, was to purge the state's antiquated eighteenth-century constitution of its "palpable defects" and open up the government to "a fresher infusion of the popular element."[46] The Coalitionists had more in mind than reform, however, when they sounded a warning to the people of central and western Massachusetts that the population flow into eastern cities and manufacturing towns was about to submerge the political influence of the interior. Nothing could be done to staunch the demographic tide, but there was a way to preserve and even amplify the political voice of rural Massachusetts, and that was by reapportioning legislative seats in their favor. That promise struck a responsive chord in the interior, where an 8,000-vote majority in favor of the referendum provided an ample enough margin to carry it statewide.[47]

In the March contest for delegates, the Coalition again played to its regional strength in the town-studded interior, its orators stumping the hinterland with the pitch that a vote for Coalition candidates was a vote for increased power in the statehouse. Everyone in the Commonwealth's 328 towns was eligible to elect at least one delegate, and all but eight did, two portentous consequences of which were a strong majority for the Coalition and a convention stacked heavily in favor of the state's rural, agrarian interests.[48] Such an outcome was inevitable in an election in which the state's 139 smallest towns, with an average population of 1,000, elected 139 delegates, while at the same time the ten largest cities, home to 295,000 people, chose 93.[49]

Overall, the convention's 419-member delegation mirrored both in composition and outlook the old agricultural, mercantile socioeconomic order of a bygone era, and even though Boston and other Whig centers had sent their usual contingents of big businessmen and lawyers to uphold the power and privileges of the industrial order's elites, they were hopelessly outnumbered. Close to a third of the delegates were farmers, by far the largest socioeconomic group present. Another third came from the ranks of lawyers, merchants, and traders. Most of the remainder were small businessmen, professional people, and small-town artisans. Only one out of ten came from the working class, and not one of them took to the convention floor as a champion of labor.[50] Career politicians like Banks and Wilson, who paraded themselves as the friends of labor when in reality they served capital, did promise to protect the worker's right to vote his conscience by writing the secret ballot into the constitution; but there was no movement within the convention to shape a program aimed at bettering the lot of the industrial worker. Indeed, on the subject of the preeminent working-class issue—the ten-hour day—the convention was as silent as the establishment press. Even less influential in his impact on the proceedings was the convention's solitary Irish Catholic delegate. Yankee Protestant Massachusetts had not activated a constitutional convention to take up the plight of the state's alien *lumpenproletariat*.

On May 4, 1853, the delegates gathered at the statehouse on Beacon Hill for the opening session of the convention. They were by and large men experienced in public affairs—over half were veteran legislators—and whether they sensed it or not, theirs was a heavy responsibility. The convention presented them with an unprecedented opportunity to achieve the kinds of fundamental reform that a society deep into its second generation of massive industrialization required.

The delegates labored well into the summer, and contrary to their instructions to revise the constitution, they brought forth a new instrument of government consisting of a constitution and seven separate amendments, all of which were to be placed on the ballot in November.

There was much in the convention's work to commend it to a people tired of status quo government. It was a Locofoco document, whose progressive features embraced three major areas of concern with regard to the state government: the need for more democracy, greater efficiency, and protection for the more vulnerable members of society.

Most of its provisions sprang from the Zeitgeist that under the rubric of Jacksonian Democracy had induced state after state during the second quarter of the nineteenth century to amend or replace their constitutions in order to lay the foundation for a more democratic and egalitarian society. The friends of constitutional reform in Massachusetts reasoned that since their state had not matched the progress made elsewhere, no less than a new framework for the government was needed to pull the Commonwealth abreast with her sister states. The convention responded with a constitutional package that if ratified would (1) establish universal male suffrage; (2) extend the ballot to include most appointive offices; (3) scrap all property and tax requirements for the suffrage and public office; (4) replace the general ticket system in the cities with election by wards; and (5) allow election by plurality for senators and executive councillors. Also in the interest of a more democratic society were proposals to (1) substitute general laws for special legislation in the establishment of corporations and banks; (2) double the state public school fund; (3) democratize the judiciary (through ten-year appointive terms for justices of the higher courts and popular election of lower-court judges); (4) schedule a referendum every twenty years on the question of convening a constitutional convention; and (5) authorize the General Court to elect the Board of Corporators of Harvard College, whose members were without exception Whig in politics and Unitarian in religion.[51]

Aimed at the creation of a more streamlined and efficient government were proposals to (1) divide the state into forty senatorial districts of equal population; (2) hold state and national elections on the same day; (3) tighten voter registration procedures; (4) establish a decennial state census, to begin in 1855; and (5) limit sessions of the General Court to one hundred days. Concerns for the welfare of some of the more vulnerable members of society were embodied in proposals to (1) abolish imprisonment for debt; (2) incorporate the secret ballot into the constitution; (3) accord state creditors standing in the courts of the Commonwealth; (4) permit state militiamen to elect their immediate officers; and—in a trade-off between Free-Soil concerns for fugitive slaves and Democratic objections to the harsh penalties of the state's temperance law—(5) expand the writ of habeas corpus and accord jurors in criminal cases the power to judge the law as well as the facts.[52] Not all of the more vulnerable members of society found favor at the convention. One provision—to prohibit the use of public funds for sectarian schools—amounted to a gratuitous swipe, under the guise of separation of church and state, at Catholic Bay Staters who had not raised the issue.[53]

In sum, the convention had produced a Locofoco agenda for change of unprecedented magnitude. It was, however, a seriously flawed agenda. Locofocoism was farmer-oriented, and the new constitution reflected the strengths and weaknesses of an agrarian radicalism that combined a progressive antimonopoly and populist spirit with a retrogressive anticity bias.

The constitution also suffered from what it did not say. Its silence on the labor question was a glaring omission, made all the more egregious in view of the fact that the delegates in the course of three months of daily sessions ranged over an impressive array of public matters without once touching on a substantive labor issue other than the secret ballot. That no delegate saw fit to raise a question pertaining to a matter like excessive hours, subminimum wages, execrable working conditions, arbitrary labor contracts, or the exploitive nature of an economic system that employed inordinate numbers of women and children exposes the inadequacy of a rural reform movement that failed to address the bread-and-butter concerns of industrial workers—the state's largest socioeconomic group. It also underscores the ideological limitations of the established parties, which wrestled with the problems of the past without touching on some of the more salient developments spawned by the forces of modernization. To grapple with the causes of working-class discontent was an improbable undertaking for a party system that refused to recognize the very existence of such a class. None of the parties— Whig, Democratic, or Free-Soil—so much as acknowledged that industrial workers were a class apart, choosing instead to lump them under the rubric of the producing classes, along with everyone who earned a living, be he farmer, fisherman, clerk, businessman, teacher, butcher, baker, or candlestick maker.

By ignoring the existence of a working class per se, the delegates avoided the necessity of confronting the special needs of that class. Silence did not signify unawareness. So long as labor remained the sleeping giant of state politics, a do-nothing policy served party ends: It quarantined from the political arena a volatile class issue—the rights of labor—that once introduced might prove uncontrollable and would certainly prove divisive; and it suited the sensibilities of the more cohesive constituency groups within each party—the probusiness Whigs, country Democrats, and Free-Soil moral crusaders—who would have regarded a shift by their party into the labor camp either as a threat to their interests or as a diversion from what for them were more pressing issues. The failure to explore working-class concerns was a failure of the party system as a whole; but it was the Coalition, and not the Whigs, that faced the task of convincing workers that it was in their interest to vote for constitutional changes that had little bearing on their daily lives.

But if the delegates were unreceptive to the idea of working-class reforms, the same could not be said of their attitude toward the interests of rural Bay Staters. It was, after all, the small-towners and farmers who had given the Coalition its majority in the convention and who, through their chosen delegates, helped set the agenda for constitutional change. It was an agenda that for all its democratic and egalitarian features represented for rural Massachusetts a last-ditch stand to retain its privileged position in the statehouse and for the Coalition a final opportunity to stage a political comeback.

More had been percolating in party caucuses at the convention, it seems, than discussions about better government. A delegate took to the floor to capsulize what lay behind the party debate: "This seems to be a question of power—how it shall be divided, and who shall get it." And indeed, partisan and regional considerations did overshadow the spirit of reform and turn the statehouse into an arena where a power struggle was waged between Coalitionists and Whigs.[54] Masterminding the Coalition's strategy was the shadowy figure of Henry Wilson, who, with the largest personal following of any political leader at the convention, exercised the greatest influence there. At stake was control of the state government.

On the surface, it was an uneven struggle in which the Coalition's advantage in numbers and the popularity of some of its proposed reforms appeared to give it the upper hand. In general, whatever its leaders wanted was written into the proposed constitution. Whig floor leaders like Charles Sumner's former law partner George Hillard and Otis Lord, a prominent Salem lawyer and veteran legislator, waged a dogged rearguard action against the Coalition phalanx only to find themselves and their cohorts on the losing end of every partisan vote. As one Boston Whig complained, "it was worse than a Sisyphean task to roll up a good, substantial, conservative, solid influence against the inclination of a majority of this Convention." A leading Locofoco newspaper, in its assessment of the convention's work, gloated that the downturn in the fortunes of those who had for too long fattened on "the fruits of special legislation" spelled the end of "the great Whig economic monopoly" and augured a golden age for "individual enterprize [sic]."[55]

The victory cry was premature, for majority support in the convention did not necessarily equate with majority support at the polls. That hinged on the quality of the product; and political considerations had outweighed those of reform in establishing that quality. Pledged to rid the constitution of its major defects, the Coalition reneged on three counts: the majority election rule, the size of the lower house, and town-based representation.

No sooner was the convention under way than the Coalition, in a power play wrapped in the rhetoric of reform, launched a drive "to secure to the rural districts and to the agricultural and mechanical population and interests a reasonable share of power in one branch of the Legislature."[56] What the Coalition really meant by "a reasonable share" was control of the state government, and to this end the Coalition exploited its numerical advantage in delegates in an attempt to rig the electoral process in its favor. Success for the plan hinged on the same two factors that had brought the Coalition to power: representation heavily weighted in favor of small towns and the election by majority rule.

In practice, the so-called majority principle was a misnomer, resulting more often than not in minority governments. Failure to obtain a majority of the vote in gubernatorial or senatorial elections threw the decision into the General Court, where partisan considerations governed the outcome.[57] Since 1848, the legislature had chosen every governor and most senators, and twice (in 1850 and 1851), Coalition legislators had selected their gubernatorial candidate (Boutwell), who lacked not only a majority of the popular vote, but a plurality as well. House races failing a majority were decided by runoffs until a majority was reached, a time-consuming, costly, and confusing practice in which light turnouts—it cost a worker a day's pay if he took time off to vote in a retrial—"open[ed] the door for intrigue and management . . . [to] the active politicians . . . who have an interest of their own to subserve." The obvious remedy for these drawbacks was to elect by plurality, and, indeed, outside New England, this was the standard procedure, four-fifths of the states having written the plurality system into their constitutions.[58]

In pre-Coalition days, the battle over plurality or majority elections had been waged along party lines, the Democrats attacking the majority rule as undemocratic and the Whigs defending it as the quintessence of *vox populi*. So long as the choice by the General Court and runoff elections favored them, the Whigs remained wedded to it. In the convention, however, there was a tidal shift. The Whigs, having discovered through bitter experience that the Coalition could manipulate the majority rule to its advantage, experienced "a sudden and miraculous conversion" to the idea that election by plurality came closest to the republican ideal of one man, one vote. "No system," a newly converted Boston Whig enthused, "can be just which will not square with this rule, equal power in each vote."[59] Their about-face drew from Ben Butler the derisive comment that "when a man cannot do as he would, he will do as he near as he can. Perhaps when the feeling of conviction comes that they [the Whigs] can no longer govern Massachusetts by a majority rule, they will do it as near as they can by plurality." Butler's taunt could have applied equally as well to his own party, which after years of clamoring for plurality elections executed an about face on the convention floor as if by military command.[60]

The Coalition labored under the disadvantage of having pledged in its report to the people to use the convention to adopt the plurality rule in all elections. The Whigs seized the initiative, pointing out that the Democratic and Free-Soil newspapers had extolled the idea and that their party orators had taken to the stump to broadcast its merits. Indeed, it was the public's positive response to that campaign, the Whigs said, that had led them to rethink their position.[61]

Twice victorious in gubernatorial elections in which their candidate ran a distant second, the Coalitionists had cause to regret their pledge, for given the Whig party's standing as *primus inter pares*, the establishment of a uniform plurality system would position that party "in a fair way to hold the reins of power, for an indefinite period." Faced with this prospect, the convention majority opted for a piecemeal resolution of its dilemma, one that applied the plurality principle to senatorial and house races but left intact the majority requirement for the all-important gubernatorial contest.[62]

The Whigs swarmed to the attack. The people had every right to expect what they had been promised and what they had voted for—a uniform plurality system—yet the best that the majority party in the convention could manage was "this fraudulent expression of the very amendment which the people have expected, and most of all desired." But what the "patchwork" proposal lacked in consistency of principle, it made up for in shrewdness of design. The proposition on elections, a Boston Whig railed, had a single purpose, and that was to confer upon the house of representatives the power "to determine that he who shall have received the highest number of the votes of the people shall not be governor, but that he who shall have a lesser number of votes shall be governor."[63]

Another change that the Whigs championed was reduction in the number of seats in the Massachusetts house. The Commonwealth, with close to four hundred representatives, was saddled with the largest legislature in the nation. Whig speakers argued plausibly that because representation was based on towns, the lower branch had grown "too great for the convenient dispatch of business" and that unless steps were taken to cap the numbers, the state would be forced to add one hundred new seats to what was already "probably the largest assembly in proportion to its population known to the civilized world."[64]

However sharp their disagreements on the mode of elections and the size of the house, almost all the speakers at the convention concurred that the chief object of their labors was to resolve the nettlesome problem of representation, which had plagued state politics since the days of Daniel Shays. They differed, however, on the remedy, the Coalitionists pushing representation based on towns and the Whigs pushing for districts of equal population. In the course of the debate, rural delegates displayed the ingrained distrust with which the country had always regarded the town. "Not a word was said about a district system, before the calling of this Convention," a country delegate recalled in explaining why rural Massachusetts went for the convention. "No, Sir; but the argument was: see to it, you of the small towns, go for the Convention that you may not be annihilated; now is your last chance to preserve town representation. That was the argument." The yeomanry were agreed that only through reapportionment in their favor could they preserve their influence in the government and counter the "great centralization of power" in the cities.[65]

Town representation would also neutralize the political consequences of an urban population growth rate that was filling house seats with Whigs. Thus, it was no surprise to the Whigs when the Coalition-controlled convention chose Democrat Whiting Griswold of Franklin County—a leading spokesman for the rural interior—to chair the committee that was to examine the representation question, or when that committee reported out a plan that even after subsequent modifications was so heavily weighted in favor of small towns that less than a third of the electorate would choose a majority of the state representatives.[66] What lay at the heart of the majority report was a scheme to shift the locus of power from Boston and coastal Massachusetts, where Whig strength centered, to Worcester and the hinterland, where the Coalition was strongest. Central and western Massachusetts, which bristled with small farm towns, stood to gain the most. Boston, as the state's major population center and headquarters to the Whig establishment, was to be hardest hit; but not even Cape Cod and the Islands (Martha's Vineyard and Nantucket)—the only distinctly rural region in eastern Massachusetts—escaped unscathed. Home to more people but fewer towns than rustic Franklin County, the Cape's portion of house seats under the proposed plan was only half that of Franklin.[67] Significantly, Franklin was agricultural and Locofoco, whereas the Cape and Islands were maritime and staunchly Whig.

The majority report triggered a floor fight that raged on day after day, consuming nearly a month of the convention's time to the virtual exclusion of all other business. It was in most respects a replay of the chronic town-versus-country rivalry that had plagued Massachusetts politics since independence. But this time there was an added dimension: Not only did the Coalition's position on representation pit the rural agrarian interests of the interior against those of their ancient rival—the Boston Money Power—it also arrayed them against those of urban industrial workers, whose limited influence in the state government would be further compromised.

So egregious a distortion of the principle of equal representation as was called for in the majority report taxed the ingenuity of those who would defend it. George Boutwell, speaking on behalf of the country Democrats, found a rationale for town representation in world history: "I venture to assert that the government of the cities . . . is shown, from the history of the world, to have been universally and uniformly bad; but history furnishes no instance in which a government vested in the country, has ever been exercised for the oppression of the city. Never!"[68]

Benjamin F. Hallett swung the Democratic urban machine behind the country side of the argument. He harbored no ill will toward cities, he told his fellow delegates, but "if there must be a guardianship, the country is better able to take care of the city, than the city is to take care of the country." Cities, said the Democratic boss, who lived in Boston, "have great sores in them, which do not exist in the country; and I say, if you must divide political power do not give it to the cities, but preserve it rather for the country."[69]

Chairman Griswold shared the Jeffersonian outlook of his urban colleagues, but preferred to couch it in republican terms. Town government, he said, is the ancestor of self-government, and town representation anteceded the birth of the republic. Where district representation is remote from the people and favors cities, town representation establishes a bond between the people and their government, because townspeople take a keener interest in public affairs when friends and neighbors represent them. Town meetings remain what they have always been—fonts of republicanism and democratic expression. So, too, with the towns themselves, each town functioning as a local assembly of the people and as "the surest guardian of liberty."[70]

Cantabrigian Richard Henry Dana, Jr., hearkened to the essentially reactionary thrust of the rustic argument. What really was at issue in this matter, the patrician Free-Soiler opined, was not the question of absolute numbers, which the Whigs raised, but the manifest differences that distinguish country from city people. Any system of representation, if it is to reflect the virtues of the people, must take into account the interests of each one of "the little towns, where every man has his property, every man his family, with his children at school, his seat in the church, and where his interest is bound up in and is identical with the interest of the town and the welfare of the State." In contrast to this state of bucolic bliss, cities served as "mere platforms on which rest the immense transient mass of immigrant population [that] is constantly pouring into the cities and manufacturing towns." Half the residents in Boston are foreigners, and there are more women in that city "whose occupation shall be nameless than there are inhabitants in the town which I have the honor to represent."[71] Political power based on such a population, Dana rationalized, does not necessarily square with democratic doctrine. "Would you count the transient alien population as it passes over your stage in its course of emigration," he asked? "You might as well count among the stock of a farmer, the crows that alight on his fields, and the wild geese that fly over them."[72]

Other speakers—Free-Soilers mostly—trod the same nativist path as Dana in an effort to link the representation question to the disproportionate number of aliens living in the cities. "Represented!" a small-town delegate exploded. "Aliens and foreigners a right to be represented in Massachusetts! When did they get that right? Where do they get the right to claim it? Why, Sir, when I hear gentlemen stating this claim, it almost makes the revolutionary blood boil."[73]

Benjamin Hallett questioned the motive behind the Whig-sponsored minority report, which advocated dividing the state into representative districts based on population. It was, he said, with more than a touch of sarcasm,

> a bold radical proposition: a manly proposition, I agree, and worthy of the most daring reformer of this reforming age. It comes, however, from a quarter that I must be allowed to say, makes such a proposition one that should be cautiously looked at. . . . I fear the Greeks, even bearing us gifts. I fear the representatives and advocates of that local majority [Boston Whiggery] who have held power in the community where I have lived, year after year, and generation after generation, by means of this very system of consolidated wealth, of trading, manufacturing, and banking corporations. I fear them when they come here . . . and say, "Oh! don't go for the corporations [towns]; do help us put down the corporations." What corporations? Why, Sir, corporations that have souls, to be put down, that those corporations may rule which are soulless.[74]

Among the Greeks bearing gifts that Hallet feared was Rufus Choate. He trumpets "God bless the country," Hallett said, even as he pleads, "but gentlemen give the cities the power."[75]

It is safe to assume that those who made up the great, floating manufacturing population—most of whom hailed originally from the New England countryside—expected neither succor nor understanding from a man like Dana, whose sympathies, in his own words, lay "with the Soil first, the Sea next, and the Loom last." Nor could urbanites in general expect much in the way of political fair play from the Free-Soil/Democratic majority in the convention, which had contrived to deny them their right to equal representation with the excuse that a district system would "in twenty years . . . put the whole power of the State absolutely, hopelessly, and forever under control of Suffolk and the suburban counties."[76]

The Brahmins, like the countrymen, feared the loss of power, and that fear, to paraphrase Dr. Johnson, concentrated their thoughts marvelously well on the virtues of republican government. Griswold, they said, was right on one point: The greatest question before the convention was representation, "because it lies at the root of all republican government." Man, and not towns, should be the sole basis of representation, declaimed the Whigs, who for a generation had ignored the Democratic dictum that man, and not capital, should be the primary subject of legislation. Cognizant that under republican government numbers are power and that the population trends favored their party, the Whigs asked only that "there should be an honest, fair, just, and righteous attempt to make [representation] nearly equal as the nature of the case will admit."[77]

Self-government by definition extends representation to all people—be they women, children, wards, aliens, or voters—on equal terms. Accordingly, the convention, if it were to conform to the principle of equality, must take into account the enormous changes in the condition of society that had transpired since the last convention (1820). Developments in transportation and machine manufacturing and the concomitant population flow into industrial areas had rendered obsolete a system of representation that discounted the factor of population in favor of towns and compelled alteration of the constitution to address "the present and prospective interests of the people." A system of government that allocated to one-third of the electorate the power to control the house of representatives, a body which since 1848 had chosen the governor and other constitutional officers, clearly did not address that need.[78]

William Schouler summoned up the authority of John Milton to alert the convention to the fact that "there can be no fundamental law which is not grounded in right reason, in justice, and in moral right." Rather than conforming to that Miltonian maxim, the proposition before the convention promulgates a system of representation pegged to "the accident of place." "I have always supposed," Schouler said, "that democracy was the supremacy of man over accidents, and yet this Report is based upon accidents, and makes accidents supreme over man."[79] The Commonwealth's premier jurist, Rufus Choate, pursued Schouler's point further, noting that the difference between district and town representation is the difference between "the advantages which history and accident have bestowed on mere place, on the one hand, and the rights of man on the other, between town lines and human beings." It was the need to exorcise the evils of unequal representation that "conduced so largely to the call of this Convention." How does the bereavement of eastern Massachusetts of its rightful voice in the government, the Whig titan queried, satisfy that need? Would not a system based on the idea that "the right of representation adheres to place and not man" aggravate the issue "a hundred fold, and perpetuate it; erecting in this Constitution a stupendous system of inequality and of the rule of the minority— unprecedented in the theory and practices of republics?"[80]

Benjamin Hallett sought to counter Choate's hyperbole with some of his own:

> What makes Boston the goodly and glorious city that she is but "place"? Is it not the privilege of place that has made the difference? Is it not the great aggregation of commerce and manufactures, and consequent wealth that has centered here; the railroads that have been created by charters

here, that have drawn everything from the country and poured it into this great mart? These are the "privileges" of Boston that draw the population to her from the small towns, and by this very means which they furnish to enlarge and enrich the great cities. And now you say to them that inasmuch as they have turned these streams into your mighty reservoir, they must go a little further, and give up the right of representation and let you have all![81]

As each side clarified and sharpened its positions on the mode of election and the representation question, it became apparent, even to the disputants, that the Whigs had the stronger case. So-called progressive Coalitionists had closed ranks behind a crude scheme to regain power by foisting on the state a reactionary representation plan. At the same time, observers at the statehouse were treated to the sight of ultraconservative Whigs like Rufus Choate and *Boston Daily Advertiser* publisher Nathan Hale, who for years had brushed aside all suggestions for constitutional change, touting elections by plurality and a district system that conformed to the democratic principle of one man, one vote.

Although both sides rooted their argument in republican principles, more was at issue than the preservation of republican government. Also at stake were the prerogatives of power. As Nathan Hale noted, elections settle more than the question of who shall occupy office. They also determine "the management of the various affairs of business, embracing the commercial policy of the State—the interests of navigation and manufacturers, questions of banking and insurance, the superintendence of all measures of public improvement, the affairs of education, and everything else which makes up the business of state legislation." Hale worried openly lest the scheme to shift power from men of property to farmers and small-towners place control over these vital matters in the hands of men who had the least acquaintance or stake in them.[82]

Regardless of their motives, however, the Whigs held the democratic ground on both issues, and they used that advantage in making their case against the proposed constitution. Their task was made easier by the reactionary stands taken by the anti-Whig elements in the convention. This was particularly true in the case of town representation, which, as elaborated by the Griswold committee, so distorted the ideal of equal representation that it provided an opening for Whig speakers to use their floor time to transform the debate into a one-sided discourse on republican principles. They accused small-town delegates of having used their leverage in the proceedings to pry loose an apportionment scheme that "is at war with the fundamental principles of republican government." A plan so contrived as to throw control of the house into the hands of the country without regard to population argues that the claims of small towns supercede the principle of equal representation; violates the doctrine of majority rule; contravenes the tenet that the people are the vessel from which all power flows; and reconstitutes a rotten borough system identical to that which England had abandoned a generation earlier.[83]

Free-Soiler Francis W. Bird tried to bury the rotten borough charge with a countercharge: "I should prefer a respectable rotten borough system, and have twenty, thirty, or forty rotten boroughs up for sale, to the district system . . . for this reason, that the rotten borough scattered over the State, might occasionally fall into the hands of representatives, who shall have some sympathy in common with the people; whereas the district system . . . would in a few years give the entire control of the State to the money power of Boston."[84]

Other Coalitionists pilloried the Whig party for having devoted its energies during its many years in power to fending off reform and attacking as reckless those who would challenge the established order. They feigned surprise that the Whigs, who for years had insisted there was no need to revise the constitution, who, in fact, at their 1851 and 1852 state conventions had attacked the Coalition's campaign on behalf of a constitutional convention as "war upon the Constitution to prostrate the bulwarks which our fathers reared," whose governor and leading journals had entertained the notion of challenging the vote in favor of the convention on the grounds of its doubtful constitutionality, and whose leading figure in the convention (Rufus Choate) had implored his fellow delegates to spare the constitution with all the "rust upon it," should now push a district system that "drives the ploughshare through the very foundation of our institutions." These are the same Whigs, the Coalitionists reminded the assembly, who had twice quashed plurality bills in the General Court and who had greeted an 1850 proposal to divide the state into single senatorial districts with "one unbroken chain of noes."[85] Dedham Free-Soiler Edward L. Keyes reproached the Whigs for having initially "appeared very much afraid that those Goths and Vandals . . . would take hold of its [the constitution's] sacred pillars and drag them to earth, and erect some socialistic fabric upon their ruins" only to come into the convention themselves eager "to tear down these venerable pillars." That so remarkable a turnaround advances their party's interests, Keyes concluded, casts doubts on the sincerity of "these new doctrines from the Boston Whigs."[86]

The Coalition's suspicions regarding Whig motives, though well-founded, begged the question of why the Coalition itself had fallen so short of the democratic ideal when it fashioned an apportionment plan that denied "equal participation in the political power to every class of people in the State and to the inhabitants of every part of it."[87] The proposed constitution, for all of its democratic and egalitarian features, was a retrogressive document. Its challenge to Whig citadels of power like Harvard College, the judiciary, and Boston, while not without popular appeal, concealed its underlying intent, which was to shore up the sagging political fortunes of the Coalition and its rural and agrarian constituents, who were rapidly losing ground to an expanding industrial order. What the farmers and small-towners wanted from this new framework of government was a greater political voice for themselves in order to counter the power of Boston capital. That entailed shifting the seat of the state government from Boston to Worcester and from the industrial east to the agricultural hinterland. Such a move, however, imposed on the Coalition the burden of having to convince eastern urbanites that they should vote for a constitution that transferred political influence from the many to the few.

In short, the Coalitionists, no less than the Whigs, were promoting party interests, but unlike the Whigs', theirs did not coincide with the public interest. On the contrary, they had managed to take a bad town representation system and make it infinitely worse. Without substantial support in urban areas—where most of the voters lived—defeat was certain. To gain that support, the Coalition somehow had to convince urban voters that it was in their best interest to surrender political influence that rightfully belonged to them. According to the Whigs, the convention majority had sweetened the constitutional pot with popular reforms as a way out of this conundrum; they hoped with this bait to entice the voters into swallowing the bitter with the sweet. George Hillard likened the ploy to the Arab who offered to sell his camel for five pieces of gold, provided the purchaser would buy a cat tied to its back for one hundred pieces. Like the camel and the cat, tying the representation plan to the new constitution created a situation where the voter "who wants only one, must take both or none."[88]

The Coalitionists' plans were in trouble, and they knew it. On the eve of adjournment, F. W. Bird, in a move calculated to shake off the camel-and-the-cat barb, introduced a proviso that would place the final determination of the mode of elections in the hands of the legislature (which the Coalition hoped to control). Again the Whigs took the popular side of the argument. They called Bird's proviso a subterfuge whose intent was to bypass the people by empowering the legislature to rig the constitution without voter approval. Its supporters dare not let the people pass judgment on their "mongrel system" for electing some officers by one rule and others by another.[89]

They were also afraid to let the people decide the representation question. Henry Wilson took to the floor on the final day to warn the friends of the new constitution that if it "goes out to the people in its present form . . . it is to encounter the fiercest opposition. Powerful interests are combining to defeat its ratification. Money will be poured out like autumnal rains to defeat it." Opposition newspapers were, according to Wilson, gearing up to pour "an unremitting fire" upon the representation plan in the hope that by targeting it "they may defeat the amended constitution and bury its friends beneath its ruins." To offset the opposition's press, moneybags, and firepower, Wilson proposed a "compromise" that would authorize the General Court to divide the state into representative districts after the taking of the state census in 1855 and to submit the plan to the people in 1856. Because his option provided for a popular referendum, he was sure that it would rally thousands of friends of the district system to the side of constitutional reform who otherwise might oppose it.[90]

Like Bird's proviso, Wilson's was steamrollered through to passage with virtually no debate, but not before the Whigs tagged it "a sham, and nothing but a sham, to get votes for the Constitution." Men do not disenfranchise themselves, the Whigs asserted, any more than they gather "grapes of thorns or figs of thistles." Wilson, they said, knew full well that under town representation, the legislature three years hence would be controlled by the friends of that system, who would not "lay their heads upon the political block, and suffer their cherished town representation to be blotted out forever." Power placed in the hands of men is not willingly surrendered; hence, the legislature, when the time came, would carve out districts in such a way "that not ten thousand men in the Commonwealth will vote for them." In effect, "the gentleman asks us to father the bastard . . . of his own begetting."[91]

Their inability to shape developments in the convention did not prevent the Whigs from carrying their case to the people. Ignoring the barbs of their critics, they chose instead to cast off their stand-pat approach to politics in favor of a new strategy—reform. During the course of the convention proceedings, they reversed themselves not only on the mode of election and representation questions, but on other selected electoral issues as well. Where in the past the Whigs as the conservative party had steadfastly opposed the popular election of executive officers and the elimination of the general ticket system and the poll tax, now as the state's newest reform party, they favored these changes. Consequently, lines that had always separated the two adversaries on matters of reform were some-times crossed in the convention, leading an anti-Whig delegate to mutter sarcastically that "one is required to believe that Boston Whig and Progressive Democrat are convertible terms."[92] But in fact, the new Whig posture did confuse their adversaries, who complained that it was "very difficult to tell who are the real reformers." "I thought I came here as one of the progressives in company with a majority of this Convention," said F. W. Bird, in commenting on the topsy-turvy consequences of the Whig strategy, "but I find that we have all turned to the 'right-about-face.' The conservatives are on the engine, and the radicals are on the brake."[93]

Even so modest a response by the Whigs to the need for change was breathtaking in its sweep when compared to past performance. More important, at least from the Whig perspective, the party's sudden metamorphosis had stolen the Coalition's thunder and allowed the Whigs to challenge the Coalition at the polls as the party of reform.

What right does the convention majority have "to appropriate the title of reformers," asked a Whig delegate? On the two major issues before the convention—majority or plurality elections and town or district representation—it was the Whigs who wanted the "sovereign people" to decide them, and it was the Coalitionists who resisted this solution. "Why this fear of the people," taunted a Boston Whig? "Why is it those considerate gentlemen [the Coalitionists] who so constantly asservate their regard for the people, all of a sudden are inspired with such dire alarm at the idea that power is to accumulate in localities where population aggregates? Dare you not trust that population?"[94]

At their state convention held in Fitchburg in September, the Whigs wrote into their platform resolutions in favor of equal representation, the plurality system, expansion of elective offices, abolition of imprisonment for debt, elimination of the poll tax, and synchronization of state and national elections; and in a move designed to relieve mounting pressure from the labor front, a number of Whig legislative candidates embraced the principle of a ten-hour day.[95] Overall, the party anticipated that the outcome of the election would hinge on the vote on the constitution, and they were confident that by pressing a campaign that highlighted its undemocratic features, they would win that vote.

The Democratic convention, in a desperate effort to reverse the trend, endorsed resolutions denouncing corporations for depressing wages, compelling excessive hours from their help, and blacklisting workers who tried to organize their fellow workers to seek better conditions.[96] This was the only forthright prolabor stance ever taken by the antebellum Democratic party, but it came on the heels of a split in the party over the constitutional question, which had resulted in the anti-Coalition, antiprohibition, national Democrats fielding a separate slate in the election.

Prominent Free-Soilers like Charles Francis Adams, John Gorham Palfrey, and Samuel Hoar joined in opposition to the new constitution. They had from the outset objected to the Coalition's diverting Free-Soilers from the antislavery cause. On the Democratic side, Marcus Morton pressed his case that President Pierce had carried "liberality" too far when he conferred so "large a portion of the offices in this state upon the Coalitionists." Attorney General Caleb Cushing agreed and issued a "ukase" from his Washington office on the eve of the state election, enjoining Bay State Democrats from further collaboration with the antislavery camp or suffer the loss of federal patronage. Contributing to the voice of the opposition was the Catholic press.[97]

It is unlikely, however, that the reactionaries in either party affected the outcome. The vote on the constitution followed regional and party lines, and this pattern favored the Whigs, who won reelection and defeated the constitution. Suffolk County (Boston) delivered a crushing 9,588 to 3,673 vote against the constitution (proposition 1), which, because it failed to carry by less than 5,000 votes, has led historians to attribute its defeat to Boston voters.[98] Their conclusion ignores the more than 6,000-vote margin that eastern Massachusetts, exclusive of Suffolk County, racked up against proposition 1. That majority exceeded Suffolk County's and came within less than a thousand ballots of offsetting the 7,000-vote advantage that the constitution had carried out of the hinterland. In sum, eastern voters, both within and outside the capital city, rejected the Coalition's handiwork.

Reverberations from the defeat of the constitution extended to the party system. Wilson and his followers had hoped to use the convention to deal Whiggery a mortal blow, only to have the Coalition and the Free-Soil party end in ruins. Anguished Coalitionists lashed out at Irish voters, some 10,000 to 12,000 of whom, they claimed, had cast a bloc vote against the constitution. "Take away the Roman Catholic vote against the New Constitution," a Free-Soil newspaper railed, "and it would have been adopted by a majority of thousands." George Boutwell singled out Boston's Bishop John Fitzpatrick for a major share of the blame, asserting that the bishop had kneaded the voting portion of his flock into an anticonstitution phalanx.[99]

Generations of historians have adopted a similar line, apparently without consulting the election returns on the entire constitutional package. Of the eight proposals on the ballot, the school fund referendum—the one that supposedly aroused the indignation of church and flock—came closest to passing. Even in Boston, the alleged epicenter of the foreign eruption, the school fund measure attracted more votes for and fewer against than any other. Kevin Sweeney, using analysis of regression, found that less than 40 percent of Boston's naturalized voters cast ballots on the constitution. He concluded that although conservatives from all parties voted against the constitution, it was a united Whig vote that crushed it. Dale Baum, on the basis of similar tests, also rejects the argument that the Irish cast the decisive vote against constitutional change. His findings show that the fate of proposition 1 was determined by turnout rates, specifically by the high rate of abstention of Democratic voters and the extraordinarily high turnout of Whigs in opposition to the constitution.[100]

Table 1 indicates that for those who did turn out on election day, party affiliation was the major dete: 'nant of the voting decision. In every county but Hampshire and Hampden, the order of rank by party vote (Whig/national Demo-

TABLE 1. Comparison of Voting Percentages and Foreign-Born Distribution in Counties and State: 1853 Constitution, 1853 Whigs and National Democrats, and Foreign-Born Residents

County[a]	Against Constitution[b]	Whig	National Democrat	Total	Rank	Foreign-Born[c]	Rank
Suffolk	72.3	60.9	6.3	67.2	1	38.1	1
Dukes	64.3	63.5	0.0	63.5	2	2.8	14
Norfolk	61.0	45.9	13.4	59.3	3	25.0	2
Nantucket	59.1	50.9	4.7	55.6	4	5.6	12
Barnstable	56.0	53.9	0.0	53.9	6	4.8	13
Middlesex	54.1	45.0	5.7	50.7	7	24.5	3
Essex	53.2	45.6	4.7	50.3	8	17.8	8
Hampshire	52.1	54.1	0.0	54.1	5	13.3	9
Plymouth	51.5	43.8	5.0	48.8	9	10.5	10
Bristol	49.8	45.8	2.0	47.8	10	18.0	6
Berkshire	45.5	46.8	0.0	46.8	11	17.8	7
Franklin	44.5	45.4	0.0	45.4	13	6.7	11
Hampden	44.0	43.7	2.0	45.7	12	21.7	4
Worcester	37.4	34.6	1.8	36.4	14	19.6	5
State	51.9	45.9	4.3	50.2	—	21.7	—

a. Arranged according to vote against the 1853 constitution. Unless otherwise noted, state election returns in this book are from Mass., "Gubernatorial Election Returns," Massachusetts State Archives.

b. Mass., *State Convention* 3:756–68.

c. Data from Francis De Witt, *Abstract of the Census of the Commonwealth of Massachusetts, Taken with Reference to Facts Existing on the First Day of June, 1855* (Boston, 1857), 98–132.

crat total) matches its ranking according to the vote against the 1853 constitution. Regional considerations, which were interconnected with those of party, also affected the outcome. In all of the interior counties except Worcester (namely, Hampshire, Berkshire, Franklin, and Hampden), a relatively small percentage of those favoring the anti-Coalition Whig or national Democratic gubernatorial candidates crossed over to vote for the regional benefits embedded in the constitutional referenda. In the counties of eastern Massachusetts, on the other hand, the contrary vote flowed in the opposite direction, with a trickle of those who supported the pro-Coalition Democratic or Free-Soil candidates voting against the constitution.

But while Table 1 underscores the connection between partisan and regional factors and the fate of the constitution, it contradicts the assumption that sizable numbers of bloc-voting naturalized citizens tipped the scales against the proposed constitution. When the proportion of foreigners residing in each county is compared with either the county's party vote or the vote against the constitution, the only match between the respective rankings occurs in Suffolk County. And it bears repeating that Suffolk's Irish Democrats had as yet to make their political presence felt in that bastion of Whiggery. Presumably, Irish voters throughout the state either were drawn to Bradford Wales, the candidate of the anti-Coalition national Democrats, or were among the small minority of Democrats who after voting for the regular party's nominee crossed over to vote against proposition 1. Wales's dismal showing (4.3 percent of the total vote) and the relatively small number of crossovers indicate that the impact of foreign-born voters in the 1853 election was marginal at best.[101] Further evidence of the irrelevance of the foreign vote can be seen in the results posted in the interior counties of Worcester and Hampden, which topped the state in support for constitutional change in spite of concentrations of foreign residents (19.6 and 21.7 percent, respectively) that were among the highest in the state.

A majority of voters in central and western Massachusetts were Coalitionists, and thus their proconstitution stance was consistent with both regional and partisan preferences. There was an exception, however. Voters in Hampshire County faced a dilemma. Hampshire alone among the interior counties had consistently cast majorities for the Whig party since the advent of the second party era. Defeat of proposition 1, however, would cost the county seats in the General Court. On election day, Hampshire's ties to the Whig party bent under the weight of this consideration but nevertheless held.

In 1852, the referendum to hold a constitutional convention had carried the state with 52.9 percent of the vote. A year later, however, the vote was reversed, when, following a campaign that exacerbated regional jealousies, 51.9 percent of the voters rejected the proposed constitution. Figure 1 illustrates that while the level of support for constitutional change held steady in the hinterland in both elections, in the cities and towns of eastern Massachusetts, it suffered a substantial drop. It was this shift on the part of eastern Bay Staters that doomed the constitution.

FIGURE 1. Comparison of Regional Votes: 1852 Convention[a] and 1853 Constitution[b]

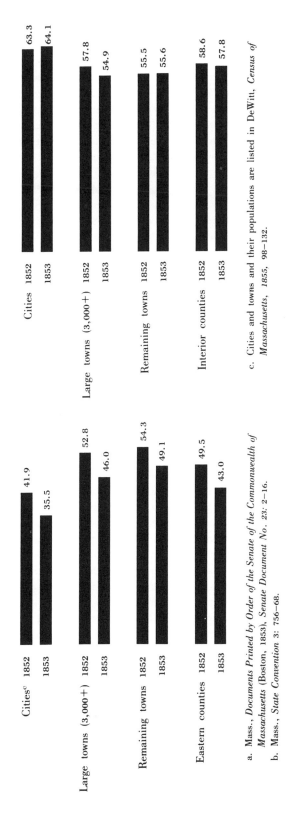

Eastern Region

Cities[c]	1852	41.9
	1853	35.5
Large towns (3,000+)	1852	52.8
	1853	46.0
Remaining towns	1852	54.3
	1853	49.1
Eastern counties	1852	49.5
	1853	43.0

Interior Region

Cities	1852	63.3
	1853	64.1
Large towns (3,000+)	1852	57.8
	1853	54.9
Remaining towns	1852	55.5
	1853	55.6
Interior counties	1852	58.6
	1853	57.8

a. Mass., *Documents Printed by Order of the Senate of the Commonwealth of Massachusetts* (Boston, 1853), *Senate Document No. 23:* 2–16.

b. Mass., *State Convention* 3: 756–68.

c. Cities and towns and their populations are listed in DeWitt, *Census of Massachusetts, 1855*, 98–132.

Support for holding a constitutional convention had cut across regional lines. Only the eastern cities among the selected types of communities shown in Figure 1 voted in the aggregate against the call, albeit the total of their negative vote (58.1 percent) was so pronounced as to cost the referendum a majority in the region. In the eastern towns, on the other hand, the aggregate vote favored holding a convention by comfortable margins. And in the hinterland, the referendum swept the vote in communities of all sizes.

Central and western Massachusetts proved as supportive of the proposed constitution (57.8 percent) as they had been for holding a constitutional convention (58.6 percent). Indeed, the aggregate results in the interior cities and towns barely changed between the two elections. Such was not the case in the east, where voters, after having divided evenly in 1852 on the question of calling a constitutional convention (49.5 percent in favor), crushed proposition 1 the following year with a resounding 57 percent voting against it. None of the selected types of communities in the east favored propostion 1. Even small-towners, who stood to gain most from the Coalition's representation plan, spurned the bait by a narrow margin. In towns with populations of three thousand or more, the 1853 results reflect a striking regional bias. Comparatively equal proportions of large-town voters in the two regions came down on opposite sides of proposition 1, with 54.0 percent of the easterners opposed and 54.9 percent of those in the hinterland in favor. In the cities, where the stakes were highest, eastern and interior voters responded to proposition 1 in inverse ratios. Nearly two out of three city voters in the east (64.5 percent) rejected the constitution, whereas their counterparts in the interior backed it by the same two-to-one proportion (64.1 percent).

Eastern city dwellers had sound reason for spurning a plan of government whose passage would have stripped them of a considerable portion of their existing share of representatives in the General Court and nullified the political advantage in house seats accruing to them from population growth. City dwellers in the interior, on the other hand, perceived the new constitution not as a threat, but as an opportunity. Through it, they hoped to shift the nexus of power from Boston to the hinterland and from the Whig party to the Coalition.

Party lines held in the 1853 election, but the eastern Whig majority, in rejecting the constitution, was not voting against reform. Bostonians, in particular, had good reasons for their action, not the least of which was the Coalition's plan to move the seat of government to Worcester. In essence, what doomed the Coalition's elaborate plans was its inability to shed its role as a country party. Wrapped inside its representation proposal were irreconcilable regional differences that pitted rural, small-town Massachusetts against the urban industrial majority. That majority overturned the work of the constitutional convention because its primary aim—the political advantage of the Coalition—came at their expense.

That the vote on the constitution was as close as it was, however, evidenced a rising tide of public dissatisfaction with status-quo politics. Regardless of party affiliation, dissident elements in all parts of the state—uprooted farmers and seafarers, hard-pressed small businesspeople, clerks and jobbers, overworked and underpaid mill hands and day laborers, and disenchanted professionals—shared an awareness that profound changes were taking place in their society and that these changes had produced social and economic dislocations that required political action. Both the Coalitionists and the Whigs sensed this restlessness and tried to respond to it, the Coalitionists by incorporating reforms within their constitutional package and the Whigs by adopting selective portions of the package. Predictably, the progressive trimmings embroidered onto the proposed constitution proved inadequate to the task of inducing a majority to vote for it. The Democracy, after all, had been running unsuccessfully for years on many of the same promises contained within the referenda. All this is not to say that the work of the 1853 convention was devoid of popular appeal. Rather, it was inadequate to the task set out for it by its authors, namely, to bring to fruition that aim which had cemented their alliance in the first place—the destruction of the Whig party.

CHAPTER THREE

Dark-Lantern Politics and the Know-Nothing Triumph

POLITICAL COMMENTATOR William S. Robinson, viewing the shambles of the reform movement left in the wake of the 1853 election, wrote:

> The coalition is completely dead; the secret ballot and ten-hour law are prostrate, the Free-Soil party disheartened, and the Democratic party good for nothing; constitutional reform will not be heard of again for many years; the fogies will frown down all attempts at agitation, whether by Democrats or liberal Whigs; the Whig party remains in complete control of Boston, and the money-bags of Boston rule the state. [1]

Even as "Warrington" penned this bleak assessment, a mysterious new organization was preparing in the privacy of its members-only lodges to challenge the Whigs for control of the state government. [2] This was the American, or Know-Nothing, [3] party, which had its roots in the anti-Catholic, antiforeign, Native American movement of the 1840s, but which, while still in its gestative stage, evolved beyond the single-issue politics of its progenitor into a new kind of political movement for Massachusetts: a populist party bent on convincing the electorate that it could "shake off the old incubus of party, which had so long tyranized [sic] over the people of Massachusetts" and put an end to the "oligarchical spirit, so long rife in the Commonwealth." [4]

From the outset, the Native American party fathers opened the lodge doors only to native-born adult male Protestants who were willing to cast off former party ties and take an oath to keep secret all lodge business, to vote the party line, and to stand vigil against the enemies of the republic, chief among whom were the Pope and the immigrant. [5] Ironically, there evolved out of these undemocratic restrictions a political party more closely attuned to the sentiments of the majority of the people than any other in the history of the state.

Conventional explanations fail to account for this unique bond between party and people. Clearly, many welcomed Know-Nothingism as the means for dealing with problems stemming from mass immigration, and others saw it as a vehicle for carrying the antislavery crusade forward. Just as clearly, people throughout the North shared these perceptions. There were, however, other compelling reasons in Massachusetts for ordinary citizens to heed the Know-Nothing call to form their own party, sweep the corridors of power clean of political hacks and unresponsive parties, and take control of the government themselves.

Bay Staters had waited in vain for more than a generation for their government to come to grips with those aspects of modernization that were disrupting their lives. Ultimately, responsibility for not having alleviated or even seriously addressed the social costs incurred in the process of radical social and economic transformation rested with the state's purblind party system. Know-Nothingism, then, represented for that generation of native-born Bay Staters their best, indeed their only, hope of overturning the unresponsive established parties. At the same time, it heightened public expectations that once the people themselves took power, they would usher in a new and brighter political age in which the people's government would serve the people's needs. That combination of promise and anticipation proved an irresistible lure.

The key to Know-Nothing organization was its lodge, or council, network.[6] Every city and virtually every town in the state had its lodge, and since the party constitution mandated that each lodge recruit members only from the community in which it was located, party ties were strongest at the neighborhood level. The constitution also accorded each lodge wide latitude in running its own affairs, a policy that fostered political activism among members, for within the confines of the lodge, any brother could speak out on issues of concern to the secret order, and all were entitled to vote on a number of important matters, such as the election of council and party officers.[7] Hence, the subordinate lodge functioned as a local branch of the party interconnected with all the other neighborhood branches contained within the cocoon of secrecy that enveloped the entire order.

Know-Nothingism, with its secret rites, binding oaths, and elaborate ceremonies, owed an obvious organizational debt to fraternal orders like the Odd Fellows and Masons; and in its preoccupation with Roman Catholic and foreign hobgoblins, it resembled the Order of United Americans (OUA), a national secret society that dabbled in nativist politics.[8] What set the Know-Nothing order apart from its fraternal cousins was its decision to build an independent political party rooted in the lodge network and to run its own slate of candidates drawn from lodge rosters. That decision was governed by the conviction that each of the established parties was run by a cabal that gathered each year in secret caucus to preselect party nominees.[9] Parties, the Know-Nothings scoffed, were the instruments by which the few manipulated the many. So were nominating conventions.

The people had as much to do with the selection of candidates as they had "with arranging the seasons."[10]

The American party, by contrast, introduced a radical change into the nominating process by conferring upon lodge members a direct and equal voice in the selection of party candidates. Each local lodge chose by majority vote its delegates to the district and state councils, or conventions, a procedure not unlike that followed by the regular parties; but once these bodies named the party's candidates for Congress, state senate, and statewide officers, they sent their choices back to the several subordinate councils for their approval or rejection. At the local level, direct democracy informed the process. Party candidates and guest speakers appeared at meetings. Lodge brothers discussed issues among themselves and chose from their own ranks candidates for state representative and local office, subject only to a *pro forma* ratification by the state convention.[11] In sum, Know-Nothing organizers, anticipating Boss Tweed's rule of thumb that whoever nominates the candidates controls the party, proposed to let ordinary native-born citizens do the job.

The ultimate purpose of the lodge apparatus was that of a bona fide political party: to acquire power by winning elections. But the American party made unprecedented demands on its rank and file: Every lodge brother was compelled under oath to "keep dark" on party matters outside the confines of the lodge and to vote the party slate. Cryptic signs, grips, and passwords distinguished the chosen from the gentile. Security was so tight that the outside world remained unaware for months that a major new party—code name "Sam"—had taken root in Massachusetts.

Opponents of Know-Nothingism carped about the undemocratic nature of its "dark-lantern" politics, that is, its use of oaths to bind members to secrecy and to vote according to party dictates. Controls like these, they said, violated the basic principles of republican government. Ralph Waldo Emerson likened the Know-Nothing voter to a man who puts his head in a bag. To Charles Francis Adams, the "essence of the secret obligations which bind these men together" was nothing less than "immoral, anti social, and unchristian—productive of nothing but fraud, corruption and treachery."[12] Such criticism missed the point that those men who joined lodges, went through the elaborate rituals, paid dues, attended weekly meetings, and took oaths to maintain silence on party matters and to vote in a bloc for its candidates did so voluntarily. It overlooked, too, that the lodge system involved members directly in important political matters and that majority rule determined most party decisions. In the absence of a responsive party system, membership in a lodge provided the ordinary citizen with a substitute means for making known his wishes and venting his grievances concerning public matters.

It was a daring organizational breakthrough. With its unique blend of populist ideology, grass-roots involvement, and dark-lantern politics, the Know-Nothing order was able to reach into practically every neighborhood in the state and offer people a political forum in which they could air their opinions. Those who responded by joining a lodge and taking part in its activities made a far greater commitment to their party than simply voting for its candidates. It was a measure of the degree of the people's determination to take control of the government that a majority of the electorate made that commitment.

"Sam's" call to the people to "take the staff in their own hands and choose from their own numbers those who shall make and execute their own laws" marked a radical departure from the Whig concept of government as a transcendent institution whose stewards decided what constituted "the greatest good for the greatest number." It was a clarion call consistent with the populist nature of the order. The Know-Nothings, by bringing out "entirely new men fresh from the temple," planned to purge from their accustomed places of power the "party hacks," "wire pullers," "money bags," and "kid-gloved gentry" who dominated public office.[13] Topping the proscription list were the leading spokesmen of the business establishment—lawyers and professional politicians. Replacing them would be the kinds of men who could be counted on to speak out on behalf of the citizenry, that is, men representative of the commonalty, who would not be swayed from carrying out the wishes of their constituents either by the prestige and emoluments of high place or by personal ambition. "Sam" was equally determined to guard against a resurgence of partisanship; thus, nominations were accorded "with a view to equalize the representation so that no one party shall have the exclusive control of the government to the exclusion of all others."[14] Once in office, nothing could prevent the party of the people from responding to the will of the people. With promises like these, "Sam" joined a Jacksonian faith in the ability of the people to govern themselves to a mood of popular rebelliousness against the status-quo politics of the Whig hegemony and the existing party system.

Whatever its merits or drawbacks, dark-lantern politics proved effective in the 1854 election campaign in neutralizing the political opposition. Secrecy shielded Know-Nothing candidates from the scrutiny of a hostile partisan press and beguiled the regular parties and their candidates into running against each other rather than against the virtually invisible Know-Nothing empire.[15] Newspapermen, whose business it was to keep tabs on political developments, missed the biggest story of the day. What little they knew about the secret order—only talk of people power and its extremist views on immigrants and Roman Catholics were on public display—led them to regard it more as a bad joke than as a political threat.

Most Know-Nothing politicking, in keeping with the order's fetish for secrecy, took place within the network of neighborhood lodges, where it was a simple matter to fan the frustrations smoldering at the grass-roots level of society into a flaming resentment of the political establishment. Each lodge functioned as a sounding board in its particular neighborhood for publicizing "Sam's" positions on issues, thus eliminating the need for the usual brouhaha of political campaigning and, not incidentally, reducing the expenses of the poor man's party. Yet, no council was isolated from its fellows. Candidates for public office delivered their campaign speeches at lodge meetings; delegates to the state council reported back to the lodge brothers who had elected them to apprise them of developments at the state level; there was a constant flow into the subordinate councils of speakers, pamphlets, and articles, all geared to educating members on the issues of the day; and the councils established committees to prepare position papers for their members and to arrange for the exchange of speakers with other councils. Annual lodge dues ($1 per member) and voluntary contributions furnished ample cash to meet such limited campaign expenses.[16]

Party prospects, of course, depended on attracting winning numbers of voters into the lodges. Obviously, something more than the ceremonial trappings of a fraternal order or the attraction of a weekly social was needed to get thousands of men to take secrecy and loyalty oaths and to vote in a bloc for party candidates, the vast majority of whom were political unknowns.

A number of reasons brought Bay Staters into the lodges. For hard-core nativists who shared an image of the American republic beleaguered by foreign hordes and the threat of international Romanism, the American party was a godsend. Their motto was "Americans must rule America," and now they had a party that they intended to use "manly [*sic*] . . . to control the election of Americans to fill all the offices."[17] Possessed either by a genuine fear of Paddy and the Pope or by a hankering to get ahead in the political world, the Native American party fathers were for the most part right-wing Whigs who had bolted their party primarily because it had failed to adopt a hard enough line on the Irish Catholic question. Prominent in this clique of long-time nativist activists were Alfred Brewster Ely, a former mayor of Springfield whose labors on behalf of the cause had earned him the post of "Sachem" of the national OUA; James E. Farwell, the publisher of a nativist newspaper and an officer in the Sons of America, an auxiliary of OUA; Samuel Bradbury, whose newspaper the *Boston Daily Bee* was slated to become the official organ of the American party of Massachusetts; and Jonathan Peirce, a Boston pump and block maker and "Grand Sachem" of all "Wigwams."[18] As party architects, these men had parlayed their control over the lodge apparatus during the party's formative phase into the acquisition of the highest party posts for themselves. From this vantage point, they imposed acceptance of their extremist views as the *sine qua non* for lodge membership. Every subordinate council had to submit its membership rolls for approval to a screening committee headed by the Grand Sachem, so that theoretically, Peirce could blackball any applicant.[19] But it is worth noting as evidence of the limitations of their actual influence that the party that they had created failed to reward these ultranativists with its choicest nominations.

This is not to say that the Native American message fell on deaf ears. Evangelical Protestant reformers, brooding over their political setbacks and smarting from the caustic attacks that the Catholic press directed against them and their causes, found in the immigrant a convenient scapegoat. Free-Soilers were particularly prone toward venting their frustrations and anger on the Irish. "Where there is base, vile work to be done for slavery," ran a typical Free-Soil diatribe, "there is your Irish Catholic . . . ready for business."[20] But it was political expediency, not bigotry, that prompted antislavery voters to join the American party. Their cause took precedence over their dislike for the Irish.

In several states, Free-Soilers and antislavery Democrats and Whigs had merged into a new antislavery party that they called Republican. Attempts to bring about a fusion of all parties in Massachusetts during 1854, however, failed to take root. Neither the Democrats nor Whigs were interested. Approached to surrender their party to fusion, the Whig leadership made a counter offer instead: If the Free-Soilers were so keen on union, let them join the Whig party; its dedication to the antislavery cause was equal to theirs, and it commanded the support of more than twice as many voters.[21] Anticipating another win in November, the Brahmins felt no compulsion to surrender their organization to an umbrella antislavery party that existed only in the minds of its proponents.

Their decision to go it alone, however, had been rendered irrelevant by the silent stream of voters from all parties that was filling the Know-Nothing lodges to overflowing. Adams detected some restlessness in the Free-Soil ranks, a condition he ascribed to Henry Wilson's "floundering around trying to find a resting place for him and his 'boys.'" Unknown to Adams, that "resting place" was the secret order. Their shift was predicated on the realization that with the Free-Soil party moribund, the Coalition unraveled, and the prospects of fusion with the Whigs bleak, there was no place else for them to go.[22]

The patrician Free-Soilers, meanwhile, swallowed their disdain for the Whig and Democratic parties and went ahead with plans to form a fusion party based on antislavery. Meetings called early in July to discuss the possibility of a fusion party drew few Whigs and Democrats. Later in the month, they assembled in Worcester at the so-called "People's Convention"; again, only a sprinkling of Whigs and Democrats attended.[23] What doomed these efforts from the outset was that the Know-Nothings had already achieved what the enemies of slavery were attempting—a fusion of the rank and file of the major parties.

Members of the antiliquor camp encountered the same problems as their antislavery brethren in their quest for a party to promote their cause. Like many Free-Soilers, they seethed with moral indignation toward Irish Catholics who mocked their crusade both by word and deed; but as was the case with the Free-Soilers, political expediency dictated their decision to attach themselves to the Know-Nothing movement. The state supreme court had rendered the 1852 prohibition law inoperative when it ruled its search-and-seizure clause unconstitutional. With the Whig party set against assuming the risk of endorsing so hazardous a cross-cutting issue as temperance, the Democratic party opposed to state enforcement of their moral notions, the Coalition dead, and the Free-Soil party dying, the Maine Law men proved ready candidates for Know-Nothing recruiters. The State Temperance Committee made it official when it endorsed the Know-Nothing gubernatorial candidate.[24]

Know-Nothing success in enrolling single-issue enthusiasts in its lodges by no means ensured victory in the forthcoming election. When politicized in the past, issues like nativism, temperance, and abolitionism had failed to rally widespread support across the broad spectrum of the electorate. However, there was a difference this time: The intensity of such causes was rising in the early 1850s. Nativism had penetrated all strata of society and had reached a pandemic stage among the lower socioeconomic orders. Yankee mechanics, factory workers, common laborers, clerks, small jobbers, tradesmen, and struggling entrepreneurs in the cities and larger towns had to live cheek by jowl with impoverished foreigners and face daily the challenge that Irish Catholics posed to their neighborhoods, job security, institutions, mores, and life-style. They blamed the Irish as well as the politicians and wealthy elites for having blocked "true reform" and for having forced American working people "to seek employment under disadvantages."[25] Such men were naturally receptive to nativist polemics, but their affinity for this kind of thinking reflected the symptoms and not the cause of what ailed the body politic in Massachusetts, namely, the wrenching social and economic changes disrupting the lives of the common people.

If Paddy and the Pope ranked high among public concerns, so did public health and safety, the deteriorating quality of urban life, and the widening gap between rich and poor.[26] Class appeals aimed at worker dissatisfaction drew far greater response in the form of labor turnouts and mass petition campaigns than did nativist harangues and demonstrations. Unregulated corporations, cyclical unemployment, and an authoritarian factory system, after all, antedated mass immigration, and conditions were worsening. California gold had unleashed an inflationary spiral that struck city dwellers and workers with particular severity. Wages failed to keep pace with the rising cost of living. Printers, carpenters, painters, hat finishers, masons, coachmen, and railway workers formed associations to back their demands for higher wages.

By the 1850s, worker unrest had reached a flash point, as evidenced by the rash of strikes launched during the decade, culminating with the Lynn shoemaker strike in 1860—the greatest industrial strike ever staged in antebellum America. Abuses inherent in the unchecked power of the industrial order was the father of the conflict between capital and labor. Workers waged these strikes in the name of equal rights and more humane working conditions, not to keep Paddy and Bridget in their place.[27] However pervasive nativism may have been in Yankee working-class circles, ethnocultural antagonisms were not an important component of labor-capital strife. In fact, Irish workers participated in a number of the strikes.

To get the Yankee Protestant majority to abandon their own parties and vote Know-Nothing, the American party had to reach out beyond the Native Americans, Maine Law men, and even the more broadly based Free-Soilers and recruit the city dwellers and rustics, fishermen and farmers, and factory workers and tradesmen who made up the rank and file of the two major parties. It hoped to accomplish this by offering them what the monocausalists did not—a viable alternative to a party system that had ceased to work in the common interest. Its promise to call out "those who have been furthest from the political cliques of the day" and to rid public life of "political hacks and trading politicians" carried its appeal beyond the circumscribed vision of the Native American fathers and cast Know-Nothingism in the mold of a populist reform party that tapped the republican and antiparty sentiments of Americans of that generation.[28]

It also tapped into the vast pool of potential voters who harbored class grievances, for implicit in the promise of Know-Nothingism was the idea that a people's government would shape economic policy in response to the reality of a society divided along class lines. Underscoring this reality was the economic recession that hit in late 1854, forcing many manufacturing establishments to suspend operations. The Whig press advised labor to accept reduced wages so as to avoid joining the growing army of unemployed. Meanwhile, the state's railroad companies were enjoying a banner year. Their volume of business and income were up. Nevertheless, the boards of directors and stockholders complained of rising costs and called for a general advance in rates. Ordinary citizens who had to deal with such realities gravitated toward Know-Nothing lodges because of their disenchantment with the established party system, and that disenchantment was rooted in the failure of the government of Massachusetts to come to grips with the tensions, pressures, and dislocations inherent in rapid industrial and urban growth. Now the bottom half of the socioeconomic strata had an alternative to a failed political system. It proved an attractive alternative, particularly so for young, poor, and working-class voters. So many workers rushed into the lodges that it prompted talk of a labor uprising.[29]

Lodge membership afforded the forgotten man the chance to do something about his circumstances other than cast ballots for candidates handpicked by his social betters. It promised to amplify his voice in those governmental decisions that affected his daily life. As a Know-Nothing, he could take an active part in a populist campaign to replace the existing party system with a political order that promised to use the state to benefit all the people.[30]

That appeal was by no means limited to the lower classes. It carried great weight in all parts of the state and among all but the most affluent, especially so in the case of the urban majority. It was this aspect of the Know-Nothing recruitment campaign that fed the ground swell of support for the new party and transformed it from the narrow, xenophobic, anti-Catholic order that its Native American fathers had fashioned into a genuine people's movement.

A few weeks after it had begun operations in the major population centers of eastern Massachusetts, the new party made its presence felt when its candidates, running on "Citizens" tickets, swept municipal elections in the Whig strongholds of Boston, Roxbury, and Cambridge. Know-Nothing J.V.C. Smith received the largest vote ever cast for a mayor in Boston, prompting a puzzled *Boston Post* to ascribe the phenomenon to a support base "composed of as many colors as Joseph's coat—abolitionists, free-soilers, Whigs, 'Native Americans', a few democrats etc.—one of the most reprehensible coalitions that we have had since the one that defeated the proposed new constitution." Over the next several months,

"Sam" won local elections in Chelsea, Lynn, Marblehead, Waltham, Stoneham, and other towns. In Whig Salem, the Know-Nothings ran a machinist for mayor who captured over 70 percent of the vote.[31] One after another, the results signaled a crisis of public faith in the established parties, but these being local elections and the new party's concealing its identity under the rubric of "Citizen," scant attention was paid by the establishment press to the first visible stirrings of political unrest.

"Sam" was intent on courting only the rank and file of the established parties, but a handful of shrewd politicians like Henry Wilson, Anson Burlingame, and Nathaniel Banks took note of the early signs of support for the mysterious new order and rushed out to join the crowd so that they might lead it. First, however, they had to satisfy the Native American fathers that their commitment to American principles was genuine. This was not always easy. Wilson, for example, was blackballed the first time he applied for admission to a lodge because his sudden conversion to nativist dogma struck the screening committee as having more the appearance of convenience than of conviction. Only after quieting Native American suspicions and swearing fealty to the proscriptive tenets of Know-Nothingism did Wilson finally gain admission.[32]

Other Free-Soil politicians, among them Edward L. Keyes, John L. Swift, Charles Slack, J.Q.A. Griffin, John W. Foster, A. W. Alford, and James W. Stone, followed Wilson into the order. So did most of the rank and file. As a group, they enjoyed an advantage over their Whig and Democratic counterparts in that their party had consistently courted the nativist vote. Some of them, like Wilson and Burlingame, were angling for high political office, and all of them accepted the ugly implications of ethnic and religious proscription.[33]

Free-Soil loyalist Edward L. Pierce, contemplating his former colleagues' pandering to the Native American mindset, exploded, "When the freedom of an empire is at issue, they run off to chase a paddy." His point was well taken. The decision by Free-Soil pragmatists to take on the freight of Native American bigotry, even if it were for the greater good of the cause, was reprehensible. As Pierce also noted, "cussed furriner" was as bigoted a sentiment as "D-d nigger."[34] But it could just as well have been said of the Free-Soil purists that while the freedom of that same empire hung in the balance, they ran off to tilt at windmills. Antislavery was a cause in desperate need of a viable political party, yet their idea of a solution to this crisis was to propose combining two moribund political organizations—theirs and the Whigs—into a new antislavery party. Power brokers like Wilson and ward boss James W. Stone of Boston nurtured more practical aims. Even if they and their followers had attached themselves to a party that did not espouse a single antislavery goal, that was a deficiency they intended to remedy.

By midsummer, some of the more prescient outsiders were groping toward the same conclusion that Wilson had reached by March—that the regular parties "seem to be approaching that happy state of solution or dissolution" and that the American party might have an important and "perhaps controlling" influence on the outcome of the state election. Charles Sumner, returning home from Washington "to take the stump during the Autumn canvass" on behalf of his party, found no party to stump for. The older parties had likewise fallen into desuetude as their rank and file stole away into the Know-Nothing lodges. Some of the shrewder (or less principled) Whig and Democratic politicians, having detected the silent erosion that was afflicting their parties, had wriggled like salmon through the nativist barriers into "the No [sic] Nothing ranks, and there they are contending for the supremacy, each to his individual notion of what is good either for himself or the nation."[35] Like antislavery reformers and prohibitionists, the sharp, trading politicians had no place else to go.

One of those who made the switch for personal reasons was Nathaniel Banks, a Democrat who had been elected to Congress by the coalition. George Boutwell told of a chance encounter with his friend and former political ally during the summer of 1854. Banks wanted to know if Boutwell were going to join the American party. Boutwell replied that he was not and that he had left politics to set up a law practice. Asked his plans, Banks rejoined, "I am in politics, and I must go on."[36] And go on he did. Earlier in the year, he had joined a Know-Nothing lodge in Washington, D.C., preparatory to his applying for admission to the lodge in his home town of Waltham. Banks's eagerness for office—he coveted the Know-Nothing nomination for Congress, but accepted renomination by the Democratic party—and his convenient conversion to nativism stirred up enough opposition to delay his admission to the Waltham lodge for several weeks. Even after his admission, the district council offered the congressional nomination to the Reverend Lyman Whiting, whose orthodoxy on nativist principles was beyond reproach. Only when the reverend turned down the honor did the nod go to Banks. Once the decision was made, however, the Waltham lodge rallied its full membership behind brother Banks, declaring the former bobbin boy a fit representative of his district's workingpeople.[37]

Not all of the self-serving politicians who gained entrance were closely associated with the working class. For example, Henry J. Gardner, a wealthy wool merchant and a Boston Brahmin, was admitted. However, Gardner had never held a major office (which, according to his former political allies, prompted him to abandon the Whig party), and, like Banks, he was a man of easy principles who ingratiated himself with the Native American clique by espousing hard-line stands on nativist issues and with antislavery Know-Nothings by professing strong Free-Soil opinions.[38]

Other than Wilson and Banks, none of the state's leading political figures had undertaken the rites of passage that would have led them into the secret world of "Sam." In a telling commentary on how far removed the Whig elite were from the commonalty, Edward Everett confessed that for him, "the course and strength of Know-Nothingism [remains] . . . wrapped in mystery." "Some claim for them 50,000 votes," he scoffed. "I doubt if they cast a fifth of that number." Everett based his estimate on the supposition that "no person of standing in the political world is known to have joined them."[39]

Not every member of the political establishment shared Everett's elitist belief that voters automatically follow leaders. Whig stalwart Ezra Lincoln, on the eve of the Whig state convention, predicted that the results of the state election would hinge on the Know-Nothings. Equally perceptive (or better informed) was C. F. Adams. His friend Charles Sumner thought that Adams had a good chance to fill the senate seat left vacant by Everett's resignation. Adams, however, had been tipped off that the Know-Nothings were going to "make a complete revolution" that fall and thus wanted no part of the contest. F. W. Bird agreed, forecasting that the "dark-lantern party" would support Wilson in the contest.[40]

Some nonmembers received privileged information from Know-Nothing friends. For example, Dr. James W. Stone wrote Sumner in mid-March disclaiming his membership in the order, which left him free, he assured the senator, to "speak to you without betraying any confidence." Stone thereupon divulged to his friend the news that Burlingame had joined the order and that other Boston Free-Soilers were doing likewise. Dr. Stone also served notice that the Know-Nothings "are destined to exert no inconsiderable control in political movements."[41]

There were also instances of unsolicited contacts with members of the state's high society. Early in the summer of 1854, two men, presumably Know-Nothings, called on C. F. Adams at his home in Quincy to sound him out on the possibility of his accepting the American nomination for the U.S. Senate. Adams would have none of it. A few weeks later, Adams received a second visit. Again the enticement was the Senate seat in return either for his joining the Order of United Americans or the American party, and again Adams rejected the offer on the grounds that he would not be party to secret obligations, nor would he condone the proscription of the rights of immigrants or Catholics. He did venture the opinion, however, that his visitors' party might achieve two beneficial results— the destruction of the old parties and the curbing of the politicians who court the Catholic vote. His visitors gone, Adams pondered the possible cost of his refusal: "There are many reasons why I should suit them [the Know-Nothings] very well at the moment, if I were willing to lend myself to their purposes, and my position away from all parties is a strong recommendation." Charles Sumner, over a cup of tea, told Adams that a delegation of Know-Nothings had made the same offer to fellow Free-Soiler Judge George Bigelow, who rejected the bait of these "fly blown" emissaries. So did Judge Charles Allen and S. C. Phillips, who were also members of the Free-Soil patrician set.[42]

The quest for famous names extended to members of the Whig ruling class as well. Edward Everett, whose senate seat these phantom missionaries were so generously offering, reported an encounter in which he was promised "everything which it [the American party] supposed itself able to bestow" if he would agree to head the order. Everett refused to be soiled by Know-Nothingism, as did Whig merchant Franklin Dexter, who was offered the Senate seat.[43] In September, a delegation waited on Robert C. Winthrop, scion of one of the Commonwealth's oldest and most prestigious families. They unfolded for him a dazzling proposal. If he would consent to lend his name to the movement, they guaranteed him leadership of their party and election as governor or, if he preferred, elevation to the U.S. Senate. The former Whig governor rejected the terms on the grounds that he was opposed to all secret societies, especially those based on religious and ethnic intolerance.[44]

There is sound reason to doubt whether the decision to dispatch these delegations on their appointed rounds originated within the official circles of the Know-Nothing order or, for that matter, whether these messengers could deliver what they promised. Apparently, the men were Native Americans seeking to attach prominent names to their cause. All of those whom they contacted—both Whig and Free-Soil—were conservative elites and leading members of the old political order that "Sam" was out to destroy. Winthrop himself had serious reservations as to "how much authority these mysterious visitants really had and how far they were in a position to carry out their promises." But Winthrop did pick up an important clue from his visitors with regard to political trends in the state: "If it be true that they have enlisted Wilson, they are not unlikely to become a power. He is far too shrewd to allow himself to be made a catspaw."[45]

Occasional leaks notwithstanding, "Sam" conducted with remarkable stealth an intensive and far-reaching campaign of mobilizing "the uninitiated" that left "each of the old parties . . . paralyzed without understanding the reason." Few outsiders had any means other than conjecture for gauging the numbers or assessing the prospects of the new party. Even seasoned political activists were left in the dark. "What duplicity this movement has introduced," a frustrated Edward L. Pierce complained to fellow Free-Soiler Horace Mann. "Men deny that they are Know-Nothings when you know they are. They say 'I don't know' when they do know."[46] Veteran newspapermen likewise missed the trend. Only scattered references to the new party appeared in the major newspapers during the first half of the year. In mid-August, the state's leading Whig journal, the *Boston Daily Advertiser*, finally took notice. The newspaper admitted that it did not have much information to go on, but it condemned the strange new party anyway for its secrecy and its "ridiculous gossip about guns, and poison, and massacre." Apparently, the secret order's chief purpose was to deprive "friendless servant girls and Irish lumpers" of their livelihood. A party so dedicated and so contrary to republican principles, the *Advertiser* assured its readers, could never win.[47]

It was in this state of blissful ignorance that the Whigs gathered in mid-August at the Music Hall in Boston for their annual state convention. They were determined to retain their own organization "at all hazards," even if that meant adopting a new identity. Promoting themselves as the party of reform, they called attention to the half dozen constitutional amendments (culled from the Coalition's 1853 proposals) that they were sponsoring and to the party's antislavery resolutions, which denounced the Kansas-Nebraska Act and called for the restoration of the Missouri Compromise, a ban on further extension of slavery into the national territories, and the repeal of the Fugitive Slave Law. As a lure for nativist voters, the platform excoriated the Democratic administration for appointing foreigners to public office "to the exclusion of native citizens of highest reputation and lofty patriotism."[48]

Know-Nothing proselytizing in the cities and large towns, which had been under way since the fall of 1853, presented a far graver threat to the urban-based Whig party than had the small-town, agrarian-oriented Coalition; yet, nothing in the convention proceedings betrayed an awareness or even an inkling on the part of the Whig leadership that they were presiding over an empty shell of a party whose rank and file had defected to the Know-Nothings months before. Quite to the contrary, "Sam's" policy of maintaining silence outside the lodges had lulled the Whig establishment into confident expectations of further victories. Hence, the *Advertiser*, in its assessment of the convention's results, confidently prattled: "We do not recollect a time at this season of the year, when the prospects were fairer for a successful result of the Autumnal election. If a judicious course is pursued by the Whig party, they are sure of an honorable triumph."[49]

The Democrats held their convention in Lowell in late September. The delegates, at the prodding of the party bosses, renominated perennial gubernatorial candidate Henry W. Bishop and produced a platform that endorsed the Pierce administration and the Kansas-Nebraska Act.[50] Neither action was calculated to stir enthusiasm on behalf of a party that had long since ceased to be competitive in the Commonwealth.

What was left of the Free-Soil organization in the wake of its humiliating failure to achieve a fusion of parties in July gathered in Worcester in September under the name Republican. The new name notwithstanding, the convention represented no more than a remnant of die-hard Free-Soilers. Their platform delivered a powerful attack against the "growing encroachments" of the slave states and urged repeal of the Fugitive Slave Law and the Kansas-Nebraska Act and abolition of slavery in the District of Columbia. One speaker envisioned the coming contest as one that would pit "Slavery, Romanism, and Rum [against] Freedom, Protestantism, and Temperance."[51] On these matters the delegates were mostly agreed; but when the convention majority chose Henry Wilson to head the party slate, it exposed deep fissures inside the antislavery movement. Wilson's membership in the American party had not prevented his laboring throughout the summer with other antislavery leaders in the cause of fusion; and his acceptance of the Republican nomination was consistent with that goal. But to the Free-Soil elite, some of whom were aware of or suspected the "Natick Cobbler's" Know-Nothing connection, Wilson was unacceptable. Judge Charles Allen took to the floor to launch a blistering attack against both Wilson and the Know-Nothing movement. His motion to drop Wilson in favor of another candidate, however, failed to carry.[52]

Wilson's double role laid him open to charges of bad faith, and Adams, for one, deemed his "intrigues . . . beyond conception." Dana agreed, faulting Wilson for having "drained the Free Soil party of its power of doing good." And a few days before the election, Wilson confirmed the worst fears of his patrician rivals when he sent word to the Republican state committee asking that it remove his name from its slate. With only a few days left before the election, the Republicans were forced to go with Wilson; but his withdrawal had obliterated what was left of an independent antislavery organization in the state. It made little difference anyway. Most Free-Soilers had stolen away months earlier to join "Sam," leaving the Republican party "a fife and drum without followers."[53]

In his memoirs, penned years later, Wilson concealed his betrayal of the 1854 Republicans behind a screen of selective recollections. For the antislavery movement to succeed, he wrote, it first had to destroy the existing party system. Only then could a new antislavery party (namely, the Republican party) arise from the ruins and sweep to power. The failure of the fusion conventions in July and September, however, made evident that only the American party could administer the coup de grace to the Whig and Democratic parties. It was with this in mind that antislavery men from all parties—Wilson among them—had flocked into Know-Nothing lodges, thereby dooming the embryonic Republican movement, but paving the way for the rise of its greater namesake.[54] What Wilson failed to mention was that he had joined the Know-Nothing order in March, months before the fusion conventions met; that he had told his friend Sumner several weeks prior to the opening of the Worcester "People's Convention" in July that unless the Whigs agreed to fusion, the Know-Nothings would carry "every city in the state"; or that he himself lacked confidence in the fusion movement, since "Whigs and Democrats are sick of politics and are going in for [the Know-Nothing] order."[55] Wilson, in other words, knew long before the stillbirth of the 1854 Republican party that "Sam" had mobilized the rank and file of all parties into a political movement that transcended the antislavery issue.

His enemies had no doubt that raw ambition had governed the decision to withdraw, timed as it was on the eve of the election to extract the maximum advantage for the American gubernatorial candidate. They accused him of sacrificing principle and cause for a seat in the U.S. Senate. A more charitable commentator, after taking stock of Wilson's deficiencies of character, concluded that although the means were questionable, the Free-Soil leader's motive for joining the American party was to advance the antislavery cause.[56] That Wilson lusted after high office there can be little doubt; but there is even less reason to doubt that he remained true to his commitment to human freedom. He had every intention, as his actions were to prove, of turning the American party into a powerful new antislavery organization.

On October 18, more than fifteen hundred Know-Nothing delegates assembled at the Tremont Temple in Boston for the opening of the party's first state convention. Their political rivals, lacking access to the secret proceedings, hardly knew what to expect. Fortunately for them and for posterity, there were informants planted among the delegates who leaked details of the proceedings to the outside world. Their accounts revealed that the convention was "a mongrel gathering" in which nativists by no means predominated.

In the jostling for place, a handful of politicians skilled in the art of trade-offs and bargains had succeeded in insinuating themselves into positions of influence. That the first manifestation of the iron law of oligarchy within the Know-Nothing movement should surface in a convention stocked with delegates who for the most part had honed their political talents among friends and neighbors in their home lodges is unsurprising. Political amateurs and even Native American leaders like A. B. Ely and Jonathan Peirce proved no match for the professionals in the internal maneuverings for place.[57] Henry J. Gardner, for example, aspired to the governor's chair, but his background as a member of the Boston Whig aristocracy—he had served as president of the Boston Common Council and as the Back Bay representative in the General Court—and his naked political ambition stirred up opposition. Maine Law and Free-Soil delegates pressed Gardner for his position on the slavery and temperance issues. "You may say," Gardner assured his interrogators, "that I have always been an antislavery man, and that I am a temperance man of fifteen years standing." Outside the convention, men familiar with the candidate's fondness for brandy and his record as a "proslavery, Fugitive Slave Law, Webster Whig" were scandalized by the "extent of Mr. Gardner's tergiversation."[58] Wilson and Burlingame did not share their repugnance, if credence can be lent to press reports that they and their fellow Free-Soil Americans voting in a bloc helped put the "wool merchant turned politician" over the top on the fourth ballot. Theirs was not a selfless act. Gardner's nomination turned on a *quid pro quo*: Free-Soil votes in return for Gardner's promise to back Wilson's bid for the vacant U.S. Senate seat and Anson Burlingame's bid for Congress.[59]

There were rumblings of discontent from rank-and-file delegates regarding the political intrigue and scrambling for office taking place in the convention and even some threats of a bolt. The Native American fathers in particular were aggrieved, complaining that the delegates had awarded the choicest nominations to "political stock-jobbers and curbstone brokers." Overall, however, the convention remained faithful to its mandate to keep Know-Nothingism a people's movement by choosing political newcomers. Ambitious politicians like Gardner, Banks, and Burlingame who won choice party nominations proved to be the exception in 1854. They had reason to consider themselves privileged. Unlike others of their calling who remained outside the order, they were privy to lodge enrollment figures and looked forward to November with confidence. A. B. Ely, for example, "as a friendly act," advised a Brahmin candidate for Congress to withdraw from the race, as he faced certain defeat. In Gardner's case, the confidence swelled into arrogance. "You had better not abuse me," he warned a Whig newspaperman whom he had chanced to meet on a Boston street, "as you are abusing me in 'The Atlas'. I shall be elected by a very large majority."[60]

By the time the American convention had released its slate in late October, the confidence that had marked earlier Whig pronouncements had subsided into more sober appraisals. Especially worrisome were the rumors that the Free-Soilers under Wilson had forged a new coalition, this one with the Know-Nothings and the state temperance organization. Still, the Brahmins took comfort in the assumption that a party ticket consisting of "spavined ministers, lying tooth-pullers, and buggering priests" and headed by "that rickety vermin of a Henry J. Gardner" could not win. R. H. Dana, Jr., went further, deeming it unlikely that "Sam" could survive such nominations.[61] As it turned out, the Know-Nothing slate, packed as it was with political unknowns, proved a source of strength, for it confirmed the party's determination to purge the state government of political careerists.

Election day opened in the midst of a deluge, which, in the words of an astonished reporter, poured "water and Know-Nothings all day." That night, as fireworks exploded and cannons thundered on the Boston Common, a crowd of Know-Nothings, its spirit in no way dampened by the still falling rain, gathered in front of Gardner's residence on Mt. Vernon Street. A spokesman for the throng read a congratulatory address to which a jubilant Gardner responded, "Whatever may be the result elsewhere in the state—of which I know nothing (laughter and cheers)—we can proudly say that in Boston our principles—and they are American principles—are triumphant."[62]

There was, as events proved, sound cause for Gardner's exuberance. In its first statewide run, the American party had managed the greatest election upset in the history of the state. Every constitutional state officer, the entire congressional delegation, all forty state senators, and all but 3 of the 379 representatives bore the Know-Nothing stamp. Gardner's 63 percent majority (the first since 1847) and his 81,500 vote total were the largest ever. He carried every city and all but twenty of the state's more than three hundred towns. All regions were caught up in the Know-Nothing tide, which swept across the state from Cape Cod to the Berkshires. Familiar landmarks on the political landscape were swept away in the flood. Whig Congregational towns went Know-Nothing by approximately the same margins as Democratic dissenting towns.[63] The tide flowed across party lines as well. The Whig vote sank to less than half of its 1853 total; the Democractic vote to just over a third; and the Free-Soil to less than a quarter. Only the Democratic party would resurface in the wake of the Know-Nothing tidal surge.

Almost everybody was taken by surprise.[64] Even C. F. Adams, who was expecting a strong Know-Nothing showing, was thunderstruck. "There has been," he penned in his diary, "no revolution so complete since the organization of government." Adams was not given to exaggeration. "Sam," in the span of a single election, had destroyed the existing party system and transformed Massachusetts into a one-party state. Indeed, the election marked the end of a political era and, as one newspaper headlined, paved the way for "A new [*sic*] Deal All Around."[65]

Members of the Whig establishment could barely grasp what had happened. The *Advertiser*, in a bitter outburst at the electorate for turning the Whigs out of power, complained, "This is the way Massachusetts rewards the faithful labors of her public men." Everett thought the election "the most astonishing result ever witnessed in our politics"; and in a letter to Winthrop, he expressed his misgivings with the people's choices: "What a political overturn! Burlingame and the other man—I forget his name [Linus B. Comins]—to represent Boston—and Gardner chosen Governor by a heavier vote and larger majority than every governor before." Winthrop, contemplating the shambles of his party and the prospects of Know-Nothing rule, voiced grief for "poor old Massachusetts."[66]

Others, too, were filled with apprehension and dismay. William Lloyd Garrison's *Liberator* explained why:

> Who was so wild, or so enthusiastic, as to dream that a party unheard of at the last election, . . . operating through invisible agencies, avowing no other object than that of proscribing men on account of their birth and peculiar religious faiths, afraid or unwilling to hold a single public meeting, and burrowing in secret like a mole in the dark, would suddenly spring up, snap asunder the strongest ties of party, enlist under its banner the most incongruous elements, absorb the elective strength of the State, and carry everything before it with the sweep of a whirlwind, leaving only the smallest fragments of the three parties which were struggling for supremacy?[67]

Those wrestling with that question identified the more highly visible social forces—sectional tensions, xenophobia, anti-Catholicism, and temperance—as the leading causes of the fragmentation. The historiographical debate ever since has hewed to the same assumptions.

Adams was satisfied that whatever other consequences might develop in the aftermath of an election that had left the American party in possession of "every office in the State," the results spelled disaster for the antislavery cause. He estimated that some 80 percent of its adherents had deserted the crusade for human freedom "to enlist . . . against a shadow."[68]

Most of Adams's contemporaries thought otherwise, arguing that what detonated the Know-Nothing explosion was not nativism but the very cause that Adams believed abandoned. They reasoned that the enactment of the Kansas-Nebraska Act and the capture in Boston of fugitive slave Anthony Burns and his forcible return to slavery, both of which occurred in May of 1854, so outraged public opinion against Southern aggression as to swing the mass of people behind the antislavery cause. "There has never been," Free-Soiler Josiah Quincy reported in the wake of the fugitive slave incident, "such a sudden change in public opinion as the rendition of Burns to slavery has produced." Even the "old-fashioned, conservative compromise, Union Whigs," according to one of their own, were transformed by the outrage into "stark mad abolitionists." "Massachusetts," Amos A. Lawrence fumed, "can never be made hunting ground for masters to pursue their slaves."[69] And if Whig leaders were agitated by the Burns incident, they were devastated by Kansas-Nebraska. Edward Everett, who had warned his Southern Whig colleagues in the Senate that the proposal would "cut the throat of every conservative Whig at the North," was convinced that its passage had killed the Whig party and "materially accelerated" the rise of the American party.[70]

On this point, angry Free-Soilers agreed with Everett, but for different reasons. For them, Congress, by its action, had driven home the lesson of the futility of working with either major party. Horace Mann articulated their sense of betrayal: "The North in 1850 invested its capital in Slavery. The Kansas-Nebraska Act is the first payment of interest." The antislavery movement in Massachusetts had reached a crossroad: Either it could pursue the quixotic course of the 1854 Republican party to certain defeat, or it could attach itself to the one organization that could advance the antislavery cause—the American party. This, claimed Henry Wilson, was what led voters from all parties "who cared less for its [Know-Nothingism's] avowed principles and purposes than for the higher claims of justice and humanity . . . to disrupt the Whig and Democratic parties, in the confident hope that out of the disorganized masses there would come a great political party antagonistic to the dominating influence of the Slave Power."[71]

Other commentators on these events were not so ready as Wilson to dismiss as irrelevant the American party's "avowed principles and purposes." "Sam," they reasoned, had capitalized on the pressures induced by mass immigration to blame the Irish for society's ills, and the order found a receptive audience. Almost everyone, it seems, bore a grudge against the Irish. Their burgeoning numbers, the bill of charges read, posed a threat to such cherished institutions as the public school system, the Protestant religion, and republican government. Paddy was stereotyped as clannish, priest-ridden, and given to drinking and brawling. Taxpayers pointed to the disproportionate numbers of Irish among the state's public charges; temperance crusaders linked Irish poverty to drunkedness; and the antislavery camp branded them tools of the slavocracy.[72] Members of the Brahmin inner circle, like Rufus Choate, Edward Everett, and Everett's brother-in-law, Nathan Hale, speculated that working-class Yankee resentment of having to compete with foreigners for jobs had combined with "the traditional New England jealousy of Romanism" to produce the potent Know-Nothing brew.[73] Recent studies, while sharing the assumption that the native working class resented foreign competition for jobs, cite the fear of the growing immigrant vote as "probably the major proximate cause of the formation of the Know-Nothing order."[74] These findings square with earlier analyses of party realignment in antebellum Massachusetts.

A number of Democrats and Free-Soilers from both wings of their parties blamed the Irish for the defeat of the constitution. C. F. Adams, still smarting over his rejection as a delegate to the convention, which he ascribed to Irish voters, lashed out at the alleged Catholic voting bloc "which had gone far to bring about in Quincy the present state of things, as many of my friends in disgust at this combined religious action had gone into the new combination to resist that dangerous influence."[75] Historians have echoed this theme. Political nativism, William G. Bean theorized, stemmed from political causes. Specifically, the Coalitionists, believing that the Irish had joined their vote to that of the Cotton Whigs to defeat the constitution, marched into the lodges to destroy Irish political power. Oscar Handlin added that when the Irish abandoned the Democratic party in 1853 to defeat the constitution and reelect the Whigs, it heralded their arrival as an independent, formidable political force, a force, moreover, whose illiberal proslavery and antireformist views threatened the traditional values of the Yankee Protestant majority. It was in response to that threat that the majority sided with the nativist order.[76]

Election returns and census data fail to sustain either the Wilson or the Bean/Handlin interpretations. Those who argue that an Irish bloc vote, by crushing constitutional reform, triggered a Coalition backlash that was responsible for the Know-Nothing landslide fall short on a number of counts. First, the constitutional question in 1853 rallied voters along party lines that "Sam" severed the following election. In fact, as many Know-Nothings had voted against the constitution as for it, which certainly would not have been the case if this were the burning issue that accounted for "Sam's" landslide. Second, the Coalition and "Sam" drew their greatest strength from different constituency bases, the Coalition from the yeomanry of the interior and "Sam" from workers and urban easterners. Third, there was no substantive Irish vote in Massachusetts in the early 1850s. It has already been noted that of the eight constitutional referenda on the ballot in 1853, the school fund proposal—the one that allegedly had stirred the wrath of Irish voters and brought them out in record numbers to vote against it— came closest to passing. More remarkable, perhaps, the foreign vote was all but invisible the following year in the face of the most ominous political threat that European immigrants have ever encountered in the United States. This may have been due to the absence of a Democratic infrastructure in Whig Massachusetts capable of speeding immigrants through the naturalization process to the polls, as was the case in other states. In any event, another quarter of a century would pass before the Irish began to make their political presence felt in Massachusetts. And finally, as Dale Baum has shown, Whig solidarity and an exceptionally high Whig turnout in 1853, not the alleged Irish swing vote, doomed the constitution.[77] Yet, in 1854, the anticonstitution Whigs contributed more votes to "Sam's" total than either the Democrats or the Free-Soilers.

Figure 2 carries the point further. Know-Nothing strength centered in the cities and large towns, which accounted for nearly two-thirds of the total Know-Nothing vote. City voters, 60.7 percent of whom had spurned the constitution in 1853, favored the American party the following year by virtually the same margin (61.4 percent). Voters in the larger towns also had rejected the constitution; yet the following year, voters in these same towns far outpaced those in the smaller towns in their support for the Know-Nothing order. The cities and leading towns contained the major concentration of Irish residents (83 percent of the state's foreign-born population); and the Irish, it is safe to say, did not vote for the xenophobic, Catholic-baiting American party.[78] Only the smaller, predominantly rural and agricultural towns, which were relatively free of a foreign presence, showed any evidence in their voting patterns of the link that Bean and Handlin theorized existed between the Coalition and the American party. Significantly, the smaller towns, which cast the strongest vote for the constitution, trailed the rest of the state in their support for the American party. Put in general terms, then, Know-Nothingism ran strongest where backing for the constitution was weakest, and vice versa, which would be odd, indeed, if the Know-Nothing triumph owed its landslide proportions to a recrudescence of the Coalition.

Nor do the data support Henry Wilson's contention that the sectional crisis and inflamed antislavery feelings suddenly converged in May of 1854 to trigger a rush

FIGURE 2. Comparison of City, Town, and State Voting Patterns:
1853 Constitution[a] and 1854 Know-Nothing

a. Mass., *State Convention* 3: 756–68.
b. DeWitt, *Census of Massachusetts, 1855,* 98–132.

of Free-Soilers, Democrats, and Whigs into the American party. Know-Nothing recruitment had begun in earnest at least half a year before the heating up of the territorial question. Mention has been made that the party had won a number of municipal and town elections by early 1854. Most of these were in cities and manufacturing towns that had never voted Free-Soil. Boston's Know-Nothing mayor, J. V. C. Smith, whom Free-Soilers tagged "the Black Huntsman of Shawmut" for having called out the militia to force Anthony Burns back to slavery, easily won reelection despite a concerted effort by the antislavery forces to unseat him.[79] Northampton Free-Soiler C. P. Huntington recalled in a speech delivered to the Massachusetts house that the pulpit, the bar, the three branches of government, most politicians, and, except Free-Soil, the parties and party press all acquiesced in the Fugitive Slave Law during the years between the Compromise of 1850 and the Kansas-Nebraska Act. Huntington doubted that either the passage of the Nebraska Act or the seizure of Burns aroused much public indignation, citing the dismal failure of the 1854 Republicans as evidence to the contrary.[80]

Figure 3 supports the contention that the degree of industrialization, urbanization, population growth, and class divisions had far greater impact on town voting

FIGURE 3. Comparison of Voting Patterns in Selected Towns: 1853 Free-Soil, 1854 Know-Nothing, and 1855 Republican

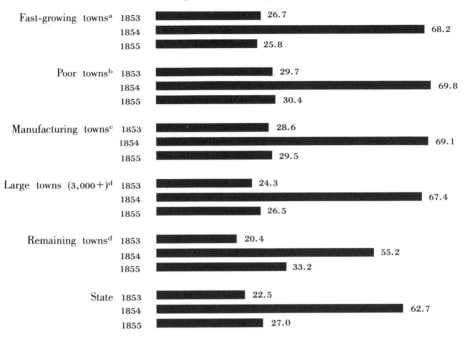

a. Towns in industrialized counties (Bristol, Essex, Hampden, Middlesex, Norfolk, Plymouth, Suffolk, and Worcester) that increased in population 20 percent or more from 1850 to 1855, including towns that lost residents because of annexation. See Oliver Warner, *Census of Massachusetts, 1865,* 240–261; Kevin H. White, *Historical Data Relating to Counties, Cities and Towns in Massachusetts* (Boston, 1966).

b. Towns with per capita distribution of personal wealth of $110 or less, except towns in which agriculture was the major industry. Data for Norfolk and Middlesex towns are in the *Gazette* (Dedham), daily issues 1855 and 1856; and the *Cambridge Chronicle,* Nov. 7, 1857. Data for other towns are in Oliver Warner, *Journal and Documents of the Valuation Committee of the Year 1860* (Boston, 1861), 70–147.

c. Towns in which the number employed full-time in the manufacture of articles amounted to 20 percent or more of the population. See DeWitt, *Statistical Information Relating to Industry in Massachusetts,* 1–650.

d. DeWitt, *Census of Massachusetts, 1855,* 98–132.

patterns in 1854 than did the sectional controversy. Nearly seven out of every ten persons voting in 1854 in the towns most affected by these conditions cast their ballots for the American party. Yet, these same towns that voted so overwhelmingly Know-Nothing failed to back the Free-Soil party in 1853 or the Republican party in 1855. To argue that Know-Nothingism in Massachusetts was a manifestation of antislavery convictions is to say that those convictions could produce a landslide vote in 1854 but not enough to attract as much as a third of the turnout the year before or the year after. Based on the election returns, it would be more reasonable to conclude that few men, other than former Free-Soilers, voted Know-Nothing because of antislavery convictions. It is also apparent that, Wilson's bombast to the contrary, the Free-Soilers, who cast only a little over one-fifth of the total Know-Nothing vote, needed the American party far more than the American party needed them. As "Warrington," who was abolitionist to the core, noted, political antislaveryism never carried an election in Massachusetts.[81]

The data, then, make clear that neither an alleged Coalition backlash against Irish voting power nor an antislavery uprising brought about the destruction of the party system. Still another explanation—that nativism was the major dynamic responsible for the electoral upheaval of 1854—demands scrutiny. Here the election returns do not provide as clear a reading, other than to confirm Oscar Handlin's finding that "Sam" had activated thousands of new or infrequent voters.[82] A number of historians, including Handlin, have pointed to this phenomenon as evidence of a sudden eruption of nativism in the political arena. Unfortunately, no polling data exist to illuminate voter motivations. There are, however, substantive reasons for challenging this interpretation.

Nativism, it is true, crossed party lines, but even if it had reached pandemic proportions in the 1850s, which seems to have been the case in Massachusetts as well as in many other parts of the country, xenophobia and religious bigotry did not necessarily translate into votes.[83] For example, other states had higher ratios of foreign-born to their total population, and higher visibility, if anything, should have intensified nativist resentment. Yet, support for "Sam" in these states fell far short of the record Know-Nothing vote in Massachusetts. Ethnocultural prejudice was but one—albeit an important one—of many competing considerations that informed the voting decision in antebellum Massachusetts. Certainly, burgeoning Catholicism and the hordes of Irish immigrants clustering into the cities and manufacturing towns of the state was an unsettling development for the Yankee Protestant majority. But the same could be said of the factory system, class divisions, urban blight, and other manifestations of the deteriorating quality of urban life, which, like the looming foreign presence, were part of a complex of issues generated by the industrial order and which, because of the symbiotic ties between the business and political communities, went unaddressed.

To get ordinary voters to abandon their own parties required something more than a diet of nativistic polemics, as the Native Americans had learned to their chagrin a few years earlier, when their efforts to build a winning coalition of voters based on harangues against popery and the foreign peril failed miserably. Another example of the limited vote-getting appeal of nativism occurred in 1853, when the voters rejected the school fund referendum despite its obvious anti-Catholic overtones. That it came the closest to passing of all the resolutions on the ballot does say something for the attraction that nativism (and the principle of separation of church and state) had for voters, but that it failed passage illustrates that the mix of regional and partisan considerations (which played on both sides of the issue) exercised far greater influence on the voting decision.

Political nativism on its own, in other words, fared poorly at the polls. The average antebellum voter may have shared some of the thinking of the hard-core bigots, but ordinarily he did not vote with them. Even when he did so in 1854, he had his own priorities. For example, nativism had little bearing on the Free-Soil decision to vote Know-Nothing in 1854 and none at all on the Free-Soil American conversion to Republicanism the following year. In the context of their overriding interest—to check the spread of slavery—nativism was of peripheral concern. Similarly, the Democratic party, plagued by the mass defection of its rank and file to "Sam" in 1854, polled a dismal 11 percent of the statewide total; but one year later, the Democratic vote had bounced back up to 26 percent of the total, which, given the interplay between the rigor of the American party's persecution of the Irish Catholic minority and the Democratic party's insistence on equal political and civil rights for immigrants and Roman Catholics, would be a study in inconsistency if nativism were the prime cause for their 1854 hiatus. The same may be said for the assertion that Democratic Coalitionists converted en masse to Know-Nothingism because of the defeat of the constitution, given the fact that the Know-Nothings implemented the Coalition's program.

Like most voters, the Democrats had reasons other than bigotry or a desire to revive the Coalition for turning against the established parties and professional politicians. The Know-Nothing call to take part in the formation of a people's party and to use that party to address some of the more pressing problems affecting their daily lives struck a responsive chord with rank-and-file Democrats. After one year of Know-Nothing rule, however, most Democrats had returned to their own party, their populist enthusiasm for the order having been extinguished by the ability of cunning politicans like Governor Gardner, Congressman Banks, and Senator Wilson to manipulate it to their own ends.[84]

Ironically, only the Whig party—the party that had dominated state politics for over twenty years—vanished completely beneath the ruins of the second party system. Expanding industries and demographic changes and their by-products— social fragmentation and ethnic and class divisions—had rendered Brahmin Whiggery, with its preachments on harmony and its politics of consensus, an anachronism. Whiggery's last-minute conversion to reform in 1853 was a case of too little, too late. The party had become the focal point of the people's resentment of political institutions because of its elitest posture on matters of governance and policy and because of its practice of status-quo politics in an age of unprecedented change.

Ethnocultural historians like Ronald Formisano, William Gienapp, and Michael Holt attribute the disintegration of the Whig party and the rapid rise of Know-Nothingism mainly to the intensification of nativist and anti-Catholic sentiments brought on by the massive influx of foreigners into the country in the 1840s and 1850s. But as Holt points out, these sentiments were the by-products of a still greater force, namely, the rapid social and economic changes that were transforming the country in these years.[85] Massachusetts, as the nation's most densely populated, urbanized, and industrialized state, was the preeminent example of this transformation. All regions of the state and all social classes were vitally affected. Social and economic dislocations on a scale exceeding those in other states exerted intense pressures for a political response. That was an imperative that the Whig-dominated second party system had to address if it were to survive. Its failure to do so doomed it.

Rank-and-file Whigs, no less than their Democratic counterparts, were drawn to Know-Nothingism as an alternative to a failed party system and by its promise of a positive government response to their needs. There was no compelling reason following "Sam's" accession to power for ordinary Whigs to support the efforts of the displaced Brahmins to resurrect a party that instead of using the state to soften the impact of modernization had wedded political power to entrenched economic interests.

Gardner's landslide showing in towns most subject to the pressures of industrialization, urban growth, poverty, and population flux underscores the dominant influence of these forces in the populist revolt against the older parties. Close to 70 percent of their voters had cast ballots for a gubernatorial candidate who was virtually unknown outside of Boston and for a party running in its first statewide election whose only announced intention, other than the promise of some kind of political pogrom aimed at the Irish, was its vow to seize control of the state from the corrupt old parties and turn it over to the native-born citizenry. Voters from all the parties and from all parts of the state answered the call, in itself a reflection of the depth of public disillusionment with the established political order. But it was in the urban and industrial towns and working-class neighborhoods of the cities, where the populist revolt against the political establishment began, where political antislaveryism, prohibition, and nativism never commanded majorities, and where the 1853 constitution was buried under an avalanche of no votes, that support for "Sam" reached its peak.

Standard explanations for the collapse of the second party system fail to account for this explosion of Know-Nothingism in urban Massachusetts, because considerations other than the sectional crisis, the defeat of the constitution, the politicization of ethnoreligious animosities, or even a general mix of these concerns also factored into the voting decision of urban Bay Staters. It was not the anticity Coalitionists, Maine Law men, Native Americans, Free-Soilers, and fresh converts to the antislavery cause who lifted the Know-Nothing majorities in these communities to such lofty heights, though all of these elements did, in fact, gather under the Know-Nothing umbrella. Even combined, they were few in number compared to their unreconstructed Whig and Democratic neighbors, who for years had remained impervious to the political appeals of the monocausalists.

That so many urban Whigs and Democrats should have suddenly abandoned their parties in 1854 in favor of "Sam," then, cannot realistically be explained in terms of an overnight conversion to political nativism or antislaveryism.[86] Ronald Formisano describes nativism and anti-Catholicism as nominally the lowest common denominator of Know-Nothingism. All Know-Nothings understood that their party was gearing up for an assault on the Irish Catholic problem. But as Formisano also notes, the grass-roots populist movement sprang from many sources.[87] Antislavery voters and prohibitionists hopped on the Know-Nothing bandwagon to implement their agendas. Rank-and-file Democrats and Whigs, on the other hand, were drawn into the secret order by its vision of a people's party enrolled in the service of the people. If the promise contained within that vision spelled hard times ahead for the state's Irish Catholic minority, it also conveyed the idea of a positive government response to the ravages of an unharnessed industrial order. Whig and Democratic urban dwellers, in particular, had cause to turn to the new party. For them, it promised relief from the festering problems of modernization, like the tyrannical factory system, slum housing, unsanitary streets, lack of public bathing facilities, and inadequate fire and police protection.

Since conditions like these were more typical in cities than towns, and since the relationship between the Know-Nothing vote and the size, wealth, amount of industry, and population growth rate in the towns is so pronounced, it might seem that the Know-Nothing vote in the cities should have run higher in the aggregate than their 61 percent posting. In fact, a close examination of city returns reveals an exceptionally strong correlation between these variables and the relative size of the Know-Nothing vote. Party recruitment of city voters was well under way even before the Kansas-Nebraska bill was introduced into Congress and at least a month prior to the defeat of the new constitution. Working-class city dwellers proved especially susceptible to the Know-Nothing alternative.[88] The leading textile and shoe cities[89] went Know-Nothing by 70 percent. Lawrence, a major national textile center and the state's poorest and fastest-growing city (having nearly doubled its size from 1850 to 1855), topped her sister cities with a 78 percent Know-Nothing vote.

Table 2 compares the 1854 Whig and Know-Nothing performances in the wards of Boston, Cambridge, Roxbury, and Salem. Prior to 1854, these old commercial cities had always registered large Whig majorities. Not surprisingly, their aggregate Whig vote in 1854 dwarfed that of the remaining cities 31.6 to 18.3 percent, even after slumping to around half of the usual average, and their Know-Nothing total fell far short of the others, 55.6 to 66.0 percent. But when the wards of these former Whig strongholds are arranged according to their per capita distribution of personal wealth, it is seen that in general, the poorer the city neighborhood, the higher the Know-Nothing vote, and, conversely, the more affluent, the better the Whig performance. The ten-point spread between the Know-Nothing totals in the poorest (A) and middling (B) wards pinpoints where "Sam" ran strongest, and the 25 percent gap between the Know-Nothing performance in the poorest wards, which contained the heaviest concentrations of working-class residents, and the wealthiest (C), which were the only ones to vote Whig, marks the presence of a class vote in these cities as pronounced as that manifested in the poorest and most industrialized towns. These cities contained almost half of the state's foreign residents, yet noticeably absent in the 1854 election was any sign of the alleged powerful Irish voting bloc that Handlin and others have cited as the major cause for the massive Yankee Protestant shift into the American party.

Implicit in the 1854 Know-Nothing call to the people was a choice between two

TABLE 2. Correlation Between Personal Wealth and Ward Voting Patterns in Whig Commercial Cities, 1854

| | Per Capita Distribution of Personal Wealth | | | | | | | |
| | A. Wards under $220 (%) | | B. Wards $220–$499 (%) | | C. Wards $500+ (%) | | Citywide Totals | |
City	KN	Whig	KN	Whig	KN	Whig	KN	Whig
Boston	65.9	23.1	53.8	32.6	41.7	46.3	56.7	31.0
Cambridge	62.1	31.3	63.4	29.3	33.7	56.0	55.1	37.0
Roxbury	76.5	5.9	54.3	23.6	40.7	51.3	60.9	21.5
Salem	53.7	40.6	58.0	36.4	45.3	47.3	54.3	39.2
Totals	66.1	22.7	56.2	32.0	41.1	47.8	56.6	31.6
Remaining cities							66.0	18.3

For ward demographic data and election returns, see the *Boston Daily Advertiser*, Nov. 14, 1854, and Sept. 17 and 20, 1855; the *Cambridge Chronicle*, Nov. 18, 1854, and April 21 and Sept. 22, 1855; the *Norfolk County Journal* (Roxbury), Nov. 18, 1854, Sept. 22, 1855, and Aug. 23, 1856; and the *Salem Gazette*, Nov. 14, 1854, and Sept. 7 and Oct. 2, 1855.

diametrically opposed philosophies of government: the status-quo paternalism of the old political order and the change-oriented populism of the challenger. On the one side lay continuation of government by "the well-born and the able"; on the other, the rule of the people. The choice between the two was an easy one for a majority of the voters who had waited in vain for the established parties to respond to the needs of a developing urban, industrial society. The political establishment never had to face such a challenge before. When it did, its defeat was sudden and complete.

Newly elected Congressman Mark Trafton made this point when he addressed his fellow Know-Nothings at their victory banquet in Boston. The people of Massachusetts, he told the celebrants, had waited twenty years "for great results and reforms from the old parties but all in vain." The triumph of Know-Nothingism, he said, was a triumph of the people and the prelude "to the second revolution." Governor Gardner struck the same theme in his inaugural address by crediting the recent election results to a united action of the people against an anachronistic party system fixated with obsolescent and irrelevant issues. By reverting to "the great primary principles of government," the governor said, the people had freed themselves from the tyranny of party.[90]

What form the people's revolution would take awaited the coming legislative year.

CHAPTER FOUR

Know-Nothing Government

KNOW-NOTHINGISM had paved the way for one-party government in Massachusetts by successfully projecting itself as a viable alternative to what was widely regarded as a corrupt and unresponsive party system. And so complete was the victory that the American party had gained over its rivals on election day 1854 that it ensured the party a minimum of one year in power unencumbered by a loyal opposition. This circumstance presented Know-Nothingism with an opportunity that other political movements could only dream of: a year's grace to enact into law its legislative goals, subject only to the constraints of factional rivalries and constitutional considerations.

Other than a general agreement to crop certain political and civil rights of Irish Catholics, however, differences of opinion quickly surfaced as to what those goals should be. Former Democrats and Whigs wanted the state government to soften the impact that rapid urbanization and industrial growth was having on their lives. Free-Soil Americans equated a strong stand in favor of the principle of free labor and against alleged Southern imperialism with the national interest. Native Americans, prohibitionists, abolitionists, and other monocausalists were just as convinced that they alone possessed the key to a better America. Farmers, fishermen, and workers anticipated legislation beneficial to their pursuits. Finally, there were those for whom personal considerations took precedence over the public interest. Swept along by the rush of the people into the lodges was an assortment of "small fry" demagogues and political adventurers like Henry J. Gardner and Nathaniel Banks, who were willing to ride the crest of any movement—or issue—that carried the promise of personal advancement.[1]

On January 3, 1855, outgoing Whig governor Emory Washburn convened the General Court, an occasion he used to remark pointedly, "So far as the oath is concerned the house of representatives is duly competent to do its business."[2]

87

Washburn was not alone in his opinion that the people had blundered when they turned to socially obscure political upstarts to conduct the affairs of state. Certainly, the task facing the Know-Nothing legislature was made more formidable by the dearth of experienced personnel.

"Dark-lantern" politics and the populist notion that the people were best served if they themselves took the reins of government had winnowed veteran politicians and their lawyer allies from the corridors of power. Lodge brothers had vented their antiparty and antipolitician feelings by turning instead to those furthest removed from the political cliques of the day, namely, to the young and inexperienced. "We come fresh from the people, with but little experience," armory worker Henry W. Benchley reminded his fellow tyros upon his election as president of the state senate. For the Know-Nothings, political amateurism was a source of pride and strength. The people had thrown off "the bonds of the Philistines" so that they themselves might rule.[3] For their opponents, it was the subject of bitter lamentation. Know-Nothingism had activated a constituency consisting of "young men, who have but little stake in the community—who usually take no interest in politics—who reside here today and there tomorrow, and make up that class of our population which . . . furnish the hangers about the corners of the streets in the cities, and loungers in taverns and stores in the country."[4]

On one point, at least, the complaints were justified. Know-Nothing government had less political experience than any other ever elected in Massachusetts. For an unprecedented number—including the lieutenant governor—this was their first venture into public life. Not one of the nine executive councillors had served in that body before, and four of them had never occupied any public office. All 40 senators were first-time members of the upper chamber, and of the 379 representatives, only 34 had previously held seats in the house. Nearly half of the solons were under forty years of age.[5]

One study of the composition of Massachusetts legislatures spanning the fifteen years from 1848 to 1862 reveals that the Know-Nothing rebellion against the political establishment swept more than professional politicians out of power. Also targeted were the other satraps of Boston capital—lawyers and merchants. Lawyers, coming as they did from the profession most closely associated with the old politics, suffered the sharpest drop in numbers elected to the General Court of any occupational group. On average, forty lawyers had held seats in each of the seven legislatures preceding the American sweep. Only eleven lawyers survived the dark-lantern purge, a reduction so drastic that it forced the 1855 legislature to hire outside legal counsel to help draft some of its major bills.[6] Next to lawyers, merchants had furnished the greatest number of legislators drawn from the professional ranks in the pre-Know-Nothing period; and like the lawyers, they suffered a setback—albeit less drastic—losing a fourth of their usual share of seats.[7]

The dark-lantern purge was by no means limited to representatives of the ruling class. Also hard hit were master mariners, whose presence in the legislature was halved, and the state's farmers, down by more than a third from their average number in the previous seven legislatures. But where lawyers and merchants stormed back into the legislature after 1855, the shakeout of the yeomanry and seafarers proved permanent.[8] Their shrunken numbers bespoke a long overdue adjustment by the political order to the diminishing stature of farm and sea in an industrializing society. The American party, itself the creature of industrial forces, was the first to respond to this reality.

A comparison of property holdings of the 1850 and 1855 memberships adds to the evidence that the undercurrent of social unrest responsible for Know-Nothingism ran strongest among urban grass-roots voters. Prior to 1855, the top echelon of the political leadership in the Commonwealth, regardless of party, was drawn almost exclusively from the ranks of wealthy urbanites.[9] City lodge members, however, swept aside these elites and replaced them with a contingent of commoners whose relatively humble station stood in stark contrast to that of their more affluent predecessors. Fewer than half of the Know-Nothing city legislators owned any real estate; only one out of twenty had holdings assessed at over $10,000; and none owned property worth more than $40,000. By comparison, nearly three-quarters of their 1850 counterparts were taxpaying property owners; a third owned property assessed at more than $10,000; and one out of sixteen had holdings valued in excess of $40,000. On the other hand, there was no appreciable difference in the value of the property owned by the 1850 and 1855 rural legislators.[10] It appears, at least according to this particular measure, that the Know-Nothing drive to humble the mighty and elevate the lowly was primarily an urban phenomenon. The net result, in any event, was a legislature in which political unknowns manned the posts formerly held by the old order's elites— wealthy businessmen, lawyers, and professional politicians.

Historians have long chuckled over the presence of two dozen clergymen in the "Praise-God-Barebones Legislature," ascribing their inflated numbers to the evangelical ardor of their antislavery, nativist, and temperance constituents. And no doubt righteous zeal and "the traditionary hatred of Popery" had helped fuel the phenomenon. However, the fact that the number of physicians and school teachers elected as legislators also reached new heights (a total of thirty) suggests that another consideration may have contributed to the summoning of so many clergymen to the statehouse: The American party, having proscribed the ruling elite of the old political order, had created a void in leadership that members of less politically objectionable professions rushed to fill.[11]

A much more significant feature of the 1855 General Court, indeed its most striking feature in terms of the occupational background of its members, was the record-breaking number of working-class solons. No other Bay State legislature came so close to mirroring in its composition the proportion of workers found in society at large.[12] Their looming presence in the 1855 body—workers held more than 100 of the 419 seats—supports the conclusion that "Sam" had accomplished what no other antebellum political party had: the mobilization of the Yankee working-class vote. That vote had been instrumental in the eviction from office of antilabor political elites and in the election of more than one hundred working-class legislators, two results that seemed to portend for the industrial workers far more access and influence in the government than they had experienced at any time during the era of the second party system.[13] In particular, the presence in the General Court of a number of ten-hour activists guaranteed that issue a top spot on the legislative calendar.

The bond between Know-Nothingism and workers calls into question the assumption that "Sam" was the offspring of the rural-centered Coalition. Know-Nothingism began and reached its peak in the mill towns and working-class neighborhoods of eastern cities, whose voters favored representatives drawn from the ranks of labor. By contrast, Free-Soil and Democratic party organizations and voters in central and western Massachusetts had relied on the union ticket system in 1850 and 1851 to flood the General Court with yeoman legislators. Farmers, hailing mainly from the hinterland, accounted for about a third of the total membership in the two Coalition legislatures, thus ensuring that calling and the back country a disproportionate influence in the government. In fact, there would have been no Coalition government without the lopsided margin of representatives elected on joint tickets in the small towns of the interior.[14]

Farmer candidates also fared well during the Whig years, which was consistent with Whiggery's preachment that the engine of progress and upward mobility joined all classes in all parts of the state in a harmony of interests. There were times in the life of the Whig party, however, when pragmatic considerations took precedence over ideological consistency. The brief restoration period (1853–1854) was such a time. A frightened Whig party, having weathered the threat of the rural-based Coalition, upped its quota of farmer candidates in a move calculated to dampen political unrest in the state's farm belt. As it turned out, Whig fears were misdirected. Their grooming of farmer candidates came at the expense of the working class, whose share of seats dropped to their lowest levels in the 1848–1854 period. That decision was ill timed, coming as it did on the eve of the urban-based Know-Nothing rebellion.

Small-town Coalitionists had contrived through manipulation of the town representation and majority vote systems to flood the General Court with more than twice as many farmers as workers in each of the four years preceding the Know-Nothing explosion. Coalition successes, however, did not rest on electoral gimmickry alone. It could not have won elections if it had lacked a broad-based appeal among voters. Its brand of "agrarian radicalism" played well with country voters, and its promise of egalitarian and democratic reforms did not go unnoticed among industrial workers. The Free-Soil wing of the partnership did its part by bringing in the antislavery vote. Nevertheless, the Coalition failed to crack the Whig power base—urban Massachusetts. Essentially a combination of agrarian preservationists and Free-Soilers in pursuit of separate priorities that largely ignored urban discontents, the Coalition fell far short of what was needed to destroy the Whig hegemony.

Know-Nothingism, by contrast, brought an end to the practice of overloading the General Court with rustics. Even the hinterland was caught up in the turnabout, pruning its share of farmer-occupied seats to the lowest level in seven years and raising that of workers to the highest. In the urban, industrial, eastern part of the state, the American party slashed the number of farmer legislators to half that of the peak level reached in 1852 (from sixty-two to thirty-one), thereby shrinking their presence in the General Court to its nadir. Statewide, the ratio of farmers to the total membership plunged from the one-third level of the Coalition years to well under one-fifth. As events turned out, Know-Nothingism was the harbinger of a permanent downturn in the political fortunes of Bay State agrarians.[15] It was no coincidence that a political movement energized by the pressures of modernization should have been the instrument of so profound a change in the political order as to lead to the dislodgement of the agrarian grip on the General Court and the election of a record-breaking number of workers.

The kinds of candidates filtered through the dark-lantern lodge system for the most part reflected the populist conviction that the best remedy for an unresponsive, elitist party system was a people's movement that opened up leadership positions in the government to ordinary men who were new to politics. Reported one Know-Nothing newspaper, "Sam" had selected candidates "for their common sense, clear judgment, and proper appreciation of the wants and feelings of the people from whose ranks they come—and whose interests they are able and willing to care for." They would take their seats fully aware that "the entire interests of the Commonwealth are not concentrated in banks or railroads or any other moneyed corporation."[16]

Most of the 1855 legislators did indeed hail from the ranks of the common people, better than one-quarter from the laboring class alone. Membership in a social class, of course, does not guarantee fidelity to the interests of that class. The Whigs, for example, had made it their practice to include on their tickets a quota of worker loyalists who could be counted on to follow the party line. Nevertheless, the political explosion of 1854, precisely because it had catapulted such an extraordinary number of political unknowns into positions of power, created a situation unique in the annals of Bay State politics: The archetypal common man, whose political wisdom the political establishment had long extolled but rarely consulted, was in a position to cut the ties between government and privilege and to use the power of the state for the advancement of the commonwealth.[17]

The American party in the 1854 campaign had demonstrated that as a vote-getting machine, it was nonpareil. But a single election is no guarantee of longevity. With power comes challenge. Party prospects over the long run hinged on the order's ability to inculcate a sense of identification and loyalty among first-time Know-Nothing voters who had flocked into the lodges on the strength of assurances that they were joining a movement to overthrow the tyranny of party and return the government to the people. Having achieved power, "Sam" could no longer parade as the antiparty champion of the outsiders. The order faced the task of establishing a new identity—that of a bona fide political party—without sacrificing its image as a people's movement. Only if a major portion of the lodge brothers accepted the idea that they were no longer Whigs, Democrats, or Free-Soilers—that, in fact, they were Know-Nothings—could the American party consolidate its initial gains and achieve permanence. Even in the absence of a loyal opposition, this was a formidable undertaking.

The threat to the future well-being of the party was gravest at its source of strength—the grass-roots organizational base anchored in the lodge network. Hunger for office, it turned out, was not peculiar to the "political hacks" of the older parties. "Sam" had come to power promising to purge public life of political careerists, only to discover there was no dearth of applicants for place within the lodges. Seasoned Free-Soilers had taken advantage of their cohesion in the midst of the confusion created by the sudden influx of thousands of men into the dark-lantern party to outmaneuver the inept Native American fathers and obtain for themselves a disproportionate share of nominations from a party that would have won without them. In the same fashion, Whig and Democratic politicians gained admittance to the conclaves and gradually assumed command over the unsophisticated majority. Henry J. Gardner was among them, and no sooner had he taken the governor's chair than he began replacing large numbers of state appointees with lodge members who were beholden to him. His intention was clear: to build a power base loyal to him, even if it meant betrayal of the populist promises that had powered the party to victory in the recent election.[18]

In the midst of these power plays, the General Court had to address the question of how best to respond to national, state, and local pressures without touching off an internecine struggle among the party's constituent groups. How well the legislators responded to the test of solidarity would also help decide the fate of their party.

It was a test that their enemies expected them to fail. Shocked members of the upper classes in particular viewed the prospects of Know-Nothing rule with grim foreboding. Charles Francis Adams, who was a Brahmin in everything but his antislavery zeal, rushed to judgment, labeling American government on its first day in office a "Saturnalia of politics." To be ruled by the hoi polloi, he sneered, "excites ridicule rather than any more grave emotion. Yet it is a pity to see Massachusetts raising such antics in this day of boasted enlightenment. I presume there is less mature education in the government than ever before at any time."[19] The passage of time did nothing to soften Adams's opinion, but not everyone of his persuasion was as dispirited. Samuel Gridley Howe hailed the "demolition" of the older parties as a golden opportunity for the antislavery movement, for, even though Know-Nothingism had brought to power a leaderless mob utterly devoid of "prestige of family—standing—respectability—character," it would prove short-lived, and out of the chaos that it had created would arise a stronger, more unified antislavery party.[20]

Whig editor Charles Congdon, shared Adams and Howe's disdain for the new legislators. Congdon blamed dark-lantern politics for having turned the state-house into a receptacle for "all the floating political rubbish" in the state. The net result of secrecy, emasculating oaths, and bloc voting, he said, was "the most ill-assorted legislative body which ever met in this country." Its members joined in the gossip "about the Pope of Rome, and the dangers to be apprehended from our foreign population; but most of them cared for none of these things, and indeed cared for nothing except place and its perquisite honors."[21] Invective aside, the despair of the patricians over the prospect of being governed by their social inferiors betrayed a bedrock conviction that if leadership by notables imbued with a sense of nobless oblige was the *sine qua non* of good government, the obverse was also true: A legislature full of ignorant and inexperienced members scrambling after their own advantage spelled disaster for the Commonwealth.

Few, if any, of the Know-Nothings who took their place in the legislature shared that sense of despair. They were for the most part men of humble station who carried with them to Beacon Hill a pledge to their constituents to build a new political order in Massachusetts. On this point, public expectations, as expressed in the election returns, were clear: an end to the Brahmin stranglehold over political life in Massachusetts and a government controlled by the people. However, a "spasm of supplication" gripped the legislature and created confusion. Petitions and orders rained down upon the solons, and a welter of conflicting demands pressed upon them from all directions.[22] Somehow the legislators had to distill from this jumble the will of the people and formulate public policy in conformity to that will.

Also crucial to the prospects of bonding the disparate elements of the Know-Nothing order into a permanent party was Governor Gardner, whose ideas on the matter were less subject to the cross-cutting pressures that afflicted the legislature because they were of a more personal nature. A professional politician of easy principles, Gardner took the oath of office more intent on building a political machine beholden to him than on consolidating a broad-based coalition behind his party. One of his fellow Brahmins explained how the governor put his formidable talents as a political organizer to work in pursuit of that goal:

> He had a book in which he had the names of men in every town in the Commonwealth whom he attached to his political fortunes by promises, or flattery, or because in some cases of their sincere belief in [nativist] doctrine. He understood better than any other man I ever knew the value of getting the united support of men who were without special influence, . . . but who united might be a very formidable force.[23]

Such machines run on the oil of patronage, a commodity readily available to the chief executive and one which, once he was in office, he dispensed liberally and with skill. Beyond the judicious use of executive appointments and the nuts and bolts of machine organization lay the matter of voter appeal. Pressure was mounting within the party to scrap the policy of secrecy and go public in the next election. Hence, if Gardner took to the hustings again, it was unlikely that he would be the beneficiary of the kind of blind bloc vote that the party's lodge network had engineered on his behalf the previous November and which had propelled the reactionary Webster Whig from the ranks of the politically obscure into the Commonwealth's highest elective office. Considerations like these are probably what prompted Gardner to use the occasion of his inaugural address to position himself for a run for reelection or for national office.

In the speech, he made plain his intention to exploit public concerns over the floodtide of immigration in order to knead the multifarious Know-Nothing mass into a coherent, unidirectional political force bonded by nativism and headed by him. The most immediate and direct threat facing the Commonwealth and the nation, Gardner declaimed, was that posed by the presence of a huge mass of unassimilated aliens; and the crisis was deepening. Four million foreigners would arrive in the United States in the 1850s alone, adding their numbers to the millions already ashore. They were a people as foreign in outlook as in origin. Hence, behind the statistics lurked the prospect of cultural mongrelization, a prospect made grimmer by the disproportionate incidence of beggary, pauperism, crime, and intemperance accounted for by the foreign-born population. Honest American taxpayers, he said, for too long have shouldered the burden of this vast army of alien ne'er-do-wells, and American workers for too long have endured the unfair competition of cheap foreign labor. It was concerns like these that had brought the people together in the great social movement that had burst the bonds of the party structure.

Still, the governor—a wool merchant who appreciated the value of cheap labor—stopped short of asking Congress to take steps to halt the foreign tide. He preferred instead that the American party of Massachusetts pioneer a crusade to "Americanize America," and he devoted most of his speech to outlining the form that the crusade should assume. The public schools could make an important contribution by dropping foreign languages from their curriculum and by continuing the practice of a daily reading from the King James Bible in the classroom. His Excellency in turn would use the power of his office to disband all foreign militia companies.

Other, more far-reaching measures were needed, of course, "to purify and ennoble the elective franchise" and otherwise "to guard against citizenship becoming cheap."[24] Specifically, Gardner had in mind constitutional amendments to exclude naturalized citizens from public office and all but strip them of the right to vote through the imposition of a literacy test in English and a twenty-one-year residency requirement as prerequisites to the suffrage. Another constitutional amendment that the governor favored—to deny public moneys to Catholic schools—had already been initiated by the previous legislature and needed only the endorsement of the present body to submit it to the people for ratification. Existing law provided the means for alleviating still another problem—the annual tab for the foreign inmates housed in state almshouses and asylums. Shipping the more "notorious" cases back to Liverpool at $20 a head, he noted, would bring immediate and sizable savings.[25]

Unfortunately, there was only so much that the state government could do. The alien threat to American institutions was a national problem requiring a national response. Congress must act, if "these and other reforms [were to] be consummated." It might start, the governor suggested, with the imposition of a head tax on immigrants and the deportation of foreign undesirables, steps that the Commonwealth had already taken.

Meanwhile, Congress's foot-dragging was Massachusetts' opportunity. The changes that the governor was proposing "constitute[d] a work transcending the ordinary platform of party," and their adoption by Massachusetts would redound to the glory of the state, for they would place her in the vanguard of a crusade for national purification that was destined to "rank with the great movements that originally found nations."[26] Unmentioned by the governor was the fact that this epic movement would also serve to divert public attention from another crusade—the one against the Slave Power.

The chief magistrate interspersed his discourse on the foreign peril with recommendations that would favor select groups within the Know-Nothing coalition, groups for whose opinions the former Webster Whig had evinced little enthusiasm in the past but whose support he now deemed important. Thus, he rekindled the hopes of antiliquor enthusiasts with a pledge to sanction any constitutional measure for the suppression of intemperance; and he courted the Locofoco vote with recommendations for a general overhaul of the usury laws, abolition of imprisonment for debt, and an improved mechanics' lien law.[27]

But it was the major theme of the address—its exposition of nativist principles and its guidelines for state persecution of the Irish minority—that signaled the direction in which Gardner wanted to move the American party of Massachusetts. By stressing nativist concerns at the expense of all others, he made clear his intention to transform Know-Nothingism from a people's movement into an ultra-nativist political party. The stakes were high—control of the party—and so were the risks. Nativism, though a widely shared sentiment, had failed as recently as 1847 to generate much support at the polls. Know-Nothingism itself had reached its current stage of development only because it had broadened its appeal beyond the precepts set by the Native American fathers. And Gardner's claim that the nation faced a crisis of unprecedented magnitude—defined as the potential for an undigested mass of ignorant aliens to mongrelize American institutions—which Congress must resolve without imposing quotas, was on the face of it as absurd as it was extreme.

His Excellency had his reasons for placing himself beyond the pale of centrist politics. In the first place, the location of the political center was by no means clear. The times, after all, were not ordinary. The collapse of the party system had left in its wake a vortex of unresolved issues, none of which seemed to promise greater popular appeal than nativism. Certainly, Gardner thought this was the case. His litany of proscriptive steps that the Commonwealth could take to meet the alleged foreign threat reflected the thinking of an ambitious politician who believed that he could establish nativism as the major dynamic in Bay State politics. It was a belief shared by those who equated Know-Nothing populism with Yankee Protestant antipathy for Irish Catholics. Second, his focus on the Irish

Catholic question was bound to attract the attention of the national American party, which was anxiously casting about for an issue with which to divert the public's attention from the slavery question. For a politician with one eye on national office and the other on a potential power base at home, these were reasons enough to take an ultranativist stance.

Gardner also tipped his hand as to his intentions by what he chose not to say in a speech purportedly dealing with the major concerns of the day. Nowhere in the address, for example, did he mention the cause that for thirty years had served as the major rallying point for organized labor—the need to limit by law the number of workday hours in the state's manufacturing establishments. That a wealthy wool merchant should remain silent on the subject of the ten-hour law, whose ramifications would be felt most in the industry that was the principal source of his fortune, was scarcely surprising. Besides, the governor was following precedent. After all, an entire generation of Bay State politicians had slipped around the issue by saying nothing. And if not bread, there was always circus. Using the power of the state to harass an ethnoreligious minority might prove popular enough to divert the attention of industrial workers from more substantive issues.

Equally revealing was Gardner's decision to downplay the interests of the party's antislavery constituency, a group that was already stipulating that the future well-being of the American party depended less on its proscriptive principles than on its stand against slavery.[28] Gardner took the opposite position, and, in fact, other than a fleeting reference to the aggressions of the slave interests and an obligatory call for the restoration of the Missouri Compromise (positions that fell within the bounds of orthodox Whig opinion), he ignored in his talk what for many members of his party was the preeminent issue of the age. It was a calculated risk on the part of the chief executive, one that was bound to offend the antislavery Americans; but it was a shrewd move nevertheless. Gardner's views on the slavery question were a matter of public record. A former Webster Whig, his comments on the fugitive slave controversy alone—he favored compliance with the law—excluded him from a position of command over the battle-hardened veterans of the antislavery crusade. No such impediment stood between him and leadership over the party's nativist elements. Compared to the politically adroit Free-Soilers, the Native Americans were crude primitives who were no match for the wiles of the governor. Finally, it is highly unlikely that so shrewd and ambitious a political opportunist as Gardner would have chosen nativism over antislavery unless he was convinced that he could get more political mileage out of hounding Paddy and the Pope than out of beating the drums for the antislavery cause.

Gardner's speech triggered speculation that the governor and the Free-Soil Americans were on a collision course. At the outset of the legislative year, however, neither side wanted confrontation. Gardner needed time to fit the parts of his political machine into place and could ill afford to have work on that project sabotaged by the party's antislavery contingent; and the latter needed the cooperation of the chief executive to implement their agenda.

Talk of a falling out between the governor and the Free-Soil Americans was not the only grist for the rumor mills. Even before the General Court convened in January, reports were circulating that a "very severe" power struggle had broken out between the antislavery and nativist forces and that "it was very doubtful which influence would prevail."[29] Commentators of all political persuasions, including some Know-Nothings, took up the theme of a bipolarized legislature in which the two warring factions vied for control. Know-Nothingism, as they saw it, was suffering from a split personality. "In Boston," wrote a Free-Soiler, "the new party is more proslavery than even the old Whig party, being either national Whigs or Yankee mechanics who equally hate a Nigger as they do an Irishman; in the state it is far more antislavery than any legislature ever elected . . . ; in the nation, I fear national, which means proslavery."[30]

The rivalry was real enough. The Native Americans, after all, had founded the party in order to deal with the foreign problem. They had intended from the outset that the party "keep mum on the subject of slavery." The Wilsonian Free-Soilers, on the other hand, had come into the party with the intention of harnessing it to their cause.[31] But the reports of a bifurcated party at war with itself reflected more the wishful thinking of the party's enemies than the actual situation. The gravitational force that had drawn most of the party's disparate elements into its orbit was neither xenophobia nor anti-Southernism per se, but the Know-Nothing pledge to dedicate their party to addressing the needs and aspirations of the Yankee Protestant common man. That promise, of course, encompassed proposals to deal with concerns over mass immigration and the slavery question. It also implied that in an age of pell-mell urban and industrial growth, the government would produce a far-reaching program to soften the impact that modernization was having on people's lives.

The antislavery Americans gave top priority to sending their leader, Henry Wilson, to join fellow Free-Soiler Charles Sumner in the Senate. That was the deal they had cut with Henry J. Gardner at the nominating convention. They had kept their end of the bargain; now they expected the chief magistrate to keep his. But by the time the legislature took up the matter, Gardner had changed his mind. The national branch of the party was opposed to Wilson, and Gardner slipped quietly over to the side of those seeking to block the Free-Soil leader's election.[32]

Also eyeing the Senate spot were the Native Americans; and when Wilson easily outdistanced their man, A. B. Ely, in a straw poll taken in the lower house, the party fathers took the offensive, concentrating their fire on what they perceived as Wilson's chief weaknesses—his antislavery zeal and his lukewarm commitment to Native American principles. To elect a Free-Soil zealot to the Senate, they contended, would send a negative message to the Southern Know-Nothings, thereby endangering the formation of a viable national party; and to elect a man who was soft on Americanism would undermine the very rationale that had called the American party into existence in the first place.[33]

The Native Americans had a point: Nothing in Wilson's public record smacked of hostility to foreigners and Catholics. Quite the contrary, he was a man who, having himself escaped from rural isolation and poverty, understood firsthand the plight of the uprooted and the disadvantaged, and on a number of public occasions, he had spoken of immigrants in warm and sympathetic terms. In the constitutional convention, he had denounced as "narrow and bigoted" a move to deny immigrants representation in the General Court. "A man is a man," he had told the delegates on that occasion, "no matter where he was born or where he resides."[34] Now, to his discomfiture, his enemies had the ill grace to jeopardize his chances for election by quoting from these speeches.

An ally in the state senate counseled Wilson to counter the Native American thrust by going public in favor of their principles. This Wilson was only too willing to do. In an open letter prefaced with the axiom that "letters written by a candidate pending an election always subject him . . . to the suspicion of insincerity in the opinion he avows," the beleaguered Wilson unveiled a hitherto concealed ardor for the American party's proposals to correct "the evils and abuses which have grown out of annual immigration into America of hundreds of thousands of men reared under the influence of social, religious, and political institutions differing or antagonistic to our own." Fortunately, the American party had it within its grasp the means to produce "wise and humane legislation" that would prevent Europe from using America as a dumping ground for her criminals and paupers, overhaul existing naturalization laws, shield the people from "the insidious and malign tendencies" of the papacy, and eliminate foreign influence in public affairs by safeguarding the sanctity of the ballot box and limiting public office to the native-born.[35]

Wilson's sudden switch to the nativist side left the Native Americans unimpressed. Why, they asked, had he as recently as 1853 fought to guarantee the right of the foreign-born to form their own militia units? Now that Governor Gardner had disbanded these units, where did he stand on the issue? Wilson took to the press again with a second letter. "The reference in my speech in the Constitutional Convention, to the organization of military companies of men of foreign birth," he explained, "was made simply as an illustration. I did not then approve, I do not now approve, and I can never approve of the organization of military companies composed of men of foreign birth."[36]

The lower house, where the Native American clique had less influence, voted first and handed the Free-Soil chieftain an easy win. In the upper body, however, where the debate over the candidacy was more heated and acrimonious (and where the battle lines were drawn tightly around the question of Wilson's dedication to American principles), Wilson won by the slimmest of margins—21 of the 40 votes cast. The "Natick Cobbler," sneered textile magnate Amos A. Lawrence, had "risen from the cowyard to the Senate" by the grace of one vote.[37]

Later in life, Wilson expressed regret for his brief affair with Know-Nothingism, but at this stage of his political career, with a U.S. Senate seat hanging in the balance, matters of conscience did not deter him.[38] More importantly, the future vice-president's groveling to nativist pressures exposed the tenuous position that the Free-Soilers occupied in the new government. While it is true that the Know-Nothing legislature did send in the person of Henry Wilson a fiery enemy of human bondage to Washington, the outcome did not hinge on Wilson's antislavery credentials, which were impeccable, but on his ability to convince the non-Free-Soil majority of the sincerity of his commitment to the American party. In the case of this foe of the Slave Power, then, the General Court had reached its decision in spite of, rather than because of, his antislavery record.

Wilson's election seemed to confirm the widely held opinion that the Free-Soil Americans had gained the upper hand in their drive to take control of the party. Unlike the Democratic and Whig Americans, who consisted almost entirely of rank and file, the Free-Soil converts included top echelon leaders whose success in infiltrating the secret order may have stemmed from their former party's pro-nativist record and from the fact that Free-Soil was more a cause than a party. These seasoned veterans of the political wars drew on their experience and skills to produce an antislavery cohort of officeholders within the Know-Nothing government, and it was no secret that they were intent on converting the American party into a national antislavery party.[39]

Nevertheless, talk of an impending Free-Soil coup was premature. In the first place, the General Court, in selecting a Free-Soiler to fill Edward Everett's seat in the U.S. Senate, was responding to the popular notion that the best forum for the debate over slavery was located in Washington and not in Boston. Second, the contest had pitted Wilson against Ely in a face-off for the Senate seat, not for control of the party. (That control, incidentally, was not the Native Americans to lose, it having slipped from their grasp while Know-Nothingism was expanding from a single-issue crusade into a mass movement.) Third, neither contestant for the post could command a majority in the General Court simply on the basis of ideology; on the contrary, both men were fronting for numerical minorities (Free-Soil and Native American) within the legislature who were dependent on the votes of other members with other beliefs and priorities. Finally, Wilson's election was more a measure of the ability of the politically seasoned Free-Soilers (who had the added advantage of the better-qualified candidate) to outmaneuver the Old Guard in lobbying for votes than of the weight that legislators attached to either cause.

All this is not to say that the majority of legislators were devoid of nativist or antislavery convictions. Quite the contrary, they evinced through their votes and their speeches on the floor of both houses strong opinions on both counts; but their concerns for these matters, unlike those of the Native Americans and Free-Soilers, did not take precedence over all other considerations. Far more than any other body of legislators that had preceded them to Beacon Hill, these men carried with them from their home towns and city neighborhoods a firsthand acquaintance with the will of the people, and this will (which had found expression in the lodges) encompassed a whole range of projects, of which the antislavery and nativist programs were but a part. Nor were the principals involved in the dispute, that is, Wilson and Ely and the core groups promoting their candidacies, mere contenders for place. Internal divisions over policy and power are endemic to party coalitions, particularly in a one-party environment like the one that the American party had fashioned in Massachusetts.

The American party coalition, however, consisted of more than a cluster of rival factions wrangling over their respective programs. By tapping into the grass roots, listening to the demands for reform, and promising action, Know-Nothingism had drawn into the lodge network thousands of rank-and-file Democrats and Whigs from all parts of the state. The party coalition cobbled together from this diffuse mass and from the Free-Soilers and interest groups that had also swarmed into the lodges was at the same time broad based and ill defined. All wanted change—that is what brought them together in the first place; they differed, however, on what kinds of changes they wanted. Adding to the confusion, the legislature that they had elected to carry out the mandate for change was awash with political tyros. It is no wonder, then, that the well-organized and cohesive Free-Soil and Native American factions leaped at the chance to focus the party on their particular causes, and this was bound to cause friction, not only between the two groups, but also between them and the amorphous Whig and Democratic majority, who had a host of other causes in mind.

It was the idea of a political party dedicated to carrying out the will of the people, coming as it did when public disillusionment with an unresponsive party system had reached pandemic proportions, that produced the Know-Nothing landslide and imbued the 1855 legislature with its sense of mission: to bring forth from the legislative chambers a new deal for the people. The portrayal of that legislature as one divided along xenophobic and antislavery lines, then, ignores the existence of that body's majority—those legislators who saw as their primary task the sorting out from the welter of claims vying for their attention what the majority of people expected from them.

There were other moderating influences at work within the General Court as well that militated against internecine factional strife. The Wilsonian Free-Soilers, for example, realized that the times—as the recent election had made clear—were not propitious for the formation of an independent antislavery party in Massachusetts and that factional warfare would preclude their chance to use the American party to promote the cause of human freedom.[40] Indeed, each of the party's constituent groups, including the Native American fathers, was inclined more to a policy of collaboration than to one of confrontation, their course dictated no doubt by an awareness that united they could use the American party as a battering ram to smash through the legislative logjam that had been blocking social reforms for more than a generation. Certainly, the spirit guiding the 1855 General Court at the outset of the legislative year was more one of accommodation between major factions than the one of bickering and mutual recrimination that rumor mongers and the anti-Know-Nothing press ascribed to it. A *quid pro quo* understanding, after all, was small enough a price to pay for legislative relief, even for rivals for power like the Native Americans and Free-Soilers.

More than goodwill, however, was called for, if the solons were to meet the demands of their constituents. Legislative productivity also hinges on the technical know-how for operating the machinery of government, and familiarity with the lawmaking process in turn requires experienced leadership, tight organization and party discipline, and adroit committee work, the very qualities that the party's detractors maintained were wanting in the 1855 body.[41] Still another difficulty facing the untested legislators was the matter of sorting out its priorities from the mountain of demands placed on it.

Some historians have described Know-Nothing populism entirely in negative terms: antiparty, antipolitician, anti-Catholic, anti-immigrant. And indeed, there was much that was negative in the Know-Nothing record. The most obvious consequence of the election of 1854, for example, was the electorate's overwhelming rejection of the political establishment. Know-Nothingism, by channeling pent-up public frustrations into the political arena, had brought crashing to the ground a party system that was widely regarded as unresponsive or corrupt. The people, with their ballots, had expressed their disillusionment with the Whig version of the positive state that allied government with business and turned a blind eye to the social costs of industrialization. At the same time, they made equally plain their distaste for the Democratic alternative—the hands-off Jeffersonian state that promised less governance and a freer rein to entrepreneurial spirits but which, like Whiggery's Hamiltonian state, paid precious little heed to the social dislocations that marked the advance of the industrial order.

One aspect of urban life—the state of public morals—evoked a strong puritanical strain within the secret order and touched off a negative campaign against sin that led to stiffer penalties for keepers of gambling dens, speakeasies, and houses of ill repute; the establishment of the state's first reform school for girls, whose charges were instructed in "piety and morality"; and fines levied on billiard rooms and bowling alleys guilty of admitting juveniles or operating on Sunday.[42] Topping the list of moral reforms was a twenty-page temperance law whose intent was to legislate moral behavior, but whose penalties were so extreme (for example, the sale of a glass of grog could net a six-month jail term) as to minimize the chances of a jury conviction, thus inviting whosesale noncompliance. Other than the Native Americans, who wanted to know if "rum and niggers" were going to crowd out all other matters pending before the General Court, there was no appreciable opposition to the prohibition measure in either house, the majority of whose members, it was said, drank "not only freely but to excess."[43]

Gardner, as he had promised, signed the bill into law, and this prompted the jubilant Maine Law men to award him the post of presiding officer at their annual convention held in May. That honor nailed down the temperance vote for the power-conscious chief executive; and he reciprocated when he greeted the assemblage of his fellow dries with the sober announcement that if the new liquor law "does not succeed in stopping the traffic in intoxicating drinks, I do not know how the ingenuity of man can devise one that will."[44] There was, in the case of the speaker, many a slip between the cup and the lip. Just a fortnight earlier, His

Excellency and other "great officers of the State" had donated their mite to the promotion of the fledgling American wine industry by polishing off a couple of bottles of domestic champagne. At about the same time, junketing legislators in another test of the ingenuity of man ran up bar bills at state expense.[45]

Those legislators who had backed the liquor law soon learned that people were upset with the idea that selling a glass of ale rated a sentence in the House of Corrections. A rally to protest the new law attracted a crowd of ten thousand to Faneuil Hall to listen to speeches denouncing the law as a gross violation of the basic rights of free men. With the exception of the Nunnery Committee, no other action taken by the Know-Nothing government caused so much controversy or provoked such a public outcry.[46]

Temperance had proved as nettlesome a problem for "Sam" as it had earlier for the Whigs. But on another social issue, all legislators were agreed: The swelling numbers of poverty-stricken Irish Catholic immigrants settling in Massachusetts cried out for state action.

The virus of intolerance that Know-Nothingism had contracted at birth coursed through the executive and legislative branches of government; and it erupted during the 1855 session in the form of a state-sponsored attack on the civil and political rights of the foreign-born and Roman Catholics that went beyond anything found anywhere else in the country.

In its drive to preserve cultural purity, Know-Nothing government indulged a mean and petty spirit that manifested itself in a callous disregard for minority rights and sensibilities. Making matters worse was the virtual absence of opposition within the one-party government to all but the most extreme nativist demands. This enabled "Sam" to launch a political assault against the Irish Catholic minority that exceeded even the stated goals of the American Republican and Native American parties of the 1840s.[47] Governor and legislature teamed up to relieve the state courts of their power to entertain applications for naturalization; to mandate a daily reading from the King James Bible in the public schools (which was offensive to Roman Catholics); to uphold "the honor of the American flag" by disbanding Irish militia units; to dismiss Irish state workers; to ban the teaching of foreign languages in the public schools; to discontinue international exchanges of books, by which the Commonwealth received public documents and scholarly material from abroad; to expunge a Latin inscription from its place above the desk of the speaker of the house; and to issue a resolve calling on the federal government to extend the residency requirement for naturalization from five to twenty-one years and to limit public office to native-born citizens.[48] More ominous were the proposed state constitutional amendments (which passed both houses with overwhelming majorities) aimed at depriving Roman Catholics of their right to hold public office and at restricting office and the suffrage to male citizens who had resided in the country for no less than twenty-one years.[49]

Pledged to separation of church and state, the Know-Nothing temporal arm lashed out at the rights of the state's Roman Catholic minority. The epitome of the Bay State's "Protestant Crusade" was the Nunnery Committee. Petitions to the

General Court, expressing concern that in "certain institutions within this state, known as convents, nunneries . . . [women] are forever barred from leaving . . . however much they desire to do so . . . [and] that acts of villainy, injustice, and wrong are perpetrated with impunity within the walls of said institutions as a result of their immunity from public inspection," prompted the legislators (or so they claimed) to establish by unanimous vote the "Joint Special Committee on the Inspection of Nunneries and Convents." A bizarre mix of concern for quality education, prurient curiosity piqued by centuries-old gossip, and a puritan penchant for minding other people's business, the Nunnery Committee, as it was popularly called, had a twofold mission: to assess the quality of parochial school education and to pry into Catholic institutions suspected of holding women against their will or of housing concealed "arms and instruments of war."[50] The Committee was the creature of a populist government that set fewer limits than had its predecessors on the power of the state and that sanctioned an unwarranted intrusion into the private lives of people. It was a charge laden with the potential for abuse.

So, too, for that matter, was the Coalition's pauper removal law by which the Know-Nothing administration during 1855 realized for the Commonwealth a savings "of at least one hundred thousand dollars" by ridding the state of more than thirteen hundred charity cases, the preponderance of whom were immigrants. Governor Gardner boasted that implementation of sound business practices had made possible these savings, and he urged extreme caution in bestowing "Christian charity" on unfortunate foreigners, lest the Commonwealth become "the receptacle of the vicious, the degraded, and the insane." The official organ of the American party was less circumspect, commending the Board of Alien Commissioners for having shipped some three hundred of "these leeches upon our taxpayers beyond [the] sea where they belong."[51] Among the "leeches" was an impoverished widow with her American-born infant and inmates from state asylums who were dumped dockside in Liverpool without any further provision for their care. A sea voyage home, the commissioners reported, would prove "conducive" to the recovery of many of them, since homesickness was the principal cause of their malady.[52]

Abuses like these aroused the ire of Peleg W. Chandler, a Whig holdover on the board. Chandler issued a separate report in which he likened the pauper removal law to the Fugitive Slave Law in its callous disregard of human rights and accused the Know-Nothing government of practicing a double standard, whereby it drove helpless foreigners out of the state, on the one hand, and provided sanctuary for runaway slaves on the other. "A black man is no better, and is entitled to no more security as to personal rights . . . than a white man," Chandler wrote.[53] Such criticism fell on deaf ears. "Sam" accelerated the removal of broken-down Irishmen and women from state institutions and sent hundreds of them "across the Atlantic with less ceremony and formality—with less of recorded and documentary evidence—than goes to the sending of a tub of butter, or a barrel or apples, from Fitchburg to Boston."[54]

Ultranativism was the dark side of Know-Nothing populism. Meanspirited and cruel, it was subversive of the rights of minorities.[55] It illustrated the danger of unchecked power inherent in all forms of government. None of the party's component groups opposed proscription, and tyranny of the majority was the result. Hostility toward the Irish Catholic minority, however, was not the *sine qua non* of Know-Nothingism. Paddy and the Pope were not the only common enemies. "Sam" had risen to power on the strength of the people's desire to shake off "the incubus of all corrupt and domineering cliques and parties," so that they might, in the words of a Know-Nothing senator, "overthrow every aristocratic and imperious power." The governing principle of American rule, he continued, "involves the promotion of all of our institutions and the principles which underlie them."[56] If the Know-Nothing government fell short in its efforts to meet the highest standards of republicanism, it was not the first to falter.

The General Court had sided with the governor on both the nativist and temperance issues, and with no loyal opposition or appreciable internal dissent present in either branch of government to counter the extension of state power into these areas, the result was the legalization of state persecution of ethnic and religious minorities and a prohibition law so draconian as to discourage enforcement. Collaboration between the two branches on these matters, however, did not signify that the General Court took its marching orders from Governor Gardner. On the contrary, serious differences between the two cropped up over the legislature's vigorous antislavery program.

Nativism illustrates Know-Nothing negativism in the extreme. "Sam's" response to the mounting national crisis over slavery, on the other hand, demonstrates that there was more to Know-Nothingism than destructive force. The 1855 Know-Nothing legislature outperformed all of its predecessors combined in its response to territorial and slavery concerns, and it did so in spite of the national American party's stricture "to keep mum on the subject of slavery."[57] One of its first actions was to elect Henry Wilson to the Senate. It also fired off resolutions urging Congress to restore the Missouri Compromise and to repeal the Fugitive Slave Law. Other resolutions targeted "Bleeding Kansas," pledging aid and calling on the state of Missouri to take whatever steps were necessary to prevent a repetition of "the gross outrages" that her native sons had perpetrated in Kansas. Not content to let the matter rest in the hands of a sister state, the General Court took the added precaution of asking President Pierce to use the power of his office to protect settlers in Kansas "against the violence and incursions of mobs from Missouri." As an earnest of its intention to accelerate the flow of free staters, including foreigners, into the Kansas Territory, the legislature granted a new charter to the New England Emigrant Aid Society.[58]

Closer to home, the General Court, in a trailblazing move, challenged the "unconstitutional and unchristian" Fugitive Slave Law by passing the Personal Liberty Bill. Designed to halt slave roundups in the Commonwealth, the bill forbade state officials from aiding federal authorities in the enforcement of the Fugitive Slave Law.[59] When the measure reached the governor's desk, he vetoed it, commenting that although many of its provisions had his "hearty approval," it was in clear violation of the Constitution and that its enforcement would place the Commonwealth on a collision course with the national government. Such was the extent of the trade-offs between the various legislative power blocs, however, that the bill was "rushed through [over the veto] by men, many of whom . . . were Union Saving Whigs and volunteers . . . in the Sims case." A companion piece setting stiff penalties for false accusation and arrest provided further protection for fugitive slaves.[60]

Having won this confrontation with the aid of newfound allies, the Free-Soil Americans turned with confidence to the next item on their agenda: the removal from the bench of State Probate Judge Edward Loring. Loring's actions as federal commissioner in the Anthony Burns affair—he had presided over the extradition proceedings—had marked him as a target for antislavery retribution. J.Q.A. Griffin insisted that Loring's removal was vital to the cause, for it would "teach the pro-slavery judges, attorneys, politicians, and divines a lesson."[61] Petitions poured into the statehouse demanding Loring's removal, and the General Court responded with a measure that would prohibit a person from simultaneously holding a state judgeship and a federal post. Governor Gardner vetoed the bill on the grounds that it threatened the independent judiciary, and this time his veto stuck. The legislature, however, was not ready to give up. It issued a joint address, authorizing the governor to remove Loring. Gardner ignored it.[62]

Gardner's willingness to take on the antislavery camp triggered speculation that he was angling for national office. "You will see . . . that Govr. [sic] Gardner has refused to remove Loring and also that he vetoed the Personal Liberty Bill," wrote antislavery leader Edmund Quincy. "He used to be called 'that Jackass' I am told by his old Whig friends . . . but jackass or not he completely took in all the Anti Slavery fellows. . . . W[ilson] will probably prevent his renomination for governor—but it puts him *rectus in curia* with the National No [sic] Nothings— which is, to be just as Pro Slavery as any of the old parties."[63] Quincy's guess that the governor had his eye on higher office was correct, but he was wrong about the amount of power and influence that Wilson and "all the Anti Slavery fellows" wielded within the party. The Free-Soil Americans had indeed sired an unparalleled record of accomplishment. Theodore Parker, who was no friend of "Sam," praised the Know-Nothing legislature as "the strongest antislavery body that had every assembled in the country."[64] But the Wilsonians had succeeded only because Whig and Democratic Americans supported them. Control of the party was another matter. On this score, the Free-Soil Americans, for all their experience and discipline, lacked the numbers necessary to win in a showdown.

Know-Nothing positive action was also directed toward solving local problems, especially those that the second party system had allowed to fester and expand during decades of neglect. Among the first tasks facing the new legislature was disposition of seven proposed constitutional reforms passed on to it by its predecessor. Two of the proposals—district representation based on population for both houses and election by plurality—were Whig measures, and the others—

holding state and national elections on the same day, a ban on the use of public funds for sectarian schools, and popular elections of the constitutional state officers, executive councillors, and county and district officers—were culled from the rejected 1853 constitutional referenda. The Know-Nothing legislature endorsed six of the seven, sending them on to the voters, who ratified them in a special election. For good reason, this series of amendments has been called the most significant expansion of democratic government in the constitutional history of Massachusetts.[65] Prior to their ratification, change had come grudgingly, the original document having been amended only thirteen times since its adoption in 1780. At the same time, it is worth noting that even though five of the amendments bore the Coalition label, they were consensus measures initiated by a Whig legislature, seconded by the overwhelming majority of Know-Nothing solons, a large number of whom were former Whigs, and ratified by the voters, who in 1853 had rejected them only because the Coalition had embedded them in a constitutional package that was unacceptable to the urban majority.

In addition to the amendments, a full docket of other reforms linked to the Coalition awaited the attention of the incoming legislature. The upper chamber acknowledged as much when it ordered for the membership individual copies of the debates and proceedings of the constitutional convention; and the General Court, following Coalition guidelines, abolished imprisonment for debt, expanded the benefits of existing homestead and mechanics' lien laws, initiated a mid-decade state census, and empowered jurors to judge the law as well as the facts in criminal cases.[66]

In making the case for the Coalition as the progenitor of Know-Nothingism, Bean and Handlin traced the roots of the 1855 legislature's antislavery, puritanical, constitutional, and Locofoco reforms back to the Free-Soil/Democratic alliance. The overall record, however, points to a different conclusion: The unprecedented volume and variety of reforms generated at the state and local levels of government in 1855 reflected an outlook on the proper functions of government that transcended the narrow vision of the Coalition's rural populists and Free-Soil moralists. At a time of general loss of faith in the existing parties, the Know-Nothing movement had responded to a fundamental urge on the part of the people for a practical means with which to voice their wishes and aspirations and to air their grievances. That function took place within the network of neighborhood lodges, one result of which was the forging of the solidarity needed for the American party to gain political power. Another result was the opening of direct lines of communication between the neighborhood lodges and the statehouse.

Know-Nothingism, unlike the Coalition, had sprung from the grass roots, and unlike the Coalition, it derived its greatest strength from the state's urban majority. It had attracted majorities from all the parties, as well, again unlike the Coalition, and by endowing all party members through the medium of its lodge system with a say in important matters directly affecting their welfare, allowed a multitude of reforms to well up from below.

Observed one Whig newspaper in the aftermath of the 1854 election, the

Know-Nothings "have produced a revolution—and there is a purpose in it, but no avowal of that purpose is made." The Know-Nothings had made public their intention to "kill off the old fogies and bring out entirely new men from the people"; but for what end was a matter for speculation. It was public knowledge, of course, that the movement had its roots in the Native American party of the 1840s and that the Wilsonian Free-Soilers had rushed en masse into the order; and this meant some kind of response to issues arising out of immigration and slavery. Beyond that, outsiders were in the dark and were forced to wait for the secret order to divulge its "distinctive principles" through its legislation.[67]

Rumor had it that the Know-Nothing legislature intended to "equalize the burden of the State and open up its benefits to all the people." That promise was a rallying point for those who believed that the state should improve the quality of life for ordinary citizens; and it was this populist upsurge that triggered the "political earthquake" of 1854 and catapulted ordinary men from their "pulpits and schoolhouses, their printing offices and farm yards, to services of public interest and trust." "Never did a legislative body meet in this hall with less experience," admitted Speaker Eddy, and, he added, "never were the people so exorbitant in their demands."[68] At last they had a party and a legislature attuned to their demands and through which they could influence the operation of government and help shape public policy to the needs of an urban, industrial society.

To this imperative, the Know-Nothings brought a radically different attitude toward the proper uses of government. Based on the republican idea of government as the servant of the people and dedicated to the Rousseauian proposition that the majority is the sole judge of what is right, the Know-Nothing populist mandate to shift the focus of government from special to general interests pushed the bounds of legislative activism far beyond the limits observed during the era of the second party system. Whatever their differences over policy matters on specific issues, most of the 1855 legislators believed in the need to use the power of the state to rectify neglected social problems and to transmit the will of the people into the statute books.

Both the president of the senate and the speaker of the house, in their maiden speeches to their respective bodies, reminded the legislators that the people had commissioned them to break with the practice of accounting to party, sect, or special interest and to legislate instead for the good of the whole. Petitions poured into the statehouse, saddling the legislators with an unprecedented volume of public business, and the General Court, in deference to the will of the people, busied itself during the third longest session since 1832 responding to them.[69]

Legislation spewed forth from the General Court in record-breaking numbers—nearly six hundred laws and resolutions in all. Their primary focus on matters of general concern reversed the policy adhered to throughout the second party era of favoring private over public interests and heralded a new deal for the common people of Massachusetts.[70] Proposals that had been rattling around legislative committee rooms for years, like safety measures at railroad crossings and abolition of imprisonment for debt, at last were given serious hearings and reported out. Popular items from the Coalition's agenda were among the changes. Many others, however, surfaced for the first time, particularly at the municipal level.

Know-Nothingism wore many faces, as befit a populist movement that pegged its appeal to the Yankee Protestant majority. Historians, however, have concentrated on the nativist and antislavery aspects of the party to the neglect of its response to urban problems. So did the *haute bourgeois*, who in passing on the written record of the times ignored the fact that urban dwellers had other problems besides the deluge of Irish pouring into their communities and the sectional crisis to worry about. Rapid and volatile changes in population, wealth, and business—industrial production alone was up 150 percent since 1846—had created a pressing need for radically different kinds of legislation than had been produced in the era of the second party system. The thousands of votes that the American party had racked up in the cities and those towns whose residents were most subject to the pressures of modernization carried with them the expectation that something would be done to meet this need; and "Sam" responded positively to this mandate.

Know-Nothingism had swept the cities in 1854 on the strength of promises to liberate them from party hacks and the cliques of powerful businessmen who controlled city hall. Victory brought anticipation of government action. As Ronald Formisano has noted, Know-Nothingism began as a lower-middle-class and working-class movement designed to influence affairs at the local level. Advertised as the party of "two dollars a day and roast beef," "Sam" had raised the expectations of the urban majority that the people's party would direct public resources toward improving the quality of urban life. The people wanted better police and fire protection, and they wanted steps taken to prevent the carnage caused by trains passing through downtown streets. Now that the people's party held power, they also wanted certain luxuries for the few made available to all, like public bath facilities, band concerts, and gas and running water piped into their residences at affordable rates. Boston's Know-Nothing mayor, Jerome V. C. Smith, responded to this expectation. He promised to cut taxes and reduce the city's water rate, and he proposed to put the city's jobless to work widening the boulevard along South Boston's shoreline and on other public works to beautify the city. Mayor Smith also wanted to sell city lots cheap to citizens of limited means and to have the city finance mortgages on extremely generous terms, so that ordinary citizens could build or purchase their own homes.[71]

The Know-Nothing legislature shared the mayor's vision. Where the Brahmins had fostered an "intimate connection" between the state and the "business prosperity of its citizens," the 1855 legislators promoted the populist ideal of the state wedded to the general welfare.[72] Given the primacy of the urban, industrial order, that meant a governmental response to the inroads of modernization.

Most of the American party's legislation in 1855, in sharp contrast to the Locofoco reforms of the Coalition, specifically addressed the needs of an industrial society. Know-Nothing enabling laws, authorizing cities and towns to lay gas and water mains and to construct highways, railway spur lines, bridges, wharves, aqueducts, drains, and the like, attested by their volume alone to "Sam's" urban focus and accelerated the expansion of the infrastructure that was vital to a rapidly expanding urban, industrial order. Know-Nothing town and municipal administrations underwrote these projects and at the same time raised essential services like police and fire protection to new heights of efficiency.[73]

All of this construction inevitably raised conflicts between public and corporate rights over matters like right of way and eminent domain. In the past, questions of this nature with rare exceptions were decided in favor of the corporations. "Sam" made an effort to right the balance. For example, in a right-of-way dispute in Boston in which the Board of Aldermen passed an ordinance investing a railroad company with the authority to close a downtown street to foot traffic, Mayor Smith intervened on the side of the pedestrians with a veto. And where the Whigs and the Coalition had left unanswered the age-old complaint regarding the size of the tolls charged to cross the two bridges connecting Charlestown and Boston, the Know-Nothings ordered the rates dropped.[74] An even more ancient grievance—sleight-of-hand market sales—led to the establishment of uniform weights and measures and to public regulation of the weighing and sale of necessities like coal, milk, corn, wheat, and other grains. Use of false weights was made a crime punishable by fine and imprisonment. The General Court also exercised the police power to regulate pawnbrokers and fortune tellers and to crack down on cardsharps, counterfeiters, and distillers who added poisonous substances in the manufacture of spirits. Another statute empowered local boards of trade to decide where abatoirs and other noisome trades might locate.[75]

"Sam" responded as well to the demand for more government regulation, creating, for example, the Board of Pilots in order to supervise and regulate harbor traffic. The major concern, however, was with the business order, and the primary focus of that concern was the railroads. Every year, an army of highly paid lobbyists descended on the statehouse in pursuit of legislation favorable to the railways and other business interests. Their importunings paid off. Legislators spent at least half of their time wrestling with private bills to create new corporations or to increase the capital stock of existing ones. Public bills, on the other hand, suffered from neglect.[76] Thus, for example, demands that the railroads take greater precautions to ensure the safety of the public went unheeded. Henry Wilson drew a line straight from the wealth of the railroad corporations to the statehouse: "I do not believe there has been a legislature during the last . . . ten years, through which we could carry any proposition against railway influence or power."[77] The record lent substance to Wilson's suspicions. Powerful lobbyists, abetted by a probusiness press, had managed to persuade successive legislatures that safety considerations were best handled by railroad management. As for the "wholesale slaughter" that aroused so much public indignation, the Whiggish press laid the blame on drunks and pedestrians "being run over in consequence of their own carelessness."[78]

That sort of callous disregard for the public safety prompted the Know-Nothing members of the Committee on Railways and Canals to report out a bill brimming with recommendations for reducing the carnage; and the General Court, in spite of an intense lobbying campaign mounted by the railroad corporations against the measure, broke precedence and followed through with statutes compelling the railroads to build bridges or tunnels wherever their lines intersected with highways; to require trains approaching grade crossings to come to a complete halt before proceeding across; and to provide attendants at drawbridges. Another law ordered railroad companies to post security to meet the contingency of court-assessed costs in cases involving land taken by eminent domain for railroad corridors.[79] Other, more far-reaching recommendations for bringing the railroads into line with the public interest—for example, motions to establish a Board of Railroad Commissioners and to set maximum fares—cropped up during the legislative session, but failed passage. Nevertheless, the Know-Nothing government had gone a great deal further than had its predecessors in imposing restraints on the industry.

Insurance companies and to a lesser extent banks were also the targets of several regulatory laws, the most important of which created the Board of Insurance Commissioners. Empowered to inspect all insurance companies operating within the state and to examine their officers under oath, the board functioned as a protector of the consumer and as a barrier to what had been a free flow into the Commonwealth of fraudulent and insolvent out-of-state companies. With more than half a billion dollars in insured property in the state, the board met a vital need for additional consumer protection. Loan and fund associations also fell under the purview of the board. And in the interest of sound insurance coverage at reasonable cost to the public, the legislature authorized voters to incorporate their towns as legal fire insurance companies.[80]

Banks had done especially well under the lobby systems, as did their shareholders, whose dividends averaged 7.64 percent per annum in the early 1850s. Because it was felt that the supply of bank capital had to grow to feed the rapid expansion of commerce and industry, cooperative legislatures had voted through 'batches" of private bills that boosted capital in Massachusetts banks to over $59 million by 1855, a total that was exceeded only by the banks of New York. Annual increases after 1850 reached $7 million and higher until the Know-Nothing legislature virtually shut down this form of state aid with its approval of a miniscule $850,000 increase. Banks, like insurance companies, had to file annual reports with the state commissioners detailing their financial condition, a requirement that the Know-Nothing legislature used to close a loophole on tax evaders by obliging the banks and insurance companies to submit to local boards of assessors the names of depositors and shareholders and the amounts that these individuals received in interest and dividends.[81]

While it cannot be said that the Know-Nothing government fashioned a regulatory state, it did bring key areas of the economy, such as harbor shipping, banking, insurance, and transportation, under increasing scrutiny. Its record of expanded state supervision, moreover, provided a counterpoise to the individual's sense of powerlessness in an increasingly impersonal world.

Public demands for new programs to address the needs of an industrial society had met with a positive response on Beacon Hill. But "Sam's" new deal for the forgotten man came with a high price tag. State spending soared, up 45 percent in a single year. The cost of running the government alone climbed to a record high of close to half a million dollars. Welfare costs jumped 40 percent above the previous year's level, mainly owing to the construction of a state hospital for the insane and a school for retarded children and to an upgrading of the state's poorhouses.[82] To the horror of fiscal conservatives, the Know-Nothing government financed these projects through a combination of deficit spending and a whopping 50 percent hike in the annual state tax on the cities and towns. Spending and taxing on so grand a scale, according to critics, came naturally to a party composed of men of little substance who took pride in spreading the wealth of others around and whose penchant for philanthropy exceeded the means to pay for it.[83]

Public school expenditures also reached record levels in a state that was already spending more per pupil than any other. To meet the costs, the legislature resorted to the largest annual raise in the school tax to that time. The legislature's willingness to pay for better education was matched by its commitment to the welfare of the school children. Owing to that concern, the legislature made vaccination compulsory; authorized the cities and towns to issue free textbooks and paper to pupils; created an annual fund to enable state institutions to procure new books for their libraries; and raised the annual appropriation for the Perkins School for the Blind by a third. Other measures, which tightened the enforcement of attendance and required factory children under fifteen years of age to attend school a minimum of eleven weeks a year, aimed at curbing the abuse of child labor. Highlighting the Know-Nothing drive for equal educational opportunity for all children was the nation's first desegregation law, which prohibited the exclusion of any child from the public schools of Massachusetts on account of race, color, or religion.[84]

"Sam" displayed a similarly enlightened approach on behalf of women's rights, producing an outstanding body of legislation that is all the more impressive when placed in the context of that male-dominated age. Several statutes redefined the marriage bond so as to undercut the primacy of the husband's position under the law. Henceforth, a married woman enjoyed the same rights as a single woman to sue, transact business, make a will, or go to work without the consent of her husband. Her earnings belonged to her, and her husband could not dispose of her property. A woman whose husband was confined to a mental institution could use up to one-third of his estate for living expenses. A wife no longer had to wait five years before filing for divorce for desertion. Obtaining a divorce was made easier, as was remarriage for divorced persons. To protect the rights of divorced women, the legislature empowered the state supreme court to assign custody of children, impose alimony, and, when necessary, attach a former husband's property to meet support payments.[85]

Reform had its limits, as the derailment of the secret ballot and ten-hour bills illustrates. Both measures lay at the heart of the labor movement's quest for a greater voice in the workplace; and given the large number of working-class and prolabor legislators on record in favor of state intervention to right the imbalance between capital and labor, passage of both proposals seemed inevitable. However, sharp differences in voting patterns in the two houses had surfaced during the legislative year. For one thing, it was easier for lobbyists to influence the 40-member senate than the 378-member house. For another, house members came directly from the local lodges with instructions to speak out on behalf of neighborhood and general concerns, whereas senators were nominated by district councils, where considerations of a more political or personal nature, like party strategy, factional alliances, political trade-offs, and self-advancement, came into play.[86]

Of all the legislation voted on during the 1855 legislative session, none was the subject of such heated and protracted debate in both houses as the ten-hour bill. It had been reported out of committee with a ringing endorsement. Majorities in both houses easily beat back amendments aimed at crippling the measure. Thus, it was particularly galling for labor when the ten-hour bill, after carrying the lower house by a wide margin, met defeat in the senate. It was widely assumed, and with good reason, that corporate gold had purchased the results in the smaller chamber.[87]

Its companion measure, the secret ballot bill, met a similar fate. After its endorsement by the house, the measure went to the senate, where the vote on it deadlocked. As was the case with the ten-hour bill, betrayal of the public trust may have decided the outcome. Senate president Henry W. Benchley, a leader in the ten-hour organization, cast the tie-breaking vote against the bill.[88] The apparent sellout of the two most important labor bills to come before the legislature in 1855 undoubtedly weakened worker support for the secret order. Nevertheless, the great majority of the Know-Nothing legislators had proved again and again by their actions during the session that they were not the captives of special interests.

"Sam" ran into trouble with the yeomanry as well, partly because they felt the government should pay less attention to urban affairs and more to agriculture. The lower house did not help matters when it buried a legislative order for the creation of state agricultural schools. Buried as well was an altered redistricting plan that favored rural Massachusetts. But it was the governor who did most to stir widespread disaffection with Know-Nothingism in the farm belt when, for budgetary reasons, he vetoed a pair of bills to provide state loans for improvements on the two railroad corridors extending westward along the upper and lower rims of the state to linkup points with other states.[89] Both lines brought the gift of growth and soaring property values to the interior sections of the state and afforded farmers access to eastern markets.

Its failures and shortcomings notwithstanding, "Sam" had turned in a remarkable performance, a performance, moreover, that contrasts sharply with the standard portraits of the party as a continuation of the Coalition or as one obsessed solely with "Temperance, Liberty, and Protestantism." Speaker Eddy and senate president Benchley, in their farewell addresses, lavished praise on their respective memberships and committees for having given due regard to "all great interests of the state" and for having, through the body of their work, expressed the sentiments of the people.[90] It was fitting praise. The Know-Nothing legislators had bequeathed an unmatched legacy of reform. The first to question the myth of the benevolent industrial order, they attempted to curb some of its excesses. If that effort proved halting and inadequate, it nevertheless broke new ground and exceeded in scope and significance the puny response of all preceding legislatures combined. And in their concern with the negative impact of modernization on the quality of urban life, the Know-Nothing lawmakers anticipated by half a century the Progressive movement. They had reached so far because they recognized that the pressures engendered by fundamental social and economic change demanded a fundamental political response. Their sensitivity to this imperative demonstrated that they had indeed listened to the voice of the people.

CHAPTER FIVE

The Republican Challenge

THE 1850S opened with a comprehensive plan drafted by national Whig and Democratic leaders to wall off the slavery question from the political arena and closed with the South on the brink of secession. Moral indignation over the fugitive slave provision of the Compromise of 1850 sparked massive protests throughout the North. Roundups of runaway slaves in the free states heightened tensions and triggered occasional violence. Passage of the Kansas-Nebraska Act four years later scuttled the principle of free soilism embedded in the Missouri Compromise and touched off protests throughout the North that underscored the failure of the bipartisan efforts to defuse the volatile slavery issue. Fusion parties materialized overnight in the free states, geared to the need of "Conscience" Whigs, "anti-Nebraska" Democrats, and Free-Soilers for a viable political organization with which to resist the spread of slavery into the national territories. Out of this flux emerged the Republican party.

As has been noted earlier, a similar development failed to take place in Massachusetts, where the rush of rank-and-file Whigs and Democrats into the American party short-circuited attempts to create an antislavery fusion party.

Remnants of the antislavery movement in Massachusetts held several meetings in the aftermath of the 1854 election in order to survey the prospects for political antislaveryism. Among those attending were three Know-nothing legislators—Dr. James W. Stone, Charles W. Slack, and Moses Kimball—whose defection from the Free-Soil party drew sharp criticism from some of the other participants. The three men "bore the attack well," explaining that their joining the American party in no way diminished their zeal for the antislavery cause. Quite the contrary, they had turned to the American party after the breakdown of the fusion movement in the belief that it alone could advance the cause. Nothing had transpired since their joining the secret order to disabuse them of this conviction. Moreover, for those present to disassociate themselves and their organization from the Free-Soil Americans who were locked in a "very severe" struggle with the Native Americans for control of the party was to risk turning the scales against the antislavery wing of the party and doom its chances for success. The others rejected the argument, deeming Know-Nothingism an unworthy vehicle to carry their cause forward. Antislaveryism, they said, had "no root in the principles of the new party," and unless the movement disclaimed "all conection with, and all sympathies in Know-nothingism . . . the cause is lost." There was general agreement, however, that any attempt to resuscitate the defunct Free-Soil party or the 1854 Republican "fraud" would prove barren. Even more frustrating, they realized that it would be premature to found an independent antislavery party so long as the American party occupied its present unassailable position in the political arena.[1] On this pessimistic note, the men broke off their discussions.

A long, gloomy winter followed for those antislavery men who held out for a fusion party independent of the Know-Nothing organization. A despondent Charles Francis Adams blamed an alleged revanchist Whiggery for the lack of progress. "The tendency of the Know-Nothing movement," he explained to a fellow Free-Soiler, "is adverse to antislavery not only because it conflicts with the first dictates of humanity, but because it helps to reinstate in a position of influence the men [Cotton Whigs] who have always resisted it." Adams believed that the antislavery cause was in great danger "of being crushed between the upper millstone of Know-Nothing Whiggery and the nether one of Douglas democracy." Only the concentration of antislavery sentiment in sufficient strength would "make it impossible for either of these parties to despise it."[2] Ironically, the Cotton Whigs blamed Free-Soil and Democratic "intriguers" for their political misfortunes.[3] That the old party elites persisted in misinterpreting the nature of the populist explosion that had destroyed the existing party system illustrates how far out of touch they were with the people. "Sam" had triumphed not through the intrigues of party professionals but by invoking a pox on all parties and politicians and by promising to replace elitist rule with people's rule. This is not to say that there were no grounds for the suspicions of outsiders like Adams. Relatively free of party professionals during its formative period, the American party, once it had gained a sizable following, had become a mecca for the politically ambitious.

As late as mid-April, Adams saw no evidence of any general interest in a concerted antislavery movement outside the American party. Edward L. Pierce offered an explanation for this state of affairs: Word had reached him that a new secret organization called Know-Something was draining off potential support by espousing nativism, temperance, and free soilism. Among those who had joined the new party was former governor George Boutwell. Adams was appalled by the news and branded the Know-Something organization a worse political blunder than Know-Nothingism, since it would serve only "to divide a falling house."[4] Adams, as usual, was overly pessimistic. The Know-Something phenomenon proved ephemeral, its ensemble of stock issues and ambitious politicians inadequate to the task of generating the kind of public enthusiasm needed to sustain a successful drive against the party in power. More important, a scandal involving the Nunnery Committee had exploded into a full-blown crisis for the American party.

The Nunnery Committee's pursuit of its commission to ferret out skullduggery behind the walls of Catholic institutions was cut short by an exposé of its own misdoings. Under the heading "Our Houses Are Our Castles," the *Boston Daily Advertiser* retraced the steps of the committee in its exploration of a Catholic boarding school for girls in Roxbury. The men had managed in their cellar-to-attic search to terrify the school children (one of whom shrieked, "The house is full of Know-Nothings!"), to flush a nun from her devotions in the chapel, and to determine that a youngster, confined to a sick bed, was, as the nuns assured them, a girl. A committee of the General Court created to investigate the Roxbury incident revealed additional details. One of the men searching the school—the party's Grand Worshipful Instructor, Joseph Hiss—had made suggestive remarks to two of the nuns, and all of the visitors upon departure had repaired to the fashionable Norfolk House, where, undeterred by the recently passed temperance law, they washed down a sumptuous dinner with copious quantities of champagne.[5]

A second special committee zeroed in on the Nunnery Committee's activities in Lowell, in particular the bill for a single night's stay at the Washington House in that city. Hiss had settled the account the following morning, charging all to the Commonwealth. The bill included meals, lodging, wine, gin, cigars, and a lady of the evening who had spent the night with the Grand Worshipful Instructor. Members who urged that the house should "not make itself a sluiceway through which to pour such dark and putrid waters upon the community" were overriden by the majority, who believed that if the scandal were "corked up now and kept corked up until next autumn the scent at election time would be rather too strong for the voters."[6] After weeks of heated debate, the house finally bent to that logic and voted to expel Hiss.

Rufus Choate seized on the scandal to draw a comparison between the old and the new politics. "Your estate is gracious that keeps you out of hearing of our politics," he informed a friend living abroad. "Anything more low, obscene, feculent, the manifold heavings of history have not cast up. Renown and grace are dead."[7] Choate spoke for an elite that was blind to Know-Nothing accomplishments. Nevertheless, the party was in trouble.

The Nunnery Committee's sorry conduct at Roxbury and Lowell had badly tarnished the American party's image as an effective, uncorrupted force for carrying out the will of the people and revived the spirits of the antislavery fusionists. Dr. Stone, reporting to his antislavery brethren from his vantage point in the state legislature, told them that the American party was "shaking to the foundation, under the odium of its follies and absurdities at the State House." Other Know-Nothings echoed that opinion, noting that the legislature was faltering badly as a consequence of its meddling in religious matters.[8] The Native Americans, too, appreciated the gravity of the situation. They lashed out at the press for having blown the incident way out of proportion for party purposes and at those legislators who in pressing for further investigations actually were seeking to gratify "certain persons outside of this House who wished to break down the power of the party in power." Hiss's lawyer, Ben Butler, seized on that point to answer his own rhetorical question of why this persecution of his client: "It is because party ends are to be answered, and these are means to party ends. He is a member of the dominant party in the State, and men hope through him to strike down the party in power."[9]

The scandals rocking the statehouse had altered the calculations of the Free-Soil Americans. Hitherto committed to working within the framework of the ruling party, they felt sufficiently emboldened by the confusion and disarray stirred up by the Nunnery Committee fiasco to embark on a policy of rule or ruin. C. F. Adams also took stock of the "travelling committees disgracing the Common-wealth, and committees of investigation which supress the evidence they cannot control." He homed in on the Nunnery Committee as if it were typical of Know-Nothing government, attributing its excesses to the license of men unrestrained by considerations of public trust and the high moral tone that had made the General Court in which he had served "one of the most respectable assemblages in the United States." It was no accident, insofar as Adams was concerned, that the "secret plotters" should have fallen from grace. Pledging votes without regard to moral distinction or individual merit, he remarked, was as likely to place the government in "the hands of knaves and idiots . . . as of honest men."[10]

But where other antislavery men saw opportunity in the American party's embarrassment, the Quincy patriarch remained immersed in gloom. In May he talked to Charles Sumner, who told him that the birth of a fusion party was imminent, albeit one with a Know-Nothing connection. Adams did not share Sumner's enthusiasm, remarking pointedly that he, for one, was disgusted with the profligacy of the Know-Nothing leadership and could never act in conjunction with them. Adams, in the privacy of his diary, ascribed Sumner's willingness to collaborate with the Know-Nothings to the sinister influence of his senatorial colleague, Henry Wilson. Know-Nothingism remained for Adams an insuperable barrier to fusion; and since there was no party of sufficient strength at the moment to topple this "secret abomination," Massachusetts had to remain at the mercy of its "demagogue agitation."[11]

Fortunately for the antislavery cause, Wilson, and not Adams, undertook the task of steering fusion through the rapidly shifting political tides. A year earlier, Wilson had chastised Summer for not speaking out against slavery, only to fall silent himself once he reached Washington. Emboldened by the Hiss fiasco, he finally decided to break his silence on the slavery question. Speaking to Know-Nothing audiences in various parts of the state, he urged them to abandon secrecy, drop religious and ethnic proscription, and unite with men of all parties behind the slavery issue.[12] At the same time, he was working behind the scenes to distance himself and his wing of the party from its nativist extremists. "As to the [twenty-one-year residency] amendment to the Constitution," he confided to a friend, "I am doing all I can to kill it. . . . Its adoption will be disgraceful to the party [and] the state. We have a class of fools in the party who have already disgraced the state and the party."[13]

Wilson's plan was to gather all antislavery groups under one roof—if not that of the American party, then that of fusion; but he went a step further in a speech delivered in Brattleboro, Vermont, on the eve of the June meeting of the American national council, at which time he warned that if the order were to ignore slavery or take a neutral stand, it would meet "a speedy death and dishonored grave." To live, the party must adopt as its watchword, "Freedom is National and Slavery is Sectional."[14]

Wilson's ultimatum was not taken lightly. Southern delegates to the American convention arrived in Philadelphia still smarting from the defeat of Know-Nothing T. S. Flournay, who had been favored to win the gubernatorial contest in Virginia. The winner of that contest—Democratic incumbent Henry A. Wise—had drawn blood by linking his American opponent to "the abolitionism of the Massachusetts Know-Nothings." Wise's upset win inspired other Southern Democrats to pin the abolitionist label on the American party.[15] The pro-Know-Nothing *Richmond Enquirer* was sufficiently alarmed by the tactic to caution the Southern delegates to beware "the Abolitionist Know-Nothings" and to "kick [Wilson] and all such out of the Convention at the outset." "Purge, purify the order at the North," the editorial advised, "and you will then construct a great national, constitutional party."[16]

Given these preconference posturings, a clash between Northern and Southern delegates was inevitable. Trouble erupted even before the opening of the proceedings, when the Southern contingent tried to bar the Massachusetts delegates from admission. That maneuver failing, a Virginia delegate took to the floor and assailed the Bay Staters as "abolitionists and disorganizers." Wilson had his reply in hand: "The past belongs to slavery—the future to freedom. The past is yours,—the future is ours." He boasted that the North had the power to end slavery in the District of Columbia, prohibit it in the national territories, repeal the Fugitive Slave Law, and defeat those trying to drag Kansas into the Union as a slave state; and, he assured the assembly, "we mean to do it."[17]

Wilson's philippic notwithstanding, the delegates elected as council president E. B. Bartlett, a Kentuckian with little sympathy for the Bay Stater's opinions. Bartlett's election also dashed Henry J. Gardner's national aspirations. Gardner had run well in the early balloting for the council presidency, but the rising anti–Bay State tide ruined whatever chance he had to win. Hard on the heels of these setbacks, the convention forced the party's national chaplain, the Reverend Henry W. Rugg of Massachusetts, to resign his post on the grounds that he was a "Universalist Abolitionist."[18]

In spite of its reversals, the Massachusetts delegation doggedly continued the battle. Former Free-Soiler and Wilson ally John W. Foster submitted a resolution to the platform committee calling for the restoration of the Missouri Compromise. The resolution was buried in committee, which instead reported out a platform tailored to Southern American predilections. Its nativist planks—a twenty-one-year naturalization period, exclusion of the foreign-born from public office, and resistance to the aggressions of the Roman Catholic Church—sat well with all the delegates, including the champions of "Human Brotherhood" from Massachusetts. But Article XII, which committed the American party to existing laws on slavery, roiled the convention. Congress, it read, lacked constitutional authority to bar slavery from the territories or abolish it in the District of Columbia or to exclude from the Union any slave state carved out of the national territories. Not even Governor Gardner was willing to swallow Article XII. Branding it "too generous" to the slave interests, he told the convention that a platform containing Article XII "could not carry a single village in Massachusetts."[19] Foster was less restrained, scoring the South for having packed the platform committee. He urged the assembly to weigh carefully the choice laid before them: Adopt Article XII and face certain defeat in next year's presidential election, or adopt "the restoration of the Missouri Compromise as our rallying cry" and "carry every free State from the Atlantic to the Mississippi." Wilson echoed Foster. The fate of the American party hinged on the convention's decision, he said. Article XII would leave the "people of the North" no recourse other than to "repudiate it, spurn it, spit upon it." The convention disregarded the warnings and adopted the platform, including Article XII, by an 80 to 59 margin.[20]

The vote left a majority of the Northern delegates in a quandary. On the one hand, they were distraught over Article XII but reluctant to break up the party by bolting; on the other hand, they could not appease the South on Article XII without alienating their constituents. They met the following morning to chart their course of action. Wilson, who chaired the meeting, wanted the dissidents to unite behind a declaration that he had drafted that demanded the restoration of the Missouri Compromise, protection for the settlers in Kansas, and a ban on further admissions of slave states into the Union. Wilson's declaration also turned Article XII on its head. Slavery being "a mere municipal regulation," Congress lacked jurisdiction under the Constitution to legalize it either in the District of Columbia or the territories.

Gardner heard Wilson out with increasing impatience, and when the senator had finished, he exploded that he, for one, would not be "abolitionized." Neither would a majority of the other free staters present, who, in the interest of unity, adopted a more moderate "Appeal to the People" that, while repeating the call for the restoration of the Missouri Compromise, the admission of Kansas and Nebraska as free states, and the protection of the right of suffrage for settlers in the territories, omitted any reference to the question of congressional jurisdiction.[21] Nevertheless, their decision to work outside the jurisdiction of the national council marked a breach with the national American party and left its plans for the forthcoming presidential campaign in ruins. The pivotal role of Wilson and the rest of the Bay State delegation in sabotaging the attempt by the Philadelphia convention to build a national base for the 1856 campaign drew from an Ohioan the caustic comment, "A d____d fool is bad enough from any region; but it does seem to me that you Boston d____d fools are the hardest cases I have ever known."[22]

Senator Wilson, for all his brave words in Philadelphia about the historical inevitability of an antislavery triumph, returned to Boston without an operative base to accelerate the inevitable. Not only had he failed to impose his antislavery views on the national order, those views by no means reflected majority opinion in the lodges of his home state. Political antislaveryism still needed a national organization if it was to bring its case to the people in the 1856 presidential campaign, and since the American party no longer met that criterion, the senator was forced to draw on other connections in an effort to salvage the drive to create a viable antislavery fusion party in Massachusetts that could merge with similar organizations cropping up in other states. He contacted two prominent antislavery Whigs, former governor Ezra Lincoln and Sam Bowles, the editor of the *Springfield Republican*, and confided to them that if the Brahmins would take the lead in consolidating the state's antislavery elements behind a united front, the Free-Soil Americans were willing to follow their lead. Bowles and Lincoln agreed that the time had come for the disbandment of the American party of Massachusetts and for the formation of an antislavery party to replace it. Wilson suggested Robert C. Winthrop for the leadership role. "Tell him [Winthrop]," Wilson said, "that we antislavery men want him and his Whig friends to take the lead in forming a victorious Republican party in Massachusetts."[23]

Wilson, in turning to the same Brahmin Whigs whom the voters had overwhelmingly repudiated the previous November, may have been signaling them that he was willing to scrap economic and social reforms in the interest of a united front on the slavery question. More likely, he was sending a message to Henry J. Gardner: If the governor did not commit his organization to fusion, he might have to face a business-backed antislavery party in the next election. Whatever the case, Wilson's machinations posed a very real threat to Gardner. A bolt of the Wilsonian Free-Soilers would deprive the governor and his party of virtually the entire antislavery vote.

Wilson was not alone in making overtures to the Brahmins. Former secretary of the Navy John P. Kennedy of Maryland implored his friend Winthrop to head up a Whig-American coalition in Massachusetts that would stand by the national council's platform and "show that the North is not wholly under the dominion of Seward, Sumner, and Wilson." Kennedy feared that "if there is no such leaven apparent [in the Northern states] . . . great embitterment will follow the secession of the North from the [American] Convention." If, on the other hand, "amongst the judicious and leading gentlemen of New England there are enough to form a respectable party in point of numbers," it was incumbent upon leaders of the proper stamp, like Winthrop, Everett, Choate, and Lawrence, to gather these numbers into "a party of dissent against Wilson and Gardner and the others . . . [and thus] raise our hopes this side of the Mason and Dixon." For the Brahmins of Massachusetts, to ignore this imperative was bound to have dangerous, perhaps even apocalyptic, consequences, for only the "friends of the new

American party as now proclaimed at Philadelphia can save—I will not say the Union for it seems profane to talk of dissolution—but the peace and prosperity of the country."[24]

Kennedy's letter reflected the thinking of a border state Fillmore Whig even more out of touch with the dynamics of Massachusetts politics than his recently ousted Brahmin friends. Bay State voters had not rebelled against the rule of the Commonwealth's "judicious and leading gentlemen" in order to reinstate that rule one year later.

It was a moot point anyway. Neither Wilson nor Kennedy's proposals stirred Brahmin interest. Winthrop and his fellow blue bloods preferred to sulk in their tents rather than consort with a tribe of politicians whom they despised as demagogues and agitators. Their decision to do nothing had no effect on the crosscurrents and rapidly shifting political tides, which, in washing away the old political order, had rendered the idea of government by the good, the wise, and the rich an anachronism. Political power in this period of transition went to the swift and the calculating—to men like Gardner, Banks, and Wilson, who carved out their own opportunities. There was no room at the top for those who waited for the call or who clung to the belief that public office still went to those who found favor within the Brahmin inner circle.

Such notions were not in evidence at the American state council when it met in special session at Tremont Hall in Boston on June 28 to hail "with pride and unanimity" the state delegation that had bolted the national convention and to issue a proclamation to the people of Massachusetts denouncing the Philadelphia platform as "utterly foreign to the convictions of the American party of Massachusetts." An ebullient Governor Gardner defined what these convictions were in a set of resolutions. The state council should (1) sever all ties with the national branch, whose Southern contingent had attempted "to send Papists [Louisiana Creoles] into the late Council at Philadelphia"; (2) support the restoration of the Missouri Compromise and protect free institutions in Kansas and Nebraska; and (3) reaffirm the principles of Americanism and call upon "men of all parties . . . [to support] the principles we profess." To that end, the governor recommended that the council drop the mantle of secrecy and open its proceedings to the public.[25]

Gardner had designed his resolutions to bridge the gap between the nativist and antislavery camps. It was a shrewd political move, and when the state council adopted the resolutions by a nearly unanimous vote, his prospects for renomination or for heading the proposed fusion party seemed assured. As an added precaution, he played down an issue that he would have to face if he were to run as an antislavery candidate: "I have heard so much about the destruction of the Union," he told his Boston audience, "that I have begun to look upon it as one of those fabulous myths we read in history. I don't believe those [Southern] gentlemen could destroy the Union . . . and I don't believe any of them would destroy it if they could. It is a grand scarecrow and means nothing. The Union to be destroyed! no—never; the idea is preposterous (great cheering)." The state council, following his recommendation, severed its connection with the "proslavery" national order.[26]

That evening, the council, in response to the governor's ecumenical call to men of all parties, ordered the doors of the Tremont Temple opened to the public. A large throng filled the seats and listened to a number of antislavery speeches, including one by the Native American hard-liner A. B. Ely. However, the American party of Massachusetts was anything but united in its stand against Southern imperialism or behind the idea of joining with others in the formation of an antislavery fusion party. The Native Americans had not suddenly seen the light. Ely's speech was in fact a disingenuous play for time. He and the other party fathers had watched with growing alarm the direction in which Wilson and Gardner were pulling the party. If fusion of all antislavery elements meant the dissolution of the American party and the abandonment of nativist principles, they wanted no part of it. They chose, however, not to speak out against fusion in the midst of the antislavery euphoria that gripped the Boston audience, preferring instead to hold their peace until the next regularly scheduled meeting of the state council.

Accordingly, when the council assembled in Springfield on August 7, the Native Americans came prepared to challenge those party members who were seeking union with other parties "on the ground of hostility to slavery." The enemies of the American party looked forward to that confrontation with glee. "There will be a quarrel in the Know-Nothing Convention . . . perhaps a split," gloated newspaper editor Sam Bowles. "It [the American party] cannot put off the end long. . . . If it denies fusion it will kill itself as the Whigs did last year."[27]

The state council was well aware of the danger, and in an effort to avoid schism, it produced a new party platform crafted to meet both nativist and antislavery concerns. A. B. Ely's blueprint for a better America was incorporated in its ethnoreligious planks: (1) exclusion of Roman Catholics from public office and of the foreign-born from office and the suffrage for a minimum of twenty-one years; (2) denial of public funds for sectarian schools; (3) retention of the King James Bible in the public schools; and (4) sweeping revision and tighter enforcement of the naturalization laws. The antislavery resolutions bore Wilson's imprint: (1) restoration of the Missouri Compromise; (2) protection provided by the national government to uphold the right of actual settlers in the territories to vote; and (3) since "freedom is national and slavery sectional," a call for the federal government to be relieved of any jurisdiction over the institution of slavery.[28]

The Springfield platform, as it came to be called, marked the culmination of a concerted effort by the Know-Nothing leadership to shape the party agenda around antislavery and nativist concerns. Crafted with the expectation that the merging of the two forces would expand the party's appeal, it proved a disappointment, because it omitted the kinds of promises that had fueled the 1854 populist explosion. A marked decline in grass-roots participation accompanied the changeover from people power to power politics. Flagging attendance and mounting debts at the lodge level signaled that those who had been drawn into the lodges with the promise of a people's government were not content to have that government controlled by cunning politicians like Wilson and Gardner. [29]

A few weeks earlier, Wilson had submitted a similar set of antislavery resolutions for the consideration of the free-state secessionists at Philadelphia, only to have the majority (including Governor Gardner) shout them down as too radical. At the time, the Wilsonians were committed to a policy of working within the state's most powerful political organization. In the subsequent weeks, however, it had become evident how difficult it was to entice nonaligned antislavery groups into the American party. More significantly, Republican organizations sprouting up in other states pointed to an attractive alternative to the scandal-racked American party. [30] Hence, the Free-Soil Americans, in spite of the insertion of their principles into the Springfield platform, shifted to a new strategy: the fusion of all antislavery groups into a new party. Wilson, having squeezed all the benefits (including his own Senate seat) that he could out of the Know-Nothing order, was now prepared to abandon it. [31]

Confident that the slavery issue would swallow nativism in the forthcoming state election, he took to the council floor to promote a fusion party and to exhort his fellow Know-Nothings not to set their faces against the dictates of "freedom, patriotism, and humanity." To do so would be contrary to their own splendid record on behalf of those noble ideals. Had not the American party of Massachusetts sent to Congress a delegation "pledged to the policy of freedom"; written "with the iron pen of history . . . declarations of principles and pledges and acts" inimical to the Slave Power; dispatched delegates to the Philadelphia convention who had "spurned the [national council's] unhallowed decrees and turned their backs forever upon that prostituted organization"; and, in league with other free-state Americans, "shivered to atoms" the pro-Southern national Know-Nothing order? And now, the American party of Massachusetts, "holding as it does the reins of power," had within its means "a glorious opportunity" to electrify the nation by setting the "magnanimous example of a great and dominant party . . . freely yielding up that power for the holy cause of freedom to the equal possession of other parties who are willing to cooperate with it upon a common platform." [32]

A political realist like Wilson could hardly have expected that his words would trigger a rush by the Know-Nothing leadership to dismantle their party in the interest of "the holy cause of freedom" without first exacting a *quid pro quo*. Even as the debate over fusion on the convention floor pitted, on the one side, delegates "who love the principles of Americanism and consider the evils of Catholicism paramount to all other evils to which this country is subjected" against, on the other side, those who scored slavery as the nation's greatest curse, Wilson, Gardner, Banks, and other power brokers were cutting deals and maneuvering for advantage behind the scenes. They finally settled on an arrangement whereby Wilson and Banks promised to work for the governor's reelection in return for his commitment to fusion. A year earlier, the people had revolted against political trade-offs and party rigging of this sort, but with some three hundred local lodges unrepresented at Springfield and with Gardner in command of the remnants of the lodge network, people power was no longer a factor in party affairs.[33]

Ely saw a way out of the ideological deadlock on the floor. Why not, he suggested, adopt a resolution that agreed to the creation of a fusionist party based on the Springfield platform? Ely's intention was obvious—to preserve the primacy of Native American principles regardless of the outcome of the decision on fusion. The delegates voted two to one in favor of the compromise, and after sanctioning a partial dismantlement of the order's dark-lantern mechanism, adjourned.[34]

The one-sided vote resulted from Gardner's having thrown his organization behind the drive for fusion. It is worth noting also that there were no paeans to the voice of the people at Springfield or any other sign of the populist ethos that was the *sine qua non* of 1854 Know-Nothingism. Instead, the convention responded to different voices—those of the party bosses—and agreed to merge their party into an antislavery fusion movement that, while deriving nothing from the populist ferment of the early lodge system or promising anything further in the way of social and economic reform, seemed to ensure His Excellency the top spot on its autumn ticket. At the same time, the settlement suited the Wilsonians, who anticipated that drawing "Sam" into the orbit of what was "substantially a movement of the old Free Soil party" would guarantee victory.[35]

The Chapman Hall Free-Soilers, as they had the year before, balked at the idea of bedding down with the Know-Nothings, choosing instead to try to form their own fusion party. Their call for a meeting of all interested parties at Chapman Hall, however, drew only a scattering of Whigs and Americans and no Democrats. Among the Know-Nothings present were Henry Wilson and his associate John W. Foster, whom Adams marked as "in training" for the governorship. Adams's sharp eye caught the detail but missed the point. Foster and Wilson, and not he or the Bird Club ideologues, commanded the allegiance of the antislavery Americans, and without them, there would be no fusion. Wilson spoke to the group, assuring them that his goal was what it had always been—a union of all parties based on the single proposition of freedom.[36]

In subsequent meetings, the Chapman Hall committee (Adams, Charles Allen, R. H. Dana, Jr., S. C. Phillips, and Judge Samuel Hoar) conferred with committees representing the Know-Nothings, Know-Somethings, and the 1854 Republicans. All were agreed on the need for an independent antislavery party, but sharp disagreement surfaced over which kind of nominating convention—delegate or open meeting—the fusionists should hold. At the heart of the dispute lay the question of control. Adams's clique insisted on a mass meeting as the best means to guard against "mere coalition with secret societies." They anticipated that a delegate convention would lead to "fraud," by which they meant that the majority American party would by virtue of its numbers elect most of the delegates and thus preempt the fusion movement for its own use. Stiffening the Chapman Hall stand was the governor's open advocacy of a delegate convention, even as "all his official dependents [were striving] to foist Mr. Gardner upon the new party as its candidate."[37] The Know-Nothing committeemen were unimpressed. They were intent on gaining concessions, not on conferring them. Asked whether, after their joining the fusion party, they planned to remain in their old party, the Know-Nothings answered yes and added that the *sine qua non* for their joining was a delegate convention. All but the Chapman Hall group consented to the demand, whereupon Foster attempted unsuccessfully to bind all the representatives to the will of the majority.[38] He managed only to widen the rift.

The apparent impasse left at least one observer of the political scene perplexed:

> Politics is in a perfect mess. Some kind of fusion will come out of it—Whig party nowhere. Demo. [sic] very small. Anti pope and antislave large. Rum party pretty large, very active. Temperance pretty large and doubtful. Pure Native American small and active. Catholic perfectly quiet, there is material to work up. Nobody knows what will come of it.[39]

Typically, the commentator omitted the state's most potent social force—populism—from his assessment of voting blocs. Every political organization in the state, including the American, either was oblivious to the existence of such a force or, what is more likely, was taking pains to conceal it. Less than a year earlier, the silent majority had made known through the medium of the Know-Nothing lodge network their desire to seize control of the government from the politicians and harness it in the service of the commonweal. Now, with the Commonwealth's several political organizations in a state of flux and groping toward realignment, party leaders took advantage of the breakdown of institutionalized political rule to redefine the political agenda in terms of three issues: nativism, temperance, and antislavery. The party press and activists of every political persuasion joined the debate swirling around the dominant triad, omitting from the public discourse or relegating to the periphery of the political arena all other public concerns.

This failure to come to grips with the everyday concerns of the people augured far more trouble for the embryonic fusion movement than did the wrangle over the convention question. Indeed, the several fusion committees resolved that impasse at their next meeting, when they all agreed to schedule two conventions—one, a delegate assembly, the other, an open meeting—to meet in Worcester on September 20.[40] Their action, however, failed to lift the spirits of the anti-Know-Nothing fusionists. Word had reached Adams and Dana that confirmed their suspicions that Gardner's people were counting on the lodge bloc vote to control the selection of delegates and thus stack the fusion convention in their favor. Adams was near panic: If successful, the Know-Nothings would renominate Gardner, tighten their grip on the state government, and place the antislavery movement "wholly at their mercy."[41]

On September 20, fusionist delegates—some one thousand strong—assembled at Worcester City Hall for the opening session of their convention. At the same time, the Chapman Hall splinter group hosted a "mass convention" gathered under a large tent pitched on Worcester Common. The main event was at City Hall, where those fearing that the antislavery movement would become entangled in an alliance with "Sam" were pleasantly surprised by early trends. A majority of the delegates voted into existence a new party—the Republican—and agreed to base it on the antislavery issue alone. With this one stroke, they destroyed the plans of the Gardner Americans to commit the fusion party to the nativist principles contained in the Springfield platform. The convention specified that no Republican need surrender his beliefs on other state or national questions, so as not to offend those who shared Native American convictions.[42]

These preliminaries settled, the convention turned to its main task: the selection of the new party's state ticket. His Excellency had agreed to abide by the outcome, confident that his nomination was preordained. On the first ballot, Gardner polled 449 of the 944 votes cast, just 24 votes shy of a majority; Julius Rockwell, an antislavery Whig, placed second with 305 votes; John W. Foster ran third with 122 votes; and the remaining 68 votes were scattered among favorite sons.[43] The balloting had carried Gardner to the brink of victory, yet there was cause for concern in the governors' camp, for the division of votes also suggested that Foster had entered the race as a stalking horse to draw off Know-Nothing votes from Gardner and thus boost Rockwell's chances.

A Gardner lackey, anxious to avoid a second ballot, moved that since His Excellency had the greatest number of votes, the convention declare him its nominee. The motion was laughed down. The Gardnerites, however, were not at the Worcester City Hall to entertain. They were bent on winning the top spot on the Republican state ticket for their ringleader or, failing that, on splitting the convention wide open. But even as the governor's men were pressing delegates for a commitment on his behalf, opposition to his candidacy mounted. A Gardner floor leader tried to deflect criticisms aimed at the former Webster Whig's equivocations on the slavery issue, assuring the convention that the governor's antislavery record "stood as fair as that of any man in Massachusetts."[44] Other delegates expressed misgivings that perhaps the governor was committed more to his own ambition than to fusion. Word had reached them that Gardner, in spite of his pledge to abide by the decision of the Worcester convention, planned to run as a Know-Nothing if the convention rejected him. Would he accept the convention's decision regardless of who headed the ticket? Gardner's friends scurried about and finally produced a letter from him that read in part: "I think that this is an honest course [acceptance of the convention's choice] and I favor it; still I will not move till I advise at home."[45] R. H. Dana, Jr., in an all-out assault against Gardner's candidacy, reminded the assembly that Julius Rockwell had committed himself without reservation to the fusionist party, whereas Henry J. Gardner had not. Dana's friends thought that his speech had "told powerfully upon many former friends of Governor Gardner."[46]

There were, however, other, more decisive influences at work in the convention. By the time the second balloting began that evening, considerable shifting of delegate pledges had taken place; and the shift proved fatal to Gardner's chance to become the first Republican gubernatorial candidate. Rockwell won a narrow majority—426 of 839 votes cast—edging out Gardner, whose 395 total was down 54 from his earlier vote; Foster ran a distant third with only 13 votes. Some attributed the turnaround to the impact of Dana's speech or to Gardner's weasel-like stands on slavery and fusion. Others—and the governor's retainers were among them—thought they detected Wilson's hand behind the push that kept His Excellency off the Republican ticket.[47] They had grounds for their suspicions. Rockwell's winning margin had come mainly from a shift into his column of Foster's early supporters, and these were mostly Free-Soil Americans marching to the sound of Henry Wilson's drum.

To George Boutwell, Gardner's debacle at Worcester signaled the passing of the Know-Nothing craze and the emergence of the slavery question as the preeminent issue in state politics. Adams, too, was both surprised and delighted with the outcome, crowing that the fusionists by their action at Worcester had thrown off "the incubus of Know-Nothingism." But the convention's decision to dump Governor Gardner by no means reflected a Republican determination to purge itself of its Know-Nothing elements. On the contrary, the convention took pains not to alienate rank-and-file Americans by placing three Know-Nothing incumbents on the Republican slate to run with Rockwell.[48] In other words, what the ouster of the governor had resolved was not the severance of the Republican/Know-Nothing connection, but the question of who was going to control the Republican party in Massachusetts. Gardner had fallen victim to a power play that left control of the fledgling party in the hands of the Free-Soilers.

Word of the Gardnerless slate was brought to the so-called "mass convention" down under the big tent on Worcester Common, which enthusiastically endorsed it. Their action, like that of the city hall delegates, underscored Republican willingness to accept nativism so long as it came without the Know-Nothing gubernatorial incumbent. Some Republicans were left with the feeling that without Gardner at the top of the ticket, their party was heading for certain defeat.[49] Sam Bowles and the *Springfield Republican* thought otherwise. Gardner's election in 1854 was the "merest accident" made possible by the absence of a viable antislavery party. If the Republican party as constituted in Worcester had been in the field, the Know-Nothing order would have served it in the capacity of a subordinate. Nathaniel Banks, on the other hand, was not so sure that antislavery would swallow nativism. A cautious man, he hedged his bet on the outcome by not attacking Gardner and by allowing some of his people to campaign actively for the governor's reelection.[50]

Where the Worcester convention received mixed reviews from the Republicans, the governor and his cohorts were united in their reaction to it. Know-Nothing converts to Republicanism were "false Americans" who had abandoned their party after having squeezed out of it all "the loaves and fishes they could get." But their betrayal of "Sam" did not sting the Gardnerites as much as their sellout of the governor. Gardner's men had no doubts about who had masterminded his downfall at the Worcester convention. "Rome had her Cataline," wrote one Gardner supporter in a letter to the editor of the *Boston Daily Bee*, "the army of the revolution its Arnold, the government of the United States its Burr, the American party of Massachusetts its Wilson, Foster [and] Co." His Excellency was more blunt. Little else should have been expected, he snarled, "from the likes of that political harlot Wilson."[51]

Though angry, the Gardnerites did not despair. They still controlled the American party apparatus. At the October 3 state convention, they renominated Gardner on the first ballot, pledged the party to the Springfield platform, and turned toward the coming campaign confident that the bulk of the 1854 Know-Nothing vote remained within reach.

There were, of course, problems. For one thing, instead of looking to the grass roots for direction, the party took its orders from one man. For another, the governor had alienated important members of the original Know-Nothing coalition. His vetoing state loans for railroad construction projects cost him support in the interior, and his veto of the Personal Liberty Bill and refusal to remove the "infamous slave commissioner" Judge Loring had earned him the enmity of antislavery voters.[52] Even without the Free-Soilers and the western farm vote, though, the Gardnerites remained confident that they would win, so long as they did not suffer any more major defections. Their man was positioned to sweep the nativist and temperance vote, thanks to his labors on behalf of their causes and to the one-note platform on which the Republicans had pinned their hopes.[53] The defeat of the secret ballot and ten-hour bills made it less likely that workers would turn out as enthusiastically as they had in 1854, but the scrapping of thoses reforms was the senate's doing, not the governor's. Any while many Whigs and Democrats were unhappy with the draconian prohibition law, those interested in populist reforms were much more likely to vote Know-Nothing than Republican.

To get out the vote, the governor had a political machine second to none. He had attached to himself a "Janissary guard" whose livelihoods rested on the political fortunes of their leader. Gardner set the record for patronage appointments, having removed more officeholders and filled more offices than any chief executive in history. These "bread-and-butter men" provided the glue for the governor's organization. He kept a book in which he listed the names of men in every town in the state whom he had recruited by flattery or promises of rewards. He took pains as well to woo those whom his enemies decried as "the knave-power and the donkey-power of the Commonwealth." More than any other politician of the day, Gardner realized that once united, the obscure, the powerless, and "even the men who were odious or ridiculous among their neighbors" constituted a formidable political force. Key staff people received special treatment. Handed lucrative patronage jobs, they were able to devote full time to election work while on the public payroll.[54] As the campaign unfolded, this army of retainers lost no time "in spending money, traversing the state, waking up the [Know-Nothing] Council and playing the deuce generally." Not surprisingly, the Gardnerites made no attempt to rekindle the kinds of populist passions that had produced such a stunning overturn in 1854, lest they themselves suffer the same fate. Instead, they shifted the party further to the right, one aspect of which was the decision to run joint legislative tickets with Whigs in a number of localities, including Boston.[55]

Administration Democrats nominated Erasmus D. Beach to run on a platform that denounced Know-Nothingism and sectionalism and endorsed the doctrine of popular sovereignty. It was a symbolic action by a party whose close ties with the South and identification with the Kansas-Nebraska Act "wholly discredited it" within the Commonwealth. Beach did benefit from one local development. Wets seeking repeal of the 1855 prohibition law had formed the Union Liberal party and endorsed him.

Former Democrat George Boutwell was convinced that the Nunnery Committee scandal had so seriously weakened "Sam" that a vigorous push would bring the party tumbling down. He did not envision such a push coming from the Democratic quarter, however, that party having been struck "nerveless" in 1854 by the Know-Nothing blow.[56]

Remnants of the Whig party decided on another run, fielding a slate headed by old-line conservative Samuel Walley and adopting a platform that scored Republican "abolitionism." The very thought of a merger either with Republican "disunionists" or with "profligate and spendthrift" Know-Nothings suggested a witches' brew to historian John Lothrop Motley:

> Black spirits and white,
> Red spirits and grey,
> Mingle, mingle, mingle,
> You that mingle may.[57]

Despite serious drawbacks—the Nunnery Committee scandals, the unpopularity of the prohibition law, the defection of the Wilsonian Americans, widespread disaffection in the back country, some highly publicized legislative boondoggling, and an unattractive candidate who personified the prototypical behind-the-scenes, wire-pulling politician that the 1854 Know-Nothings had rebelled against—the American party had not disintegrated, and its gubernatorial candidate, with the best organization among the aspirants, approached the election ahead of the pack. Charles Francis Adams, scanning the field, saw the race going to "the poorest nag [Gardner]."[58] Adams's call betrayed his sense that in a campaign that pitted nativism against antislavery, the former would prevail because of the "deep sympathy among the masses" for the "Native American idea." This "false idea," this "madness which rules the hour," this "balloon," he railed, "is raised only to catch the eyes of the multitude, and carry up a few chance adventurers high enough to see the world."[59]

Like most of his peers, Adams never challenged a premise that tarred the Yankee Protestant common man with a nativist brush nor bothered to probe for other sources of Know-Nothingism's popularity. The idea that the ordinary working person might have been at least as unhappy with his lot in the workplace—for example, with the drudgery, insecurity, low pay, unhealthy environment, and excessive hours of his job—as he was with Paddy and the Pope never seems to have occurred to him. Nor did he or others of high station seem to entertain the notion that the American party in its first year in office had chalked up a record of positive accomplishments that was bound to appeal to the hoi polloi. Quite the contrary, their portrait of Know-Nothing government was unremittingly bleak.

Ironically, the very failings of the party that most offended Adams's sensibilities—its raw bigotry, demagoguery, and scandalous misconduct—his Brahmin Whig counterparts discerned in equal measure in the newborn Republican party. "To rid the Commonwealth of Jack Cadism under which it now suffers," John Lothrop Motley sniffed, "is the first and great political duty—and yet not one word of disapprobation, direct or implied can be found in the doings of the new party styling itself Republican to any of those abominations of the last legislature, but on the contrary some of the leading men of that scandalous legislature are to be retained with the endorsement 'Well done good and faithful servants!'"[60]

Motley's point, that the Republicans, by pandering to the Know-Nothing yahoos, had taken on their baggage, had merit. Lost in the observation, however, was the fact that Know-Nothingism consisted of more than bigotry and sleazy politicians or that more separated the American and Republican parties than the respective weight that each attached to the territorial and Irish Catholic questions. In fact, the American party alone of the four parties in the field could point with pride to an unparalleled record of democratic and working-class reforms. That was a record that the Republicans could ill afford to challenge or even mention. On these issues, a gulf lay between the two major contenders— American and Republican—that was plainly visible to ordinary voters if not to Adams or to historian Motley or even to the Whiggish Know-Nothing newspapers that pressed Gardner's candidacy on the basis of his commitment to the antislavery and nativist principles contained in the Springfield platform.

On election day, Adams, after arriving at the Quincy polling station and finding Know-Nothings predominant among those filing in to vote, feared the worst. The returns confirmed his apprehensions. Gardner topped the field, winning by a plurality. His 51,305 share (37.7 percent) of the 136,146 votes cast was down more than 30,000 from his 1854 showing. Nevertheless, only around one-fifth of his 1854 supporters had defected to the Republicans, and the preponderance of them were former Free-Soilers. Republican candidate Julius Rockwell trailed with a disappointing 36,622 votes (26.9 percent), no better than the mark set by the first Free-Soil gubernatorial candidate in 1848. As expected, he ran well in those pockets of the state, like Worcester County, where the Free-Soilers had been strongest. He also attracted substantial numbers of Whig farmers in western Massachusetts, many of whom had not voted Know-Nothing in 1854. Rockwell's inability to siphon off appreciable numbers from the vast pool of the 1854 Whig and Democratic Know-Nothings, however, cost him the election.[61] His defeat demonstrated the difficulty, if not impossibility, of carrying the Commonwealth on the single issue of no more slave states. Hard on Rockwell's heels came Erasmus Beach with 34,641 votes (25.4 percent). His third-place finish heralded a comeback for his party from the 1854 disaster. Samuel Walley placed last with only 13,332 votes (9.8 percent), underscoring what all but the most myopic Whigs had long known—that their party had received its death blow a year earlier. Its commonwealth ethos rendered impotent by populist ferment and heightened class consciousness, Whiggery had failed to make the necessary adjustments to a rapidly changing political environment that would have transformed it into a viable alternative to the American and Republican parties.

On the whole, the election was an impressive Know-Nothing victory. The party had swept all the statewide contests, retained control over both houses of the General Court, and administered a thorough drubbing to political antislavery-ism.[62] Moreover, it had accomplished all this by adding enough new and inactive voters to its roll of 1854 repeaters to compensate partially for the losses that the party had sustained from defections to the Republicans and the resurgent Democracy. Gardner told a jubilant throng of supporters gathered outside his Beacon Hill home on election night that the win was more significant than that of 1854 because it proved that the American party had taken its place in Massachusetts as a great and permanent party.[63]

Edward Everett found one aspect of the election results "most gratifying": they had "utterly discredited" the "boasting" and "lying" and "lecturing" of the "fusionist fraud." C. F. Adams shared Everett's conclusion, if not his sentiments. He saw the Republican defeat as having set the antislavery cause back five years, for it "sadly cloud[ed] the prospect of united action" in the next year's presidential election.[64]

Adams was saturnine by nature. The election had by no means dashed the prospects of the Republican party in Massachusetts. The process of party dealignment triggered by the Know-Nothings in 1854 was still in progress. Party lines were fluid, and if anything, the Republicans had greater cause to feel confident about the future of their party than the Know-Nothings of theirs. The Republicans had succeeded where the Know-Nothings had failed in fashioning a national base for their party. Republican expectations ultimately were pinned to the party's performance nationally, and at this level the Republicans had far better reason than the divided Americans to look forward with optimism to 1856—a presidential year, when national concerns would dominate the political debate.

At the state level, the Republicans had picked up almost the entire Free-Soil American contingent, and even though they attracted few Whigs and fewer Democrats, their Know-Nothing rival, plagued by defections, retained the support of only around half of the original party voters.[65] Other forces were at work that also boded well for the Republicans. The lodge network that had been so instrumental in the Know-Nothing triumph a year earlier was unraveling. Reports in the daily press told of lodges being disbanded or reorganized. Mounting dissension and plummeting membership sapped the secret order's strength. In 1854, the order's dark-lantern method of nominating political unknowns and making their names public on election day worked because a majority of voters had pledged their ballots beforehand. A year later, "Sam" lacked the numbers to spring the same "midnight trap."[66] In fact, many (and probably most) of those voting Know-Nothing in 1855 neither belonged to a lodge nor swore an oath to vote for the party's candidates sight unseen.

The bolt of the Free-Soil Americans to the Republican party only partly accounts for the drop in lodge membership. An even larger number of Whigs and Democrats had also abandoned "Sam." In western Massachusetts—hitherto the least responsive region in the state to political antislaveryism—former Whigs deserted the American party in droves to vote Republican, their decision prompted by resentment of the urban bent of Know-Nothing policies and gubernatorial vetos of railroad projects beneficial to that region rather than by a sudden conversion to the antislavery cause.

A more significant indicator of the growing alienation with Know-Nothingism was the comeback of the Democratic party, which was staged at the expense of "Sam." Almost as many former Democrats had returned to the party fold as there were Free-Soil American converts to Republicanism.[67] Close to thirty-five thousand Bay State voters, or more than a quarter of the total turnout, ignored nativist, temperance, and free-soil appeals, opting instead to back a party that sided with immigrants, Catholics, wets, and the South. Among them were many of the Democrats who had voted for Gardner in 1854. Their return to the Democracy after a year in which the Know-Nothing government of Massachusetts had pushed nativism far beyond the limits reached in any other state demonstrates that these voters had been drawn to "Sam" by something other than ethnocultural battle cries. The same may be said for the temperance cause. Bishop's surprisingly strong showing owed much to his outspoken opposition to the Maine Law, which had proved as divisive for "Sam" as it once had for the Whigs.[68] Nor do the election returns support the idea that most Democrats had turned to the Know-Nothing party in 1854 out of frustration with their own party's inability to enact the traditional Jacksonian principles embodied in the 1853 constitutional referenda. "Sam" had consummated the work of the constitutional convention and had chalked up an unparalleled record for reform, which, in spite of the failure to pass ten-hour and secret ballot laws, should have nailed down the Locofoco vote. That some two-fifths of the Democratic Americans should have returned to their former party in the face of this record suggests that they had something more in mind than the Coalition's reform program when they turned to "Sam."[69]

Overshadowing the partisan flux present in the 1855 campaign was a sense of betrayal on the part of rank-and-file Whig and Democratic Know-Nothings, who witnessed the transmutation of the people's movement of 1854 into a patronage machine that, if anything, was more inimical to the ideal of a people's government than the political parties that the voters had displaced when they raised "Sam" to power. In place of the populist ideal of a people's party that had illuminated the dark-lantern lodges and galvanized the voters in 1854 was a patronage machine whose chief function was to advance the political career of Henry J. Gardner. Just how extensive their alienation with these developments was came to light a month after the state election, when nonpartisan "Citizen's" candidates defeated American incumbents in municipal contests held in cities across the state.[70] Ironically, it was in these same cities where Know-Nothingism had first taken root two years earlier and where the party had enjoyed its initial victories.

Part of "Sam's" problem at the municipal level was that party candidates had overpromised during their first run for office. It will be recalled that Mayor Smith had proposed the sale of city lands to the humble at affordable prices and below-market carrying terms and the launching of a public works program to provide jobs for the unemployed. Boston's city council, however refused to appropriate sufficient funds to implement the mayor's grandiose plans; and instead of fulfilling the mayor's promise to cut taxes and reduce the city's water rate, the city council raised them. Even so, the Know-Nothings were not the first to sweep into power on the wings of inflated promises. Moreover, some of the city administrations that were turned out of office had chalked up some impressive reforms.[71] That they lost in spite of their accomplishments suggests a waning of the public's faith in the Know-Nothing concept of a people's party.

At the same time, the dissatisfaction with "Sam" evidenced in these municipal elections did not herald a turn to the Republican party. The American party might have lost its majority in the cities, but not its plurality. The Know-Nothing incumbents had been turned out by an opposition united behind the nonpartisan citizens' tickets. And several weeks earlier, nearly twice as many city voters cast ballots for Gardner as for Rockwell.

Know-Nothingism had risen to power through a combination of opportune timing and its image as the people's party. Its successful dark-lantern campaign in the lodges in which it billed itself as a genuine people's movement came at a time of extreme alienation with political parties and electrified a people who for a generation and more had waited in vain for the old parties to grapple with the problems endemic to rapid urban and industrial growth. Through "Sam," they would regain the power that the politicians had stolen from them and use that power to right wrongs long ignored. But the lodge network had proved just as susceptible to the iron law of oligarchy as the committee rooms, caucus meetings, and stacked conventions of the second party system. A year of intraparty politicking in which the lodge amateurs were shunted aside had given rise to a new generation of opportunistic, manipulative politicians bearing the Know-Nothing label. Eventually, even the lodge system fell victim to this syndrome, as the chief magistrate gradually shifted the party's organizational base from the local lodges to his "bread and butter men," that is, to state and local appointees anxious to hold on to their jobs.[72]

Gardner had survived the political infighting and party struggles of 1855, and in fact, he remained the most powerful politician in the state. The mass defection of the Free-Soil Americans had removed the only formidable obstacle to his takeover of the American party. Nevertheless, his position was anything but secure; for in the process of shifting control from the lodges into his own hands, he had destroyed "Sam's" *raison d'être*, namely, to safeguard the rule of the people by quarantining ambitious politicians from political office.

.

CHAPTER SIX

Gardner Republicans, Fremont Americans, and the Election of 1856

W ITH THE RECENT election behind it, the Know-Nothing state council turned to the task of charting the party's strategy for the next one. It was a relatively simple task, insofar as the decision-making process was concerned, since there no longer was any doubt as to who was in control of the party apparatus. This the council made clear when, as its first order of business, it filled its top three posts—vacant since their former occupants had defected to the Republican party—with Gardner loyalists.[1] The principal order of business before the council, however, was the question of whether to open negotiations with the national chapter in the interest of reunification, a matter of special concern to the governor. His party, having dropped its populist message, had sunk into a state of lassitude, punctuated by declining enrollments and a sharp drop in lodge membership. December and January brought more bad news. The party, as usual, had announced its candidates for municipal offices at the last minute; only this time, with lodge membership plummeting, the results were disastrous. Candidates running for mayor on nonpartisan Citizens' tickets defeated their Know-Nothing opponents in Boston, Roxbury, Charlestown, Newburyport, Lynn, Worcester, Springfield, Cambridge, and Lowell.[2]

That these losses had occurred precisely where the Know-Nothing order had first manifested its strength lent a sense of urgency to His Excellency's quest for higher office. His national ambitions remained very much alive in spite of the troubles experienced at the late Philadelphia convention. This being a presidential year, the vice-presidential position was open, but for the Bay State's chief magistrate to gain a spot on the American national ticket, he first had to mend political fences with Southern and "doughface" Americans at the next national council meeting, which was scheduled to open in Cincinnati in a fortnight.

A less ambitious man might have declined so challenging an undertaking, given the fact that Gardner, along with the rest of the Massachusetts delegation, had bolted from that body the previous February. He had boasted of that action that it was "of prime significance for the future" and that "I am glad that I was there and do not regret the part I took."[3] His words were part of the public record and thus posed an obstacle to rapprochement with the pro-Southern national order. Moreover, any such attempt on his part would offend those members of the state party who wanted nothing to do with the national order. To ease their concerns, he characterized the forthcoming Cincinnati meeting as a rump convention of the Northern secessionists. For that very reason, the national American faction of the state party opposed sending delegates, calling it "a fusion trick." Gardner, however, brushed aside their objections and instead dipped into the "dirty pool" of state politics and came up with a delegation of "chosen ones" to represent his interests at Philadelphia. Those interests centered on two possibilities—either the nod from his party as its vice-presidential candidate or his replacing Charles Sumner in the U.S. Senate.[4]

At Cincinnati, the delegates, cognizant of the high stakes involved in a presidential year, glossed over the sectional differences that had ruptured the body at its last meeting and issued an invitation to all state councils—North and South—to attend a special national council meeting in Philadelphia in February. The meeting was timed so that if all went as planned, a reunited national council could reassemble on Washington's Birthday as the American National Convention.[5]

Gardner's courtship of the national Know-Nothings was conducted on several fronts simultaneously, as he made evident in his inaugural address. He allowed in the speech that there should be no extension of slavery into the national territories formerly covered by the Missouri Compromise, but otherwise skirted that divisive question. No mention was made of the deteriorating situation in Kansas, and to the delight of the national Americans, he recommended that the General Court repeal the "unconstitutional" Personal Liberty Law, whose passage in 1855 had antagonized Southerners of all political persuasions.[6]

As in his first inaugural, the governor held that foreigners and the Roman Catholic Church posed the gravest and most immediate threat to American institutions. Thus, it was incumbent upon the present body to carry on the work of its predecessor in combating this menace—and that meant specifically the endorsement of the amendments aimed at stripping naturalized citizens and Roman Catholics of the right to hold public office and limiting the vote to male citizens with a minimum of twenty-one years of residency in the United States. The principles embraced in these proposals were "of the deepest importance to the preservation of a republican government." Disregard these truths, he warned, and face the certainty "that liberty under democratic institutions will degenerate into anarchical license or give place to slavish and bigoted superstition." Massachusetts, while willing to extend "Christian charity" on behalf of immigrants, was not prepared to become "the receptacle of the vicious, the degraded, and the insane whom foreign parsimony and cruelty might send to our shores." For this reason, the state government during the past year had removed 295 aliens from the state's welfare rolls and shipped them back to Liverpool at an immediate savings to the taxpayers of $100,000.[7]

His Excellency was playing to a wider audience than that of the legislators seated in front of him. His offering up Paddy and the Pope as surrogate targets for Northern concerns addressed the most pressing need of the national American party about to enter its first presidential campaign—an issue powerful enough to divert the public's attention from the crippling sectional divisions that bedeviled the established national parties. Such a ploy, if it worked, was bound to advance Gardner's chances for being tapped for the second spot on the national ticket. He had already made progress in that direction with his veto of the Personal Liberty bill.[8]

There remained the matter of obtaining the cooperation of the Great and General Court. A similar gubernatorial plea for action against the foreign peril delivered the year before had triggered a favorable response in that body, but the 1856 legislature bore little resemblance to its predecessor. For one thing, only 64 of the 419 members of the 1855 legislature had returned to their seats; and for another, even though the American party, with 173 seats in the house and 30 in the senate, enjoyed a majority in both houses, its margin in the lower branch was slender thanks to the election of 33 Democrats, 60 Republicans, and 63 Whigs, whose election on union tickets had been engineered by the governor's machine.[9] The partisan turnover was matched by the change in the occupational mix. Twenty percent fewer workers occupied legislative seats than in 1855. Even harder hit were the less politically sophisticated professionals like teachers and clergy, whose numbers were halved. On the upside, the old political elites—lawyers and merchants—staged a comeback that increased their share of seats by 80 percent and signaled an end to the short-lived experiment with populist government.[10]

The radical alteration in the composition of the legislature reflected in part a waning public interest in a lodge network that no longer catered to the man in the street and in part interparty developments that had produced an election campaign in which the candidates competed for votes on the basis of conflicting positions on ethnoreligious and sectional issues. None of them—candidates nor parties—availed themselves of the opportunity to return to the populist themes that had suffused the 1854 Know-Nothing dark-lantern campaign. They had their reasons for ignoring these themes. In Gardner's case, the diminished role of the people in party matters served his purpose, which all along was to transform the party from a people's movement into a political machine headed by him. His placing that machine at the disposal of conservative Whig legislative candidates, for example, was part of a gubernatorial push to shift "Sam" to the right. Populism, if uncorked again, would abort his power play and almost certainly sweep him from power. Hence, the American party, after a year of alterations carried out under the chief magistrate's direction, bore little resemblance to the 1854 original. He had successfully co-opted the dark-lantern mechanism, first by seeding the lodges with his adherents and then by shifting the organizational base of the party into his own hands.

In the case of the Democratic and Republican leadership, they were playing for much higher stakes than Gardner—namely, control of the national government. Populism, as the election of 1854 clearly demonstrated, packed enough explosive power to ruin their plans. The promise of political solutions for the social costs of modernization had fueled the political uprising of 1854, and that uprising could be repeated. It therefore behooved the party leaders to keep so potent a force bottled up, lest it draw the people away from the political agenda that they had laboriously framed within a national context and which they wanted to be the focus of the political debate in the forthcoming presidential election. Thus, the leadership, while quite prepared to debate the rights of free-state settlers in Kansas, was reluctant to take up matters closer to home, like the rights of workers. This strategy meant limiting discussion of local issues to a narrow range of relatively noncontroversial subjects, like the popular constitutional amendments pending before the 1856 legislature.[11]

National political considerations affected Republican stands on ethnocultural issues as well. Under ordinary circumstances, the antislavery camp might have indulged its nativist bent in support of the governor's recommendations, but the national Republicans, who were more concerned with the midwestern German vote than with Gardner's warnings about the imminence of "anarchical license" and "slavish and bigoted superstition," prevailed on the state party to ease up on nativism. Consequently, most of the Republican legislators joined with the Democrats and some of the Whigs to block two of the three nativist amendments launched in 1855—the exclusion of Catholics and the foreign-born from public office. The third proposal, because its twenty-one-year residency requirement for the suffrage was pared to fourteen years, was passed on to the next legislature. The only concession by the legislature to the governor's requests was to initiate an amendment to the constitution that would impose a literacy test for the suffrage.[12]

A more immediate concern for Gardner than the legislature's partial dismantlement of his nativist program was the American national council meeting that had assembled in Philadelphia to lay the groundwork for a united front on the American national ticket. To carry this off, the delegates first had to mute the sectional uproar that had shattered the body the previous June. Four days of wrangling and trade-offs between Northern and Southern delegates produced a new platform pledging the party to God, country, and the proposition that "Americans must rule America." In keeping with its newfound spirit of compromise, the council replaced the controversial Article XII, which had triggered the Northern bolt at its last gathering, with a resolution endorsing popular sovereignty in the national territories. But the spirit of compromise proved fleeting. Planks aimed at mollifying the Southern wing of the party called on the Congress to observe and enforce all constitutional laws (namely, the Fugitive Slave Law) and not to intervene in the internal affairs of the several states. Understandably, these pro-Southern resolutions sparked resistance within the thirteen-man Massachusetts delegation, only five of whom signed the proposed platform. Nevertheless, they held their peace at the urging of the governor's hand-picked functionaries among them.[13]

The Bay Staters were not the only ones unhappy with the tentative platform. When the national council reassembled on Washington's Birthday as the American National Convention, some of the Northern delegates took the opportunity to submit a proposal to limit party nominations to candidates who accepted the Missouri Compromise. The Southern and "doughface" majority, however, moved quickly to cut off the Northern attempt at an end run by voting to accept without change the platform on the floor. Thereupon some fifty Northern delegates stormed out of the convention, their action precluding any chance that the American party might have had to enter the 1856 presidential campaign as a united, national party.[14] It also virtually eliminated Gardner's chances for a place on the national ticket.

The convention, purged of its disruptive elements, indulged a death wish by nominating former Whig president, Millard Fillmore, the signer of the Fugitive Slave Law, to head the ticket. Then, to the chagrin of the Massachusetts delegation, who were still "looking out for Mr. Gardner," the convention chose as its vice-presidential candidate Tennessean Andrew Jackson Donelson, the slave-holding nephew of "Old Hickory."[15]

Several days later, the Northern bolters gathered in a Philadelphia hotel to protest the national convention's actions and to ponder the future. They justified their secession from the national body in a set of resolutions that berated the late American convention for having refused to pledge the national party to the restoration of the Missouri Compromise and for having admitted delegates from Louisiana who represented "a Roman Catholic constituency." Having struck a balance in their manifesto between nativist and territorial concerns, the seceders issued a call for a nominating convention of "independent" Americans to meet in New York City on June 12.[16]

The second breakdown of the national American party, accompanied as it was by the nominations of Fillmore and Donelson and the rejection of Gardner, profoundly affected the political situation in Massachusetts. Free-Soiler Seth Webb reported Know-Nothing legislators divided "down to the very roots," with many of them contemplating a bolt to the Republicans. Neither the Know-Nothing state organization nor its leader was willing to conform to the national party's dictates, preferring instead to pursue other options, such as a possible linkup with the Republicans. Gardner's personal ambitions, however, ran counter to the wishes of those Republicans who were wedded to the idea that the actions taken at Philadelphia would define party lines more sharply in terms of freedom or slavery and "put a final extinguisher upon all notions of combination" between the Republicans and "Sam."[17] A number of national Republicans shared their optimism. "Fillmore's nomination seems to have fallen dead," exulted Ohioan Ben

Wade. "There can be but two parties in the next campaign. Those who are for the institution of slavery and those who are for restricting it."[18]

Wade's opinion notwithstanding, there was a third position. Fillmore's nomination sat well with some of the "old-line Whigs," who were counting on the former president to rally his fellow Whigs and the Northern and Southern wings of the American party behind his candidacy.[19] Amos A. Lawrence, for one, had contributed generously to the drive to secure the nomination for Fillmore and "some reliable Southern man" in the expectation that such a ticket would "temper the asperity of parties [and] calm the sectional animosities that threatened to engulf the Union." He thought that Fillmore could win if the American party solidified behind him, and he counted it a certainty if Fillmore gained the combined backing of the Whigs and Americans.[20]

The dream of a Whig restoration and of the Union saved may have clouded Lawrence's political vision. Upon receipt of the news from Philadelphia, he arranged for the firing of a one-hundred-gun salute on the Boston Common to honor "the most fit thing" accomplished by any national convention in years. "This [cannonade] will wake up the Whigs and the Americans too," he crowed. Lawrence counted everyone in Boston as being in the Fillmore column except the Democrats "who are few" and the Republicans "who can never carry much force in this seat of hunkerism." In the state, he expected that all "Whigs and Natives" would swing behind the American team.[21]

Lawrence was wrong on both counts. The Brahmins were anything but united behind a party that had sent Henry Wilson to the U.S. Senate and "placed on the statute books many strange enactments." They wrote off Know-Nothingism in Massachusetts "as an equal mixture of blind machinery, imbecility, and craft." Some were equally unimpressed with the national ticket. "I cannot see the . . . probability, no, not even the possibility of electing Mr. Fillmore," Hamilton Fish confided to R. C. Winthrop. What particularly galled Fish was that the former Whig president, having submitted to the secret oaths of the Know-Nothing order, was now obliged, if victorious, to staff his administration with members of a party "of secrecy and of intolerance, bigotry, and proscription. . . . As he now stands before the country I do not see how old-fashioned Whigs like you and me can give support to Fillmore." Winthrop, too, had been shocked when he learned that Fillmore had "undergone the initiatory humiliation." "I should as soon expect," he said, "to see him submit to the old iniquities of crossing the line."[22]

And if the American nominations failed to ignite the enthusiasm of the Brahmins, they fell "like a wet blanket" on the Gardnerites, who were looking for something more than Fourth of July oratory or artillery salutes on the Boston Common. Even Lawrence grasped that those who, like himself, were bent on "nationalizing" the American party of Massachusetts faced a touchy situation: The failure of the national order to tap Gardner for the vice-presidential slot had alienated the governor and his powerful machine. Lawrence took comfort in the thought that since bolting would avail the Gardnerites nothing, they had no recourse other than to "fall into line and throw up their hats for Fillmore."[23] He failed, however, to reckon either with the ingenuity of the Commonwealth's chief magistrate or with the general willingness of key power brokers in the American and Republican parties to let bygones be bygones if it served their purpose to do so.

Gardner, Wilson, and Banks had entered into secret negotiations, hoping to unite their respective parties behind freedom in the national territories and opposition to "malign foreign and ecclesiastical influences" at home. Such a union would ensure Gardner's reelection and a Republican win in the Massachusetts presidential election. Lawrence's cheerful assessment notwithstanding, the fact remained that the Fillmore-Donelson ticket without the backing of His Excellency was not going to "wake up the Whigs and the Americans too" in the Commonwealth of Massachusetts.[24]

Early in March, the Bay State American delegates reported back from Philadelphia to the state council and urged it to reject the national ticket as inimical to the future of freedom in the territories. Their recommendation stunned the national Americans. "If you won't take Mr. Fillmore," A. B. Ely queried, "what on earth will you do?"[25] Ely's question touched off a marathon debate that revealed the council divided "down to the very roots." Not until two o'clock the following morning did the council bring the proceedings to a close with the adoption of resolutions pledging the American party of Massachusetts to the 1855 Springfield platform and withholding council support from Fillmore and Donelson until they committed themselves to American principles and to the protection of the rights of Northern freemen in the territories.[26] The council's decision to withhold its endorsement clearly suited the governor's purposes. He was not about to commit his forces gratis to the presidential campaign.

In May, the council again took up the question of the national ticket at its regular quarterly session, and again two sets of delegates—pro- and anti-Fillmore—argued their respective positions. Motions introduced by the anti-Fillmore bloc to reject the national party's standard bearer for want of commitment to "those principles to which the American party of Massachusetts stands pledged" and to endorse the North American National Convention scheduled to meet in New York in June threw the council into "real confusion." Though taking neither side openly, Henry J. Gardner orchestrated the proceedings to his advantage. This became evident when the council tabled a motion to repudiate the Philadelphia nominations. The antislavery minority stormed out of the hall, whereupon the council voted to adjourn without having committed the order (or the governor) for or against the national ticket.[27]

That evening, the bolters gathered to issue a declaration rejecting the American national ticket and endorsing the forthcoming North American convention. There was more to their action than a simple reaffirmation of their antislavery principles. A scheme was afoot to transform the rump convention into a front for the Republican party, which, if successful, would rally free-state Know-Nothing voters to the Republican national ticket.[28]

Unaware of these subterranean maneuverings, the Fillmore Americans continued to work for a rapprochement with the unreconstructed Whigs. Prospects for some kind of an understanding seemed good, although there were obstacles: The Bay State American party did not "command much respect" among the lofty Brahmins, and memories of how the Know-Nothings turned them out of office still rankled. Still, with the American party purged of its abolitionist firebrands and with a former Whig president in nomination, the party's promise of Fillmore and the Union exerted a powerful appeal among Whig elites.[29] Neither the Brahmins nor the Fillmore Americans appeared concerned with the role of another Whig—the one who occupied the governor's chair and who commanded far many more votes than they did combined.

National developments, however, shattered their reverie. On May 21, a pro-slavery gang sacked Lawrence, Kansas; and on the following day, Preston Brooks of South Carolina brutally assaulted Charles Sumner in the chamber of the U.S. Senate. So far as the Brahmins were concerned, the two events spelled the "beginning of the end" for the Fillmore party in Massachusetts and dashed whatever hopes they had for a political comeback.[30] Edward Everett, in a near panic, described the mood of the people as so ugly that if a "reckless leader" were to seize the moment, he could raise a mighty host and "march on Washington." Everett, who consistently lent greater weight to national over state influences in his political analyses, was convinced that the caning of Sumner had done more to strengthen "the abolition party" in the Commonwealth and to diminish Whig influence there than any other occurrence. On the strength of that conviction, he wrote to Fillmore, telling him that it was no longer possible for the conservative Whigs to rally the people to the former president's candidacy. Everett was speaking for a party that had rallied less than 10 percent of the total vote in its last outing, a point that he himself made when he confessed that their beloved party could not significantly effect the outcome in Massachusetts, since "we were a fragment last year, and this year shall be a fragment of a fragment."[31]

Republican leaders confirmed Everett's fears that they were anxious to capitalize on the Sumner incident. Deeming the assault "an epoch in the antislavery movement," they expected the antislavery Know-Nothings to be "swept by the late hurricane" into the Republican ranks. "And thus from the wickedness of our opponents," Dr. Stone consoled the grievously wounded Sumner, "does the Almighty Arm evolve good to our great cause."[32]

If Sumner paused to wonder whether his present misery were part of a Divine plan, he was not alone. Amos A. Lawrence, for example, had drawn a different conclusion from the recent events than had the pious Stone, although like Stone and most other political commentators, he failed to distinguish between national and state politics. A major sponsor of the New England Emigrant Aid Company, Lawrence viewed the outbreak of violence in Kansas rather than the caning of Sumner as the key to political developments in the Commonwealth. Unlike Everett, he remained convinced that Fillmore could still carry Massachusetts, but only if Congress admitted Kansas into the Union as a free state.[33]

Such musings were largely academic for the delegates to the North American rump convention who assembled in New York City on June 12. Their principal order of business was the selection of a national ticket for the forthcoming presidential campaign, and as they had made clear when they bolted the late Philadelphia convention, Millard Fillmore was not under consideration. They leaned instead toward an alliance with the Republicans, although one based on their terms irrespective of Sumner or Kansas. They tipped their hand by scheduling their convention five days prior to that of the Republicans, anticipating by that move to pressure the Republicans into accepting their choices.[34] Their plan hinged on the expected nomination of Congressman Nathaniel Banks, who topped their list of favorites, but unwittingly they were playing into the hands of the Republicans. Banks already had volunteered to play straw man for his friend John C. Fremont. If, as expected, the North Americans nominated him, Banks would withdraw in favor of the Pathfinder, thereby securing for the Republicans the advantage of Northern Know-Nothing backing without the cost of saddling their party with a nativist presidential candidate. At least one Know-Nothing smelled a rat. A Banks constituent asked the congressman, if he were nominated by the Know-Nothings and not by the Republicans, would he stand as the "distinctive American candidate."[35] Banks was too clever by half to answer that one.

Everything went according to plan. The New York convention nominated Banks and Governor W. F. Johnston of Pennsylvania, but no sooner had the applause of the delegates subsided than a Banks supporter rose to be recognized. Banks, he told the assembly, had instructed him to withdraw his name and to urge the nomination of John C. Fremont in his place. A majority of the delegates accepted the *fait accompli* and nominated Fremont. A handful, however, stalked out of the convention hall and held their own meeting, at which they announced a third American presidential ticket—Commodore R. F. Stockton of New Jersey and Kenneth Rayner of North Carolina.[36] The Commodore and his North Carolinian running mate excited little interest either during the campaign or on election day.

Hard on the heels of these developments, the Republicans followed through with the nomination of Fremont, a move that satisfied C. F. Adams that the antislavery cause was "at last . . . established on a solid footing."[37] In the case of his own state, at least, the usually cautious Adams had rushed to judgment. Bay State Know-Nothings, in spite of Banks's wire-pulling, were by no means united behind Fremont.

Neither presidential organization—Republican nor American—had yet to reach an accord with the state's favorite son, an oversight that could affect the election results in the Commonwealth. Sooner or later, the national Republicans and Americans, to boost their chances, had to take into consideration Governor Gardner's formidable political machine and his proven record as a vote-getter. It was apparent, as well, from his refusal to commit himself that His Excellency's endorsement—whether for Fillmore (whom he personally favored) or Fremont—belonged to that side which came in with the best offer. The national Americans, by turning down his bid for the vice-presidential spot on their ticket, had tipped him toward the Republicans. His friend Lawrence's caveat that the emergence of a sectional party would endanger the nation failed to budge him. But the assault on Sumner did. Sumner's martyrdom aborted his scheme to move into the Senate and forced Gardner to fall back on a bid for reelection.[38]

Thus, the governor finally tipped his hand at the American state convention, which met in Springfield "to harmonize, if possible, the views of the party" on a presidential ticket. Presiding over the proceedings was Gardner's lieutenant, Moses G. Cobb. In a straw vote, Fremont and Fillmore ran neck and neck, with the Republican pulling ahead at the final count to edge out his opponent by a mere 3 votes. Prior to the taking of the formal ballot, however, a large number of the governor's supporters "hauled down the Fillmore flag," their last-minute switch enabling Fremont to win by a comfortable 280 to 187 margin.[39] Fillmore's supporters—raising a cheer for their favorite—stalked out of the convention and marched in a body to the nearby Free Will Baptist Church, where they declared their intention to carry out "true Americanism." True Americanism, Native American style, featured a speech calling Fremont a Roman Catholic, the speaker having seem him "partake of the sacrament [of the Holy Eucharist] at a church of that persuasion." Fired by this latest revelation, the bolters nominated Fillmore and Donelson by unanimous vote.[40]

His Excellency expressed himself satisfied with the results of the state convention. Fillmore, he explained to a bitterly disappointed Amos A. Lawrence, though "second to no man," could not obtain the backing of the American party in Massachusetts following "the troubles of last month in Kansas"; hence, the action taken by the American state convention was both "unavoidable [and] wise." Moses G. Cobb, echoing his patron, told Lawrence that since no presidential candidate could win in Massachusetts unless he was "unqualifiedly in favor of the admission of Kansas with its free state constitution," the nomination of Fillmore, who opposed such a step, "would be playing . . . directly into the hands of the democrats."[41]

What Gardner really had in mind was to board the Fremont bandwagon. In exchange, he was willing to commit his organization to the fray in support of the Republican presidential candidate. Reelection was the primary consideration. Even the future of the American party was negotiable. A year earlier, Gardner had offered to sacrifice the Know-Nothing order on the altar of fusion in return for the Republican gubernatorial nomination. The offer still held.

There remained the problem of the Fillmore, or national, Americans. At the next state convention, which met in Faneuil Hall on July 24 to nominate the state ticket, Fillmore's backers, drawn mostly from the Native American wing, took to one side of the hall and the governor's people to the other. There ensued one of the most disorderly conventions ever held in the state—one in which only the most leather-lunged delegates could make themselves heard above the din of hisses, catcalls, booing, and foot stomping. Calls to send for the police went unheeded, perhaps unheard, above the tumult, and the near-riot continued.[42]

Leading the Native American claque were standbys Jonathan Peirce, James

Farwell, and A. B. Ely, who, furious over their having been eased out of the inner circle of the party that they had founded, were beyond polite exchange. A plea from the chair that the convention had met not to debate the national ticket but to choose the state one failed to mollify them. Neither did the chair's plugging Governor Gardner's renomination. Ely took to the floor to denounce Gardner as a man who was "true to himself but not the American party." His toadying to the Fremont party, Ely said, was self-serving, but if the Republicans dump him, he will come knocking for entry into the Fillmore organization. Peirce leaped onto a chair and bellowed out to the mob whether there was a "way for the American party to be rid of the American traitors."[43]

There was a way: control of the delegate seats. This touched off a heated contest, with each side challenging the credentials of the other's delegates. Again the Gardnerites had the advantage, having taken the precaution of packing the credentials committee, and when that body ruled in favor of their delegates, the Fillmore Americans stormed out of the hall. The remaining delegates dutifully renominated Gardner by acclamation, a step that triggered a second bolt—this one by a handful of Republican-leaning delegates who preferred a candidate more committed to the antislavery cause. Their action had no impact on the proceedings. His Excellency's warm endorsement of Fremont in his acceptance speech put the Republicans on notice that he was a candidate for their nomination as well.[44]

Two weeks later, the Fillmore Americans had another chance to argue their case, this time at the state council's quarterly session. On this occasion, both sides observed parliamentary procedure. A. B. Ely spoke for the minority. He recalled for the delegates how the council earlier had withheld endorsement from Fillmore pending his placing himself "unequivocally upon the Springfield platform." Fillmore having since fulfilled that requirement, Ely moved that the council, in accordance with its own directive, nominate Fillmore. The Gardner-dominated council, however, had no intention of being held hostage to its word, reaffirming instead its support for the national and state slates headed by Fremont and Gardner. A Fillmore American delegate thereupon produced an order from the national council president revoking the charter of the Massachusetts state council. Unimpressed, the Gardnerites rejected the "bull" on the grounds that the national organization had no jurisdiction over the Know-Nothing order in Massachusetts, the state council having severed all connections with it during "the twelfth section troubles" the previous year. Frustrated at every turn, the Fillmore Americans withdrew to form their own council and to name Ely its president.[45]

A fortnight later, the rump council of "the pure Native American party" gathered at the Music Hall in Boston to name its candidates for state office. In a move calculated to enhance the chances of a joint Whig-American venture "provided the Whigs take the right ground," the national Americans by a nearly unanimous vote nominated as their standard bearer Amos A. Lawrence—a favorite of both the Brahmins and Native Americans.[46] No sooner had the Fillmoreites announced their choice than Gardner's liaison, Major Cobb, had a letter in the mail to Lawrence informing the Brookline Whig American that the newspaper accounts of the proceedings were garbled. Cobb gravely cited as an example that 7 ballots cast for Henry J. Gardner went undeclared. He alleged, moreover, that fewer than 300 delegates attended the meeting rather than the 550 reported by the press. He was passing this information on to Lawrence "so that your determination heretofore not to run for public office may not be changed by false appearances."[47]

Cobb's exercise in civic responsibility was coupled with a concern that a challenge from the right might jeopardize the chances of his patron. As it turned out, neither the major nor the governor had anything to worry about from that quarter. Lawrence had come under increasing pressure from his friends in the New England Emigrant Aid Company to reject the nomination. He was told that if he were to accept the nomination of "the Know-Nothing pro-slavery party" it would have a "disastrous" effect on the company and would prove "seriously injurious to the cause of Kansas." "If you want to give Dr. Robinson [the director of the company in Kansas] a blow equal to the stroke with a sledge hammer," wrote a fellow member, "you will accept the Fillmore nomination and thus add your influence to the faction that are doing all they can to perpetuate the tyranny in Kansas."[48]

Lawrence, who had gone so far as to draft an acceptance speech, bent to the pressure and rejected the nomination. His decision to withdraw stunned his supporters. Ely pleaded with him to reconsider: "You leave us as sheep without a shepherd! Without you we will be defeated."[49]

The threat from the right, such as it was, having unraveled, the Gardnerites were now free to concentrate their efforts on securing a linkup with the Republicans. "There is great pressure on our folks [the Republicans] to nominate Gardner or set nobody up against him," newspaperman Sam Bowles reported. Bowles expected that the Republicans would withstand the pressure and run their own gubernatorial candidate, even though "there is not a candidate on whom we can command a union of the Fremont vote against Gardner—none but Sumner, and I suppose it would be hard to get him."[50] Gardner's supporters, who were worried over the possibility of a Sumner challenge, had continued to float rumors that their man might still make a run for the Sumner seat. It was a bluff, but the ploy got the attention of certain Republicans. Sumner's friends, in particular, feared that the chief magistrate was indeed "making a desperate effort" to gain the seat.[51] Sam Bowles complained about an apparent willingness to appease Gardner on the basis of that fear. "The fellows [the Republican leadership] are putting the screws on me to go for Gardner; they got Dana of the *Tribune* to believe that opposition to Gardner will endanger Sumner's reelection." Bowles, for one, would have nothing to do with any arrangement with the Know-Nothing chieftain. "I will see them [those Republicans countenancing a deal with Gardner] in a very hot place before I will support Gardner."[52]

Adams, like Bowles, had gotten wind of a Know-Nothing/Republican understanding: Republican support for the Gardner American state ticket in return for a united front in the presidential election and no American entry in three congressional district races. Such a bargain, in spite of the advantages accruing to the Republican side, carried too steep a price for Adams, since it would be purchased "at the heavy expense of assuming the liabilities of the present bankrupt concern." Adams feared that since his name was among those being considered as the Republican candidate in one of the open congressional districts, "any action of mine . . . which should look like acquiescence in the nomination of such a man as Gardner . . . would seem to others, and might savor even to myself of a participation in some of the bargaining spirit by which I might benefit."[53] Adams's crisis of conscience was misplaced; he did not get the nomination. In a political environment peopled with schemers like Gardner, Wilson, and Banks, public office—if it ever did—no longer sought the man.

As it turned out, there was more to the fears of Republicans like Adams and Bowles than the rumors of a Gardner bid for Sumner's Senate seat. National Republican leaders, worried that if the governor were to mobilize his formidable political machine behind Fillmore, it might cost the party the state's electoral votes, pressured the state Republicans into reaching an understanding with the Know-Nothing chieftain.[54]

Edward Everett had prophesied during the 1855 political season that regardless of the bitterness of their falling out, the Wilson and Gardner Americans would coalesce again if ever it served their interests to do so, since "all [were] veteran intriguers."[55] For once, Everett was right. The Republican and American conventions opened simultaneously in Worcester, thus affording "weak-backed Republicans" under the watchful eye of Henry Wilson the chance to scurry back and forth between the two bodies, carrying with them the torch of unity. Nathaniel Banks materialized before his former Know-Nothing brothers with the message that Fremont was a true American and "no more a Catholic than Buchanan is a married man." The delegates received the news with enthusiasm, their late differences with "the black agitators" having been replaced by a newfound spirit of unity. Wilson, meanwhile, was counseling Republican conventioneers in somewhat contradictory terms that even though the American party was "a broken and scattered party that can never rally again," its support would magnify Fremont's impending victory in the Commonwealth.[56]

The Republican convention, in order to pursue the matter further, established a committee chaired by John W. Foster to confer with the Gardner Americans. The Foster committee, after being hailed with enthusiasm upon its appearance at the American convention, closeted with Gardner's henchmen. When the negotiating teams emerged, it was to announce a union ticket: Fremont for president, Gardner for governor. Once again, His Excellency had bedded down with those "political harlots" Wilson and Foster.[57]

All was not bliss, however. When the Foster committee reported back to the Republican convention with its proposal to adopt the American state ticket, they were met with a storm of protests made more raucous by fears that union with "Sam" would jeopardize the foreign antislavery vote in the Midwest. Faced with a possible rupture in their ranks, the Republican leadership fell back to a secondary position—a resolution to make no nominations for state offices.[58] The resolution passed with little opposition. Even so straitlaced a Republican as Charles Francis Adams, who had been holding out for a "proper" Republican gubernatorial candidate, hailed the compromise, "as no responsibility is assumed for his [Gardner's] conduct, and there is no obligation to vote for him." Sam Bowles, on the other hand, grumbled that the Republicans had paid a stiff price: "It shows the overriding importance of the national election . . . that such men as met in Worcester yesterday were willing to throw away the certainty of flaxing out Gardner, for the sake of the moral effect abroad of a grand union and peace here in Massachusetts against the Administration party." It showed also that the man who had stage-managed the accord, namely Henry Wilson, was the dominant force in building the Republican coalition.[59]

A sprinkling of Republican ideologues who called themselves the Bird Club after their leader, Francis W. Bird of Walpole, spurned the compromise settlement on the grounds that the moral effect of the decision made in Worcester would weigh the Republican party down with baggage of Know-Nothing bigotry. Sound in principles but weak in numbers, the Bird Club entered its own slate headed by Josiah Quincy, the former mayor of Boston.[60]

The national Americans were also given to tilting at windmills. Their efforts to build a party coalition having come a cropper when Lawrence rejected their nomination, they opened negotiations with another Whig blue blood, William Appleton. The former congressman, however, disappointed his Native American supplicants by refusing to swallow their nativistic principles. A. B. Ely was incensed. Appleton must accept the Philadelphia platform whole, he snapped, if he wished the nomination, for the national Americans had no intention of endorsing "an old Hunker Whig anymore than an old Hunker Democrat." According to Ely's logic, Whigs who repudiated the Fillmore American party—the only national party in opposition to the administration—were carrying water for the Democracy. Thus: "If Mr. Appleton is not for us, he is against us."[61]

Having failed to secure a Brahmin luminary to head their state ticket, the national Americans turned to a lesser light, George W. Gordon, a nondescript Whig businessman who had served as postmaster under Fillmore. Gordon pledged action against foreign paupers and criminals, opposition to the right of naturalized citizens and Roman Catholics to hold public office, and elimination of "unnecessary and reckless" state spending.[62] The Brahmins, in turn, fielded their own candidate, Luther V. Bell, whose background as the chief administrator of an insane asylum presented an irresistible target for political punsters. Nevertheless, the negotiations between the national Americans and the "pure Whigs" did produce a partial union slate of congressional candidates. Even in union, however, the Brahmins "held themselves aloof" from their allies and treated them "as if we [the national Americans] who number more than three to their one were of a [sic] inferior race." Ely, who was running for Congress, was not inclined to allow the Brahmins to plug into "the living galvanism of our Fillmoreism to give temporary life to the dead and decaying body of Whiggery," once he learned that "these everlastingly prating Whigs . . . [had] put a man in nomination in my district in opposition to me." It struck Ely as ironic that if it had not been for his good offices and hard work, the Whigs "would not be a corporal's guard of the National Americans in the State." His expenditure of "some thousands in money" on behalf of the cause disposed him even less "to submit to Whig superciliousness [or to] Whig treachery or dishonesty." Vowing "to fight all Whigs as inimical to myself as well as to the American party and Mr. Fillmore," the Native American leader urged "the true men of the party" to break with their imperious allies and "stand by their own guns and fight their own battles."[63] The fight that Ely envisioned was against a phantom, the Whig party for all practical purposes having ceased to exist after the 1854 Know-Nothing knockout blow.

There never was much doubt how Massachusetts would vote. This being a presidential year, national politics dominated the canvas. The Republicans seized the advantage by drumming on the twin themes of "Bleeding Sumner" and "Bleeding Kansas." The antislavery cause had its martyr in the wounded Sumner and its campaign issue in the turmoil in Kansas. What was at stake in the election, they said, was "clearly and fully, slavery and freedom" in the territories, and that left the electorate with a choice between Fremont and Buchanan, since Fillmore and the national Americans dodged the issue.[64] Most Bay Staters, regardless of political persuasion, agreed. Edward Everett regretfully informed Fillmore that even his brother-in-law Nathan Hale—the publisher of the staunchly Whig *Boston Daily Advertiser*—was "leaning towards Fremont." And while Hale leaned, Samuel Walley, the Whig gubernatorial candidate in 1855, along with a number of other "old-line" Whigs announced for the Republican. C. F. Adams watched the trend, content that victory was at hand. He had no doubts about the outcome of the election in Massachusetts "from the day of the assault upon Sumner" and predicted that "Whiggery and Fillmore Know-Nothingism will find no soil to sustain any crop at election."[65]

At the state level, the Gardner Americans faced a weak and divided opposition, their only formidable potential competition—the Republicans—having taken themselves out of the race. The Democrats, though recovered from the 1854 disaster, remained a minority party; the Whigs and Bird Club, with their independent slates, were putting a brave face on lost causes; and the Native Americans had only their peculiar ideology and Unionism to offer the electorate. Political nativism did have an appeal for a generation of native-born buffeted by the forces of industrialism, urbanization, and mass immigration, but not enough to command a majority of votes on its merits alone. Besides, the Native Americans had to compete with the governor for the anti-Catholic, xenophobic vote.

Election day in Massachusetts brought no surprises other than the margin of the national Republican win. Fremont won a stunning victory, garnering 108,190 votes, or nearly two-thirds of the 167,000 votes cast. Buchanan lagged far behind with only 39,240 votes, or less than a quarter of the total. Fillmore trailed the field, and his 19,626 votes, amounting to less than 12 percent of the turnout, was one of his worst showings in a Northern state. Expectations that the Know-Nothings and former Whigs would rally to appeals of Unionism and nativism proved baseless. Nearly three-quarters of the Know-Nothings and a similar proportion of former Whigs voted for Fremont. Fremont's huge majority—close to 25,000—was the largest ever tallied in the Bay State to that time and placed beyond doubt where public opinion stood on national issues. The results would have been much closer, however, if it were not for the mutually advantageous arrangement between the Republicans and the Americans. Fremont matched the governor's showing among Know-Nothing voters, attracting 72 percent of the 1854 Know-Nothings and 95 percent of those who voted for Gardner in the state election.[66]

Gardner also made an impressive showing, carrying every county in the state with a total vote of 92,576. His 72 percent share of the vote of the original Know-Nothings marked a comeback from 1855, when only around half of them voted for him. Gardner also fared well with the Republicans, garnering the votes of more than half of those who had voted for Rockwell in 1855 and an impressive 83 percent of the Fremont Republican voters.[67] Among the other gubernatorial candidates, only Democratic Erasmus Beach drew a respectable vote, thanks to the return of most Democrats to the party fold. His more than 40,000 total, which topped his party's presidential ticket, points to the influence of local considerations in the state contest. In an inverse way, so did the performance of the other three candidates—Gordon, Bell, and Quincy—whose inability to garner as much as 15 percent of the total vote between them demonstrated the difficulty, if not impossibility, of cobbling together a viable coalition based on ideological commitment alone.

Fremont's running 15,614 votes ahead of Gardner and the Republicans' sweeping majorities into both houses of the General Court (albeit many of them ran on joint Republican-American tickets) denoted a popular swing to that party. Their unofficial coalition with the Gardner Americans reflected a Republican belief that they would best succeed if they adopted the "general doctrine of Native Americanism."[68] For this reason, they relied on former Know-Nothing leaders like Banks and Burlingame to set a nativist tone for their party. Members of the Bird Club were furious with the leadership for dabbling "in the dirty pool of Know-Nothingism" and thus having thrown away the chance to take control of the state government. Ideological purity, however, is not a prescription for winning elections. The Bird Club's gubernatorial candidate, Josiah Quincy, finished a distant last with only 3.6 percent of the vote.

The life-and-death struggle between the American and Republican parties as to which one would survive to contend with the Democracy for national supremacy was decided by the 1856 presidential election. The Republicans prevailed by adroitly exploiting nativism as well as heightening sectional tensions, a strategy that they continued to pursue for the rest of the decade. In Massachusetts, as elsewhere in the North, Know-Nothing converts to Republicanism made the difference. Over 70 percent of the 1854 Know-Nothings—some 58,000 in all—turned their backs on the American candidate Millard Fillmore to vote for the Republican standard bearer John C. Fremont. Their votes added up to a majority of the Pathfinder's total.[69]

CHAPTER SEVEN

The Collapse of the American Party

THE STATE election returns did not augur well for the Gardner Americans, despite their leader's having chalked up his third straight win. In the North, the Republicans had replaced the Democrats as the majority party; and in Massachusetts, their capturing control of both houses of the legislature and Fremont's outdistancing the Know-Nothing state ticket by 15,600 votes sent a strong signal to the governor's clique that their party was in trouble. After taking stock of the situation, an alarmed American state council ordered "immediate measures [be taken] for a thorough and effective organization of the party throughout the commonwealth."[1] Their overriding concern was how best to deal with the likelihood of a Republican bid to replace them as the state's dominant party.

Having neglected the populist spirit that had lifted Know-Nothingism from obscurity to omnipotence and unable to match the Republican appeal in the antislavery quarter, the Gardnerites remained fixed to an ultranativist position. They realized that this was too narrow a base on which to pin their hopes for the perpetuation of their own distinct organization. Some kind of adjustment was needed either to broaden the party's base or to solidify their alliance with the Republicans. With the latter goal in mind, the American council abandoned secrecy, pledged support for candidates of all parties who were in sympathy with the aims of Know-Nothingism, and approved a modified Springfield platform that toned down the party's ultranativist posture.[2] At the same time, the council stipulated that if the Republicans were serious about "the continuance of the union of the friends of freedom" they must meet their commitments to Americanism. Otherwise "Sam" would seek alliances elsewhere.[3] The council's ultimatum was more a sign of weakness than a serious threat. With its original coalition in tatters, the party's inner circle was reduced to scrambling around for outside help in an effort to retain power.

Governor Gardner, in his inaugural address, as much as admitted the straitened circumstances of the once mighty American party when he announced that he would not run for reelection. He called on the Republicans to reaffirm the arrangement that had joined their respective parties in common cause against the Democrats and Fillmore Americans. Nativism was again the centerpiece of the governor's talk, but this time he adroitly grafted it to the slavery question. Fremont's defeat and the corresponding successes of the Slavocracy and its Democratic henchmen, he declaimed, were made possible by the "votes of aliens born, aliens unnaturalized, and aliens entirely ignorant of our institutions and grossly callous to the vast interests involved in this [antislavery] stupendous issue."[4] Moreover, the "horde of foreign born," having dealt the cause of freedom a damaging blow in the presidential contest, stood poised to repeat its work, because "the foreign vote . . . always has been, and in the nature of things ever will and must be attracted to that party [Democratic] which, under high-sounding generalities on the abstract rights of man, always practically cooperates with the Slavery at the South, and banishes from its platform the moral questions, and nobler instincts, and more enlightened sentiments of the age."[5]

Gardner contended that those for whom such instincts and sentiments were part of their birthright (namely, the Yankee Protestant majority) should deny or at least delay the naturalized citizen's right to vote, since foreigners "born and brought up under totally dissimilar principles of government . . . are unfitted to appreciate or rightly use the great trust, in the exercise of which they are unwisely permitted to participate." In their deliberations on these matters, the legislators should bear in mind the dangerous mix of religion and politics that informs the foreign vote in the Commonwealth, for "while we would grant them . . . the enjoyment of their religious belief . . . we may properly . . . remember that the class of aliens to whom we specially refer [Irish Catholics] are blindly attached to a religious faith whose cardinal principle is implicit obedience to its temporal head, and that temporal head a foreign potentate . . . which arrogates to itself . . . a potent and malign political influence at war with the teachings of our Constitution and the essence of our government."[6] To deny office and the suffrage to new arrivals like these was neither intolerant nor oppressive; nor would it interfere with existing rights. Immigrants would continue to enjoy all the rights and privileges of native-born citizens "subject to the sole condition that they shall take no part in the selection of our rulers or the administration of our government until they are fitted by experience to understand its workings and appreciate its blessings."[7] Considerations such as these dictated withholding "for a suitable period" eligibility for the suffrage and public office. Gardner urged the General Court to take prompt and favorable action on the two articles of amendment pending before it regarding qualifications of voters and the right to hold office, and he cautioned the legislators that not a line could be changed, not a word expunged, lest the measures suffer yet another year's delay and the crisis facing republican institutions deepen.[8]

Notwithstanding his vow to step down, Gardner had by no means slammed the door on a fourth term. His speech made it plain that he hoped to entice the Republicans into renewing their alliance with his organization on the basis of a shared commitment to political proscription and antislaveryism. His supporters in the General Court, taking their cue from the governor, joined with the Republicans to reelect Charles Sumner, thereby putting to rest the fears of a Gardner run for the Senate seat.[9] Gardner had other reasons as well to hope for a favorable Republican response to his overtures. Both of the proposed constitutional amendments targeted the vote of Irish Catholic Democrats, a prospect that had to please the new party. National Republicans, it is true, were uneasy with the reading and writing proposition, fearing that it might exclude German-speaking voters who were unfamiliar with English.[10] But the number of naturalized German voters in Massachusetts was minuscule, and the amendment clearly targeted the Irish Catholics in the state, whose numbers were large, whose literacy rate was low, and whose party of choice was the Democracy. Moreover, most Republican legislators had run on union tickets with Know-Nothing backing. Some of them had promised to vote for the amendments, and the rest, by implication at least, had committed themselves to a policy of political proscription.

A large majority in both houses found these reasons compelling enough to vote for the literacy amendment. The more extreme residency amendment, however, encountered such stiff opposition that it forced supporters to drop the waiting period from twenty-one to fourteen years. Their concession failed to mollify the national Republicans, who feared a backlash from midwestern German Republicans. Henry Wilson blasted the measure as a "disgrace [to] the state" and called for its defeat. Wilson's denunciations infuriated hard-core nativists, some of whom demanded that the American party break with the Republicans. The more moderate majority, however, realizing that they had much to lose and nothing to gain from so drastic a step, stipulated that if there were to be a split, let it be the Republicans' doing.[11]

The 1857 legislature, in keeping with its reputation for "vacillation and timidity," entertained a compromise proposal to reduce the waiting period further from fourteen years to two. Hard-to-please ideological Republicans groused over their party's "timid policy" of swallowing proscription to placate the Know-Nothings, but most of them accepted it on the grounds that "perhaps it is the only way to quiet honest nativism."[12] Their pragmatic brethren were even less discriminating. Henry Wilson, whose earlier objections to the principle of proscription were so profound that no "consideration on earth would induce [him] to vote for the fourteen year proposition," found sufficient merit in the two-year substitute to back it without reservation. Know-Nothing hard-liners, however, proved less pliable than their former colleague. They held fast to their demand for fourteen years, and backed by the governor, they succeeded in blocking the passage of the watered-down two-year version.[13]

Republican ambivalence toward the suffrage amendment reflected more an uneasiness with their association with the American party than with the principle of proscription. No longer needing Know-Nothing support or a political arrangement encumbered by obligations to the governor, they rebuffed Gardner's efforts to clamber aboard their bandwagon. The final rupture came in mid-April, when the Republicans posted a notice in the daily press outlining plans to rally all opponents to the spread of slavery behind their party; in a not-too-veiled dig at Know-Nothing taxes and deficit spending, they promised to reduce the size of government and slash state expenditures. Left with no other recourse, the Gardnerites accused the Republicans of having broken faith on the fourteen-year amendment and declared their alliance at an end.[14]

The falling out between the Gardnerites and the Republicans illustrates the first of two major political developments that emerged during the first half of the year: the Republican decision to sever their ties with the Gardner-led American party. It was a decision based on their expectation that they could achieve an independent and dominant status for their party without the governor. Unlike the false hope of 1855, this time the Republicans had good reason for optimism. They had learned from their mistake of running on the slavery issue alone, and thus, in addition to capitalizing on "Bleeding Sumner" and "Bleeding Kansas," they had wooed the nativist and temperance vote in the 1856 campaign. That courtship had paid off with large enough numbers of Know-Nothing converts to give the Republican party the advantage in the state. In democratic politics, votes are destiny, and now that the Republicans had more of them than "Sam," they no longer needed the governor.[15]

The second development was the product of the first: Gardner's reversion to an ultraconservative position on slavery and other issues. Spurned by the Republicans, and with no national base to hook onto, he was forced to seek alliances elsewhere, and this brought him into contact with antireformist and Unionist elements outside the Republican party.

The General Court's appropriation of $100,000 for the aid of "Bleeding Kansas" brought matters to a head. Gardner's initial reaction was to try to scotch rumors that he would "put his veto upon it and then raise the flag of opposition to the reckless extravagance of the republican party."[16] Newspaper speculations to that effect, he assured an interested inquirer, were "all bosh." The demands of his office had deprived him of sufficient time to scrutinize the Kansas Resolves "critically," but when they reached his desk, he would "give them careful attention." His Excellency was afforded the opportunity shortly after penning these words. He vetoed the appropriations, and in so doing, declared war on the Republican party.[17]

The executive veto reflected the governor's predicament: Without Republican backing, he had little choice other than to turn to the task of patching up his own splintered party, a task made all the more difficult by the absence of a national organization to promote his plans. Never an antislavery enthusiast, the former Webster Whig cast off all pretense of sympathy for that cause once it became evident that he could not find a place for himself in the Republican organization. Gardner's refusal to accommodate the legislature on the Judge Loring matter and his veto of the Kansas Resolves widened the split between the two former allies, but the rupture was not of his making and probably could not have been avoided.

He was, however, responsible for the alienation of the populist elements within his own party. Gardner had built his gubernatorial career on the premise that ethnocultural divisions constituted the major dynamic in Bay State politics. Now with that career in jeopardy, he continued to beat the nativist drum, oblivious to the fact that his best chance for staying in office lay not in harassing Irish Catholics but in repeating the Know-Nothing promise of 1854 to open up the government to the people. Instead of making such an appeal, he shifted further to the right. He vetoed a proposed $2 million state loan for the construction of the Hoosac Tunnel as well as a $2,500 grant to a school for retarded children in the name of cost cutting in a depression year. The vetoes betrayed a blind spot in the governor's political vision, violating as they did the populist spirit that had informed the Know-Nothing movement at its height.[18] Whatever claim he had on any remaining reform-minded voters in the American party died with those vetoes.

The governor evidently hoped to recoup any losses by mending political fences in other quarters. His softening stance on the South and his calling for a reduction in the size of government, for instance, had a Democratic ring. He reached out as well to reestablish a working relationship with his former allies, the Unionist Whigs and Fillmore Americans, whom he had estranged in 1856 when he cast his lot with the Fremont Republicans.

While Gardner was reestablishing relations with the ultraconservatives, the Republicans, in a maneuver to undercut support for the incumbent within his own party, scheduled their annual convention for June, several months ahead of the customary nominating season. At about the same time, a group of Fremont Americans working in tandem with the Republicans announced that the American convention would meet on June 16, one week earlier than the Republicans. Hard on the heels of these two announcements came a political bombshell: The state's leading Know-Nothing journal, the *Boston Daily Bee*, endorsed Nathaniel C. Banks for governor.[19] Banks was already being touted as the favorite to win the Republican nomination. Now the governor had a double worry: The likely Republican nominee was also angling for the American endorsement.

The *Bee*'s action triggered a swift response from Gardner's headquarters, which, in spite of the chief executive's assurances that he was not a candidate, was nevertheless concerned enough to caution party members not to participate in the "fraudulent" June 16 convention.[20] But the warning came too late to abort a joint Banks American–Republican venture on foot for months to consolidate "the Fremont party of last year under the name of Mr. Banks."[21] Hence, the Banks Americans met as scheduled in Boston on June 16 with the expressed purpose of incorporating the concentration of nativist and antislavery sentiment in Massachusetts within the Republican fold. It was the sort of power play that the original Know-Nothings had rebelled against three years earlier. Only around one-quarter of the towns had bothered to send delegates, leading one small-towner to complain that the convention's organizers had rounded up men in the streets of Boston to speak for the country people. His point was well taken. The convention's "programme [was] cut and dried beforehand" and the delegates were screened in order to rig the results. To the surprise of no one, Banks received 219 of the 229 votes cast. The party's sitting governor drew 5.[22]

Banks accepted the nomination in a public letter, underscoring the major themes that he planned to address in the forthcoming campaign, namely, opposition to the extension of slavery and to foreign influence in elections. He called on the Republicans and Americans to put aside their bitter squabbling and jockeying for position and join in a united action for "higher purposes."[23] Longtime ally and fellow townsman Gideon Haynes made it clear in a speech touting his neighbor's virtues that he understood the higher purposes to include the consolidation of the Republican and American forces behind the candidacy of the "Iron Man." Banks's staff thought enough of the suggestion to adopt the name American Republican for their organization and pledge it to the Springfield platform.[24]

Their venture had the backing of Henry Wilson, who, as usual, was pulling strings in both the American and Republican camps. Not all Republicans, however, were thrilled with the prospect of a Know-Nothing heading their ticket. Adams, in a jab at archrival Wilson, described Banks's following as "small both in numbers and character."[25] Other Republicans criticized the proposed coalition on the grounds that no party can long survive without its own organization and platform. Last year, they said, the party had compromised its principles and forfeited certain victory when it entered into an arrangement with the Know-Nothings. Henceforth, the party must eschew such bargains and go it alone with candidates who are wedded to Republican principles irrespective of whether or not they are acceptable to other parties. Specifically, they wanted no part of a candidate like Banks who stood with "one foot on the [Republican national] Philadelphia platform and the other on the Springfield platform."[26]

At the Republican convention, which opened in Worcester on June 24, that line of reasoning failed to elicit much support, except from members of the Bird Club, whose bitter opposition to Banks, in the opinion of some, threatened a serious division. Given to an idealistic viewpoint of how the political system should work, these "radical" Republicans were disgusted by the prearrangements set in place by their own party to anoint the candidate of the sham American convention.[27] Club leader Francis W. Bird labeled the ploy "the old game . . . of a coalition with K. Nism [*sic*]" and denounced Banks as a man with "the unerring instincts of an original Know-Nothing." "I see constant illustration," he would later remark, "of the melancholy fact that when 'one has learned to discriminate between a native and foreigner, it becomes easy to discriminate between a white man and a negro.'"[28] Bird also questioned the wisdom of his party's truckling to a candidate who could accept two nominations and stand on two platforms at the same time or to Wilson and the other connivers who had "sold out the Republican party last year."[29]

Bird's stinging rebuke stirred Wilson to a defense of pragmatic politics. Men like himself, he said, had "felt impelled by an imperative sense of duty to advise the Republican State Convention of last year to avoid a controversy with the Fremont Americans by adopting their state ticket or by making no nominations at all." Admittedly, the Republican party could have fielded a slate that would have swept "the American State ticket, like chaff, out of the field." To have done so, however, would have detracted from the more critical Fremont run for the presidency. But that was last year. The presidential election now behind them, the Republicans had an unparalleled opportunity to welcome all friends of freedom (including the Know-Nothings) into "one harmonious party."[30] In private, Wilson was as contemptuous of his "radical" critics as they were of him. "In my opinion," he confided to Sumner, "the antislavery cause would be advanced if some of them were ever more to keep silent."[31]

Most of the delegates, as it turned out, preferred unity to mutual recrimination; and when one of the leading "radical" Republicans, Judge Charles Allen, announced for Congressman Banks, those opposing any link with Know-Nothingism were thrown into confusion.[32] Allies of Banks, sensing victory, intensified the drive for his nomination. Among them was fellow congressman and political careerist Anson Burlingame, whose nomination speech on behalf of Banks was "more American than against Slavery." Even some of the "intractables" who would have preferred a purely antislavery party consoled themselves with the thought that Banks's nomination would quite likely result in the "ejection of the present incumbent from the place which he has so unfortunately occupied."[33] For those anticipating a serious division over the nomination, the vote proved anticlimactic: the convention endorsed the Know-Nothing on the first ballot by a 337 to 94 margin. Some of the Bird Club members expressed disappointment with the decision; but since the rest of the slate was "purely republican" and since they did not bolt, it was assumed they would support the ticket.[34]

In July, the Gardner Americans issued a call for a September meeting of "the American party of Massachusetts and all others who agree with the principles of the Springfield platform." Also included in the invitation were "all who deem a paramount issue in the approaching election to be retrenchment and reform in the expenditures of the Commonwealth."[35] Thus, the party made clear its intention to appeal to conservatives of all kinds—Unionist Whigs, Fillmore Americans, small-government Democrats, and cost-conscious taxpayers—to unite in opposition to the Republicans.

They kicked off their campaign at a party rally in Dorchester that was packed with Gardner loyalists. The featured speaker was the governor himself, who arrived to the strains of "Hail to the Chief" and strode to the rostrum. He reminded his audience that he was not a candidate for reelection and that he was pledged to his party's nominees, providing they were true Americans. His pledge, he hastened to add, did not include the "recreant" who had prostituted the principles of the American party by accepting the Republican nomination (the same nomination, incidentally, that Gardner had eagerly solicited prior to the Republicans' casting him adrift). Banks was no more American, Gardner scoffed, than his partners in deceit—Henry Wilson and John Foster. But this time, these political wire-pullers had overreached themselves, for not even the nimble "Bobbin Boy" could stand on the American and Republican platforms at the same time. His candidacy, moreover, lacked focus as well as principle. Important state issues stood in the forefront of public concerns, yet who knew Banks's position on matters like the Hoosac Tunnel, the Loring case, and the Kansas Resolves?[36]

Gardner's audience responded to his prodding by endorsing as their gubernatorial choice "our present worthy Chief Magistrate." Companion resolves severed all connections with the Republican party, repudiated the "irregular and unauthorized" June 16 convention of "so-called Americans," and rejected "any candidate who attempts to deceive by pretending to support two sets of principles and two sets of candidates at the same time."[37]

The indignation vented at the Dorchester gathering over the cynical bargain that bound together Republicans and Banks Americans barely had time to dissipate before the governor's staff took up the question of reaching a similar understanding with the Fillmore, or national, Americans. Negotiations produced an agreement to hold their respective conventions in Boston on the same day. But the Fillmore Americans set a price for reconciliation: the Gardnerites must modify the Springfield platform so as to soften its "harsh stand against the South."[38] His Excellency, who, as recently as the Dorchester rally, had excoriated the Banks Americans for having "eviscerated, castrated, [and] altered [the] Springfield platform," agreed to make the necessary adjustments. Leaving nothing to chance, his henchmen labored diligently during the time left prior to the opening of the two American conventions to stack both bodies with Gardner loyalists. As F. W. Bird had surmised months earlier, "Gardner . . . goes to the Hunkers."[39]

The Gardner "Fremont Americans" assembled in Boston's Tremont Temple on September 10. In a display of disciplined response every bit as precise as that evidenced at the convention of the Banks "Fremont Americans" in June, they renominated the governor with 676 of the 682 ballots cast; and even as the delegates reaffirmed without debate the party's commitment to the Springfield platform, they dropped the preamble of that document, which had paired the Slavocracy with the papacy as twin foes of the republic. Dropped also were last year's denunciations of the Democratic and Fillmore American platforms.[40] What took their place—as might be expected from political careerists anxious to give their flagging party a new identity—was an open invitation to all nativists and conservatives to back a program of ethnic and religious proscription, Unionism, and fiscal responsibility. A series of resolutions singled out state spending as "an issue of vital and absolute importance," rapped Republican legislators for having brought on the budgetary crisis through extravagances like the Kansas Resolves, which had earmarked $100,000 to be transferred from the "impoverished treasury" of the Commonwealth to the citizens of a "foreign State," and promised to bring runaway expenditures under control through "economy, retrenchment, and reform."[41]

While these platform matters were being settled, conference committeemen were scurrying from the Tremont Temple over to the nearby Music Hall, where the national Americans were convened, to relay His Excellency's reaffirmation of the Native American ideals that "Americans must rule America" and "none but

Americans should be elected to office." Sufficiently impressed, the Music Hall delegates endorsed Gardner by acclamation.[42]

The bargain reunited the national and state branches of the Massachusetts American party behind His Excellency's bid for a fourth term. Later that afternoon, all the delegates reassembled in Faneuil Hall to hear Gardner's acceptance speech. The honor accorded him, he told them, came at "great personal sacrifice." His business affairs perforce must suffer. Still, the contest pitting as it did "Americanism against the opponents of Americanism" left him no choice but to shoulder the burden once again.[43]

His Excellency's skipping from convention to convention, like his Republican opponent's standing on two platforms at the same time, was an exercise in political opportunism totally out of keeping with the rebellious spirit that had energized the early Know-Nothing movement. That spirit had been kindled precisely by the kinds of maneuverings and accommodations that the American and Republican power brokers were engaged in on the eve of the 1857 election campaign. Gardner did try to distance himself from Banks by preaching the preeminence of state issues over national ones, but his positions on the very issues that he cited as most germane—Judge Loring, the Kansas Resolves, the Hoosac Tunnel, and the School for Idiot Children—placed him outside the pale of the antislavery and populist camps. He sought to compensate for his weaknesses in these quarters with overtures to "doughface" voters. Kansas, he pontificated, is a "dead horse," the question of freedom or slavery there having been settled by the federal government. That pronouncement, however, was unlikely to win many converts, especially from Democrats whose own party was the architect of that settlement.[44] Ultimately, the governor's strength lay in his organization, his political acumen, and his strong nativist stance; but he was facing, in the forthcoming campaign, his strongest challenge in all three areas.

The Bay State Republicans, fresh from their outstanding performance in the presidential election, had the advantage of momentum; and in their gubernatorial nominee, they had a politician every bit a match for Gardner in the demogogic arts and his superior as a campaigner. "He came," wrote Banks's biographer, "not as a crusader, but as a young man in search of a profession. . . . He had an arresting personality, an excellent speaking voice and manner. . . . More valuable still were a capacity for political intrigue . . . and a readiness to sacrifice principles for political advantage."[45] Banks had joined the Know-Nothing party to save his political career. From the outset, the former Democrat had gravitated toward the Free-Soil wing of the party in anticipation of rewards to be gleaned from that sector. A cautious man, however, he had retained his connections with the governor's camp while awaiting a more opportune moment to commit himself unqualifiedly to the antislavery cause.[46] That moment arrived in 1857, when the Republicans decided to dump Gardner.

Some of the more ideological Republicans remained unreconciled to their party's choice. The Bird faction, which from the first recoiled at the idea of having to abide a candidate who openly lusted after the bigot vote instead of concentrating solely on the antislavery cause, announced their intention to take to the field as "Straight Republicans." They drew up a slate headed by Caleb Swan of Easton to run on a platform that espoused human freedom and condemned Know-Nothing bigotry. Their purpose was to offer voters an alternative to the two leading candidates who pretended that "two millions of foreigners can swallow nineteen millions of free Americans." But for all its purity of motive, theirs was a token gesture that elicited criticism even from fellow travelers like the aristocratic stalwarts of the old Free-Soil party.[47] Charles Francis Adams, who in the past had castigated Wilson and other pragmatic Free-Soilers for following the path of expediency, now counseled the same policy himself. In an exchange of views with one of the Bird "intransigents," Adams asserted that while it was true that the Republicans could have made a better choice, Banks's nomination was not sufficient reason to split the antislavery party and endanger its cause. Wilson-like, Adams reasoned that the party could extract its measure of advantage from its unsavory candidate without sacrificing principle. It boiled down to a matter of Banks needing the support of the friends of freedom more than their needing him. If he were to betray the cause, they could "push him aside as an obstacle in the way."[48]

Adams's newfound enthusiasm for pragmatic politics was tempered by a patrician overview. He regarded the unfolding campaign "to all intents and purposes . . . a Native American quarrel" which, by plunging the quality of political discourse to the depths of "vulgarity," alienated "the great body of intelligent voters." He ascribed this unhappy aspect of a changing political culture to Banks's lieutenants, men whom he judged as being of "scarcely higher calibre" than those serving Gardner.[49]

The Quincy patriarch's low opinion of Banks's entourage was of little concern to the Republican nominee, who, in spite of his efforts to project a bandwagon image, was running scared. The "Bobbin Boy" was too clever a politician to repeat the Republican error of 1855 and base his appeal to voters solely on territorial and slavery considerations. He was particularly sensitive to Gardner's proved record of support among nativist voters, a concern that led him to bump the Republican nominees from the party slate and replace them with "straight American" candidates. To bind his constituency to the new "union ticket" called for the agility of a dancing master, which Banks once was. The "old line democrat—coalitionist—Know-Nothing—fusionist—all in 6 years with one or two accessory changes" proved equal to the task.[50] He did it primarily by pegging his campaign to the same triad of issues on which Gardner had based his 1856 run— antislavery, temperance, and nativism.

Banks enjoyed certain advantages over his opponent on all three counts. First, as the Republican candidate, he preempted the antislavery vote. Gardner, of course, had won without that vote two years earlier, but the American party had suffered other defections in the interim, and it faced a more broad-based Republican foe. Second, Banks's unflagging advocacy of prohibition (he had presided over the Maine Law convention in 1851, and the following year he had in contradistinction to his own party's laissez-faire policy used his influence as speaker of the house to shepherd the Coalition's controversial temperance bill around legislative roadblocks to enactment) and his lifelong practice of abstinence stood in stark contrast to the discrepancy between His Excellency's professions of orthodoxy, on the one hand, and his highly publicized affinity for brandy and fine wines, on the other. The Republicans did not hesitate to exploit the contrast during the campaign. Finally, Banks's attacks on the Irish Catholics, whose vote he once courted (and would court again), scored well with the nativist crowd.[51] Moreover, memories of the governor's betrayal of the Fillmore Americans still rankled. Embittered Native American leaders A. B. Ely and Jonathan Peirce announced for Banks. "I do not deem it necessary for me to vote for a bad man," Ely snarled. "I do not believe," added the Native American ideologue with unintentional irony, "in perpetuating a malicious despotism."[52]

Gardner's overtures to former Whigs also met with a mixed reception. Remnants of the old Brahmin ruling clique agonized through the summer and autumn months over their conundrum: choosing the lesser of several evils. Edward Everett summarized the difficulty of their choice. Banks was the least appealing in a field of undesirables. A man of the "most barefaced tergiversation," the Republican candidate wanted principle. What was worse, his party pointed "directly and inevitably to disunion." A vote for Democratic candidate Erasmus Beach, on the other hand, was tantamount to an endorsement of the national adminstration and its odious Kansas-Nebraska Act, which was the source of "all our present disorganization." And Henry J. Gardner, though a clever man and responsible for some "praiseworthy" acts, was "as much an adventurer in politics as Mr. Banks." To make matters worse, he had "coquetted" with the "disunion" party when it had served his purpose to do so. Rufus Choate seconded Everett's assessment of the incumbent, marking Gardner as a "light, ambitious, vain man" who showed "utter want of principle" in his scrambling after office. Faced with these choices, a disillusioned Everett, for the first time since reaching his majority, could not bring himself to vote.[53]

A few Whig luminaries like Robert C. Winthrop, George Hillard, and former congressman William Appleton swallowed their reservations and announced for their fellow Brahmin, but by 1857, it no longer mattered where the Winthrops, Appletons, and Hillards or the Everetts and Choates placed their support. Certainly, Governor Gardner had more pressing concerns than how his fellow Brahmins were lining up in the campaign. His opponent was making inroads among nativist and temperance voters, and the chief magistrate was also losing his hold on the bedrock of the original Know-Nothing coalition—the native-born working class.[54]

The Gardnerites having transformed Know-Nothingism from a people's movement into a political machine had long since diverted it from its original populist goals. As the party increasingly fell under the control of the chief magistrate, it ceased responding to public opinion and followed instead a strategy aimed at enhancing the governor's power. Substantive worker discontents remained unaddressed. The drive for the ten-hour day, which had come so close to fruition in 1855, petered out through lack of response at the statehouse. That the force underlying that drive—a militant concern for workers' rights—should again have been deflected once it reached Beacon Hill is scarcely surprising. Workers' rights was far too controversial an issue for that generation of politicians even to admit its existence. Besides, the concept of collective bargaining had as yet to be formulated, let alone addressed. Even more pernicious insofar as working conditions were concerned was the sudden collapse of the economy.

In 1857, a nationwide financial crisis had triggered a sharp economic downturn. Its impact on the industrially advanced Commonwealth was devastating. Bankruptcy stalked the business community in Boston, striking wholesale clothiers, dry goods jobbers, and commission houses with particular severity. Within weeks, the pattern of business failures and massive layoffs had spread misery to every corner of the state. By late autumn, around one-quarter of the state's manufacturing concerns had shut down, and almost all of those still operating had cut back on production. Hardest hit were mechanics and laborers. Manufacturing villages in the largely rural western part of the state reported 8,500 mill hands out of work. Three thousands workers lost their jobs in Fall River alone. Workers lucky enough to hang on to their jobs were put on a shortened week and had their wages slashed. Three weeks before the election, the state's banks were forced to suspend payments of species.[55] With the depression deepening and winter approaching, prospects for relief were bleak.

Incumbency in a depression year compounded the difficulties that the governor faced in his bid for reelection. Unemployment and taxes stood at all-time highs; and both opposition parties turned the hard times to their advantage by fixing the blame on the administration. Gardner sought to counter their efforts by sponsoring the creation of an ad hoc legislative committee to prepare a list of recommendations on how to prune government programs and spending and bring the budget into balance.[56] He followed that up with the vetoes of the Hoosac Tunnel, Kansas Resolves, and School for Idiot Children proposals, which he applied in the name of cost cutting. His actions were consistent with orthodox economic doctrine, which held that a free-floating debt, when combined with deficit spending, spelled eventual bankruptcy of the state. However, there was nothing in this budget-balancing scenario of high taxes and reduced government expenditures that promised relief to the victims of the depression.

In any event, Gardner's rivals took the issue of fiscal responsibility away from him. Both Banks and Beach, in accepting the endorsement of their parties, echoed Gardner's pledge to shrink the budget; but where the governor blamed profligate Republican legislators for the deficits, his opponents had a field day pointing out the incongruity of the administration's efforts to wrap itself around the issue of budget cutting after having presided over the largest accumulation of government costs in the history of the state.[57] The ultraconservative *Boston Daily Advertiser* (which had recently converted to Republicanism) drove that point home when it reminded its readers that the governor had inherited a surplus when he entered office, only to plunge the state into debt when he signed the 1855 appropriation for $200,000 to build an insane asylum.[58] Spending had in fact doubled since Gardner had taken office, sending the state debt spiraling upward to record heights and prompting fears of the government going bust.[59] Taxes also had soared to new levels under Gardner. High taxes and hard times combined to accelerate the erosion of an already crumbling Know-Nothing base.

The economic downturn enhanced Republican prospects. The Republicans had hoped to win labor over through warnings that the spread of slavery into the territories would imperil the status of free labor everywhere; but worker distress presented them with a more immediate and graphic issue that they were quick to exploit.[60] They paraded the Waltham "Bobbin Boy" (who was closely associated with the corporate interests) as a former factory operative and a friend of the working man. Banks himself delivered speeches out on the hustings that were long on sympathy for the plight of the workers but short on specifics on just how he intended to improve conditions. A testimonial letter from factory employees expressing faith that Banks as governor would champion their cause drew from the candidate the admission that he was indeed a man of the people and that some of his best friends were mechanics.[61] There was no need for specific proposals like the jobs program and government relief projects that Boston's Know-Nothing mayor had spelled out in 1854, for even though the Republican response to the victims of the depression lacked substance, the Know-Nothing incumbent had even less to offer. Gardner's sole promise—fiscal restraint—failed to lift the spirits of the legions of unemployed men and women and bankrupted business-men and tradesmen.

Economic hard times, however, were only part of the governor's problems. In 1854, he had risen from relative political obscurity to the highest elective state office by way of dark-lantern politics. Three years later, the Know-Nothing organization that had produced that stunning upset lay in shambles, the chief magis-trate's having co-opted the more talented lodge activists to serve in his administra-tion. The lodge system in its initial state of development had provided ordinary citizens with a forum in which to air their ideas for better government. Gardner's preempting that forum for his own purposes triggered an exodus of rank-and-file Know-Nothings from the lodges and contributed to the party's dismal performance in the municipal elections in late 1855. Gardner's machine had turned out win-ning numbers in the general election that year, thanks in part to the Republican decision to run on the single issue of no more slave states. Gardner won again in 1856 by intertwining his organization with that of the Republicans. Their com-bined appeal on state and national issues in a presidential year mobilized a majority against their Democratic and Fillmore American opponents.

In 1857, however, state issues once again dominated the canvas, and Gardner's situation was desperate. The party that he presided over was a hollow shell of its former self, a majority of its original supporters having deserted it. Gardner's tightening grip on the party apparatus, while enabling him to consolidate his position as party leader, had the additional effect of loosening his hold on the voters. Many of the abler members of his administration had likewise drifted away in hopes of catching on with the Republicans.[62] Gardner himself had set a precedent for them in 1855 and again in 1856, when he openly pursued the Republican nomination. Measured in this context, the depression had the effect of making a bad situation worse. As a Banks supporter enthused, Gardner "with all his cuteness and chicanery [is on] his last political legs—legs which will convey him to the tomb of the Capuletts [*sic*]."[63]

One hour after the polls closed in Boston, the political cognoscenti were predicting Governor Gardner's defeat. The early trends held, and the Republicans did indeed score an impressive win. They elected Banks and the entire "union ticket" of Know-Nothing/Republican legislative candidates, which in conjunction with victorious Republican aspirants who had no ties to the Know-Nothings ensured them commanding majorities in both houses of the General Court.[64] Banks failed a statewide majority, but thanks to the Know-Nothing reform, a plurality now elected. His 60,000 total dwarfed Gardner's 37,500 and Democrat Beach's 31,000. "Straight Republican" candidate Caleb Swan's 216 votes (0.1 percent of the total) once again illustrated the futility of a purely ideological approach to electoral politics.

The 1857 campaign was the last serious run by the American party. Gardner had based his hopes on the appeal of nativism, the promise of reduced state spending, and Unionism, a strategy that failed not only to attract appreciable numbers of new supporters, but also to keep intact his own party's coalition. Lodge membership, which had begun to decline sharply even before the first face-off with the Republicans in 1855, was no longer a major factor in state politics. Only around half of the original Know-Nothing voters had supported the governor's bid for reelection in 1855, and this number had shrunk still further by the time he made his final run. In fact, in just three years, Gardner had lost the support of some two-thirds of the 1854 Know-Nothings.[65]

Voters had swarmed into the Know-Nothing movement in 1854 in response to its promise to liberate the people from the tyranny of party and corrupt politicians. They had expected that through such a movement they would control the state government. Three years later, they had no compelling reason to endorse either of the two self-serving Know-Nothing politicians running for governor. Neither the nativist and anti-Catholic harangues of the campaigners nor the debate over the respective merits of a policy of appeasement or a hard-line stand toward the South reignited the populist passions that carried the Know-Nothings to victory in 1854.

Republicans of all stripes including those who despised Banks and his Know-Nothing cronies, celebrated the outcome. Anyone who appreciates artistry in politics, "Warrington" wrote, has to admire "the exquisite way in which the breath has been beaten out of Henry J. Gardner."[66] Gardner conceded as much by later turning Democrat, and, in what has to be the supreme irony of antebellum party politics, most of the Know-Nothing hierarchy followed their leader into the party that championed the ideal of cultural pluralism.[67]

"Sam's" fall from grace, like that of the Whigs, was as complete as it was sudden. Rendered feeble and ineffectual by the disintegration of its 1854 coalition, the party survived its defeat only as a "miserable delusion." A residue of Unionist Whigs and Native Americans remained to keep alive the dream of restoration. It was a false hope. Henry Gardner, who had not yet joined the Democrats, was chosen to preside at their nominating convention, a choice that provided some unwelcomed excitement. A Native American leaped to his feet to berate the former governor for having conspired with the Republicans in 1856 to betray the American party. Efforts to calm the delegate having proved fruitless, he was dragged from the hall still screeming invectives at the presiding officer. The incident augured ill for the party. Not even the Native Americans were united behind it. The probusiness, "doughface" party fielded in 1858 under the American rubric bore no resemblance to the people's party of 1854, a point made clear by the last-place finish in the general election of its gubernatorial candidate. "Amos A. Lawrence," the *New York Times* chortled, "is left so dismally out in the cold that he will one day be obliged to procure affidavits that he was ever a candidate at all."[68] The rest of the ticket fared no better.

C. F. Adams hailed the results as "exclusively a triumph of antislavery sentiment," unmindful of the fact that former Know-Nothing Nathaniel Banks, like his predecessor, had used the governor's office to build a powerful patronage machine whose primary purpose was to keep him and his lieutenants in power. However, the party's chalking up it first statewide majority in the election did lend credence to Adams's observation that "the last traces of third parties are setting in."[69]

The 1859 election settled that point, at least for the tattered remnants of the American party. Former Whig governor George W. Briggs stood for election as the American candidate. Billed as "a plebeian beloved of the patricians," the once invincible Briggs—he had won seven straight gubernatorial elections—fared no better than had Lawrence.[70] His humiliation marked the end of the short-lived American party.

Its passing was celebrated by its elitist enemies, and it was they who first wrote its story. Nothing in their negative commentaries and selective recollections adequately explains the party's phenomenal success in Massachusetts or its rapid collapse. They left, instead, an account of a party that ascended to great heights on a tidal wave of ethnocultural resentments only to be dashed from the pinnacle of power three years later by the still greater force of antislaveryism.

Know-Nothingism in Massachusetts was unique not only in the extent of its power, but also in how it wielded that power. It had chalked up a record for change unsurpassed in state history, a record, moreover, that encompassed unprecedented gains on behalf of the trio of issues—temperance, nativism, and antislaveryism—that allegedly bore most heavily upon political developments in the Commonwealth. It had wrestled with the problems of pell-mell urban and industrial growth that the other antebellum parties had ignored, and while its reforms did not go far enough to relieve the pressures and ease the pain induced by wrenching change, the American party more than any other had listened and responded to the will of the people. Despite these accomplishments, however, the party lost its popular mandate in 1857 and rapidly faded into oblivion.

The answer to why this happened lies partly in the appeal of Republicanism, which enabled that party to monopolize the antislavery vote and to compete with the Gardnerites for temperance and nativist support. After their 1855 defeat, the Republicans took pains to broaden their appeal and to reach out to voters from all parties, including "Sam." Their focus on "Bleeding Sumner" and "Bleeding Kansas" in the 1856 presidential campaign brought fresh recruits to the antislavery cause; and their choice of Nathaniel Banks to head their state ticket helped lure most Know-Nothings into the Republican camp. Approximately two-thirds of the Know-Nothings still participating in the electoral process in the late 1850s cast their ballots for Banks.[71]

Nathaniel Banks was better suited both in life-style and personal commitment to lead the antiliquor crusade than his opponent. As the "American Republican" candidate, his hold on the antislavery camp went unchallenged, whereas he was able to compete for the yahoo vote by directing a steady stream of attacks against the Irish *lumpenproletariat*.[72] Regional resentments added to the Republican advantage. Farmers and small towners in the interior had led the march of voters into the Republican camp in 1855, transforming the anti-Boston hinterland into the vanguard of the new party. Also making things easier for the Republicans was the fact that the airtight security and voting controls that the American party had used to such great advantage in its first campaign broke down under the pressures of a democratic environment and the scrutiny of a partisan free press. Far more damaging still was the steady erosion in lodge membership that deprived the governor of the kind of automatic bloc vote delivered on election day 1854. Hence, the Gardner Americans had to campaign on their own merits. But their merits, such as they were, were lost in a swirl of campaign billingsgate. Mudslingers on both sides indulged a talent for personal invective in waging the dirtiest campaign in memory. In the war of words, Banks relied on his Ironsides Clubs, which were active in all parts of the state all the way down to the precinct level. Staffed with job-hunting activists drawn from all the parties, they proved more than a match for the governor's vaunted patronage machine in getting out the vote.[73]

On a larger scale, the same national developments that had strengthened the Republican hand proved deleterious to the American party. The life-and-death struggle at the national level between the American and Republican parties as to which would survive to contend with the Democracy for supremacy had been decided by Fremont's strong showing in the 1856 presidential race. The Republicans had outdistanced Fillmore by exploiting civil strife in Kansas and the brutal assault on Sumner while at the same time currying favor with the nativists, anti-Catholics, and prohibitionists.[74] And where the Republicans drew strength from the heightening sectional tensions, the national Americans were irreparably weakened. The national council's decision to ram through a "doughface" platform in 1855 had triggered a bolt by Northern delegates that left the party in Massachusetts bereft of a national organization. Gardner's efforts to effect a rapprochement with the national council prior to the opening of the presidential campaign had proved futile. Thus, when the Gardner Americans broke with the Republicans in 1857, it was too late for them to hearken to the siren call of their Southern brethren: "Return, then, Americans of the North, from the paths of error . . . to the sound position of the American party—silence on the slavery question."[75] There was no national organization for them to return to. The national council had met for the last time in Louisville in June, 1857, only to recommend "that the organization in each State be permitted to adopt such platforms and pursue such policies as it deemed fit."[76]

By the time national politics and the ascendant Republican party took the measure of the American party in Massachusetts, it bore little resemblance to the movement that had galvanized the voters in 1854. Indeed, the internal stresses and fissures that finally caused the order to shatter antedated the rise of the Republican party. Excepting antislavery voters, what led to the shearing off of much of the party's constituency base after 1854 was the party's transformation from a grass-roots movement into what the original Know-Nothings had rebelled against—a vote-getting machine staffed and run by professional politicians.

As soon as the political careerists began to consolidate their hold on the party, disillusionment set in at the grass roots. As a consequence, the rise of politicians to the top of the party corresponded to an erosion of support at its base.[77] In Massachusetts, the effects of the iron law of oligarchy were especially pernicious. Gardner had won in 1855 despite his losing around half of his original supporters. He owed his victory primarily to the weakness of the opposition. In 1856, the Republican decision not to enter their own ticket removed the only formidable obstacle to his reelection. Most of the Republicans and Know-Nothings who turned out in record numbers for Fremont on election day also cast ballots for Gardner, thus enabling him to rack up a landslide win. That inflated vote, however, concealed a pervasive disenchantment among the rank and file. The following election sounded the depths of their discontent. Only around a third of the original 81,500 Know-Nothings voted for Gardner in 1857. Many of the erstwhile Americans turned Republican. Many others were former Democrats returning to the party fold. Thousands more were Whig and Democratic Americans who expressed their disillusionment with "Sam" and the other political parties by staying home on election day.[78]

Even as a new party system was crystallizing in the years between the presidential elections of 1856 and 1860, some 40,000 of the original Know-Nothing voters stopped participating in electoral politics. More than one out of five of them abstained in 1857, setting a trend that accelerated in the next two years, when nearly half of them sat out the election.[79] Those dropping out were almost entirely former Whigs and Democrats, the Free-Soil Americans having switched to the Republican side in 1855. Defections and abstentions on so massive a scale could have taken place only if the American party had alienated its initial supporters.

Gardner's Republican successor in the statehouse was as anxious as the Know-

Nothing chieftain had been to avoid another populist explosion. He took care not to stir up class resentments of the industrial order, concentrating instead on solidifying his standing with temperance, antislavery, and nativist voters. He set the tone for the crusade to dry up the state through personal example and through vigorous enforcement of the 1855 prohibition law. To the delight of antislavery enthusiasts, Banks committed his administration to the passage of the Kansas Resolves and ordered the removal of Judge Loring. Nativists likewise were pleased when the new governor backed the two-year amendment and, to the dismay of the national Republicans, helped push it through to ratification. Banks also reached out to members of Gardner's patronage machine still in office. Demands from within his own party that he apply "the gubernatorial foot to the backsides" of Gardner holdovers and thus put an end to their "miserable intriguing in . . . state affairs" went unheeded. Instead, Governor Banks put his predecessor's "set of Hessians" to work on the task of expanding and solidifying his hold on the nativist vote.[80]

Banks's strategy of courting the Know-Nothings had paid off in majority support at the polls. It was a strategy, moreover, that the Republicans had pursued with similar success in other northern states.[81] Yet, the Banks administration, for all of its labors on behalf of its nativist, antislavery, anti-Southern, and Maine Law constituents, failed to excite the general electorate. Quite the contrary, voter apathy and alienation were more in evidence during Banks's tenure in office than at any time since the advent of the second party system. The high voter turnouts in 1856 and 1860 are misleading, since voting totals in gubernatorial elections peaked in the presidential year of every quadrennial cycle since 1832. Participation in the off-year elections of the late 1850s, when state issues dominated the canvas, tell a different story. Only 41 percent of the adult male population voted in 1857, the smallest proportion in eight years. Total voter turnouts in 1858 (119,249) and 1859 (109,051) sank to their lowest point in the decade, even as the number of potential voters continued to rise; and with only 37 percent of the adult males voting in 1858 and a mere third of them in 1859, the rate of participation dropped to its lowest level in the entire antebellum period (1830–1860), which is all the more remarkable since 1858 and 1859 were realigning years, when voter excitement should be at a fever pitch.[82]

Such a dismal record of participation makes it obvious that realignment in Massachusetts took place in an atmosphere of voter apathy and alienation. Nearly half of the 1854 Know-Nothings dropped out of the electoral process. These were, for the most part, former Whigs and Democrats who had backed the people's party in 1854 in the expectation that they would help shape public policy, only to have their expectation turn sour as opportunistic politicians transformed the party into a vehicle for self-advancement. Unlike former Free-Soilers, most Whig and Democratic Americans had no compelling reason to turn to the Republican party. Its response to the social and economic problems that plagued them was to dust off the commonwealth ethos and preach harmony of interests.[83] On the basis of the record, it would appear that the Republicans of Massachusetts had achieved political ascendancy at the state level without having overcome formidable political opposition or having generated enthusiasm at the grass roots. They had no need to, once their principal rival, the American party, began to disintegrate. In the context of local politics, the Republicans had replaced the Whig hegemony in Massachusetts by default. On the other hand, the record-breaking numbers who turned out for Fremont and Lincoln leave no doubt as to how most Bay Staters felt about national politics.

Epilogue

ELECTORAL POLITICS shapes the relationship between the government and the major interests of the state, and the voters of Massachusetts displayed their disposition on this crucial point by voting year after year for the Whigs to administer the government and set policy with regard to manufacturing, commerce, finance, trade, the fisheries, agriculture, public education, communication, and transportation. In part, the lopsided pattern of partisan politics in Massachusetts stemmed from the positive appeal of Whiggery's record on behalf of growth and development, and in part it reflected voter antipathy or indifference to the Locofoco alternative, which, no less than Whiggery, failed to take into account the salient problems of the industrial age. Explosive industrial growth, urbanization, and population flux had accelerated the velocity of social and economic change to a bewildering pace in antebellum Massachusetts, creating in the process tremendous strains within the society and the need for the government to adopt new policies to relieve the pressure. Both parties claimed to be defenders of the republican faith, yet both preferred a policy of indirection and drift or outright avoidance to one of coherent response to that imperative.

At midcentury, reform elements in the Free-Soil and Democratic parties coalesced to drive the Whigs from power and to end a generation of status quo politics. But the inability of the Coalitionists to rise above the limitations of their moral zeal and agrarian biases and appeal to the urban majority with programs aimed at the most serious problems vexing their society and lives proved fatal. In their place arose a new reform party, the first ever built around the democratic ideal that the people themselves must rule.

The American party swept like a summer storm across the nation in the middle years of the 1850s, and like a summer storm, its force was great, its passage turbulent, and its duration brief. Know-Nothing lodges sprang up like mushrooms along its path, enabling the secret order to forge from its network of local and state organizations a national coalition with which it hoped to challenge the Democracy for dominance over an emerging third party system. Internal divisions and the poor showing in the 1856 presidential election, in which Know-Nothing hopeful Millard Fillmore ran a distant third behind winner James Buchanan and runner-up John C. Fremont, however, dashed its prospects of becoming the national rival of the Democracy, and the party rapidly faded into oblivion. Voter enthusiasm for Know-Nothingism varied from state to state, but its extraordinary, albeit short-lived, popularity in Massachusetts, where the movement reached its apogee, suggests that a more volatile mix of social, economic, cultural, and political ingredients was at work in the Commonwealth to have produced the unprecedented grass-roots eruption of 1854, in which nearly two out of every three voters chose "Sam" in preference to the established parties.

House Speaker Daniel Eddy, in his farewell address to his colleagues, distilled from the countless speeches and multitude of laws that he had stood witness to during the 1855 legislative session what for him were the outstanding accomplishments of Know-Nothing government. The speaker (who was also a Baptist minister) reported with pride that the legislators had "spoken for Temperance, Liberty, and Protestantism, a threefold principle which embodies the highest and truest Americanism."[1] And indeed they had, advancing each of these causes to its high water mark in the antebellum period. Moreover, the diaries, letters, memoirs, speeches, and newspapers of the day make evident that virtually all members of the professional and upper classes, regardless of party affiliation, shared the speaker's assumption that contained within this troika were the issues that generated the force behind such major political developments as the rise of the American and Republican parties. Historians, taking their cue from the written record, continue to debate party transformation in antebellum America on both sides of the same line that divided contemporary political commentators: whether sectional divisions or ethnocultural tensions brought about the collapse of the second party system. Over the years, variations on these two themes and the introduction of several new schools of interpretation have enriched the historiographical debate.

The orthodox historical viewpoint links the fate of the second party system to sectional divisions over slavery. Fueling tensions in the South was the growing conviction that the antislavery crusade threatened her rights and way of life. Correspondingly, the antislavery movement in the North found its widest audience when it warned that the spread of slavery into the territories would undermine the nation's republican institutions and the status of free labor. Public disillusionment with the inadequate response of the major parties to the deepening sectional crisis so weakened partisan attachments that it led to the disintegration of the party system and paved the way for the election of Abraham Lincoln in 1860.[2] That victory, in turn, led ineluctably to secession, the formation of the Confederacy, and the firing upon Fort Sumter.

Most practitioners of "the new political history"—so called because of the reliance on quantitative methodology—have formulated an explanation for partisan preferences in antebellum America based on the idea that ethnic and religious affiliations were the most powerful determinants of voting behavior. Their data show a strong bias among evangelical Protestants in favor of Whiggery, whereas most dissenters and Catholics attached themselves to the Democracy. Mass immigration beginning in the late 1840s brought millions of Germans and Irish Catholics to America and added a new dimension to the ethnocultural factor: The looming presence of so many foreigners and their apparent unassimilability challenged the basic tenets of the core culture and exerted unbearable pressure on the party system, causing it to buckle and finally to collapse in the mid–1850s.[3]

A third school, dating back to the Progressive historians of the early twentieth century, postulates that pocketbook concerns governed voter choices in the Jacksonian period.[4] The socioeconomic interpretation lost favor after Edward Pessen and others demonstrated that not only was the urban labor vote not solidly Democratic, but except for the staunchly Whig upper crust, native-born voters divided their allegiance between the two major parties, regardless of social station.

More recent commentators have returned to the theme of economic determinism. Historians like Alan Dawley, Jonathan Prude, and Sean Wilentz, have relied heavily on social analysis to make the case that the industrial revolution was the spawning ground of class conflict. However, the concept of a systemic class struggle was foreign to the middle-class outlook of the political establishment and never took root in the political parties of the antebellum period. Hence, the parties, though willing to take an occasional prolabor stance for tactical reasons, never committed themselves to the cause of labor; and since the political environment in America militated against the formation of a viable labor party, workers remained politically impotent and their cause unredressed. But even though the party system effectively muted labor's voice in matters of governance and policy-making, labor was not passive. Workers found outlets for their grievances through political action such as petition drives, mass rallies, and local political struggles or by job action in the form of absenteeism, quitting, industrial sabotage, and strikes.[5]

It is worth noting that in an age when poverty was generally ascribed to flaws in the character of the poor, the American party touched a responsive chord in the manufacturing towns and cities when it said that the gulf between the rich and powerful and the poor and dispossessed stemmed from a corrupt party system that, having usurped power from the people, ruled on behalf of "the money bags" and "kid-gloved gentry."

Finally, there is the realignment school of history, which bases its interpretation on V. O. Key's theory of critical, or realigning, elections. Social and economic changes over a period of time transform the socioeconomic environment and render many party issues anachronistic or irrelevant. Pressure builds within the party system to formulate new governmental policies that address the problems generated by radically altered conditions. Parties that ignore this imperative do so at the risk of triggering a realigning election or series of elections in which huge numbers of frustrated voters cast off their party ties and shift to another party to give new direction to matters of governance and public policy.[6] In the 1850s, disillusionment with parties and politicians by all accounts had reached pandemic proportions throughout the country. Instead of responding to the causes of this crisis of confidence, the major parties tended to downplay them and continued to compete on the basis of the outmoded and largely irrelevant issues and policies of the Jacksonian era. As a consequence, the party system lost its legitimacy in the eyes of the voters, who turned elsewhere for solutions.

Components of each theory of party transformation help explain the American party's rise to power in Massachusetts.[7] However, not all played an equal part, nor did any one of them account for why support for "Sam" was so much greater in the Commonwealth than anywhere else.

Among the more serious problems vitally affecting the lives of the people were those relating to immigration. The massive influx of poverty-stricken foreigners into the Commonwealth and the alien ways of the newcomers impinged on the core culture and stirred widespread resentments among the Yankee Protestant majority. It was a situation ready-made for exploitive politicians, and Know-Nothing candidates made the most of it by appealing to widely held ethnic and religious prejudices. But the order was not primarily a hate group; nor did ethnoreligious prejudice govern the voting decision of most lodge members. If it had, then native-born voters in states like New York and Pennsylvania, with even larger proportions of foreigners, would have been at least as enthusiastic about Know-Nothingism as were Bay Staters.

There were varying degrees of conviction among the rank and file with regard to the gravity of the Irish Catholic problem. And while there was little serious opposition to Native American extremism within the party, it is doubtful that most Know-Nothings swallowed their ideas whole. The Native American monomania— that Paddy and the Pope constituted a clear and present danger to the republic— exhibited a pathology more characteristic of a paranoid fringe group than of a mass following of a major political party. This was especially true in Massachusetts, where the foreign-born lacked political clout. What is clear from the record is that raw bigotry was but part—and not the major part—of the populist Zeitgeist that had stirred so many ordinary voters into abandoning their parties in favor of Know-Nothingism. The reverse is also true. The 1854 Know-Nothing voters would have had no compelling reason to desert a party that had posted the most far-reaching nativist record in the nation if proscription of the rights of the Irish Catholic minority were the *sine qua non* for their original commitment to "Sam."

The Free-Soil Americans, it is true, left the party in 1855 despite its having chalked up major gains for their cause. But what governed that decision was a preference for a viable, national antislavery Republican organization over an American party that, like the Whig party before it, had divided into an antislavery Northern wing and a proslavery Southern wing. Antislavery currents ran strongly in the Massachusetts political arena. For example, the Free-Soil vote from 1848 to 1853 ranged around one-quarter of the total, well above the free-state average. Nevertheless, the Know-Nothings proved by their landslide win in 1854 and their defeat of the Republicans in 1855 that they could carry the state without the antislavery vote.

The voter rebellion against the regular parties was national in scope and reflected a crisis of public confidence in a party system that was perceived as unresponsive or irrelevant. Nevertheless, the level of intensity of antiparty sentiment varied from state to state, depending on the mix of social, economic, and political conditions. If the crisis of confidence was particularly severe in Massachusetts, it was because the pace of social and economic change was greater there and her party system less sensitive to the disruptive impact of industrialization and urbanization on the lives of the ordinary people. On the surface, this seems to suggest that class divisions spawned by industrialization lay at the heart of that crisis in the Commonwealth.

Conflict between capital and labor was on the rise in the early 1850s. Symptomatic of this unrest was the spate of strikes staged in these years, the most significant of which closed down operations in the textile mills of Amesbury and Salisbury and other North Shore towns in 1852. The strike, which was provoked by petty tyranny on the part of management, was crushed, but at the cost of poisoned relations between the workers and the owners and a drop in worker support for the probusiness Whig party in local elections. The controversial municipal election in Lowell a year earlier, in which manufacturers and their agents threatened to fire workers who voted for the ten-hour ticket, had the same impact.

Both of these crises stemmed from the momentum building behind the drive for the ten-hour day. Alarmed by its inroads among their employees, the major industrialists of the state, in an effort to derail the drive, shortened the workday in their plants to eleven hours. The ploy proved futile. But so did labor's strategy of backing candidates of the regular parties who promised to vote for a ten-hour measure. Too often, office-seekers taking the pledge honored it only in the breach. Their duplicity exacerbated the distrust with which labor had always regarded politicians and parties and primed the working class for a shift into a new political party.

The phenomenon of the class-blind vote that had characterized electoral politics in the era of the second party system ended abruptly in Massachusetts in 1854. Dale Baum speaks of the slavery issue moving politics from below, but only one political party in antebellum Massachusetts mobilized the urban poor and working class behind it, and that was the American party. Even so, the idea of a class struggle also falls short as an explanation for "Sam's" phenomenal success in the Commonwealth. Support for the order was so broad-based among all classes, excepting the wealthiest, as to discount talk by Edward Everett and others who equated Know-Nothingism with a labor uprising. Workers and the urban poor were indeed among the party's most enthusiastic converts, but they were not alone. Joining them to form the people's party were a majority of farmers and fishermen, "wets" and "dries," evangelicals and dissenters, townsmen and city dwellers, and Whigs, Free-Soilers, and Democrats from all walks of life and all regions of the state.

"Sam" alone among the major antebellum parties sympathized with the plight of labor. But the true essence of Know-Nothingism was its faith in the ability of the people to rule themselves. Where the Jacksonians preached that doctrine, the Know-Nothings practiced it. Those who controlled the institutions of power in Massachusetts had more to fear from its brand of grass-roots politics than from a voter backlash against Kansas-Nebraska or from political proscription of an alien *lumpenproletariat*. Once unleashed, the order displayed an anti-establishment bent, crushing the party system and purging public office of political careerists. Major economic interests also came under attack. No longer connected to a friendly, responsive government, the state's corporations had to adjust to a legislature predisposed to curb the power and abuses of big business. Like the Coalition, "Sam" expanded regulation of the business order, and while it is too much to say that Know-Nothingism replaced the positive state with a regulatory one, it did succeed—even if only temporarily—in loosening the grip of the business elite on the state government. No previous legislature, when faced with the perennial choice between private and public interest, had come down so often on the public's side as did the 1855 General Court. Even on the occasion of its most notable failure to do so—the defeat of the ten-hour bill—the measure carried the lower house by a wide margin.

A grass-roots political movement that brought the second party system crashing down, purged professional politicians and lawyers (albeit temporarily) from public life, replaced the elitist commonwealth concept with egalitarian populism, challenged the privileged status of the state's vested interests, and wrote into law a new deal for the common people cannot accurately be characterized as one whose energies were consumed by an obsession with Irish Catholics, intemperance, and sectional concerns. Yet, this is precisely how its contemporaries and historians have portrayed it.

One-party government, it is true, produced bitter fruit as well—in particular, the Nunnery Committee and all of its attendant follies, which threw the nativist apologists into disarray and steeled the resolve of the Wilsonian Americans to desert the party and join their Free-Soil colleagues in building a fusion antislavery party. The bulk of the politically experienced American personnel being "rank free soil," their departure left the Gardnerites free to stamp their brand on the party. It did not matter. The party had already lost its *raison d'être*.

Like an iceberg whose great mass is concealed beneath the water, Know-Nothingism poses problems for those who would see it whole. Obstructing the view is the cloak of secrecy that enshrouded the order during its formative period. Thousands of men met weekly in hundreds of lodges throughout the state to chart the course for the new party; yet, other than a few sparse comments by a handful of members of a Worcester lodge, an occasional aside written into the minutes of an East Boston lodge, and some leaks that found their way into newspapers, no firsthand account of their discussions survives to tell the historian what inspired that generation of Bay Staters to abandon the established parties in favor of "Sam."

Edward Everett, in the aftermath of the 1854 election, had to admit to Millard Fillmore that he was unable to enlighten the former president on the results, since even "the wisest are in the dark."[8] A prominent Whig journalist, recounting his own experience, credited the uncanny ability of the Know-Nothings to "keep dark" on party matters for the impenetrable ignorance that enveloped the old political order on the eve of its own destruction:

> I went down to Boston . . . late in the autumn of 1854, without the slightest idea of the impending catastrophe and actually entertaining the belief that Emory Washburn, the Whig candidate for governor, would either be elected by the people or the Legislature. He lacked only about 50,000 votes of achieving that success. At this moment, more than a quarter of a century afterward, I blush for the simplicity with which I anticipated a widely different result. I knew there was a Know-Nothing organization; I was in the way of picking up whatever political intelligence that might be floating about; yet, associating every day with men who were in the Know-Nothing lodges, and, . . . having every incentive to be vigilant and wary, I no more suspected the impending results than I looked for an earthquake which would level the State House and reduce Faneuil Hall to a heap of ruins. I mention the fact to show how faithfully a political secret shared by thousands upon thousands—some 80,000 in all—was kept.[9]

Know-Nothing secrecy, however, only partly accounts for the surprise. More significantly, the fact that the fourth estate and party elite missed these developments exposes their lack of contact with the common people and the bankruptcy of a party system that in its last year of existence remained unaware of the depth of public resentment toward it or of the shifting tide of voters that presaged its doom.

Another impediment to a clearer view of the secret order is the upper-class bias that colors much of the primary source material. The common man seldom leaves a written record, and unfortunately, rank-and-file Know-Nothings did not prove an exception to this rule. Contemporary accounts of the movement, written almost entirely by the haute bourgeois, are negative in the extreme and either skirt or fail to mention the positive side of the Know-Nothing record. Worrisome matters pertinent to the lives of the common people, like the loss of social status, deteriorating working conditions, or the economic squeeze that was uprooting thousands of artisans, farmers, and seafarers, rate peripheral mention at best in the extant accounts. Farmers, mariners, and workers of that generation carried their opinions to the grave, but it is safe to assume that most of them had strong opinions about the unsettling changes taking place in their lives.

Students of the period have tried to rectify the distortion by acknowledging the existence of a sizable populist element within the American party and crediting it with important reforms. But on balance, historians like Speaker Eddy and his peers have concentrated on the tip of the Know-Nothing iceberg—the interest groups and party factions that pushed legislation pertaining to slavery, temperance, and Irish immigrants—to the neglect of its greater mass—the populist contingent that gave to the Know-Nothing movement its unique purpose and winning numbers and produced its greatest successes: the creation of an enormously popular people's party, the destruction of an elitist, unresponsive political order, and the massive breakthrough on the reform front.

The American party in Massachusetts was spawned and nourished in the matrix of a rapidly expanding industrial order. Its lodges served as greenhouses for the cultivation of republican ideas at a time when such ideas were widely disseminated and informed the political beliefs of the common people. Within the secret chambers of the lodges, a vision of a new political culture emerged, one in which a party drawn from the ranks of the ordinary people would topple the ruling elite from the citadels of power and return the government to the people. In a state where industrialization and sprawling, unregulated urban growth had made their greatest inroads, and where party leaders had turned a blind eye to the wrenching social and economic dislocations that had cropped up in their wake, that vision acted as a lightning rod, drawing into the lodges a majority of native-born voters who had lost faith in their own parties and who shared a belief that acting in concert they could regain control of their government and harness it to the task of responding to their needs and aspirations.

As a social movement, Know-Nothingism was rooted in the populist tradition of American politics. It had enjoyed in its gestative stage the advantage of targeting an elitist party system more attuned to special interests than to the great multiplicity of interests that exist in a complex, pluralistic, industrial society. "Sam" was able, through the implementation of participatory democracy in the local lodges, to tap neighborhood sentiment and develop a sensitive relationship between the order and the grass roots. Even the American party's virulent nativism reflected the bond between party and people. Populist upheavals, as Richard Hofstadter and other historians have pointed out, commonly juxtapose the illiberal prejudices of the ordinary people with their progressive impulses. [10]

As a political movement, Know-Nothingism was an anomaly: an antiparty party. The care taken to select political amateurs for candidates reflected the populist vision of Know-Nothingism as more a people's movement than a political party. But if the spirit that imbued the politics of "Sam" was anti-establishment and antipartisan, it was not antipolitical. Quite the contrary, the party's dark-lantern brand of politics "to choose officers to govern our way" fired the hopes of a people longing for new governmental approaches to old social and economic problems. Its policy of excluding political careerists from its lodges and its promise to crush out the "corrupt" old parties and turn the state government over to the people so that they themselves might rectify the problems and abuses that the older parties had allowed to fester proved an irresistible lure to a people steeped in a belief in the virtues of republicanism. No issue or set of issues could match so transcendent an appeal. It drew the restive majority into its lodges and armed the party with mass support; and it did so without alarming either the party elites or party press, which continued to rattle on about equality of opportunity, upward mobility, and the dignity of labor.

Know-Nothingism, as shaped within the lodge network, was to be the ultimate expression of republicanism. To a generation that had lost faith in the old order because that order had failed the ultimate test of democratic politics—the successful resolution of conflicting claims—the American party's proposed remedy— a government purged of elites and controlled by the common people—had produced the greatest landslide win in the state since the advent of party politics; and its coming closer than any other party to the realization of that republican ideal constitutes its greatest achievement, a point that some of the less hostile newspapers alluded to on election day 1854. Even the establishment press conceded that the people had spoken, albeit, it was said, on behalf of ethnocultural prejudices.

Shortly after the American party took office, however, a cloak of silence descended on the subject of a people's government. Saying nothing can serve important ends in public life. In the 1840s, for example, the older parties had systematically quarantined volatile issues like slavery, prohibition, and the ten-hour law from the political arena. In a more open (and self-defeating) fashion, the American national council publicly proclaimed that the national interest demanded silence on the slavery question. Similarly, avoiding public discussion of grass-roots populism benefited powerful interests inside as well as outside the American party.

"Sam" had come to power in Massachusetts promising government of, by, and for the people. The secret order's antiparty, antipolitician posture, however, was compromised the moment it took control of the statehouse. Under any political system, power attracts the politically skillful. Running a government effectively takes administrative and legislative talents and experienced leadership, qualities that were in short supply among the ordinary citizens who had flocked into the lodges. Inevitably, a new generation of politicians, businessmen, and lawyers infiltrated the party and shouldered aside the lodge amateurs in the competition to fill the command posts left vacant by the Know-Nothing purge of the old party war horses.

Henry J. Gardner, taking advantage of the confusion amidst the jostling for place, rapidly established control over the executive branch and began expanding his influence into the General Court by means of patronage appointments. There he encountered a rival expansionary force—the Free-Soil Americans. Possessed of the largest and most cohesive contingent of experienced personnel in the legislature, they stood between the chief magistrate and his goal of control of the state government. Both sides wanted power, the governor for his personal ends, the Free-Soil Americans to advance the antislavery cause. Neither side had a vested interest in prolonging the populist government that the Know-Nothing uprising had produced. Quite the contrary, people power, because it diverted the business of government from territorial concerns and because it represented the antithesis of the kind of machine politics that the governor and his cronies were putting into practice, was expendable. In the ensuing power struggle, the two sides drew the battle lines around the issue triad. Governor Gardner staked out the strongest claim to the nativist vote; the Free-Soil Americans co-opted the antislavery issue; and both courted the Maine Law men. Whether by accident or by design, their limiting the public agenda to these three issues excluded the kind of examination of the nature and proper functions of republican government undertaken by the 1853 constitutional convention and by the secret order during its formative period.

The gradual displacement of neighborhood amateurs from the decision-making process went unremarked by the party's enemies, for all of their patronizing references to the collective power and wisdom of the people. Instead they riveted their attention on the same circumscribed agenda as did the warring Know-Nothing factions. Perhaps the failure of the older parties to unearth and discuss the ultimate source of Know-Nothing strength was unintentional. Perhaps Whig and Democratic leaders really meant it when they blamed ethnocultural resentments for having drained their parties of their rank and file. Confusing the lesser part of the Know-Nothing phenomenon (nativism) for the greater (populism) remains common practice. Henry J. Gardner's strategy of concentrating almost exclusively on the Irish Catholic question, for example, suggests that he, too, may have misread the nature and intent of the transcendent force that had catapulted him into the governor's chair. But the closed-mouth reaction of party professionals and their lawyer and journalist auxiliaries to a political movement aimed at radically reforming the political and economic systems suggests that many, if not all, were silent not out of ignorance but out of fear. Nativism did not threaten entrenched interests; populism did.

William Hickling Prescott had greeted the dawn of the Know-Nothing era with the bitter words of one who spoke for the old order and who grasped neither the origins nor the significance of the new. Know-Nothingism, he told fellow historian George Bancroft in the wake of the 1854 election, was "but a rope of sand . . . made up of discordancies, without any settled principles to hold them together."[11] Within months, Prescott's words took on a significance that they lacked when he wrote them. The impact of the iron law of oligarchy in the intervening period had altered the fundamental nature of the American party. Its corrosive inroads into the lodge apparatus ate away at the vital organizational base of the order and caused the gradual shutdown of the lines of communication between lodge members and party leaders. Sealing off the opportunities for mass participation in important party matters, in turn, drained the order of its vitality. Signs of deterioration were already visible in the early weeks of the 1855 legislative session as the Wilsonians and Gardnerites struggled for control. As the order became less of a people's party and more a vehicle for the advancement of ambitious politicians and selective causes, disillusionment spread among the rank and file. This was evidenced in the 1855 municipal elections when city voters, ignoring the party's manifold accomplishments, evicted Know-Nothing incumbents from city halls all over the state.

Dark-lantern politics and the lodge network had proved at least as conducive to manipulation and rigged results as had the committee rooms, secret caucuses, and stacked conventions of the old political order that the voters had rebelled against in 1854. The politicians, in taking control of the party apparatus, however, did so at the cost of alienating the rank and file. Newspaper reports of occasional lodge closings during 1855 hinted that all was not well. The "more active and clever portion" of the party picked up on the downward trend and began to cast about for a sounder organization.[12] That proved to be the Republican party, which had already replaced "Sam" as the chief adversary of the Democracy in the national arena. Governor Gardner thought to appease party members and stanch the hemorrhage in the ranks by equating Know-Nothingism with nativism, Unionism, and fiscal conservatism. It was a desperate strategy doomed to fail, not because it omitted slavery, but because Gardner himself had already mortally wounded the order when he converted it from a people's party into a political machine.

In the beginning, a meteoric, grass-roots rebellion against status quo government and self-serving, opportunistic politicians, Know-Nothingism ended in the clutches of a reactionary Brahmin Whig. Charles Sumner may have sensed the irony of the party's fate when he scoffed: "You have no real principles on which you stand. You are nothing but a party of Gardnerites."[13] Sumner's words echoed Prescott's earlier assessment, but where Prescott's judgment was premature, Sumner's, delivered just three years later, was an epitaph.

Notes

Introduction

1. William E. Gienapp, *Origins of the Republican Party, 1852–1856* (New York, 1987), 7–8; Michael F. Holt, *The Political Crisis of the 1850s* (New York, 1978), 14–16.

2. The pioneer historian of Know-Nothingism in Massachusetts, George H. Haynes, attributed the party's success solely to its exploitation of rampant anti-immigrant and anti-Catholic sentiments. Other early historians of the movement like Ray Allen Billington, while agreeing that bigotry was the leitmotif of Know-Nothingism, pinpointed anti-Catholicism as the mainspring of the new party, since it provided what the other parties lacked: a bond between the party and the electorate. William G. Bean was the first historian to acknowledge that the American party was the product of positive forces as well as negative ones, pointing out that the party championed antislavery and Locofoco reforms as well as nativism. Indeed, Oscar Handlin concluded that reform rather than nativism was the hallmark of the American party. Like Bean, Handlin saw Know-Nothingism as a bridge over which the Coalitionists marched into the Republican party. Irish voters, he asserted, by tipping the scales against constitutional reform triggered a backlash among the Coalitionists who turned first to the American party and later to the Republican party. See George H. Haynes, "A Chapter from the Local History of Knownothingism," *New England Magazine* 15 (September 1896): 82–96; Haynes, "The Causes of Know-Nothing Success in Massachusetts," *American Historical Review* 3 (October 1897 to July 1898): 67–82; Ray Allen Billington, *The Protestant Crusade, 1800–1860*, rev. ed. (Chicago, 1964), 385–87; William G. Bean, "Party Transformation in Massachusetts with Special Reference to the Antecedents of Republicanism, 1848–1860" (Ph.D. diss., Harvard University, 1922), chaps. 8–10. Oscar Handlin, *Boston's Immigrants: A Study in Acculturation*, rev. ed. (Cambridge, Mass., 1959), 195–204.

3. Kevin Sweeney, "Rum, Romanism, Representation, and Reform; Coalition Politics in Massachusetts, 1847–1853," *Civil War History* 22 (June 1976): 36; Dale Baum, *The Civil War Party System: The Case of Massachusetts, 1848–1876* (Chapel Hill, N.C., 1984), 29–30, 33.

4. Baum, *Civil War Party System*, 6–7, 26–43.

5. Gienapp, *Origins of the Republican Party*, 92–100, 419–23.

6. Ronald P. Formisano, *The Transformation of Political Culture: Massachusetts Parties, 1790s–1840s* (New York, 1983), 330–36.

7. Michael F. Holt, "The Politics of Impatience: The Origins of Know-Nothingism," *Journal of American History* 60 (September 1973): 324–25.

8. Gienapp, *Origins of the Republican Party*, chap. 13.

9. Ibid., 419–20, n. 27.

Chapter One

1. Oliver Warner, *Statistical Information Relating to Certain Branches of Industry in Massachusetts for the Year Ending May 1, 1865* (Boston, 1865), xxv; Myron Lawrence, "Address of the Chairman of the Valuation Committee," Massachusetts, General Court, *Ms. Journal of the Valuation Committee of Massachusetts, 1850* (State Archives), 132–33; Gov. Henry J. Gardner, "Inaugural Address of 1857," Mass., *Acts and Resolves Passed by the General Court in 1857* (Boston, 1857), 714; Paul Goodman, "The Politics of Industrialism Massachusetts, 1830–1870," in Richard L. Bushman et al. (eds.), *Uprooted Americans: Essays to Honor Oscar Handlin* (Boston, 1979), 164; Francis DeWitt, *Statistical Information Relating to Certain Branches of Industry in Massachusetts for the Year Ending June 1, 1855* (Boston, 1855), xiii–xiv, 642–43. Ranked third behind New York and Pennsylvania in total value of industrial production and second only to New York in the number of hands employed in manufacturing, Massachusetts, with a much smaller population than either, topped the nation as the most thoroughly industrialized state. See J. D. B. DeBow, *Statistical View of the United States . . . Being a Compendium of the Seventh Census* (Washington, D.C., 1854), 179, and Carroll D. Wright, *The Industrial Evolution of the United States* (reissued New York, 1967), 139.

2. Mass., *Official Report of the Debates and Proceedings in the State Convention, 1853*, 3 vols. (Boston, 1853), 3:175–76; DeBow, *Compendium of the Seventh Census*, 180; Wright, *Industrial Evolution*, 171; Albert Bushnell Hard (ed.), *Commonwealth History of Massachusetts*, 5 vols. (New York, 1927–1928), 4:403, 408, 412–16; 5:430; Douglass C. North, *The Economic Growth of the United States, 1790–1860* (New York, 1966), 161–64; Sarah S. Whittelsey, "Massachusetts Labor Legislation: An Historical Study," *Annals of the American Academy of Political and Social Science*, (Philadelphia, 1901), 17:53; Albert Fishlow, *American Railroads and the Transformation of the Ante-Bellum Economy* (Cambridge, Mass., 1965), 251, 257; Victor S. Clark, *History of Manufactures in the United States*, 3 vols. (New York, 1929), 1:453, 470, 474, 479, 515–16, 518, 520, 532, 545, 567, 570, 574; Caroline Ware, *Early New England Cotton Manufactures* (New York, 1966), 224–44; George R. Taylor, *The Transportation Revolution, 1815–1860* (New York, 1951), 283–84.

3. Thomas Cochran, *The Frontiers of Change: Early Industrialism in America* (New York, 1981), 10; Fishlow, *American Railroads*, 7–8, 237; Edward C. Kirkland, *Men, Cities, and Transportation: A Study in New England History, 1820–1900* (Cambridge, Mass., 1948), 92, 284–85; Mass., *State Convention* 3:12; Gov. John W. Davis, "Inaugural Address of 1842," Mass., *Acts and Resolves, 1842* (Boston, 1842), 612; Gov. George N. Briggs, "Inaugural Address of 1844," Mass., *Acts and Resolves, 1844* (Boston, 1844), 361–62; *Lowell Weekly Journal and Courier*, July 25, 1851; *Boston Daily Advertiser*, Sept. 18, 1851, and Feb. 20, 1856; Lawrence, "Valuation Committee," 133–34.

4. Glyndon G. Van Deusen, "Major Party Thought and Theory," in Edward Pessen (ed.), *New Perspectives on Jacksonian Parties and Politics* (Boston, 1969), 146; Hart, *Commonwealth History* 5:429; Samuel Eliot Morison, *The Maritime History of Massachusetts, 1783–1860* (Boston, 1921), 213; Taylor, *Transportation Revolution*, 8, 224; Mass., *State Convention* 2:337; 3:175; *Boston Daily Advertiser*, Aug. 31, 1855.

5. Oliver Warner, *Abstract of the Census of Massachusetts, 1865: With Remarks on Same, and Supplementary Tables* (Boston, 1867), 275; Mass., *State Convention* 1:662, 948; 2:411, 417–18; Mrs. William S. Robinson (ed.), *"Warrington" Pen-Portraits* (Boston, 1877), 419; Arthur B. Darling, *Political Changes in Massachusetts, 1824–1848* (reissued Cos Cob, Conn., 1968), 8–9, 183; Cochran, *Frontiers of Change*, 110; Formisano, *Transformation of Political Culture*, 121, 172–78, 263, 283, 314–15; Charles E. Persons, "The Early History of Factory Legislation in Massachusetts from 1825 to the Passage of the Ten-Hour Law in 1875," in Susan M. Kingsbury (ed.), *Labor Laws and Their Enforcement with Special Reference to Massachusetts* (reissued New York, 1971), 22; William Gray, *Argument of Hon. William Gray on Petitions for a Ten-Hour Law before the Committee on Labor* (Boston, 1873), 22; Daniel Howe, *The Political Culture of the American Whigs* (Chicago, 1979), 182; Goodman, "Politics of Industrialism," 180.

6. Mass., *State Convention* 1:583–84.

7. Gov. John H. Clifford, "Inaugural Address of 1853," Mass., *Acts and Resolves, 1853* (Boston, 1853), 695; Darling, *Political Changes in Massachusetts*, 21–2; Glyndon G. Van Deusen, "Some Aspects of Whig Thought and Theory in the Jacksonian Period," *American Historical Review* 43 (Jan. 1958): 308; Paul Faler, "Cultural Aspects of the Industrial Revolution: Lynn, Massachusetts, Shoemakers and Industrial Morality, 1826–1860," *Labor History* 15 (Summer 1974): 368; Carl Siracusa, *A Mechanical People: Perceptions of the Industrial Order in Massachusetts, 1815–1880* (Middletown, Conn., 1979), 13, 87–88; Ray Ginger, "Labor in a Massachusetts Cotton Mill, 1853–60," *Business History Review* 28 (March 1954): 67–68.

8. Gov. John W. Davis, "Inaugural Address of 1841," Mass., *Acts and Resolves, 1841* (Boston, 1841), 467; Van Deusen, "Whig Thought and Theory," 308, 321; Howe, *American Whigs*, 101–02, 217. For an excellent analysis of the relationship between the commonwealth ethos and government policy, see Oscar Handlin and Mary Flug Handlin, *Commonwealth, A Study of the Role of Government in the Economy: Massachusetts, 1774–1861* (Cambridge, Mass., 1969).

9. *Springfield Republican*, Nov. 1, 1849; *Boston Daily Journal*, Aug. 7, 1854; *Boston Daily Advertiser*, Oct. 11, 1853, and Aug. 15, 1855; Lawrence, "Valuation Committee," 133–34; Davis, "Inaugural Address of 1841," 465–68; Davis, "Inaugural Address of 1842," 606–07; Clifford, "Inaugural Address of 1853," 695–97.

10. Handlin and Handlin, *Commonwealth*, 53; Van Deusen, "Major Party Thought and Theory," 142; Goodman, "Politics of Industrialism" 270–71; *Boston Daily Advertiser*, Oct. 11, 1853; *Boston Daily Journal*, Nov. 9, 1853; Lawrence, "Valuation Committee," 133–34; Mass., *State Convention* 3:175; Clifford, "Inaugural Address of 1853," 695–96.

11. Mass., *State Convention* 1:882.

12. George S. Boutwell, *Reminiscences of Sixty Years in Public Affairs*, 2 vols. (New York, 1902), 1:71; Charles T. Congdon, *Reminiscences of a Journalist* (Boston, 1880), 70; George F. Hoar, *Autobiography of Seventy Years*, 2 vols. (New York, 1903), 1:133; Lynn L. Marshall, "Opposing Democratic and Whig Concepts of Party Organization," in Pessen (ed.), *New Perspectives on Jacksonian Parties and Politics*, 57–58; Van Deusen, "Major Party Thought and Theory," 143–44; M. J. Heale, *The Making of American Politics, 1750–1850* (New York, 1977), 64, 185, 188–89.

13. *Boston Daily Advertiser*, Oct. 11, 1853, Nov. 4 and 11, 1854, and Aug. 31, 1855; *Boston Daily Journal*, Nov. 2, 1853, and Aug. 7, 1854; Mass., *State Convention* 1:882; Clifford, "Inaugural Address of 1853," 695–97; Gov. Emory Washburn, "Inaugural

Address of 1854," Mass., *Acts and Resolves, 1854* (Boston, 1854), 458; Lawrence, "Valuation Committee," 132–35.

14. Mass., *State Convention* 1:902–03; 2:531–33, 703–06; George S. Boutwell, *Address of the Hon. George S. Boutwell to the People of Berlin upon the Provisions of the New Constitution, October 3, 1853* (Boston, 1853), 9; Robinson, *"Warrington" Pen-Portraits*, 122; Goodman, "Politics of Industrialism," 180.

15. Francis W. Bird, *Address of Hon. F. W. Bird to His Constituents upon the Provision of the New Constitution* (Boston, 1853), 10; *Boston Daily Journal*, Nov. 6, 1849; *South Boston Gazette*, Nov. 11, 1854; *Worcester Palladium*, Nov. 22, 1854; David Donald, *Charles Sumner and the Coming of the Civil War* (New York, 1961), 147.

16. Hoar, *Autobiography* 1:133; Briggs, "Inaugural Address of 1844," 360–61; Gov. George N. Briggs, "Inaugural Address of 1850," Mass., *Acts and Resolves, 1850* (Boston, 1850), 534–37; DeBow, *Compendium of the Seventh Census*, 180; Handlin and Handlin, *Commonwealth*, 167, 180; *City Advertiser* (Charlestown), April 23 and May 7, 1856; *Lawrence Courier*, June 24, 1853; *Boston Daily Journal*, Nov. 6, 1849, and Nov. 9, 1853; *Yarmouth Register*, Sept. 20, 1849; Lawrence, "Valuation Committee," 132–35.

17. Hoar, *Autobiography* 1:133; Heale, *Making of American Politics*, 188; Boutwell, *Address to the People of Berlin*, 9; Edward Pessen, "Did Labor Support Jackson? The Boston Story," *Political Science Quarterly*, 44 (June 1949): 267; Goodman, "Politics of Industrialism," 165–66, 170; Howe, *American Whigs*, 300; *Yarmouth Register*, Sept. 20, 1849; *Massachusetts Spy*, Sept. 8, 1852; *Boston Daily Journal*, Nov. 2, 1853; *Springfield Daily Republican*, July 11, 1853.

18. Mass., *State Convention* 1:948; Robert Kelly, *The Cultural Pattern in American Politics: The First Century* (New York, 1979), 20–22, 144; Jonathan Prude, *The Coming of Industrial Order: Town and Factory Life in Rural Massachusetts, 1810–1860* (Cambridge, Mass., 1983), xii–xiii, 19, 33, 45.

19. Oliver Warner, *Abstract of the Census of Massachusetts, 1860, from the Eighth U.S. Census, with Remarks on the Same* (Boston, 1863), 286, 293–94, 298–99; DeWitt, *Industry in Massachusetts*, xiii–xiv, 642–43; Gardner, "Inaugural Address of 1857," 714; North, *Economic Growth*, 258; C. Ware, *Cotton Manufactures*, 246. In 1850, industrial workers made up 44 percent of the state's total work force. The proportion of the population employed in manufacturing in New England was one to eight; in the middle states, the proportion was one to fifteen; in the West, it was one to forty-eight; and in the South, one to eighty. See Siracusa, *Mechanical People*, 33–38; Clark, *History of Manufactures* 1:580.

20. *Boston Daily Journal*, Nov. 15, 1850; Benjamin F. Butler, *Butler's Book: A Review of His Legal, Political, and Military Career* (Boston, 1892), 89–91; Wright, *Industrial Evolution*, 133–34; O. Handlin, *Boston's Immigrants*, 74–79; Howe, *American Whigs*, 102–04; Siracusa, *Mechanical People*, 4–9, 36–39; Prude, *Industrial Order*, 110–13, 128–31, 201–02.

21. Wright, *Industrial Evolution*, 201–04, 219; Gov. George S. Boutwell, "Inaugural Address of 1851," Mass., *Acts and Resolves, 1851* (Boston, 1851), 899–900; *The Worcester Palladium*, April 27, 1853; *South Boston Gazette*, April 28, 1855; Butler, *Butler's Book*, 86–91; Handlin and Handlin, *Commonwealth*, 189–92; Clark, *History of Manufactures* 1:375–78; Formisano, *Transformation of Political Culture*, 285; Robert H. Wiebe, *The Opening of American Society, from the Adoption of the Constitution to the Eve of Dissension* (New York, 1984), 322–35.

22. Prude, *Industrial Order*, chap. 4; Siracusa, *Mechanical People*, 108–11; DeBow, *Compendium of the Seventh Census*, 129; Nathaniel B. Shurtleff, *Abstract of the*

Census . . . of Massachusetts Taken . . . the First Day of June, 1855 (Boston, 1857), 199. The number of Bay Staters emigrating during the 1850s exceeded that of immigrants entering the state. See Warner, *Census of Massachusetts, 1865,* 292–94.

23. Taylor, *Transportation Revolution,* 266–67; Norman Ware, *Industrial Worker, 1840–1860,* rev. ed. (Chicago, 1964), 71–78; Handlin and Handlin, *Commonwealth,* 189–91; Goodman, "Politics of Industrialism," 166–67.

24. Mass., *State Convention* 2:451.

25. Lemuel Shattuck, *Report to the Committee Appointed to Obtain the Census of Boston for the Year 1845* (Boston, 1846), 37; DeBow, *Compendium of the Seventh Census,* 123; Shurtleff, *Census of Massachusetts, 1855,* 132, 233, 236; Josiah Curtis, *Report of the Joint Special Committee of the Census of Boston, May, 1855* (Boston, 1856), 9; DeWitt, *Industry in Massachusetts,* 643; Warner, *Abstract of the Census, 1860,* 293–94, 299; Warner, *Abstract of the Census, 1865,* 292; William G. Bean, "Puritan Versus Celt, 1850–1860," *New England Quarterly* 7 (March 1939): 71.

26. Laura E. Richards (ed.), *Letters and Journals of Samuel Gridley Howe,* 2 vols. (Boston, 1909), 2:280; Charles Francis Adams, Diary, April 10, 1856, Adams Family Papers, Massachusetts Historical Society (hereafter cited as MHS); DeBow, *Compendium of the Seventh Census,* 163–65; Warner, *Census of Massachusetts, 1860,* 335, 360–61; John P. Sanderson, *Republican Landmarks—The Views and Opinions of American Statesmen on Foreign Immigration* (Philadelphia, 1856), 204; Constance M. Green, *Holyoke, Massachusetts: A Case Study of the Industrial Revolution in America* (New Haven, 1939), 37–91; Arthur L. Eno, Jr. (ed.), *Cotton Was King: A History of Lowell, Massachusetts* (Lowell, Mass., 1976), 98–99; O. Handlin, *Boston's Immigrants,* 54–87, 100, 117–22, 250–53; Hart, *Commonwealth History* 4:157; Hoar, *Autobiography* 2:280–81; *Worcester Palladium,* June 28 and Aug. 30, 1854.

27. Persons, "Factory Legislation," 56–58; C. Ware, *Cotton Manufactures,* 3, 11, 230–32; Green, *Holyoke,* 30–31; N. Ware, *Industrial Worker,* 117, 149–53; Eno, *Cotton Was King,* 94, 110–23; Siracusa, *Mechanical People,* 169, 174–75; Taylor, *Transportation Revolution,* 282–87, 292–300; *Barnstable Patriot,* March 27, 1855; O. Handlin, *Boston's Immigrants,* 64, 70, 83, 253; Faler, "Cultural Aspects," 374; Bean, "Party Transformation in Massachusetts," 209.

28. Jack Larkin, "The View from New England: Notes on Everyday Life in Rural America to 1850," *American Quarterly* 34 (1982): 255–56; Mass., *State Convention* 1:948; 3:4; U.S., *Compendium of the Enumeration of the United States . . . from the Returns of the Sixth Census, 1840* (Washington, D.C., 1841), 107–8; DeBow, *Compendium of the Seventh Census,* 170–74; Shurtleff, *Census of Massachusetts, 1855,* 244; Joseph G. Kennedy, *Agriculture of the United States in 1860; Compiled from the Original Returns of the Eighth Census* (Washington, D.C., 1864), 74–75; Lester Earl Klimm, *The Relation Between Certain Population Changes and the Physical Environment in Hampden, Hampshire, and Franklin Counties, Massachusetts, 1790–1925* (Philadelphia, 1933), iii, 9, 45, 48, 68, 71, 107; Percy Bidwell, "The Agricultural Revolution in New England," *American Historical Association* 26 (1921): 683, 688–90; The Western Railroad, extending from Worcester to Albany, was completed in 1841. Three years later, it hauled three hundred thousand barrels of western flour into New England. Bay State farmers were especially hard pressed by the competition. Wheat production in the state plummeted from 101,178 bushels in 1840 to 28,487 bushels in 1850. In the same decade, the number of sheep dropped from 343,390 to 179,537. See *Boston Daily Journal,* Nov. 15, 1850; Hart, *Commonwealth History* 4:427, 430.

29. Bidwell, "The Agricultural Revolution," 693–96; 700–702; Handlin

and Handlin, *Commonwealth*, 187–214. See DeBow, *Compendium of the Seventh Census*, 128–29; Shurtleff, *Census of Massachusetts, 1855*, 242–43.

30. Blanche Evans Hazard, *The Organization of the Boot and Shoe Industry in Massachusetts Before 1875* (Cambridge, Mass., 1921), vii, 112–13, 147; Wright, *Industrial Evolution*, 340–41; Morison, *Maritime History*, 303; Foster Rhea Dulles, *Labor in America* (New York, 1960), 77; Clark, *History of Manufactures* 1:444; Siracusa, *Mechanical People*, 19–20, 117; Alan Dawley, *Class and Community: the Industrial Revolution in Lynn* (Cambridge, Mass., 1976), 29, 55, 57–58, 77.

31. Mass., *State Convention* 2:308; Morison, *Maritime History*, 311, 352–57; *The Barnstable Patriot*, March 21, 1854, and Jan. 6, 1857; *Worcester Palladium*, July 13, 1853.

32. DeBow, *Compendium of the Seventh Census*, xxxiii; DeWitt, *Industry in Massachusetts*, xiii–xiv; Shurtleff, *Census of Massachusetts, 1855*, 199, 231–33; Warner, *Census of Massachusetts, 1860*, 286, 289, 294–95, 335; Warner, *Census of Massachusetts, 1865*, 292–94; Taylor, *Transportation Revolution*, 246; North, *Economic Growth*, 258; Robert F. Dalzell, Jr., "The Rise of the Waltham-Lowell System and Some Thoughts on the Political Economy of Modernization in Ante-Bellum Massachusetts," in Donald Fleming and Bernard Bailyn (eds.), *Perspectives in American History* (Cambridge, Mass., 1975), 229–30.

33. Howe, *American Whigs*, 35–37; Formisano, *Transformation of Political Culture*, 181, 271; Van Deusen, "Major Party Thought and Theory," 151–52; Heale, *Making of American Politics*, 185, 187; Handlin and Handlin, *Commonwealth*, 189–94, 205–6; Hoar, *Autobiography* 1:133–34; Dalzell, "Some Thoughts on Political Economy," 266–68; Ronald G. Walters, *American Reformers* (New York, 1978), 8–9, 16–17, 210.

34. Mass., *State Convention* 1:235, 565, 590; 2:236–37, 242–43, 713, 782–91; 3:53, 192, 197–98, 407–8, 485; N. Ware, *Industrial Worker*, 125, 203, 208; Dulles, *Labor in America*, 45, 49–50, 63; Joseph G. Rayback, *A History of American Labor* (New York, 1959), 59, 65–67, 72, 89–92, 96–97; Douglas T. Miller, *Jacksonian Aristocracy: Class and Democracy in New York, 1830–1860* (New York, 1967), 43–44; Charles Sellers (ed.), *Andrew Jackson: A Profile* (New York, 1971), 147–48, 191–92; Edward Pessen, *Most Uncommon Jacksonians, The Radical Leaders of the Early Labor Movement* (Albany, 1967), 40–41; Edwin T. Randall, "Imprisonment for Debt in America: Fact and Fiction," *Mississippi Valley Historical Review* 39 (June 1952–March 1953): 102.

35. *Springfield Republican*, Nov. 1, 1849; Mass., *State Convention* 2:20–1, 286, 668; 3:53–54, 319; Henry Wilson, *Address Delivered by Hon. Henry Wilson to His Constituents Explanatory of the Proposed Constitutional Amendments* (n.p., n.d.), 15; Bird, *Address of Hon. F. W. Bird*, 4–12; Boutwell, *Address to the People of Berlin*, 14; Goodman, "Politics of Industrialism," 189.

36. George S. Boutwell, "State Constitutional Convention of 1853," *Groton Historical Series*, 4 (n.d.): 409; Bird, *Address of Hon. F. W. Bird*, 4–12; *Gazette* (Dedham), Nov. 13, 1852; *South Boston Gazette*, Nov. 4, 1852; Hart, *Commonwealth History* 3:443–44; Samuel Shapiro, "The Conservative Dilemma: The Massachusetts Constitutional Convention of 1853," *New England Quarterly* 33 (June 1960): 208–9.

37. Butler, *Butler's Book*, 89–91, 99; Darling, *Political Changes in Massachusetts*, 167–71; *Boston Daily Journal*, Nov. 8, 1850; *Worcester Palladium*, Feb. 9 and March 9, 1853; Gov. Marcus Morton, "Inaugural Address of 1840," Mass., *Acts and Resolves, 1840* (Boston, 1840), 311; Mass., *State Convention* 1:235, 565–69, 590, 639–40; 2:317, 333; 3:192. The Democrats repealed the "sunset" law in 1843.

38. Marcus Morton to J. Harrington, Feb. 13, 1854, Marcus Morton Papers, MHS.

39. Mass., *State Convention* 1:881–82.

40. Formisano, *Transformation of Political Culture*, 222–26; Edward Pessen, "The Workingmen's Movement of the Jacksonian Era," *Mississippi Historical Valley Review*, 43 (Dec. 1956): 432; Darling, *Political Changes in Massachusetts*, 98–99; Wright, *Industrial Evolution*, 238; Persons, "Factory Legislation," 10–11.

41. *South Boston Gazette*, April 28, 1855; Persons, "Factory Legislation," 4–8, 23; Wright, *Industrial Evolution*, 242; Gray, *Hon. William Gray on Petitions for a Ten-Hour Law*, 4, 9, 22; Butler, *Butler's Book*, 89–91; N. Ware, *Industrial Worker*, 4–9, 208–9; Pessen, "Workingmen's Movement," 288–93; *Lawrence Courier*, Feb. 7, 1852; Faler, "Cultural Aspects," 389.

42. *Daily Herald* (Newburyport), Feb. 24, 1855; Dulles, *Labor in America*, 63, 84, 86; Rayback, *History of American Labor*, 25, 59, 77, 88, 90–92, 96–97; N. Ware, *Industrial Worker*, 125–26, 144, 202–3; Persons, "Factory Legislation," 54, 76–78; William Gray, *Labor: The Ten-Hour System* (n.p., 1871), 629. The ten-hour day was in force in the building trades in New York City before 1820. See Sean Wilentz, *Chants Democratic: New York City and the Rise of the American Working Class, 1788–1850* (New York, 1984), 191, n. 40, 192; Walters, *American Reformers*, 188.

43. Siracusa, *Mechanical People*, 58–60, 71–74, 89–90, 106–12.

44. Ibid., 159–62, 185, 197–200; Wright, *Industrial Evolution*, 231–36; 239–42; Charles Cowley, *Ten-Hour Law: Argument Delivered before the Joint Special Committee of the Massachusetts Legislature, upon the Hours of Labor, in Behalf of the Petitioners for a Ten-Hour Law, March 22d, 1871* (Lowell, Mass., 1871), 1–2; *Massachusetts Spy*, June 1, 1853; N. Ware, *Industrial Worker*, 125–56; Dulles, *Labor in America*, 77, 84.

45. Formisano, *Transformation of Political Culture*, 224, 229–30; Dawley, *Industrial Revolution in Lynn*, 8–9, 56, 68–70, 96; Wilentz, *Chants Democratic*, 219–20, 233, n. 15, 235, 338, 395; Walters, *American Reformers*, 110–11; Goodman, "Politics of Industrialism," 166–67.

46. N. Ware, *Industrial Worker*, 106–17, 150–51; Eno, *Cotton Was King*, 121–22; Howe, *American Whigs*, 103; *Springfield Republican*, Aug. 19, 1853; Walters, *American Reformers*, 110, 173.

47. C. Ware, *Cotton Manufactures*, chap. 9; John T. Cumbler, "Labor Capital, and Community: The Struggle for Power," *Labor History* 15 (Summer 1974): 397–402; Dawley, *Industrial Revolution in Lynn*, 2–9, 58, 68; Wilentz, *Chants Democratic*, 128–29; Prude, *Industrial Order*, 98, 118–36, 143.

48. Holt, *Political Crisis of the 1850s*, 31–33; Kelly, *Cultural Pattern in American Politics*, 272–76; Edward Pessen, *Jacksonian America*, rev. ed. (Homewood, Ill., 1978), 278, 293, 296; Wright, *Industrial Evolution*, 237; *Worcester Palladium*, Jan. 26, March 23, April 27, and Oct. 19, 1853; *Barnstable Patriot*, Oct. 28, 1851; *Bunker Hill Aurora*, Feb. 26, 1848; *South Boston Gazette*, March 17, 1853; *City Advertiser* (Charlestown), May 18, 1853; Morton, "Inaugural Address of 1840," 293, 296–301; Gov. Marcus Morton, "Inaugural Address of 1843," Mass., *Acts and Resolves, 1843* (Boston, 1843), 128; Mass., *State Convention* 3:327, 329.

49. Mass., *State Convention* 2:418.

50. Morton, "Inaugural Address of 1840," 298–302, 310–12; Morton, "Inaugural Address of 1843," 118–24, 128.

51. Morton, "Inaugural Address of 1840," 301; Morton, "Inaugural Address of 1843," 123; Carl N. Degler, "The Less Than Radical Locofocos," in Pessen (ed.), *New Perspectives on Jacksonian Parties and Politics*, 229; Goodman, "Politics of Industrialism," 176; Darling, *Political Changes in Massachusetts*, 255–57.

52. Van Deusen, "Major Party Thought and Theory," 142; Pessen, *Jacksonian America*, chap. 10; Formisano, *Transformation of Political Culture*, 259; Siracusa, *Mechanical People*, 59–60; Wilentz, *Chants Democratic*, 213–14.

53. Wilentz, *Chants Democratic*, 7, 174–75; Joseph Dorfman, "The Jackson Wage-Earner Thesis," *American Historical Review* 54 (Jan. 1949): 305–6; Siracusa, *Mechanical People*, 121–31, 136; Formisano, *Transformation of Political Culture*, 192–93; Goodman, "Politics of Industrialism," 176, 189; Heale, *Making of American Politics*, 176–77.

54. Boutwell, *Reminiscences* 1:114, 195; Hart, *Commonwealth History* 4:78–81; E. W. Emerson and W. E. Forbes (eds.), *Journals of Ralph Waldo Emerson*, 10 vols. (Boston, 1914), 6:276; 9:85; *Boston Daily Journal*, Sept. 28, 1854.

55. Darling, *Political Changes in Massachusetts*, chap. 5; Handlin and Handlin, *Commonwealth*, 200–1; Formisano, *Transformation of Political Culture*, 196, 248–49, 258–60, 272–73; Pessen, *Jacksonian America*, 223–24; Van Deusen, "Major Party Thought and Theory," 148–50; Butler, *Butler's Book*, 117; *South Boston Gazette*, Nov. 13, 1848; Morton to George Bancroft, May 11, 1846, Marcus Morton Papers.

56. Congdon, *Reminiscences*, 61; *Worcester Palladium*, Oct. 4, 1854; Mass., *State Convention* 3:278.

57. Morton to Granite Club No. 1, Aug. 24, 1852, Morton Papers.

58. Heale, *Making of American Politics*, 175–76; Arthur B. Darling, "Jacksonian Democracy in Massachusetts, 1824–1848," *American Historical Review* 29 (Jan. 1924): 286–87; Howe, *American Whigs*, 21–22; Goodman, "Politics of Industrialism," 170–76; Arthur B. Darling, "The Workingmen's Party in Massachusetts 1833–1834," *American Historical Review* 29 (Oct. 1923–July 1924): 84–85.

59. Mass., *State Convention* 1:229, 813; 2:144–47, 316, 324, 342; Walters, *American Reformers*, 177.

60. Mass., *State Convention* 1:830, 896, 940–41; 2:164, 339, 354; Charles Allen, *Speech of Hon. Charles Allen at Worcester, Nov. 5, 1853* (pamphlet), 5.

61. Darling, "Jacksonian Democracy in Massachusetts," 275; Holt, "Politics of Impatience," 328; Formisano, *Transformation of Political Culture*, 149, 268.

62. Darling, *Political Changes in Massachusetts*, 3, 39, 83; *Boston Daily Advertiser*, Aug. 10 and 15, 1855; Prude, *Industrial Order*, 52–54, 60, 106.

63. Darling, *Political Changes in Massachusetts*, 100; Siracusa, *Mechanical People*, 56–60; 71–79, 127–30; Wilentz, *Chants Democratic*, 235; Holt, *Political Crisis of the 1850s*, 33.

64. Darling, *Political Changes in Massachusetts*, 83, 87; Hart, *Commonwealth History* 4:77–81; *Worcester Palladium*, Oct. 12, 1853, and Oct. 4, 1854; Morton to F. A. Hildreth, Aug. 18, 1849, Morton Papers.

65. *Massachusetts Spy*, Oct. 30, 1839; Congdon, *Reminiscences*, 81–82, 104; Darling, *Political Changes in Massachusetts*, 239–43, 286–89; Goodman, "Politics of Industrialism," 178–79; Formisano, *Transformation of Political Culture*, 299. Marcus Morton, the Democratic victor in both elections, stands proof that every vote counts. His popular majority in 1839 was one vote, and his margin of victory in the lower house of the legislature in 1842 again was one vote. See Alfred S. Roe, "The Governors of Massachusetts," *New England Magazine* New Series, 25 (Jan. 1902): 541–44.

66. Persons, "Factory Legislation," 24–27; Pessen, *Jacksonian America*, 207–8; Formisano, *Transformation of Political Culture*, 223, 319. The 1843 legislature did abolish the poll tax for males under twenty-one and repeal the "sunset" law. However, the Democratic leadership and press reinforced labor's jaundiced view of their party by their extended silence on the ten-hour question. Not until 1850, when the issue had reached a fever pitch in the industrial towns, was it incorporated into the Democratic platform, and even then it was so carefully worded as to cast doubts upon the sincerity of the party's commitment. See Formisano, *Transformation of Political Culture*, 336; Siracusa, *Mechanical People*, 134; Hart, *Commonwealth History* 4:92.

67. Winfield Scott to Robert C. Winthrop, Dec. 17, 1844, Robert C. Winthrop Papers, MHS; Amos Abbott to William Schouler, Nov. 16, 1844, William Schouler Papers, MHS; *Massachusetts Spy*, Oct. 29, 1845; *Boston Daily Advertiser*, Feb. 22, 27, and 28, 1845; Hector Orr, *The Native American* (Philadelphia, 1845), 150–62; John Hancock Lee, *The Origin and Progress of the American Party* (Philadelphia, 1855), 248–52.

68. Hart, *Commonwealth History* 4:95; Darling, *Political Changes in Massachusetts*, 328–29; Bean, "Party Transformation in Massachusetts," 228–35.

69. Moorfield Storey and Edward W. Emerson, *Ebenezer Rockwood Hoar, A Memoir* (Boston, 1911), 42–44; George S. Merriam, *The Life and Times of Samuel Bowles*, 2 vols., (New York, 1885), 1:45–46; Hart, *Commonwealth History* 4:93–96; Martin B. Duberman, *Charles Francis Adams, 1807–1886* (Boston, 1961), 108–29; Bean, "Party Transformation in Massachusetts," 4–5, 23; Holt, *Political Crisis of the 1850s*, 44; Joel H. Silbey, *The Partisan Imperative: The Dynamics of American Politics before the Civil War* (New York, 1985), 94; Eric Foner, *Free Soil, Free Labor, Free Men: The Ideology of the Republican Party before the Civil War* (New York, 1970), 78, 81–82, 190.

70. Congdon, *Reminiscences*, 131; Hoar, *Autobiography* 1:134–35, 145–46; Storey and Emerson, *Ebenezer Rockwood Hoar*, 52–55; Duberman, *Charles Francis Adams*, 155–56; Joseph G. Rayback, *Free-Soil: The Election of 1848* (Lexington, Ky., 1970), vii–ix, 26–27, 56, 230, 265, 299–302; James L. Sundquist, *Dynamics of the Party System: Alignment and Realignment of Political Parties in the United States* (Washington, D.C., 1973), 53–54. Dale Baum estimates that around one-third of the 1848 Bay State Free-Soil voters were Democrats. Kevin Sweeney puts their number somewhat lower at 29 percent. See Baum, *Civil War Party System*, 25; Sweeney, "Rum, Romanism, Representation, and Reform," 117, n. 3.

71. V. O. Key, *Politics, Parties, and Pressure Groups* (New York, 1964), 208.

72. Adams to the Editor of the *Commonwealth*, Sept. 12, 1853; Adams to John A. Andrew, July 23, 1854; Adams to D. G. Bailey, Sept. 2, 1855, Letterbooks, Adams Family Papers; Henry Wilson, *History of the Rise and Fall of the Slave Power in America*, 3 vols. (Boston, 1872), 2:342; Frank Otto Gatell, *John Gorham Palfrey and the New England Conscience* (Cambridge, Mass., 1963), 178, 192.

73. The societal dynamics described above correspond to that part of the theory of critical elections that holds that party realignments "arise from emergent tensions in society, which not adequately controlled by the organization or outputs of party politics as usual, escalate to a flash point." See Walter Dean Burnham, *Critical Elections and the Mainsprings of American Politics* (New York, 1970), 10.

Chapter Two

1. Sweeney, "Rum, Romanism, Representation, and Reform," 117; Mass., *State Convention* 1:316, 398.

2. *Yarmouth Register*, July 5 and Sept. 27, 1849; George S. Boutwell, "State Constitutional Convention of 1853," *Groton Historical Society* 4 (n.d.): 409; Wilson, *Slave Power* 2:339; Bean, "Party Transformation in Massachusetts," 33–37; Ernest McKay, *Henry Wilson: Practical Radical, a Portrait of a Politician* (Port Washington, N.Y., 1971), 60.

3. R. H. Dana, Jr., to Samuel Hoar, Oct. 24, 1850, Richard H. Dana, Jr., Papers, MHS; *Boston Daily Journal*, Nov. 1, 1849; Wilson, *Slave Power* 2:339, 341; Boutwell, *Reminiscences* 1:115, 216–17; Sweeney, "Rum, Romanism, Representation, and Reform," 120.

4. Edward Everett to Winthrop, Sept. 23, 1850; Abbott Lawrence to Robert C. Winthrop, Oct. 31, 1850; George Hillard to Winthrop, May 14, 1850; John W. Davis to Winthrop, Sept. 6, 1851, Winthrop Papers.

5. Hart, *Commonwealth History* 4:474.

6. Ibid., 98, 128; Merriam, *Samuel Bowles* 1:90–91; Robinson, *"Warrington" Pen-Portraits*, 405, 430, 432; Wilson, *Slave Power* 2:343.

7. Robinson, *"Warrington" Pen-Portraits*, 405. Many Free-Soilers were former Democrats attuned to Locofoco positions; and all Free-Soilers drew the connection between the profits of the Cotton Whigs and slave labor. Thus, like the Locofocos, they chafed under the rule of the Boston "monied interest." In addition, they were anxious as the country Democrats to clip urban wings because of the opposition that they encountered from Bostonians and the Irish to their antislavery and temperance crusades. See Mass., *State Convention* 2:355.

8. Everett to Winthrop, Dec. 4, 1850, Winthrop Papers; R. H. Dana, Jr., to R. H. Dana, Sr., July 22, 1848, Richard Henry Dana, Sr., Papers, MHS; Mass., *State Convention* 2:235; *Springfield Daily Republican*, Nov. 1, 1849; Boutwell, "State Constitutional Convention," 409; Butler, *Butler's Book*, 94; Robinson, *"Warrington" Pen-Portraits*, 543; Bean, "Party Transformation in Massachusetts," 33–34.

9. *Massachusetts Spy*, Oct. 29, 1851; *Gazette* (Dedham), Nov. 13, 1852; *Daily Herald* (Newburyport), Nov. 3 and 22, 1853; Mass., *State Convention* 2:147; Wilson, *Slave Power* 1:111–12, 339; Butler, *Butler's Book*, 93; Bean, "Party Transformation in Massachusetts," 34–35, 62; Donald, *Charles Sumner*, 177–82; Goodman, "Politics of Industrialism," 188–89; Silbey, *The Partisan Imperative*, 110. Wilson and Banks paraded themselves as self-made men who were friends of the working man. In fact, both men were probusiness. See McKay, *Henry Wilson*, 22–23, 40–41.

10. Adams to John Bolles, April 28, 1851; Adams to Enos P. Brainerd, L. W. Hall, and Ira Gardner, June 12, 1851; Adams to D. G. Bailey, Feb. 2 and April 5, 1852; Adams to Charles Sumner, Jan. 1 and June 11, 1852, and Nov. 21, 1853; Adams to Henry Wilson, Aug. 23, 1854, Letterbooks, Adams Family Papers; Robert F. Lucid, *Journal of Richard Henry Dana, Jr.*, 3 vols. (Cambridge, 1968), 1:391; Boutwell, *Reminiscences* 1:246–47; 2:98; Wilson, *Slave Power* 2:342; Gatell, *John Gorham Palfrey*, 178, 192.

11. Morton to B. V. French, Nov. 22, 1850, Morton Papers; R. H. Dana, Jr., to Samuel Hoar, Oct. 24, 1850, Richard H. Dana, Jr., Papers; Richard Henry Dana, Jr., *Speeches in Stirring Times and Letters to a Son* (Boston, 1910), 145–46; Storey and Emerson, *Ebenezer Rockwood Hoar*, 98–100; Gatell, *John Gorham Palfrey*, 167, 178–79; Duberman, *Charles Francis Adams*, 66–67; 74, 159.

12. Lucid, *Journal of Richard Henry Dana, Jr.* 2:599, 622; Adams, Diary, Sept. 16, 1853; Adams to D. G. Bailey, April 5, 1852, and Sept. 2, 1855, Letterbooks, Adams Family Papers.

13. Adams, *Diary*, May 5, 1853, Adams Family Papers.

14. McKay, *Henry Wilson*, 42–43, 60–61, 64. Free-Soil journalist William S. Robinson (a.k.a. "Warrington") judged Adams no less flexible than Wilson on matters of principle, asserting that the Quincy patriarch's reputation as a rigid doctrinaire cloaked the reality of a "diplomatic and expedientist turn of mind." Adams's biographer, on the other hand, described him as "primarily a moralist who entered politics at the dictation of his conscience and to whom the calculations and bargains of the real world were always repugnant." See Robinson, *"Warrington" Pen-Portraits*, 543; Duberman, *Charles Francis Adams*, 47, 186.

15. Wilson, *Slave Power* 2:110–12, 152; Boutwell, *Reminiscences* 1:228–29.

16. *Salem Gazette*, Jan. 16, 1855; Lucid, *Journal of Richard Henry Dana, Jr.* 2:565; Mass., *State Convention* 1:228; 2:760. Wilson was the quintessential self-made man. He was born in Farmington, New Hampshire, and was hired out as a farmhand at the age of ten. Upon reaching his majority, he struck out on his own, walking all the way from Farmington to Natick, Massachusetts, where he settled and where eventually he started his own shoe business. See the *Boston Daily Advertiser*, Feb. 1, 1855.

17. Richard H. Abbott, *Cobbler in Congress: The Life of Henry Wilson, 1812–1875* (Lexington, Ky., 1972), 35–36; Robinson, *"Warrington" Pen-Portraits*, 428; Hoar, *Autobiography* 1:132, 153, 217–18; Edward Everett, *Diary*, Feb. 23, 1855, Everett Papers, MHS; Congdon, *Reminiscences*, 132.

18. Robinson, *"Warrington" Pen-Portraits*, 405; Hart, *Commonwealth History* 4:98–99.

19. *Yarmouth Register*, Sept. 26, 1850; *Boston Post*, Nov. 18, 1850; *Daily Herald* (Newburyport), Nov. 22, 1853; Boutwell, *Reminiscences* 2:98; Hart, *Commonwealth History* 4:474; Abbott, *Cobbler in Congress*, 40–41; Sweeney, "Rum, Romanism, Representation, and Reform," 123–24.

20. *Massachusetts Spy*, Oct. 29, 1851; Everett to Winthrop, Sept. 23, 1850; Abbott Lawrence to Winthrop, Oct. 31, 1850, Winthrop Papers; R. H. Dana, Jr., to Samuel Hoar, Oct. 24, 1850; R. H. Dana, Jr., to Edmund Dana, Nov. 12, 1850, R. H. Dana, Jr., Papers.

21. Adams to D. G. Bailey, April 5, 1852 Letterbooks, Adams Family Papers; *Boston Pilot*, Nov. 8, 1851; Mass., *State Convention* 1:631; Boutwell, *Reminiscences* 1:123.

22. Henry Adams, *The Education of Henry Adams* (Boston, 1918), 49; Richards, *Samuel Gridley Howe* 2:331, 345; Congdon, *Reminiscences*, 137.

23. Robinson, *"Warrington" Pen-Portraits*, 500; Boutwell, *Reminiscences* 1:112; Hart, *Commonwealth History* 4:481; Winthrop to John H. Clifford, Nov. 12, 1850; Abbott Lawrence to Winthrop, Jan. 8, 1851, Winthrop Papers.

24. *Boston Daily Advertiser*, Aug. 21, 22, and 23 and Oct. 4, 1851; Boutwell, *Reminiscences* 1:100, 116, 119–20; Hoar, *Autobiography* 1:185–86; Wilson, *Slave Power* 2:349; Claude M. Fuess, *The Life of Caleb Cushing*, 2 vols. (New York, 1923), 2:102–4, 107–8; Bean, "Party Transformation in Massachusetts," 64–70; Everett to Winthrop, Dec. 4, 1850, and Jan. 4, 1851, Winthrop Papers.

25. Morton to Francis R. Gourgas, Jan. 18, 1852; Morton to Frederick Robinson, Nov. 22, 1850; Morton to Edward Cazneau, March 25, 1851; Morton to George Hood, March 26, 1851; Morton to B. V. French, Nov. 22, 1850; Morton to John B. Alley, March 21, 1851, Morton Papers.

26. Richards, *Samuel Gridley Howe* 1:326, 336, 338; Robinson, *"War-*

rington" Pen-Portraits, 543; *Gazette* (Dedham), Jan. 3, 1853; Wilson, *Slave Power* 2:342, 350–51.

27. Mass., *State Convention* 1:581; 2:535; *Boston Post*, May 26 and Sept. 9, 1852; *Massachusetts Spy*, Oct. 10, 1851; *Boston Daily Advertiser*, Oct. 3 and 4 and Nov. 10, 1851; *Yarmouth Register*, May 29, 1851; *Springfield Daily Republican*, March 7, 1853.

28. Bean, "Party Transformation in Massachusetts," 88; *Barnstable Patriot*, June 3, 1851.

29. *Massachusetts Spy*, Oct. 29, 1851.

30. Amos A. Lawrence to A. E. Hildreth, March 27, 1855, Letterbooks, Lawrence Papers; *Boston Daily Advertiser*, March 9, 1855; Butler, *Butler's Book*, 91–92; William Gray, *Labor: The Ten-Hour System* (n.p., 1871), 631–32; Persons, "Factory Legislation," 24–27, 49–51, 79–81.

31. Persons, "Factory Legislation," 81; Cowley, *Ten-Hour Law*, 6–7; *Quincy Patriot*, April 30, 1853; *Woburn Journal*, Nov. 13, 1853.

32. Persons, "Factory Legislation," 86; Butler, *Butler's Book*, 92–93.

33. Everett to Winthrop, Feb. 10, 1851; John Davis to Winthrop, Sept. 6, 1851, Winthrop Papers.

34. Robinson, *"Warrington" Pen-Portraits*, 36, 48; Butler, *Butler's Book*, 98–99; Sweeney, "Rum, Romanism, Representation, and Reform," 127–28.

35. Persons, "Factory Legislation," 70–73; Butler, *Butler's Book*, 99; Mass., *State Convention* 1:594–95, 615–16, 658–61.

36. Mass., *State Convention* 2:526; Butler, *Butler's Book*, 100–104; Winthrop to John H. Clifford, Nov. 15, 1851, Winthrop Papers. Butler denounced as craven the unwillingness of the Coalition and Democratic city committees to stand up to the corporations and publicize the notice about firing workers. See *Butler's Book*, 99, 105.

37. Mass., *State Convention* 1:657, 663; *Boston Post*, March 10, May 26, and Sept. 9, 1852; *Boston Daily Advertiser*, April 21, 1855; Hart, *Commonwealth History* 4:386–87.

38. Bean, "Party Transformation in Massachusetts," 117–20. Bean incorrectly labeled both of these Free-Soil measures "Locofoco."

39. *Boston Post*, Sept. 9, 1852; Persons, "Factory Legislation," 87; Siracusa, *Mechanical People*, 162; Formisano, *Transformation of Political Culture*, 336–39. Shortly before the fall election in 1853, the major textile corporations went to an eleven-hour day.

40. Mass., *State Convention* 3:461; Adams, Diary, Nov. 8, 1852, Adams Family Papers; Lucid, *Journal of Richard Henry Dana, Jr.* 2:505–6; *Boston Post*, Feb. 26, 1852; *Barnstable Patriot*, June 1, 1852; Bean, "Party Transformation in Massachusetts," 113–17; Sweeney, "Rum, Romanism, Representation, and Reform," 128–30.

41. *Barnstable Patriot*, April 3, 1855; *Boston Post*, Feb. 26, 1852. Adams and Dana helped engineer Mann's nomination, much to the disappointment of Wilson, who was angling for the party's nod himself. See Lucid, *Journal of Richard Henry Dana, Jr.*, 2:506.

42. Mass., *State Convention* 1:631; *Boston Daily Advertiser*, April 24, 1855.

43. *Boston Post*, Sept. 25, 1852.

44. *Gazette* (Dedham), Nov. 13, 1852; Morton to Franklin Pierce, Nov. 28, 1852; Morton to Caleb Cushing, Nov. 28, 1852, Morton Papers; Adams to D. G. Bailey, April 5, 1852; Adams to Charles Sumner, April 7, 1852, Letterbooks, Adams Family Papers.

45. Robinson, *"Warrington" Pen-Portraits*, 543; Boutwell, *Reminiscences* 1:233; McKay, *Henry Wilson*, 80.

46. Mass., *State Convention* 3:102–3; *Boston Daily Advertiser*, Oct. 4, 1851, and Sept. 9, 1852.

47. *Boston Post*, April 26 and Sept. 25, 1852; *Yarmouth Register*, Oct. 21 and Nov. 18, 1853; Edward L. Pierce, *Memoirs and Letters of Charles Sumner*, 4 vols. (Boston, 1893), 3:325–26; Samuel Eliot Morison, *A Manual for the Constitutional Convention of 1917* (Boston, 1917), 41–43, 49; Sweeney, "Rum, Romanism, Representation, and Reform," 132–33. A few days before the election of delegates, the Whig legislature, in a fit of "party-madness," repealed the secret ballot law. Its action had no bearing on the outcome, since it was the small rural towns, whose voters were not subject to employer pressures, which dominated the delegate selection process. See Mass., *State Convention* 1:181–82, 581, 631.

48. *Yarmouth Register*, Oct. 21 and Nov. 18, 1853; Shapiro, "Conservative Dilemma," 211. The state constitution limited the number of years in a decade in which a town with fewer than twelve hundred inhabitants could send a representative to the statehouse. Since the towns themselves chose which years they would exercise that option, the number doing so indicated the degree of interest in the small towns in a given election.

49. Mass., *State Convention* 1:99, 838; *Yarmouth Register*, March 11 and Oct. 21, 1853; *Springfield Daily Republican*, Feb. 5 and March 8 and 11, 1853; Morison, *Manual*, 43–45, 49.

50. *Boston Daily Advertiser*, Aug. 9 and Nov. 14, 1853; Horace B. Davis, "The Occupations of Massachusetts Legislators, 1790–1950," *New England Quarterly* 24 (March 1951): 92; Alexis Poole (comp.), *Poole's Statistical View of the Convention for Revising the Constitution of Massachusetts, 1853* (Boston, 1853), 17–25.

51. Mass., *State Convention* 2:236–37; 3:35, 231, 254–55; Pierce, *Charles Sumner* 3:332; Hoar, *Autobiography* 1:28–29. The Whigs, upon returning to office in 1853, ignored the Coalition's general incorporation and banking laws, which were optional. See Mass., *State Convention* 3:168.

52. Mass., *State Convention* 3:453, 476, 613–23; Mass., *The Constitutional Propositions Adopted by the Delegates . . . A.D. 1853 and Submitted to the People for Their Ratification* (Boston, 1853), iii–vii, 15–49; Morison, *Manual*, 42, 49, 52, 56–57; Louis A. Frothingham, *A Brief History of the Constitution and Government of Massachusetts* (Boston, 1925), 53–54.

53. For the Democratic and Free-Soil agendas, see Mass., *State Convention* 2:758; *Springfield Daily Republican*, July 11, 1853.

54. Mass., *State Convention* 2:227; Morison, *Manual*, 49; Frothingham, *Constitution and Government of Massachusetts*, 52.

55. McKay, *Henry Wilson*, 82; Pierce, *Charles Sumner* 3:328; Mass., *State Convention* 1:712; *Worcester Palladium*, Oct. 19, 1853.

56. Mass., *Constitutional Propositions*, 46.

57. The emergence of the Free-Soil party in 1848 introduced a three-party system in which no one party commanded the required majority.

58. Mass., *State Convention* 1:235–36; 241–42; 261–62, 294–95, 315–16, 376–88; 2:393; 3:98–99, 103, 114, 154–155.

59. Ibid. 1:268, 312–13, 382, 386; 3:93, 102.

60. Ibid. 1:382, 386, 415, 633; 3:276.

61. Ibid. 1:241, 377–78, 387; 3:103–5, 112, 114; Morison, *Manual*, 58.

62. Mass., *State Convention* 3:138; Morison, *Manual*, 57–58.

63. Mass., *State Convention* 3:89, 92, 105.

64. Ibid. 1:836–37, 849; 2:224–26, 236–37, 256–57, 403.

65. Ibid. 1:229, 881, 926; 2:148, 292; 3:574–75.

66. Ibid. 3:102–3, 704; *Lawrence Courier,* June 28, 1853.

67. Morison, *Manual,* 50–51; *Springfield Daily Republican,* July 11, 1853; Mass., *State Convention* 1:838, 840–41, 846–47, 854, 857, 871–72, 879–80; 2:375; 3:492.

68. Mass., *State Convention* 1:898.

69. Ibid. 1:924.

70. Ibid. 1:816, 825–30.

71. Ibid. 1:942, 947. Dana was one of a number of prominent delegates who, because they could not win an election in their own communities, were elected from safe towns. In Dana's case, the town was Manchester.

72. Ibid. 2:451.

73. Ibid. 1:211.

74. Ibid. 1:908–9.

75. Ibid. 1:921.

76. Ibid. 1:849, 940–41, 948; 2:151, 154.

77. Ibid. 1:850, 854; 2:224–26, 402–3.

78. Ibid. 1:836, 842; 2:224–26, 403, 587.

79. Ibid. 1:852–54.

80. Ibid. 1:877–84.

81. Ibid. 1:924.

82. Ibid. 1:840–41.

83. Ibid. 1:836–40, 850–53, 858–59, 868, 877–78; 2:347–49.

84. Ibid. 2:158.

85. Ibid. 1:120, 180–83, 936–37; 2:57; 3:115–16, 124.

86. Ibid. 1:903, 926; 2:39, 57.

87. Ibid. 1:837.

88. Ibid. 3:676–77.

89. Ibid. 3:546–49, 556–57, 560–62, 566.

90. Ibid. 3:581–83.

91. Ibid. 3:492, 586, 589, 600–9.

92. Ibid. 1:855, 860, 889, 936.

93. Ibid. 1:675, 891.

94. Ibid. 2:39, 158; 3:557, 560, 562.

95. *Boston Daily Advertiser,* Sept. 20, 1853; *Springfield Daily Republican,* Oct. 27, 1853; *Salem Gazette,* Nov. 18, 1853; John Sargent to Emory Washburn, Nov. 8, 1853, Emory Washburn Papers, MHS.

96. *Boston Daily Post,* Sept. 23, 1853.

97. Adams to Charles Sumner, Jan. 1, 1852; Adams to D. G. Bailey, Feb. 2 and April 5, 1852, Letterbooks; Adams, Diary, Nov. 15, 1853, Adams Family Papers; Pierce, *Charles Sumner* 3:338–39; Lucid, *Journal of Richard Henry Dana, Jr.* 2:602; *Boston Daily Journal,* Nov. 2 and 5, 1853; Wilson, *Slave Power* 2:342; Fuess, *Caleb Cushing* 2:141; Bean, "Party Transformation in Massachusetts," 174–78; Sweeney, "Rum, Romanism, Representation, and Reform," 135.

98. For example, see Bean, "Party Transformation in Massachusetts," 173; O. Handlin, *Boston's Immigrants,* 197, 354, n. 74.

99. Bean, "Party Transformation in Massachusetts," 174, 179, n. 2, 180, 236—37; *Gazette* (Dedham), Nov. 19, 1853; Pierce, *Charles Sumner* 3:339—41; Boutwell, *Reminiscences* 1:220. Oscar Handlin attributes the alleged mobilization of the Irish vote against the proposed constitution to the relentless assaults upon it by Orestes Brownson and the Catholic newspaper *Pilot*. See O. Handlin, *Boston's Immigrants*, 196—97.

100. Sweeney, "Rum, Romanism, Representation, and Reform," 136; Baum, *Civil War Party System*, 29—30, 33. Proposition 1 failed passage by 4,928 votes; the school fund referendum lost by only 401 votes.

101. Dale Baum estimates that fewer than 4,000 Democrats crossed over to vote against proposition 1. See Baum, *Civil War Party System*, 29.

Chapter Three

1. Robinson, *"Warrington" Pen-Portraits*, 205.

2. The Solomon Bradford Morse, Jr., Papers, MHS. These papers contain the constitutions for the state and local Know-Nothing lodges and the minutes and membership roll of an East Boston lodge kept over a three-year period. The first entry is dated October 12, 1853. Two Know-Nothing publicists, Anna E. Carroll and Thomas R. Whitney, also dated the beginnings of the order in Massachusetts in the fall of 1853. See Carroll, *The Great American Battle* (New York, 1856), 269—70 and Whitney, *A Defence of American Policy* (New York, 1856), 84, 294.

3. So called because its members, when asked about their secret organization, answered, "I know nothing."

4. From a speech by Know-Nothing state senator Robert Hall, quoted in part in the *Boston Daily Advertiser*, Feb. 22, 1855, and in the *Worcester Palladium*, Feb. 23, 1855. Among the works tracing the rise of the American party in Massachusetts are Dale Baum, "Know-Nothingism and the Republican Majority in Massachusetts: The Political Realignment of the 1850s," *Journal of American History* 64 (March 1973): 959—86; Baum, *Civil War Party System*, chap. 2; Bean, "Party Transformation in Massachusetts," chaps. 8—10; Bean, "An Aspect of Know-Nothingism: The Immigrant and Slavery," *South Atlantic Quarterly* 23 (Oct. 1924): 319—34; Bean, "Puritan Versus Celt," 70—89; Billington, *Protestant Crusade*, chap. 15; Formisano, *Transformation of Political Culture*, chap. 14; O. Handlin, *Boston's Immigrants*, chap. 7; William E. Gienapp, "Nativism and the Creation of the Republican Majority in the North before the Civil War," *Journal of American History*, 72 (Dec. 1985): 529—55; Gienapp, *Origins of the Republican Party*, 133—39; Haynes, "Causes of Know-Nothing Success," 67—82; Haynes, "Local History of Know-nothingism," 82—96; Siracusa, *Mechanical People*, chap. 6; Wilson, *Slave Power* 2:chap. 32. The best account of the rise of Know-Nothingism nationwide is contained in Holt, "Politics of Impatience," 309—331; Holt, *Political Crisis of the 1850s*, chaps. 5 and 6.

5. Morse Papers, subordinate council constitutions: *Barnstable Patriot*, June 12, 1855; *Barre Patriot*, Jan. 12, 1855. The editor of the Barre newspaper, Nahum F. Bryant, was a prominent Know-Nothing. For admission requirements and rituals, see Thomas V. Cooper and Hector R. Fenton, *American Politics* (Philadelphia, 1892), 60—64.

6. The following analysis of Know-Nothing organization draws heavily on Maurice Duverger, *Political Parties: Their Organization and Activity in the Modern State* (New York, 1954); Key, *Politics, Parties, and Pressure Groups*; and E. E. Schattschneider, *Party Government* (New York, 1942).

7. Morse Papers, April 25 and May 2, 1855, subordinate council constitutions; *City Advertiser* (Charlestown), Dec. 23, 1854. A Free-Soil newspaper with Know-

Nothing connections reported in September that the secret order claimed 325 councils and seventy thousand members. See the *Gazette* (Dedham), Sept. 1, 1854.

8. Everett to H. W. Trescot, Oct. 20, 1854; Everett to Sir Henry Holland, Jan. 11, 1855, Letterbooks; Everett, Diary, Nov. 28, 1854, Everett Papers.

9. Adams to F. W. Bird, Oct. 16, 1854, Letterbooks, Adams Family Papers; *Daily Herald* (Newburyport), May 10, 1855; *Worcester Palladium*, Nov. 22, 1854; *Westfield News Letter*, Sept. 27, 1854; Mass., *State Convention* 2:341; Bird, *Address of Hon. F. W. Bird*, 10.

10. Holt, "Politics of Impatience," 315–16; *Lynn Reporter*, Aug. 19 and Nov. 4, 1854; *South Boston Gazette*, Nov. 11, 1854. Both the *Reporter* and the *Gazette* were Know-Nothing newspapers.

11. Morse Papers, May 17 and Nov. 1, 22, and 29, 1854, and Oct. 10, 1855; *Yarmouth Register*, Oct. 20, 1854; Robinson, *"Warrington," Pen-Portraits*, 436–37. The promise to return power to the people came at a time of pandemic disillusionment with politicians and the established parties brought on by wrenching social and economic change. See Holt, "Politics of Impatience," 313–17; Holt, *Political Crisis of the 1850s*, 132–37.

12. *Worcester Palladium*, April 14, 1855; Everett to Mrs. Charles Eames, Nov. 13, 1854, Letterbooks, Everett Papers; Adams to George Bradburn, April 20, 1855, Letterbooks, Adams Family Papers.

13. *Boston Post*, Nov. 16, 1854; *National Aegis*, Dec. 13, 1854; *Cambridge Chronicle*, Nov. 18 and Dec. 9, 1854; *Gazette* (Dedham), Oct. 14, 1854; *Massachusetts Spy*, July 4, 1855; *Lynn Reporter*, Nov. 3, 11, and 25, 1854; *South Boston Gazette* (quoting the Know-Nothing *American Patriot*), Sept. 16, 1854. The editor of the South Boston newspaper, Albert J. Wright, was a Know-Nothing candidate for the state senate.

14. Samuel Bradbury to Amos A. Lawrence, Nov. 27, 1854, Lawrence Papers. Party organizers meant what they said. Only 11 of the 419 American legislative candidates in 1854 were lawyers; less than 10 percent of the aspirants had ever served in the General Court; and only 5 of the 132 Boston candidates for state representative in 1853 ran for that office as Know-Nothings the following year. See Alexis Poole (comp.), *Statistical View of the Executive and Legislative Departments of the Government of Massachusetts* (Boston, 1855), 6, 14.

15. Adams to Bradburn, April 20, 1855, Letterbooks, Adams Family Papers. The Know-Nothings defended their use of secrecy on the grounds that the only way to secure good men for office was to shield them from the outrageous lies of a partisan press and party hacks whose sole object was to canonize their own candidates and vilify their opposition's. They complained that not only did the party battles that dominated election campaigns fail to enlighten the public, they left the voters knowing as much about the issues and candidates "as they do about the man in the moon." *Lowell Daily Advertiser*, Oct. 17, 1854; *South Boston Gazette*, Nov. 11, 1854; *Lynn Reporter*, Aug. 19, 1854.

16. Morse Papers, Sept. 12 and 26, 1855, and subordinate council constitutions; *South Boston Gazette*, Nov. 11, 1854; *Mercury* (Dorchester), Feb. 23, 1856.

17. Haynes, "Local History of Knownothingism," 90.

18. Holt, "Politics of Impatience," 319–20; Carleton Beals, *Brass-Knuckles Crusade: The Great Know-Nothing Conspiracy: 1820–1860* (New York, 1960), 105; Carroll, *Great American Battle*, 266; *Boston Daily Bee*, Dec. 15, 1855; James W. Stone to Charles Sumner, March 15, 1854, Charles Sumner Papers, Houghton Library.

19. *Lowell Weekly Journal and Courier*, Oct. 13, 1854; *Boston Daily Advertiser*, May 19, 1855; *Boston Daily Bee*, Nov. 6 and Dec. 15, 1855.

20. Gienapp, *Origins of the Republican Party*, 136; *Gazette* (Dedham), July 1, 1854. The *Gazette*'s editor, E. L. Keyes, like most Free-Soilers, turned Know-Nothing.

21. Washburn to Julius Rockwell, June 1854, Julius Rockwell Papers (New York Historical Society); Adams to John A. Andrews, July 23, 1854, Letterbooks, Adams Family Papers; *Boston Post*, July 19, 1854; E. L. Pierce, *Charles Sumner* 1:256; 3:400; Wilson, *Slave Power* 2:414; Elias Nason and Thomas Russell, *The Life and Public Service of Henry Wilson* (Boston, 1876), 118; Gienapp, *Origins of the Republican Party*, 82, 84.

22. Adams, Diary, June 1, 1854, Adams Family Papers; Everett to Mrs. Eames, Aug. 31, 1854, Letterbooks, Everett Papers; Henry Wilson to Sumner, July 2, 1854, Sumner Papers; Gienapp, *Origins of the Republican Party*, 133.

23. Wilson, *Slave Power* 2:414; Hoar, *Autobiography* 1:30–31; Lucid, *Journal of Richard Henry Dana, Jr.* 2:617; *Boston Post*, July 10, 20, and 22, 1854.

24. Gienapp, *Origins of the Republican Party*, 137–38; *Middlesex Journal*, Nov. 11, 1854; *Yarmouth Register*, June 30 and Nov. 3, 1854; *Boston Daily Advertiser*, Aug. 15, 1855.

25. Holt, "Politics of Impatience," 312–14, 322–23, 330–31; Billington, *Protestant Crusade*, 391; John Hancock Lee, *The Origins and Progress of the American Party in Politics* (Philadelphia, 1855), 222–23; *Worcester Palladium*, May 24, June 28, and July 21, 1854; *Daily Herald* (Newburyport), Sept. 23, 1854; *City Advertiser* (Charlestown), Nov. 15, 1854; speeches of Know-Nothing officeholders J.V.C. Smith and A. C. Carey quoted in part in *Boston Daily Advertiser*, Jan. 17, 1854, and Feb. 14 and 18, 1856.

26. Assessed personal estate in Boston's three wealthiest wards amounted to just under 60 percent of the city's total in 1840 and 1845. By 1855, it had climbed to 77 percent. See Shattuck, *Census of Boston for the Year 1845*, 15, 18, Appendix JJ, 62; Curtis, *Census of Boston, May 1855*, 7–8; Josiah Curtis, *Documents of the City of Boston for the Year 1859*, 2 vols. (Boston, 1859), 2:Doc. No. 41, 26; *Boston Daily Advertiser*, Sept. 20, 1855.

27. *Springfield Daily Republican*, April 15, 1853; *City Advertiser* (Charlestown), May 21 and Dec. 7, 1853; Butler, *Butler's Book*, 106; John T. Cumbler, "Labor, Capital, and Community: The Struggle for Power," *Labor History* 15 (Summer 1978): 401–2; Faler, "Cultural Aspects," 393; Dawley, *Industrial Revolution in Lynn*, 80–89, 182, 230; Goodman, "Politics of Industrialism," 191, 201.

28. Amos A. Lawrence to Charles Wild, Dec. 26, 1854, Letterbooks, Lawrence Papers; Circular of Council No. 57 (Brookline), Nov. 24, 1854, Lawrence Papers. Lawrence was a member of this council.

29. *Boston Daily Advertiser*, Dec. 12, 1854, and Jan. 30 and Feb. 5 and 8, 1855; Holt, "Politics of Impatience," 319, 329; Edward Everett supposed the rank and file of the lodges "almost wholly made up of the laboring classes." See Everett, Diary, Nov. 13 and 18, 1854, Everett Papers. Records of the East Boston and Worcester lodges show a surge of workers and boardinghouse transients into the secret order that began in October 1853 and peaked in December 1854. See Morse Papers, Oct. 12, 1853, and Haynes, "Local History of Knownothingism," 85, 88.

30. *Gazette* (Dedham), Nov. 19, 1854; *Bunker Hill Aurora*, Dec. 2, 1854; *Massachusetts Spy*, July 4, 1855; *Salem Gazette*, March 7, 1856; *City Advertiser* (Charlestown), Nov. 15, 1854; *South Boston Gazette*, July 29, 1854; *Bunker Hill Aurora*, Dec. 2, 1854; Holt, "Politics of Impatience," 330.

31. *Boston Post*, Dec. 26, 1853, and March 9 and 15, 1854; *Barnstable Patriot*, April 11, 1856; *Gazette* (Dedham), March 12, 1854; *Boston Daily Advertiser*, Jan. 10 and July 12, 1854; *Lowell Daily Advertiser*, March 15 and 30, 1854; *Salem Gazette*, March 10, 1854; James W. Stone to Sumner, March 15, 1854, Sumner Papers.

32. Stone to Sumner, March 15, 1854, Sumner Papers; Everett to H. Trescot, Oct. 20, 1854, Letterbooks, Everett Papers; James M. Bugbee, "Memoir of Edward Lilie Pierce," *Massachusetts Historical Society Proceedings* 31 (1896–1897): 393; Merriam, *Samuel Bowles* 1:132; Hoar, *Autobiography* 1:249; Congdon, *Reminiscences*, 146.

33. Adams, Diary, Oct. 25, 1854, and June 16, 1856, Adams Family Papers; Merriam, *Samuel Bowles* 1:124–25; Gienapp, *Origins of the Republican Party* 137.

34. E. L. Pierce to Horace Mann, Jan. 18, 1855, Horace Mann Papers, MHS.

35. Seth Webb to Sumner, July 14, 1854, Sumner Papers; Samuel Downer to Horace Mann, Oct. 25, 1854, Mann Papers.

36. Boutwell, *Reminiscences* 1:238.

37. *Boston Evening Transcript*, Nov. 14, 1854; Robinson, *"Warrington" Pen-Portraits*, 436–37.

38. Robinson, *"Warrington" Pen-Portraits*, 436; *Boston Daily Advertiser*, Oct. 19, 1854; Everett, Diary, Nov. 15, 1854; Everett to Millard Fillmore, Dec. 16, 1854, Letterbooks, Everett Papers; Gienapp, *Origins of the Republican Party*, 136.

39. Everett to Mrs. Eames, Aug. 31 and Sept. 30, 1854, Everett Papers.

40. Gienapp, *Origins of the Republican Party*, 100; Ezra Lincoln to William Schouler, Aug. 14, 1854, Schouler Papers; Adams, Diary, Sept. 16 and 25, 1854, Adams Family Papers.

41. Stone to Sumner, March 15, 1854, Sumner Papers. There was an implicit *quid pro quo* for Stone's disclosures. He wanted Sumner to relay to the order's "Grand Sachem," Jonathan Peirce, that he, Stone, had requested the senator to look into the matter of a possible pension for Peirce's mother. "I have," Stone added cryptically, "a particular reason for desiring to do a favor for Mr. Peirce." The "particular reason" may well have been Peirce's approval of Stone's application for admission to the Know-Nothing lodge in Boston's ward 4.

42. Adams, Diary, July 5, Aug. 30, Nov. 15, and Dec. 16, 1854, and March 1, 1855, Adams Family Papers.

43. Everett to James Buchanan, Jan. 19, 1857, Letterbooks: Everett, Diary, Nov. 25, 1854, Everett Papers; Adams, Diary, Dec. 16, 1854, Adams Family Papers.

44. Winthrop to John H. Clifford, Nov. 16, 1854, Winthrop Papers; Robert C. Winthrop, Jr., *A Memoir of Robert C. Winthrop* (Boston, 1897), 168.

45. Winthrop, Jr., *Memoir of Robert C. Winthrop*, 168.

46. Adams to Bradburn, April 20, 1855, Letterbooks, Adams Family Papers; E. L. Pierce to Horace Mann, Jan. 18, 1855, Mann Papers.

47. *Boston Daily Advertiser*, Aug. 15, 19, 21, and 22, 1854.

48. C. P. Huntington to Sumner, July 2, 1854; Henry Wilson to Sumner, July 2, 1854, Sumner Papers; Merriam, *Samuel Bowles* 1:122; Virginia C. Purdy, "Portrait of a Know-Nothing Legislature: The Massachusetts General Court of 1855," (unpublished Ph.D. diss., George Washington University, 1970), 73–74; *Boston Post*, Aug. 17 and 18, 1854; *Yarmouth Register*, Aug. 25, 1854.

49. *Boston Daily Advertiser*, Aug. 15, 1854.

50. *Boston Post*, Sept. 27, 1854; *Boston Daily Journal*, Sept. 28, 1854.

51. Merriam, *Samuel Bowles* 1:121; Henry G. Pearson, *The Life of John A. Andrew*, 2 vols. (Boston, 1904), 1:64; Wilson, *Slave Power* 2:414; Hoar, *Autobiography* 1:30–31; *Boston Daily Advertiser*, Sept. 8, 1854; *Boston Post*, Sept. 7 and 8, 1854; *South Boston Gazette*, Sept. 9, 1854.

52. *Boston Post*, July 10, 1854; Boutwell, *Reminiscences* 1:228–29; Adams, Diary, Sept. 7 and Oct. 10 and 25, 1854, Adams Family Papers.

53. Adams, Diary, Oct. 25, 1854; Adams to F. W. Bird, Oct. 16, 1854, Letterbooks, Adams Family Papers; Lucid, *Journal of Richard Henry Dana, Jr.* 2:67; *Boston Daily Advertiser*, Nov. 3, 1854; Pierce, *Charles Sumner* 3:401; Pearson, *John A. Andrew* 1:65.

54. Wilson, *Slave Power* 2:414–15.

55. Henry Wilson to Sumner, July 2, 1855, Sumner Papers.

56. *Yarmouth Register*, Nov. 3, 1854; Everett, Diary, Feb. 9, 1855, Everett Papers; Pearson, *John A. Andrew* 1:65; Hoar, *Autobiography* 1:31, 139, 189, 216; Pierce, *Charles Sumner* 3:400.

57. Congdon, *Reminiscences*, 145; *Daily Herald* (Newburyport), Oct. 21, 1854; *Boston Daily Bee*, Nov. 6, 1855; Haynes, "Causes of Know-Nothing Success," 81. Ely wanted his party's backing for the U.S. Senate, and Peirce was angling for the gubernatorial nomination. *Daily Herald* (Newburyport), Oct. 7, 1854.

58. *Boston Daily Advertiser*, Oct. 19 and 30 and Nov. 2, 6, 7, and 8, 1854; Congdon, *Reminiscences*, 145–46; Everett, Diary, Nov. 3 and 14, 1854, Everett Papers. Gardner claimed that the Whig party's rejection of fusion led him to join the American party. His former colleagues thought it more likely that his appetite for high office dictated the move, pointing out that their party had rejected Gardner's bid to be named candidate for the state senate. According to Everett, Gardner had opposed surrendering the Whig party to fusion. See the *Boston Daily Advertiser*, Oct. 19, 1854; Everett, Diary, Nov. 3, 14, and 15, 1854; Everett to Millard Fillmore, Dec. 16, 1854, Letterbooks, Everett Papers.

59. Robinson, *"Warrington" Pen-Portraits*, 428, 436; Merriam, *Samuel Bowles* 1:125; Everett, Diary, Jan. 12, and Feb. 9, 1855; Everett to Mrs. Eames, Nov. 16, 1854; Everett to Millard Fillmore, Dec. 16, 1854, and April 11 and Nov. 11, 1855, Letterbooks, Everett Papers; *Boston Daily Journal*, Oct. 27, 1854; *Lowell Daily Advertiser*, Nov. 7, 1854; *Boston Daily Advertiser*, Oct. 30 and 31 and Nov. 4, 1854. At this early stage of party development the professional politicians by no means controlled events. The contest for the gubernatorial nomination, for example, was fiercely waged. Wilson was one of five contenders for the top spot on the party ticket but withdrew after trailing the field on the first ballot. The front-runner also withdrew when it was revealed that he had enrolled in his lodge only a few days earlier. Gardner was a dark-horse entry who joined the contest on the third trial and gained the required majority on the fourth. Unlike Wilson, he was a relatively obscure politico and thus less likely to provoke an antipolitician response from the delegates. See the *Daily Gazette* (Taunton), Oct. 23, 1854; *Springfield Weekly Republican*, Oct. 28, 1854.

60. *Springfield Weekly Republican*, Oct. 28, 1854; *Daily Herald* (Newburyport), Oct. 21, 1854; A. B. Ely to Amos A. Lawrence, Oct. 16, 1856, Lawrence Papers; Congdon, *Reminiscences*, 144–45.

61. Pierce, *Charles Sumner* 3:401; *Boston Daily Advertiser*, Oct. 9 and 30, 1854; Everett to Mrs. Eames, Aug. 31 and Sept. 30, 1854, Letterbooks, Everett Papers;

Ezra Lincoln to William Schouler, Oct. 25, 1854, Schouler Papers; R. H. Dana, Jr., to R. H. Dana, Sr., Oct. 6, 1854, Dana Papers.

62. *Lowell Daily Advertiser*, Nov. 14, 1854; *Cambridge Chronicle*, Nov. 18, 1854; Downer to Mann, Nov. 13, 1854, Mann Papers; *Boston Daily Advertiser*, Nov. 14 and 15, 1854.

63. Mass., *Senate Journal, 1856* (Boston, 1856), 18; Horace Greeley, ed., *The Whig Almanac and United States Register* (New York, 1853), 53; Goodman, "Politics of Industrialism," 187.

64. See, for example, R. H. Dana, Jr., *Journal*, Nov. 15, 1854, Dana Papers; *Lowell Daily Advertiser*, Nov. 14, 1854; *Boston Daily Advertiser*, Nov. 16, 1854.

65. Adams, Diary, Nov. 14, 1854, Adams Family Papers; *Boston Daily Advertiser*, Dec. 18, 1854; *National Aegis*, Nov. 22, 1854.

66. *Boston Daily Advertiser*, Nov. 14, 1854; Everett, Diary, Nov. 14, 1854, and Feb. 7, 1855, Everett Papers; Everett to Winthrop, n.d., Winthrop Papers; Winthrop to Everett, Nov. 16, 1854, Everett Papers.

67. *Liberator*, Nov. 17, 1854.

68. Adams, Diary, Nov. 14, 1854, Adams Family Papers.

69. Downer to Mann, June 10, 1854; Josiah Quincy to Mann, March 17 and June 6, 1854, Mann Papers; Amos Lawrence to Giles Richards, June 1, 1854; Amos A. Lawrence to William Appleton, July 20, 1854, Letterbooks, Lawrence Papers.

70. Everett to Caleb Cushing, Oct. 11, 1854; Everett to J. A. Hamilton, Nov. 10, 1855; Everett to R. Hawes, May 10, 1856; Everett to J. J. Crittenden, Jan. 3, 1857, Letterbooks, Everett Papers.

71. Mann to Theodore Parker, May 30, 1855, Mann Papers; Wilson, *Slave Power* 2:414–15, 418–20. For comments of others who shared the Wilsonian view that the sectional crisis was the principal agent for the disruption of the established parties, see Lawrence to Appleton, July 20, 1854, Letterbooks, Lawrence Papers; Quincy to Mann, June 6, 1854; Downer to Mann, Nov. 13, 1854, Mann Papers; Stone to Sumner, March 15, 1854, Sumner Papers; Lucid, *Journal of Richard Henry Dana, Jr.* 2:637–38. The leading exponent among recent historians of the claim that the slavery question was the mainspring of party realignment in Massachusetts is Dale Baum. He neglects in his analysis the sizable contribution of the American party to that process, especially its role in mobilizing and unleashing the grass-roots rebellion that destroyed the second party system. See Baum, *Civil War Party System*, 24–43. William Gienapp convincingly argues that Baum and other historians have downplayed the enthusiasm with which rank-and-file Free-Soilers embraced Native American doctrines. See Gienapp, *Origins of the Republican Party*, 138, nn. 35 and 37. Nevertheless, I agree with Baum that the Free-Soilers turned Know-Nothing primarily for reasons of political expediency. For them, the crusade to halt the spread of slavery overshadowed all other considerations.

72. Haynes, "Causes of Know-Nothing Success," 75–79; Bean, "Party Transformation in Massachusetts," 205–6; Gatell, *John Gorham Palfrey*, 221.

73. Everett, Diary, Nov. 13, 18, and 28 and Dec. 8, 1854; Everett to Mrs. Eames, Sept. 30, 1854; Everett to Trescot, Oct. 20, 1854, Letterbooks, Everett Papers. See also speeches by Know-Nothings J.V.C. Smith and A. C. Carey in *Boston Daily Advertiser*, Jan. 17 and Feb. 14 and 18, 1854, and Carey's attack on foreign job competition in Hale, *Report on the Massachusetts Legislature, 1856*, 86. For a fine exposition on the link between ethnocultural antagonisms and the rise of the American party, see Gienapp, *Origins of the Republican Party*, 92–97.

74. Gienapp, *Origins of the Republican Party*, 96; Seymour Lipset and Earl Raab, *The Politics of Unreason: Right-Wing Extremism in America, 1790–1970* (New York, 1970), 50; Holt, "Politics of Impatience," 523–24.

75. Butler, *Butler's Book*, 119–20; Duberman, *Charles Francis Adams*, 186; Pierce, *Charles Sumner* 3:400; Adams, Diary, March 8, 1853, and Nov. 12, 1854, Adams Family Papers. Adams's quarrel was with the alleged Catholic bloc vote, but not with opposition to the constitution, which he, too, opposed.

76. Formisano, *Transformation of Political Culture*, 330–32; Bean, "Party Transformation in Massachusetts," 89, 210–19, 223, 236, 261–62, 378; O. Handlin, *Boston's Immigrants*, 191–201. Fewer than 4,000 Democrats crossed over to vote against proposition 1. See Baum, *Civil War Party System*, 29.

77. Baum, *Civil War Party System*, 29–34, 232, n. 25; Sweeney, "Rum, Romanism, Representation, and Reform," 136–37. Sweeney argues that although the Irish vote was not instrumental in the defeat of the proposed constitution, the public's perception that it was triggered a massive backlash and led ineluctably to the Know-Nothing sweep in 1854. William G. Bean likewise theorized that this public perception of the Irish role in the defeat of the constitution transformed the Coalition overnight into the Know-Nothing party. See Bean, "Party Transformation in Massachusetts," 223. There are several reasons for rejecting that conclusion. First, it conflicts with the fact that as many opponents of the constitution as proponents voted for "Sam." Second, many, if not most, of the Coalitionists voting Know-Nothing were Free-Soilers whose wholesale conversion to the new party stemmed primarily from their desire to advance the antislavery cause. And finally, most of the Democrats who voted Know-Nothing in 1854 returned to the party fold after a year in which "Sam" enacted most of the constitutional reforms.

78. Baum, *Civil War Party System*, 33–34. Lawrence, with the highest proportion of foreign-born (42 percent) of any city, cast a 78 percent vote for "Sam." Lowell, with 35 percent of her residents foreign-born, went Know-Nothing by 68 percent.

79. *Boston Daily Advertiser*, Dec. 12, 1854; Lucid, *Journal of Richard Henry Dana, Jr.*, 2:632. Oscar Handlin asserted that the Free-Soilers, furious at Irish support of the Kansas-Nebraska Act and the fugitive slave law and the use of Irish military units (which Mayor Smith had called out) to conduct the hapless Burns to the ship waiting to carry him back to slavery, joined with constitutional reformers in an all-out assault against the obstructionist Irish that galvanized a latent nativism and culminated in the Know-Nothing triumph in November 1854. See O. Handlin, *Boston's Immigrants*, 197–201. Mayor Smith's easy win in his reelection bid just one month later, however, despite the furious campaign waged against him for his role in the Burns episode, demonstrates that it took more than fugitive slave roundups and Free-soil protest rallies to mobilize electoral majorities in the capital city.

80. Huntington's speech quoted in the *Boston Daily Advertiser*, April 24, 1855.

81. Baum, *Civil War Party System*, 33; Robinson, *"Warrington" Pen-Portraits*, 482.

82. O. Handlin, *Boston's Immigrants*, 200–1. Dale Baum's approximations that some 12 percent of the 1854 Know-Nothings had sat out the 1852 presidential election and that 25 percent of the 1852 Free-Soilers had abstained in 1854 suggests that the Know-Nothings were more interested in local politics and the Free-Soilers in national politics. See Baum, *Civil War Party Systems*, 33; Baum, "Know-Nothingism and the Republican Majority," 966.

83. Baum, "Know-Nothingism and the Republican Majority in Massachusetts," 963. The Native American party, after its initial flare-up in the 1840s, rapidly lost favor. It ran a separate slate in 1852 that attracted a mere 184 votes. See Greeley, *The Whig Almanac and United States Register, 1853* (New York, 1853), 49.

84. Holt, *Political Crisis of the 1850s*, 174; Holt, "Politics of Impatience," 320.

85. Holt, "Politics of Impatience," 312–13.

86. Free-Soil ward boss James W. Stone, who was himself swept into office by the Know-Nothing tide, estimated that some 25,000 Whigs and Democrats voted "blindly" for "Sam" out of disgruntlement with the "old order of things" and in the hope for "better things" from their government. See Stone to Charles Sumner, Dec. 29, 1854, Sumner Papers.

87. Formisano, *Transformation of Political Culture*, 320, 331.

88. The press to join the lodge in Boston's solidly working-class ward 2 (East Boston) was so great that lodge officers twice had to declare a moratorium on initiations into the order during the months leading up to the 1854 election. See Morse Papers, Feb. 1 and July 12, 1854. More than eight hundred men had joined the lodge when it opened in October 1853. One month later, East Boston voters rejected the proposed constitution by a 546 to 343 margin, and only 71 of the 992 East Bostonians voting for governor opted for Free-Soil candidate Henry Wilson. Two months later, in January, three-quarters of ward 2's voters backed the Know-Nothing candidate for mayor, and the following November, 70 percent of them voted for Henry J. Gardner.

89. Lowell, Lawrence, Fall River, Newburyport, and Lynn.

90. *Yarmouth Register*, Dec. 8, 1854; *Boston Daily Advertiser*, Dec. 6, 1854, and Jan. 10, 1855; Gov. Henry J. Gardner, "Inaugural Address of 1855," Mass., *Acts and Resolves, 1855* (Boston, 1855), 984.

Chapter Four

1. *Lynn Weekly Reporter*, Dec. 30, 1854, and Jan. 6 and March 24, 1855; Everett to Mrs. Eames, Sept. 30, 1854, Letterbooks, Everett Papers.

2. George H. Haynes, "A Know-Nothing Legislature," in American Historical Association, *Annual Report, 1896*, 2 vols. (1897), 1:179.

3. Amos A. Lawrence to Charles Wild, Dec. 26, 1854; Lawrence to Henry J. Gardner, Dec. 28, 1854, Letterbooks, Lawrence Papers; Everett, Diary, Jan. 3, 1855, Everett Papers; *Lynn Weekly Reporter*, Nov. 25, 1854, and Jan. 6, 1855; *Yarmouth Register*, Nov. 10, 1854.

4. Everett, Diary, Nov. 14, 1854, Everett Papers; *Lynn Weekly Reporter*, Nov. 25, 1854.

5. Alexis Poole, *Annual Register of the Executive and Legislative Departments of the Government of Massachusetts, 1855* (Boston, 1855), 3–14; Haynes, "A Know-Nothing Legislature," 185; *Boston Daily Advertiser*, Feb. 7, 1855.

6. Purdy, "Portrait of a Know-Nothing Legislature," 148–49, 155, 163–67, 218–19. One of the eleven lawyers was J.Q.A. Griffin, who, running for the house as a Republican in Charlestown, trailed the field with 12 percent of the vote. No majority obtaining in the initial contest, Griffin ran again in the retrial a fortnight later, this time as a Know-Nothing. Thanks to the backing of his newly adopted party, Griffin's total vote rose from 294 to 1,042, which was enough to win him a seat in the legislature. See the *Bunker Hill Aurora*, Nov. 18 and 25 and Dec. 2, 1854; Robinson, *"Warrington" Pen-Portraits*, 485.

7. Purdy, "Portrait of a Know-Nothing Legislature," 163–67; Poole, *Annual Register, 1855*, 15.

8. Poole, *Annual Register, 1855*, 15; Haynes, "A Know-Nothing Legislature," 178; Purdy, "Portrait of a Know-Nothing Legislature," 165–67.

9. Purdy, "Portrait of a Know-Nothing Legislature," 229.

10. Ibid., 132–34, 140.

11. *Boston Pilot*, Jan. 27, 1855; Everett to Millard Fillmore, Dec. 16, 1854, Letterbooks, Everett Papers; Haynes, "A Know-Nothing Legislature," 178; Purdy, "Portrait of a Know-Nothing Legislature," 166–69, 216. The disproportionate number of clergymen was not unique to the Know-Nothing legislature. The 1853 constitutional convention also included two dozen ministers among its 422 delegates. See the *Gazette* (Dedham), Feb. 17, 1855.

12. Purdy, "Portrait of a Know-Nothing Legislature," 210; Poole, *Annual Register, 1855*, 15. In 1855, there were more than twice as many mechanics and factory workers in the male work force as farmers and farm laborers. See Warner, *Census of Massachusetts, 1860*, 306.

13. *Amesbury and Salisbury Villager*, Dec. 28, 1854.

14. Purdy, "Portrait of a Know-Nothing Legislature," 173–210; Sweeney, "Rum, Romanism, Representation, and Reform," 124, 127–128.

15. Purdy, "Portrait of a Know-Nothing Legislature," 163–210, 262–65.

16. *South Boston Gazette*, Dec. 2, 1854.

17. Edward Pessen has amply demonstrated that government by elites in the Age of the Common Man was by no means confined to Massachusetts. Party leaders nationwide made sure that the ordinary people never exercised meaningful power. See, for example, Pessen, *Jacksonian America: Society, Personality, and Politics* (Urbana, Ill., 1985), 170.

18. *Gazette* (Dedham), Oct. 14 and Nov. 19, 1854, and Feb. 24, 1855; *Boston Daily Advertiser*, Dec. 28, 1854, and Sept. 11, 1857; *Bunker Hill Aurora*, Nov. 10, 1855; *Lynn Weekly Reporter*, March 8, 1856; *Salem Gazette*, Nov. 6, 1857.

19. *Lynn Weekly Reporter*, March 1, 1856; Adams, Diary, Jan. 3, 1855, Adams Papers.

20. Richards, *Samuel Gridley Howe* 2:403.

21. Congdon, *Reminiscences*, 146–47.

22. *Bunker Hill Aurora*, Dec. 2, 1854; Mass., *House Journal, 1855*, 1730–31.

23. Gienapp, *Origins of the Republican Party*, 136; Hoar, *Autobiography* 1:189.

24. *Boston Daily Advertiser*, Jan. 9, 1855; Gardner, "Inaugural Address of 1855," 978–80.

25. Gardner, "Inaugural Address of 1855," 986–88.

26. Ibid., 980, 990.

27. Ibid., 990–95.

28. Haynes, "A Know-Nothing Legislature," 179–86; Hart, *Commonwealth History* 4:490–91.

29. Adams, Diary, Nov. 15 and 22 and Dec. 27, 1854, Adams Family Papers; Everett to Fillmore, Dec. 16, 1854, and April 11, 1855, Letterbooks, Everett Papers, Stone to Sumner, Jan. 13, 1855, Sumner Papers.

30. Downer to Mann, Jan. 7, 1855, Mann Papers.

31. Abner Phelps to Adams, March 23, 1855, Adams Family Papers; Wil-

son, *Slave Power* 2:415; Hoar, *Autobiography* 1:139; Haynes, "A Know-Nothing Legislature," 180–81.

32. Stone to Sumner, Dec. 22, 1854, Sumner Papers; Lawrence to Appleton, Dec. 23, 1854, Letterbooks, Lawrence Papers; Gienapp, *Origins of the Republican Party,* 176.

33. *Springfield Weekly Republican,* Jan. 13, 1855; *Boston Daily Advertiser,* Jan. 13, 17, and 19, 1855; *Worcester Palladium,* Jan. 17, 1855; *Gazette* (Dedham), Jan. 20, 1855.

34. Robinson, *"Warrington" Pen-Portraits,* 544; Hoar, *Autobiography* 1:217; *Boston Daily Advertiser,* Jan. 12 and 19, 1855; *Boston Daily Courier,* Jan. 13, 1855; *Gazette* (Dedham), Jan. 27, 1855; Mass., *State Convention* 1:193–94.

35. *Boston Daily Courier,* Jan. 24, 1855.

36. *Boston Daily Advertiser,* Jan. 24 and 27, 1855.

37. Ibid., Jan. 24, 1855; *Boston Daily Courier,* Feb. 1, 1855; Amos A. Lawrence to his wife, Feb. 1, 1855, Letterbooks, Lawrence Papers.

38. Hoar, *Autobiography* 1:216; Hart, *Commonwealth History* 4:490–91.

39. *Boston Daily Advertiser,* Jan. 19, 1855; *Boston Daily Courier,* Feb. 1, 1855; *Worcester Palladium,* Jan. 24, 1855; Robinson, *"Warrington" Pen-Portraits,* xv, 416, 542, 544; Richards, *Samuel Gridley Howe* 2:409–10; Haynes, "A Know-Nothing Legislature," 181; Bean, "Party Transformation in Massachusetts," 271–72; Baum, *Civil War Party System,* 26; Gienapp, *Origins of the Republican Party,* 136.

40. Adams, Diary, Dec. 27, 1854, Adams Family Papers; Stone to Sumner, Jan. 13, 1855, Sumner Papers; Everett, Diary, Jan. 3, 1855, Everett Papers.

41. Everett, Diary, Jan. 3, 1855, Everett Papers; *Worcester Palladium,* Jan. 10, 1855.

42. Mass., *Acts and Resolves, 1855,* 803–4, 843; *Boston Daily Advertiser,* March 30, 1855.

43. *Boston Daily Advertiser,* March 28 and May 24, 1855; *Salem Gazette,* May 25, 1855; Bean, "Party Transformation in Massachusetts," 285–86, 334; *Boston Pilot,* March 16 and April 14, 1855; Mass., *House Journal, 1855,* 1038, 1731; Lincoln to Schouler, May 24, 1855, Schouler Papers. In the original version, the liquor bill banned the sale of wine for sacramental purposes. This provision was inserted by the Native Americans in an effort to kill the measure. See *Boston Daily Advertiser,* March 22, 1855.

44. George F. Clark, *History of Temperance Reform in Massachusetts, 1813–1883* (Boston, 1888), 89–92; *Boston Daily Bee,* May 10, 1855; *Gazette* (Dedham), May 12, 1855.

45. Lawrence to Giles Richards, March 29, 1855, Letterbooks, Lawrence Papers; Mass., *Documents Printed by the Order of the House of Representatives of the Commonwealth of Massachusetts* (Boston, 1855), *House Document No. 263:*1–12.

46. *Boston Daily Advertiser,* May 22 and 24, 1855. Know-Nothing attorney general John H. Clifford pronounced the efforts to dry up the state by law "an expensive failure," citing as evidence for his disappointment the fact that nearly half of the criminal cases tried in the state courts involved alleged violations of the 1852 and 1855 prohibition laws. See Charles Hale, *Report on the Debates and Proceedings of the Massachusetts Legislature, 1856* (Boston, 1856), 119.

47. For the principles of the nativist parties, see *Address of the Executive Committee of the American Republicans of Boston to the People of Massachusetts* (Boston, 1845), 12; Hector Orr, *The Native American* (Philadelphia, 1845), 150–62; John Hancock

Lee, *The Origins and Progress of the American Party in Politics* (Philadelphia, 1855), 21, 243–44, 248–52.

48. Formisano, *Transformation of Political Culture*, 333; *Boston Daily Advertiser*, Jan. 13, Feb. 20, May 23, and Aug. 10, 1855; Mass., *House Journal, 1855,* 1730–31; Mass., *House Doc. No. 132* (1855), 2–3; *Senate Docs.*, 1855; Everett to A. deVattemere, April 18, 1855, Letterbooks, Everett Papers. Everett expressed concern that the Bible issue might stir up so great a fury between Catholics and Protestants as to endanger the entire public school system. See Everett to Edward Turleston, Feb. 2, 1855, Letterbooks, Everett Papers.

49. *Boston Daily Advertiser*, April 10 and June 4, 1855; Gov. Henry J. Gardner, "Inaugural Address of 1856," Mass., *Acts and Resolves, 1856* (Boston, 1856), 302; Mass., *House Doc. No. 274* (1855), 2–3; Mass., *House Journal, 1855,* 1741–42; Mass., *Senate Journal, 1855,* 859–60. Bean is less than persuasive when he cites the Free-Soil American push to substitute the twenty-one year residency provision in place of total exclusion as an example of their moderation. See Bean, "Party Transformation in Massachusetts," 279–82. A companion measure to exclude illiterates from the vote failed to muster the necessary two-thirds majorities, even though it clearly targeted immigrants, who made up 93 percent of the adult illiterate population. The following two legislatures made up for the oversight, and the proposition was added to the constitution in 1857.

50. *Boston Daily Advertiser*, Jan. 13, 1855; *Boston Daily Courier*, May 29, 1855; *Boston Daily Bee*, Dec. 19, 1855; Mass., *House Journal, 1855,* 58–59, 165; Mass., *House Doc. No. 262* (1855), 1–7 and *House Doc. No. 263* (1855), 1–12.

51. *Boston Daily Advertiser*, Jan. 4, 1856; Gardner, "Inaugural Address of 1856," 308–9; *Boston Daily Bee*, Dec. 19, 1855.

52. *Boston Daily Advertiser*, May 31 and June 7, 1855; *Boston Daily Courier*, May 29, 1855; Hale, *Report on the Massachusetts Legislature, 1856,* 42–43; "Report of the Commissioners of the Alien Passengers and Foreign Paupers," in Mass., *House Doc. No. 41* (1856).

53. Mass., *House Doc. No. 123* (1855); *Boston Daily Advertiser*, March 7, 1855; *Boston Daily Courier*, May 29, 1855.

54. *Boston Daily Courier*, May 29, 1855; *Boston Daily Advertiser*, May 16, 1855.

55. Handlin dismissed "Sam's" nativist record as insignificant, citing as its most egregious action the disbandment of the Irish militia companies. He further asserted that since the American party had a clear mandate to curb Irish political power, its failure to do so in spite of its absolute control of the state government suggests that its reputation for bigotry was overblown. See O. Handlin, *Boston's Immigrants*, 202–3. This conclusion overlooks the changing nature of Know-Nothingism. The 1855 legislature did in fact make clear its intention to strip naturalized citizens and Roman Catholics of their political rights, launching three constitutional amendments for that purpose. When the amendments came before the 1856 legislature for the constitutionally required second vote of approval, however, they encountered difficulties. That body bore little resemblance to the Know-Nothing original—only 64 of the 419 Know-Nothing legislators had returned to their seats. It tabled the resolution to bar Catholics from office and dropped the residency requirement for office and the suffrage from twenty-one to fourteen years. The 1857 legislature defeated the residency amendments, but in 1858 they were resuscitated in the form of a two-year waiting period before naturalized citizens could either vote or hold office. This amendment was ratified in 1859. See Hale, *Report on the Massachusetts*

Legislature, 1856, iii, viii, 87, 320, 349, 355, 417–20; Bean, "Party Transformation in Massachusetts," 330–31; Baum, *Civil War Party System*, 43–45.

    56. *National Aegis*, Feb. 28, 1855.

    57. Wilson, *Slave Power* 2:423–24; *Gazette* (Dedham), Aug. 4, 1855; Abner Phelps to Adams, March 23, 1855, Adams Family Papers.

    58. Mass., *Acts and Resolves, 1855*, 941, 946–47; Mass., *House Doc. No. 45* (1855), 2–3; and *No. 109* (1855), 2–3; Mass., *Senate Doc. No. 203* (1855), 1–2; *Boston Daily Courier*, June 2, 1855; *Boston Daily Advertiser*, Feb. 14, 1855. Even hard-line nativists agreed in principle to the sending of foreigners into the territories so that they could fill the kinds of dangerous, physically demanding construction jobs that Americans tended to avoid. See the *Gazette* (Dedham), Feb. 17, 1855.

    59. Mass., *Acts and Resolves, 1855*, 506, 941, 946–47; Mass., *Senate Doc. No. 162* (1855), 12; Merriam, *Samuel Bowles* 1:134–35.

    60. *Lynn Weekly Reporter*, Feb. 24, 1855; Mass., *Senate Journal, 1855*, 855–58; Mass., *House Journal, 1855*, 1721–26; Lincoln to Schouler, May 24, 1855, Schouler Papers. C. F. Adams denounced the Personal Liberty Bill as too extreme. It was, he told a Know-Nothing legislator, symptomatic of a concept of government in which "the grand panacea for every difficulty is a law, and the longer and more stringent its provisions the better." See Adams to Charles A. Phelps, March 1855, Letterbooks, Adams Family Papers.

    61. Benjamin F. Hallett to Caleb Cushing, April 3, 1855, Caleb Cushing Papers, Library of Congress.

    62. Mass., *Senate Doc. No. 66* (1855), 2–3; Mass., *House Doc. No. 93* (1855), 1–43; *Boston Daily Advertiser*, May 11, 1855; *Liberator*, May 18, 1855; Robinson, *"Warrington" Pen-Portraits*, 21; Merriam, *Samuel Bowles* 1:132–35. The Loring controversy dragged on for the remainder of Gardner's stay in office. Each successive legislature mounted a drive to unseat him, only to be blocked by the governor. Not until Nathaniel Banks assumed the office was Loring removed. See Pearson, *John A. Andrew* 2:71–72. Dale Baum asserts that Gardner's opposition to the removal of Judge Loring and his veto of the Personal Liberty Bill opened up "an irrevocable breach" between the governor and the Wilsonian Americans. See Baum, *Civil War Party System*, 31. Actually, each was willing to work with the other when it served their purposes to do so. Thus, for example, they formed an alliance in 1856 that proved mutually advantageous in the election that year.

    63. Letter of Edmund Quincy (no addressee), May 27, 1855, Edmund Quincy Papers, MHS.

    64. Wilson, *Slave Power* 2:415.

    65. Mass., *Acts and Resolves, 1855*, 954–57; *Boston Post*, Aug. 17 and 18, 1855; *Boston Daily Advertiser*, May 23, 1855; Hart, *Commonwealth History* 4:22–29, 43. The one amendment failing passage—the proposal on representation—had been altered so as to relinquish the principle of apportionment based on population and thus was unacceptable to urban Know-Nothings. The next legislature recast it in the form of two propositions that divided the state into 40 senatorial districts and 240 house districts based on equal numbers of voters. See Mass., *House Journal, 1855*, 1659–62; Hale, *Report on the Massachusetts Legislature, 1856*, 242, 250, 329, 377. When ratified in 1857, the two amendments finally resolved the representation question, which had plagued state politics since the birth of the republic.

    66. Mass., *Senate Journal, 1855*, 45; Mass., *Acts and Resolves, 1855*, 826, 853; *Boston Daily Advertiser*, May 23, 1855. The statute pertaining to jurors fell victim to

the law of unintended consequences. Conceived initially to protect fugitive slaves, its enactment made extremely unlikely jury convictions of violators of the 1855 liquor law. See Bean, "Party Transformation in Massachusetts," 734.

67. *Bunker Hill Aurora*, Nov. 18 and Dec. 2, 1854; *City Advertiser* (Charlestown), July 13, 1853; *Yarmouth Register*, Nov. 10, 1854.

68. *Bunker Hill Aurora*, Dec. 2, 1854; *Yarmouth Register*, Nov. 10 and 17 and Dec. 1, 1854; *City Advertiser* (Charlestown), July 13, 1853; Formisano, *Transformation of Political Culture*, 335; Mass., *House Journal, 1855*, 1730–31.

69. Mass., *Senate Journal, 1855*, 866–68; Mass., *House Journal, 1855*, 1855.

70. Mass., *House Journal, 1855*, 1731, 1739, 1749; Mass., *Senate Journal, 1855*, 866–69; Goodman, "Politics of Industrialism," 196–97.

71. Formisano, *Transformation of Political Culture*, 335; *City Advertiser* (Charlestown), July 13, 1853; *Boston Daily Advertiser*, Jan. 17 and Dec. 6, 1854; *Salem Gazette*, March 7, 1856; *Boston Daily Bee*, Jan. 17, 1855.

72. Gov. Emory Washburn, "Inaugural Address of 1854," Mass., *Acts and Resolves, 1854*, 455; *City Advertiser* (Charlestown), July 13, 1853.

73. *Cambridge Chronicle*, Dec. 29, 1855.

74. *South Boston Gazette*, Sept. 30, 1854; *Boston Daily Advertiser*, Oct. 19, 1855; *Bunker Hill Aurora*, May 5, 1855.

75. Mass., *Acts and Resolves, 1855*, 567, 577, 600, 610, 654–55, 755, 797; *Boston Daily Advertiser*, Jan. 31, 1855; *Cambridge Chronicle*, March 5, 1855.

76. *Worcester Palladium*, Jan. 26, 1853; Wilson, *Address of Hon. Henry Wilson*, 15; Morton, "Inaugural Address of 1840," 299–300; Mass., *State Convention* 1:785; 2:7, 122–24; 3:51–52, 67–71, 168–70. By one measure, legislators lavished four times more attention on private measures than public ones. The special laws passed by the General Court in the quarter century preceding the constitutional convention fill eight volumes; the general laws for that period occupy two volumes. See Mass., *State Convention* 3:168.

77. Mass., *State Convention* 2:259–65, 283–85, 291, 311, 417, 607, 667; 3:465.

78. *Boston Daily Advertiser*, Aug. 23, 1855.

79. *Boston Daily Advertiser*, March 23 and May 19 and 23, 1855; Mass., *Senate Journal, 1855*, 207–8, 363–64, 445; Mass., *Acts and Resolves, 1855*, 498, 666–68, 749–51, 829–30, 869.

80. Mass., *Acts and Resolves, 1855*, 569–72; Hale, *Report on the Massachusetts Legislature, 1856*, 380; Gardner, "Inaugural Address of 1856," 310; *Salem Gazette*, March 14, 1856; *Worcester Palladium*, Oct. 17, 1855.

81. *Worcester Palladium*, Jan. 26, 1853; *Boston Post*, May 2, 1854; *Boston Daily Advertiser*, April 29, 1856, and April 25, 1857; Wilson, *Address of Hon. Henry Wilson*, 15; Mass., *Acts and Resolves, 1855*, 555–56, 645.

82. Mass., *Acts and Resolves, 1856*, 306–7; Gardner, "Inaugural Address of 1856," 307; Hale, *Report on the Massachusetts Legislature, 1856*, 379; *Salem Gazette*, May 1, 1857; Goodman, "Politics of Industrialism," 198.

83. Goodman, "Politics of Industrialism," 39; Mass., *Acts and Resolves, 1855*, 889; Mass., *Acts and Resolves, 1856*, 306; Mass., *Acts and Resolves, 1857*, 719; *Boston Daily Advertiser*, Jan. 17, 1854, May 23 and Oct. 20, 1855, and June 27, 1856; *Salem Gazette*, Jan. 25, 1856; Goodman, "Politics of Industrialism," 196–99.

84. Gardner, "Inaugural Address of 1856," 312–13; Mass., *Acts and Resolves, 1855*, 674–75, 716, 766–67, 812–13, 833, 954, 966; Mass., *School Laws, 1860; Being All the Provisions Relating to Schools* (Boston, 1860), 214–17.

85. Mass., *Acts and Resolves, 1855*, 513, 579, 710–11, 733, 873.

86. *Lynn Weekly Reporter*, March 24, 1855. Rumors of widespread dissatisfaction among rank-and-file Know-Nothings with the senatorial nominations in various districts cropped up at the time of the state nominating convention. Delegates from local lodges, it was said, met at Chapman Hall in Boston to discuss the nominations. After a heated session that lasted until close to midnight, it was decided to refer all senatorial nominations back to the subordinate councils for approval or rejection. See *Yarmouth Register*, Oct. 20, 1854.

87. Charles Cowley, *Illustrated History of Lowell* (Lowell, 1868), 149; Formisano, *Transformation of Political Culture*, 340. A long-time champion of the ten-hour reform, Senator Albert J. Wright, of South Boston, played a critical role in the upset defeat of the ten-hour bill in the senate. Wright's working-class constituents demanded to know why he had "squizzled out" on his commitment, only to be treated to a discourse in the pages of his newspaper on the right of workers to negotiate their own contracts free from government restraints. *Boston Daily Bee*, April 14, 1855; *South Boston Gazette*, April 14 and 28 and June 2, 1855.

88. For an incisive analysis of the complexities of the secret ballot and ten-hour issues and their impact on state politics, see Formisano, *Transformation of Political Culture*, 227–38, 335–40.

89. Mass., *House Journal, 1855*, 1433–40. Gov. Gardner vetoed four bills in all—the Personal Liberty bill, the resolution for the removal of Judge Loring, and the two railroad loans—while approving 488 acts and 88 resolves. Mass., *House Journal, 1855*, 1749. This record hardly comports with the contention that Gardner used his veto power to block a number of important reforms. See, for example, O. Handlin, *Boston's Immigrants*, 202, and Baum, *Civil War Party System*, 31.

90. Mass., *House Journal, 1855*, 1730–40; Mass., *Senate Journal, 1855*, 866–69.

Chapter Five

1. Adams, Diary, Nov. 14, 15, and 22 and Dec. 27, 1854, and Jan. 10, 1855; John Greenleaf Whittier to Adams, Feb. 27, 1855, Adams Family Papers; Richards, *Samuel Gridley Howe* 2:408.

2. Adams to Bradburn, April 20, 1855; Adams to Bird, April 2, 1855; Adams to D. G. Bailey, Jan. 20, 1855, Letterbooks, Adams Family Papers.

3. Everett to C. G. Baylor, Sept. 19, 1853; Everett to Mrs. Eames, Sept. 30, 1854; Everett to Trescot, Oct. 20, 1854; Everett to Fillmore, Nov. 10, 1854, Letterbooks; Everett, Diary, Nov. 14, 1854, and Dec. 24, 1854, Everett Papers.

4. *Boston Daily Bee*, June 15, 1855; *Boston Daily Advertiser*, June 18, 1855; *Daily Evening Traveller*, July 11, 1855; Adams, Diary, April 14, 1855; Adams to Bailey, April 15, 1855, Letterbooks, Adams Family Papers.

5. *Boston Daily Advertiser*, March 31, April 2, 11, and 13 and May 2, 1855; Mass., *House Doc., No.* 263 (1855).

6. Mass., *House Doc., No.* 263 (1855); Mass., *House Journal, 1855*, 1290, 1306, 1558–83; *Boston Daily Bee*, April 23, 1855; *Boston Daily Advertiser*, April 16, 23, 24, and 28 and May 9, 1855; *Boston Investigator*, May 16, 1855.

7. Robinson, *"Warrington" Pen-Portraits*, 63, 461.

8. Donald, *Charles Sumner*, 273; Adams, Diary, April 20, 1855, Adams Family Papers; Amos A. Lawrence to Henry J. Gardner, April 24, 1855; Lawrence to William B. West, May 31, 1855, Letterbooks, Lawrence Papers.

9. O. Handlin, *Boston's Immigrants*, 203; *Boston Daily Bee*, April 3, 1855; *Boston Daily Courier*, April 24 and 25, 1855; *Boston Daily Advertiser*, April 23 and 24 and May 7, 1855.

10. *Boston Daily Bee*, June 29, 1855; Adams to Bradburn, April 20, 1855; Adams to Bailey, April 15, 1855, Letterbooks, Adams Papers.

11. Adams to Bird, April 2, 1855, Letterbooks; Adams, Diary, May 24, 1854, and June 6, 1855, Adams Family Papers; Adams to Richard Henry Dana, Jr. (n.d.), Dana Papers.

12. Everett to Fillmore, April (n.d.) 1855, Letterbooks, Everett Papers; *Boston Daily Advertiser*, May 4 and Oct. 10, 1855; *Gazette* (Dedham), May 5 and 20, 1855; Abbott, *Cobbler in Congress*, 71–77.

13. Henry Wilson to Schouler, April 16, 1855, Schouler Papers.

14. *Boston Daily Advertiser*, May 4 and June 6, 1855; *Gazette* (Dedham), June 9, 1855; Wilson, *Slave Power* 2:423–24.

15. J. P. Kennedy to Winthrop, April 22 and June 18, 1855, Winthrop Papers; Aaron V. Brown, *Speeches, Congressional and Political, and Other Writings* (Nashville, Tenn., 1855), 18.

16. Quoted in the *Boston Daily Courier*, June 5, 1855.

17. W. Darell Overdyke, *The Know-Nothing Party in the South* (Baton Rouge, La., 1950), 128; William G. Bean, "An Aspect of Know-Nothingism—The Immigrant and Slavery," *South Atlantic Quarterly* 23 (1924):328, 331–32; *Boston Daily Courier*, June 8 and 23, 1855; *Gazette* (Dedham), June 9, 1855; Wilson, *Slave Power* 2:423–25.

18. *Daily Evening Traveller*, June 9, 1855; *Boston Daily Advertiser*, June 11, 1855; *Boston Daily Courier*, June 8 and 12, 1855.

19. William G. Brownlow, *Americanism Contrasted with Foreignism, Romanism and Bogus Democracy* (Nashville, Tenn., 1856), 58; *Boston Daily Courier*, June 12 and 13, 1855; *Boston Daily Advertiser*, June 13, 1855; *Daily Evening Traveller*, June 12, 1855; *Gazette* (Dedham), June 16, 1855; *South Boston Gazette*, Aug. 4, 1855.

20. *Daily Evening Traveller*, June 12, 1855; *Boston Daily Advertiser*, June 13, 14, and 19, 1855; *Boston Daily Courier*, June 13 and 14, 1855; *Gazette* (Dedham), June 16, 1855; *South Boston Gazette*, Aug. 4, 1855; Wilson, *Slave Power* 2:426–31.

21. Wilson, *Slave Power* 2:431–32; *Boston Daily Advertiser*, June 15, 1855; *Boston Daily Bee*, June 15, 1855.

22. *Boston Daily Advertiser*, June 19, 1855; Lewis Campbell to Schouler, June 26, 1855, Schouler Papers.

23. Bean, "Party Transformation in Massachusetts," 303; *Boston Daily Advertiser*, Oct. 10, 1855; Wilson, *Slave Power* 2:431, 433.

24. Kennedy to Winthrop, April 22 and June 18, 1855, Winthrop Papers.

25. *Boston Daily Bee*, June 29, 1855; *Boston Daily Advertiser*, June 29, 1855; *Bunker Hill Aurora*, June 30, 1855.

26. *Boston Daily Bee*, June 29, 1855; *Boston Daily Courier*, June 30, 1855; *Daily Evening Traveller*, June 29, 1855.

27. *Daily Evening Traveller*, Aug. 7, 1855; Merriam, *Samuel Bowles* 1:139, 168.

28. Merriam, *Samuel Bowles* 1:140; *Daily Evening Traveller*, Aug. 7, 1855; *Boston Daily Advertiser*, Aug. 8 and 10, 1855.

29. Haynes, "Local History of Knownothingism," 84–87, 90, 93; Morse Papers, Sept. 12, 1855.

30. Bean, "Party Transformation in Massachusetts," 305–6.

31. McKay, *Henry Wilson*, 97; Merriam, *Samuel Bowles* 1:132; *Boston Daily Advertiser*, Aug. 18, 1855.

32. Gienapp, *Origins of the Republican Party*, 221–22; J. B. Mann, *The Life of Henry Wilson, Republican Candidate for Vice-President* (Boston, 1872), 142–45.

33. McKay, *Henry Wilson*, 101–2; Adams to R. H. Dana, Jr. (n.d.), Dana Papers; Mass., *State Convention* 1:924; *Boston Daily Advertiser*, Aug. 11, 1855.

34. *Daily Evening Traveller*, Aug. 8, 1855; *Boston Daily Bee*, Aug. 9, 1855. The new rules left secrecy optional and abolished oaths. Applicants for admission henceforth needed only to receive a majority vote and to sign the party constitution and platform.

35. Everett to J. Thomas, Esq., Feb. 2, 1856, Letterbooks, Everett Papers.

36. *Daily Evening Traveller*, Aug. 16, 1855; *Boston Daily Advertiser*, Aug. 17, 1855; Adams, Diary, Aug. 16, 1855; Adams to Bailey, Sept. 2, 1855, Letterbooks Adams Family Papers; R. H. Dana, Jr., *Journal*, Aug. 16, 1855, Dana Papers; Gienapp, *Origins of the Republican Party*, 215.

37. Gienapp, *Origins of the Republican Party*, 216–17; *Daily Evening Traveller*, Aug. 22, 1855; *Boston Daily Advertiser*, Aug. 24, 1855; Adams, Diary, Aug. 20, 22, 23, 25, and 29 and Sept. 3, 1855; Adams to Bailey, Sept. 2, 1855, Letterbooks, Adams Family Papers; R. H. Dana, Jr., *Journal*, Aug. 22, 1855, Dana Papers; Hoar, *Autobiography* 1:31.

38. Gienapp, *Origins of the Republican Party*, 217; Merriam, *Samuel Bowles* 1:140–41; *Boston Daily Advertiser*, Aug. 24, 1855.

39. Downer to Mann, Aug. 25, 1855, Mann Papers.

40. Gienapp, *Origins of the Republican Party*, 217; Merriam, *Samuel Bowles* 1:140–41; *Boston Daily Advertiser*, Aug. 30, 1855.

41. T. D. Eliot to R. H. Dana, Jr., Aug. 24, 1855, Dana Papers; Adams, Diary, Aug. 23 and Sept. 3, 11, and 17, 1855; Adams to Bailey, Sept. 2, 1855, Letterbooks, Adams Family Papers.

42. *Boston Daily Advertiser*, Sept. 21, 1855; Bean, "Party Transformation in Massachusetts," 323.

43. Samuel Bowles to R. H. Dana, Jr., Sept. 15, 1855, Dana Papers; *Boston Daily Advertiser*, Sept. 21, 1855; *Daily Evening Traveller*, Sept. 21, 1855; *Amesbury and Salisbury Villager*, Sept. 27, 1855.

44. Bean, "Party Transformation in Massachusetts," 319–20; Merriam, *Samuel Bowles* 1:142–43; *Boston Daily Bee*, Sept. 21, 1855.

45. R. H. Dana, Sr., to R. H. Dana, Jr., Sept. 8, 1855; Bowles to R. H. Dana, Jr., Sept. 15, 1855, Dana Papers; *Daily Evening Traveller*, Sept. 20 and 21, 1855; *Daily Herald* (Newburyport), Sept. 22, 1855; *Gazette* (Dedham), Oct. 10, 1855.

46. Adams, Diary, Sept. 21, 1855, Adams Family Papers; R. H. Dana, Sr., to C. S. Henry, Oct. 2, 1855; R. H. Dana, Sr., to Mrs. G. R. Arnold, Oct. 8, 1855; Letter to R. H. Dana, Jr. (illegible signature), Sept. 23, 1855, Dana Papers.

47. *Boston Daily Bee*, Oct. 6, 1855; *Daily Evening Traveller*, Sept. 21, 1855; *Amesbury and Salisbury Villager*, Sept. 27, 1855; *Boston Daily Advertiser*, Oct. 9 and 23, 1855; Adams, Diary, Sept. 21, 1855, Adams Family Papers. My conclusion that

Henry Wilson was the prime mover behind the overturn of Gardner differs from the conventional opinion that Dana engineered it. See, for example, Gienapp, *Origins of the Republican Party*, 219.

48. George S. Boutwell to R. H. Dana, Jr., Sept. 22, 1855, Dana Papers; Adams, Diary, Sept. 21, 1855, Adams Family Papers; *Boston Daily Advertiser*, Sept. 21, 1855. William Gienapp effectively rebuts Dale Baum's assertion that the radical Bird Club was a major force and nativism a minor one in the new party, pointing out that the events that transpired at the Republican convention show just the opposite. See Gienapp, *Origins of the Republican Party*, 219–20, n. 93.

49. Gienapp, *Origins of the Republican Party*, 219–20, n. 93; C. P. Huntington to R. H. Dana, Jr., Sept. 10 and 13, 1855, Dana Papers.

50. *Springfield Republican*, Sept. 19, 1855; Gienapp, *Origins of the Republican Party*, 221; McKay, *Henry Wilson*, 102.

51. Gienapp, *Origins of the Republican Party*, 221; *Daily Evening Traveller*, Oct. 3 and 4, 1855; *Boston Daily Bee*, Sept. 26 and Oct. 4 and 6, 1855.

52. *Middlesex Journal*, May 12 and 19, 1855; Merriam, *Samuel Bowles* 1:154. It is widely held that Gardner retained the support of substantial numbers of antislavery voters in 1855 because of the American party's strong antislavery record. For example, see Gienapp, *Origins of the Republican Party*, 220. The party's record, however, stands in contradistinction to that of the Governor, who vetoed the Personal Liberty Bill and refused to remove Judge Loring from the bench.

53. *Boston Daily Advertiser*, Oct. 4, 1855. For the second year in a row, Governor Gardner presided at the annual state temperance convention. He was warmly applauded when he told his audience that the American party had kept its pledge to enact a tough prohibition law and that his administration intended to enforce it. See *Bunker Hill Aurora*, May 12, 1855.

54. Gienapp, *Origins of the Republican Party*, 220–21; Huntington to R. H. Dana, Jr., Sept. 13, 1855, Dana Papers; *Boston Daily Advertiser*, Sept. 11, 1857; *Worcester Palladium*, Sept. 20 and Oct. 31, 1855; *Barnstable Patriot*, June 12, 1855; *Massachusetts Spy*, Oct. 10, 1855; Hoar, *Autobiography* 1:189; *Gazette* (Dedham), Nov. 10, 1855, and Oct. 24 and 3, 1857.

55. Bowles to R. H. Dana, Jr., Oct. 15, 1855, Dana Papers; *Gazette* (Dedham), Nov. 3, 1855; Merriam, *Samuel Bowles* 1:144; Bean, "Party Transformation in Massachusetts," 330.

56. Everett to Caleb Cushing, Oct. 11, 1855, Letterbooks, Everett Papers; *Daily Herald* (Newburyport), Aug. 23, 1855; Merriam, *Samuel Bowles* 1:141; Boutwell, *Reminiscences* 1:238, 246.

57. Merriam, *Samuel Bowles* 1:143; *Boston Daily Advertiser*, Oct. 4, 1855; John Lothrop Motley to Winthrop, Oct. 20, 1855, Winthrop Papers.

58. Boutwell, *Reminiscences* 1:238; Adams, Diary, Oct. 5, 1855, Adams Family Papers.

59. Adams to Hon. Julius Rockwell, Nov. 9, 1855; Adams to Bailey, Jan. 16, 1856, Letterbooks, Adams Family Papers.

60. Motley to Winthrop, Oct. 20, 1855, Winthrop Papers.

61. Hale, *Report on the Massachusetts Legislature, 1856*, 3; Adams, Diary, Nov. 6, 1855, Adams Family Papers; Baum, *Civil War Party System*, 34–35; Gienapp, *Origins of the Republican Party*, 221–23.

62. *Daily Evening Traveller*, Nov. 7, 1855.

63. Gienapp, *Origins of the Republican Party*, 222–23; *Boston Daily Advertiser*, Nov. 8, 1855.

64. Everett, Diary, Nov. 7, 1855, Everett Papers; Adams, Diary, Nov. 10, 1855, Adams Family Papers. See also *Boston Daily Advertiser*, Nov. 8, 1855; *Boston Daily Bee*, Nov. 8, 1855; Merriam, *Samuel Bowles* 1:144.

65. Baum, *Civil War Party System*, 35–37; Gienapp, "Nativism and the Creation of a Republican Majority," 533, 540.

66. Haynes, "Local History of Knownothingism," 84–86, 90, 93; Morse Papers, Sept. 12, 1855; *Barnstable Patriot*, July 3, 1855; *Middlesex Journal*, Sept. 8, 1855; *Worcester Palladium*, Sept. 19, 1855; *Boston Daily Bee*, Sept. 29, 1855; *Bunker Hill Aurora*, Dec. 15, 1855.

67. Baum, "Know-Nothingism and the Republican Majority," 965–68; Geinapp, *Origins of the Republican Party*, 222.

68. Haynes, "A Know-Nothing Legislature," 186.

69. Baum, *Civil War Party System*, 34–36.

70. Holt, "Politics of Impatience," 319–20; *Gazette* (Dedham), Nov. 3, 1855.

71. *Boston Daily Advertiser*, Dec. 6, 1854; *Cambridge Chronicle*, Dec. 29, 1855.

72. *Daily Herald*, (Newburyport), Oct. 31, 1854; *Lowell Weekly Journal and Courier*, Dec. 11, 1855; *Boston Daily Advertiser*, Dec. 12, 1855.

Chapter Six

1. *Boston Daily Advertiser*, Nov. 15, 1855.

2. Ibid., Jan. 7 and 25, 1856; *Lowell Weekly Journal and Courier*, Dec. 11, 1855; *Bunker Hill Aurora*, Dec. 11 and 15, 1855.

3. Henry J. Gardner to Schouler, June 15, 1855, Schouler Papers.

4. *Boston Daily Bee*, Nov. 14, 1855; *Daily Evening Traveller*, Nov. 14 and 19, 1855; *Boston Daily Advertiser*, Nov. 15 and 23, 1855; F. W. Prescott to A. A. Lawrence, Dec. 25, 1855; Lawrence to Prescott, Dec. 17, 22, 25, and 29, 1855, Letterbooks, Lawrence Papers; Stone to Sumner, Jan. 25, 1856, Sumner Papers.

5. Prescott to Lawrence, Feb. 5, 1856, Lawrence Papers; *Daily Evening Traveller*, Nov. 19, 1855, and Feb. 6, 1856; *Boston Daily Advertiser*, Nov. 23, 24, and 26, 1855.

6. Gardner, "Inaugural Address of 1856," 304; *Boston Daily Courier*, Jan. 4, 1856; Merriam, *Samuel Bowles* 1:146; Gienapp, *Origins of the Republican Party*, 387.

7. Gardner, "Inaugural Address of 1856," 300–2; *Boston Daily Advertiser*, Jan. 4, 1856. The dispatch of nearly three hundred aliens overseas marked a sharp upturn in the enforcement of the pauper removal law under the Know-Nothings. The previous legislature, for example, had sent 113 back to Ireland. See Mass., *Senate Doc. No. 29* (1855), 5.

8. Everett, Diary, May 21, 1855, Everett Papers; Stone to Sumner, Jan. 25, 1856, Sumner Papers.

9. Hale, *Report on The Massachusetts Legislature, 1856*, iii, viii, 320, 417; *Boston Daily Advertiser*, Jan. 11, 1856; *Gazette* (Dedham), April 5, 1856.

10. Stone to Sumner, March 25, 1856, Sumner Papers; Alexis Poole, *Annual Register of the Executive and Legislative Department of the Government of Massachusetts, 1856* (Boston, 1856), 15; Haynes, "A Know-Nothing Legislature," 186; Purdy, "Portrait of a Know-Nothing Legislature," 163–64.

11. Julius Rockwell to Winthrop, Feb. 6, 1856, Winthrop Papers.

12. *Boston Daily Advertiser*, March 28, 1856; Mass., *Journal of the House of Representatives, 1856* (Boston, 1856), 497–98, 603–4, 1104–6; Mass., *Senate Doc. No. 43* (1857), 2–4; Hale, *Report on The Massachusetts Legislature, 1856*, 87, 152, 188, 339, 349, 355, 419–20. The literacy test was seconded by the 1857 legislature and ratified by the voters, but the more extreme fourteen-year amendment failed passage. The following year, a Republican-sponsored two-year amendment took its place and was ratified in 1859. These two amendments are the only constitutional changes aimed at curbing the political power of naturalized citizens that originated in the Know-Nothing period. Some historians cite the failure of the Know-Nothings to capitalize on their three-year reign of power to reduce the Irish Catholic minority to the status of second-class citizens as evidence that party policy on this matter was much more moderate than party rhetoric. See, for example, O. Handlin, *Boston's Immigrants*, 202–3. This assumption ignores the fact that only the constitutional provision that an amendment must receive a two-thirds majority in both houses in two consecutive legislative sessions prevented their passage. An overwhelming majority of the legislators sent from the dark-lantern lodges to the General Court in 1855 endorsed constitutional proposals designed to preserve the Yankee Protestant monopoly of political power by depriving Irish Catholics of the power of the vote and the right to hold public office. Succeeding legislatures, however, which bore little resemblance to the original Know-Nothing body, rejected these extreme measures in favor of the more moderate approach mentioned above.

13. Brownlow, *Americanism*, 12–15; *Daily Evening Traveller*, Feb. 18, 1856; *Boston Daily Advertiser*, Feb. 22, 1856; *Boston Daily Courier*, Feb. 23, 1856; *Worcester Palladium*, Feb. 27, 1856. For a copy of the Philadelphia platform, see Cooper and Fenton, *American Politics*, 57.

14. *Boston Daily Advertiser*, Feb. 23 and 26, 1856; Wilson, *Slave Power* 2:509. Only two of the thirteen Bay State delegates joined the bolters. The majority remained in hopes that the convention might still tap their chief for the second spot on the national ticket. Brownlow, *Americanism*, 15–16.

15. Prescott to A. A. Lawrence, Dec. 17, 1855; Lawrence to Prescott, Dec. 29, 1855; Lawrence to Judge H. E. Davies, Feb. 26, 1856, Letterbooks, Lawrence Papers; *Boston Evening Transcript*, Feb. 26, 1856. Gardner received only eight votes in the balloting for the vice-presidential nomination. Horace Greeley and John F. Cleveland, *A Political Text-Book for 1860* (New York, 1860), 23.

16. Brownlow, *Americanism*, 15–16; *Daily Evening Traveller*, Feb. 26, 1856; *Boston Daily Advertiser*, Feb. 27, 1856.

17. T. P. Chandler to Sumner, March 3, 1856; Seth Webb to Sumner, March 19, 1856, Sumner Papers; Adams, Diary, Feb. 25, 1856, Adams Family Papers.

18. Benjamin F. Wade to Schouler, March 11, 1856, Schouler Papers.

19. Everett, Diary, Nov. 30, 1855; Everett to J. A. Hamilton, Dec. 3, 1855; Everett to Winthrop, Dec. 31, 1855, Letterbooks, Everett Papers; J. J. Crittenden to Winthrop, March 1, 1855; Fillmore to Winthrop, Sept. 26, 1856, Winthrop Papers; S. T. Dana to Lawrence, Feb. 26, 1856, Lawrence Papers.

20. Amos A. Lawrence to Prescott, Nov. 7, 1855; Lawrence to John Carter Brown, Nov. 9, 1855, Letterbooks, Lawrence Papers.

21. Lawrence to Judge Davies, Feb. 26, 1856, Letterbooks, Lawrence Papers.

22. Hamilton Fish to Winthrop, March 19, 1856, Winthrop Papers; Everett

to Prescott, Jan. 20, 1856, Letterbooks; R. C. Winthrop to Everett, Nov. 16, 1854, Everett Papers.

23. Thomas J. Marsh to N. P. Banks, March 19, 1856, Nathaniel Prentiss Banks Papers, Essex Institute; Lawrence to Davies, Feb. 26, 1856, Letterbooks, Lawrence Papers.

24. Stone to Banks, April 14, 1856, Banks Papers; McKay, *Henry Wilson*, 14.

25. *Daily Evening Traveller*, March 5, 1856.

26. Seth Webb to Sumner, March 19, 1856; Stone to Sumner, March 25, 1856, Sumner Papers; *Boston Daily Advertiser*, March 5, 1856; *Gazette* (Dedham), March 15, 1856. Those pondering the sincerity of Fillmore's commitment to "American principles" had cause for concern. He was on a European tour that included an audience with the Pope when word reached him of his nomination. See *Daily Evening Traveller*, March 5, 1856.

27. John A. Sanborn to Banks, April 9, 1856, Banks Papers; Lawrence to Appleton, May (n.d.) 1856, Letterbooks, Lawrence Papers; *Boston Daily Courier*, May 7, 1856; *Daily Evening Traveller*, May 7, 1856; *Salem Gazette*, May 9, 1856; Gienapp, *Origins of the Republican Party*, 387.

28. *Boston Daily Courier*, May 7 and 8, 1856.

29. Lawrence to Appleton; May (n.d.) 1856, Letterbooks, Lawrence Papers; Everett to R. Hawes, May 10, 1856, Letterbooks, Everett Papers.

30. One sign of the impact of the Lawrence, Kansas, and Charles Sumner incidents on state politics was the decision by the Massachusetts house to reverse its vote to repeal the Personal Liberty Law. See *Boston Daily Advertiser*, May 23 and 28, 1856; Hale, *Report on the Massachusetts Legislature, 1856*, 318–21, 337–39.

31. Everett, Diary, May 25, 1856, Adams Family Papers; Everett to Horace Maynard, Oct. 3, 1857; Everett to Earl Stanhope, Jan. 12, 1857; Everett to Fillmore, July 16, 1856, Letterbooks, Everett Papers.

32. Hale, *Report on the Massachusetts Legislature, 1856*, 330–34; Adams, Diary, May 23, 1856, Adams Family Papers; Everett to Hamilton, June 30, 1856, Letterbooks, Everett Papers; Stone to Sumner, May 22, 1856, Sumner Papers.

33. Lawrence to Appleton, May (n.d.) 1856, Letterbooks, Lawrence Papers. Most historians agree that the "sack" of Lawrence and the assault on Sumner vastly improved the Republican party's chances in the forthcoming presidential election. See, for example, Gienapp, *Origins of the Republican Party*, 299–303; Holt, *Political Crisis of the 1850s*, 194–96.

34. Adams, Diary, June 7, 1856, Adams Family Papers.

35. Holt, *Political Crisis of the 1850s*, 177; Fred H. Harrington, *Fighting Politician: Major General N. P. Banks* (Philadelphia, 1948), 36–38; Stone to Banks, June 14, 1856; Ezra Clark to Banks, June 14, 1856, Banks Papers.

36. George Law to Banks, June 23, 1856, Banks Papers; *Boston Daily Courier*, June 17, 1856.

37. Adams to J. G. Palfrey, July 13, 1856, Letterbooks, Adams Family Papers.

38. Lawrence to Henry J. Gardner, April 4, 1856, Letterbooks, Lawrence Papers; Gienapp, *Origins of the Republican Party*, 387.

39. *City Advertiser* (Charlestown), July 12, 1856; *Daily Evening Traveller*, July 1 and 2, 1856; Lawrence to S. G. Haven, July 5, 1856, Letterbooks, Lawrence Papers.

Lawrence attributed the switch to Fremont to the arrival of news from Washington that Congress had voted against the admission of Kansas as a free state. A more plausible explanation is that Gardner's lieutenants manipulated the convention's votes in order to impress the Republicans. On another front, for example, the party's official organ, the *Boston Daily Bee*, which had endorsed the Fillmore-Donelson ticket, struck their names from the top of its editorial page and raised those of Fremont and Johnston in their place. See the *Salem Gazette*, July 11, 1856. *Bee* publisher Samuel Bradbury was a Gardner ally.

40. *Daily Evening Traveller*, July 2, 1856.

41. Gardner to Amos A. Lawrence, July 5, 1856; Moses G. Cobb to Lawrence, July 5 and 10, 1856, Lawrence Papers.

42. *Boston Daily Advertiser*, July 25, 1856; *Bunker Hill Aurora*, July 26, 1856.

43. *Boston Daily Advertiser*, July 25, 1856; *Daily Evening Traveller*, July 24, 1856. Peirce had earlier confided to Banks that he preferred a Fremont-Banks ticket to that of Fremont-Donelson because he was confident that if the former were elected "no Alians [sic] or Roman Catholicks [sic] would be retained in office." See Jonathan Peirce to Banks, Feb. 25, 1856, Banks Papers.

44. *Daily Evening Traveller*, July 25, 1856; *Worcester Palladium*, July 30, 1856; *Boston Daily Advertiser*, July 25, 26, and 30, 1856; *Bunker Hill Aurora*, Aug. 16, 1856.

45. Bean, "Party Transformation in Massachusetts," 343–44; *Worcester Palladium*, Aug. 13, 1856; *Boston Daily Advertiser*, Aug. 6, 1856; *Daily Evening Traveller*, Aug. 6, 1856.

46. *Daily Evening Traveller*, Aug. 21, 1856; *Boston Daily Advertiser*, Aug. 21, 1856.

47. *Boston Daily Advertiser*, Aug. 21, 1856; Cobb to Lawrence, Aug. 20, 1856, Lawrence Papers. For a conflicting account of the national American convention, see J.D.W. Jay to Lawrence, Aug. 20, 1856, Lawrence Papers.

48. Dr. LeBaron Russell to Amos A. Lawrence, Aug. 29, 1856; J.M.S. Williams to Lawrence, Aug. 21, 1856, Lawrence Papers.

49. *Boston Daily Advertiser*, Sept. 1, 1856; Amos A. Lawrence to Committee of Fillmore Americans, Aug. 26, 1856, Letterbooks; A. B. Ely to Lawrence, Aug. 26, 1856, Lawrence Papers.

50. Donald, *Charles Sumner*, 318; Merriam, *Samuel Bowles* 1:193.

51. Donald, *Charles Sumner*, 320–21; Adams to Sumner, April 16, 1856, Letterbooks; Adams, Diary, Sept. 5 and Nov. 20, 1856, Adams Family Papers.

52. Merriam, *Samuel Bowles* 1:193.

53. Adams to Palfrey, July 29, 1856, Letterbooks; Bird to Adams, July 28, 1856; Adams, Diary, Sept. 15, 1856, Adams Family Papers.

54. Gienapp, *Origins of the Republican Party*, 387–88.

55. Everett to D. D. Barnard, Nov. 22, 1855, Letterbooks, Everett Papers.

56. *Bunker Hill Aurora*, Aug. 2, 1856; Robinson, *"Warrington" Pen-Portraits*, 437; *Daily Evening Traveller*, Sept. 16, 1856; *Boston Daily Bee*, Sept. 17, 1856; *Boston Daily Advertiser*, Sept. 17, 1856.

57. The leading role of former Americans Wilson, Foster, and Banks in patching up the differences between the governor and the Republicans contradicts the assertion that Gardner's removal of Judge Loring and his veto of the Personal Liberty Bill

had opened up an"irrevocable breach" between himself and the Free-Soil Americans a year earlier. See, for example, Baum, *Civil War Party System*, 31.

58. Bean, "Party Transformation in Massachusetts," 344; *Boston Daily Advertiser*, Sept. 17, 1856; *Daily Evening Traveller*, Oct. 2, 1856.

59. Adams, Diary, Sept. 16, 1856, Adams Family Papers; Merriam, *Samuel Bowles* 1:174–75. "Warrington" was so furious with Wilson's bargain with the Know-Nothings that he rushed home from the convention, ripped his friend's picture from the wall, tore it in half, and hurled it to the floor. See Robinson, *"Warrington" Pen-Portraits*, 63–64. Wilson's boast to the contrary, the Know-Nothings were a vital political force whose support was essential if the Republicans were to carry the state. See Gienapp, *Origins of the Republican Party*, 378, 387–88.

60. *Daily Evening Traveller*, Oct. 3, 1856; Pearson, *John A. Andrew* 1:66.

61. A. B. Ely to Lawrence, Oct. 27, 1856, Lawrence Papers.

62. State Executive Committee of the National American Party in Massachusetts, *the Record of George Wm. Gordon* (Boston, 1856), 16; *Boston Daily Advertiser*, Sept. 1 and 4, 1856; *Daily Evening Traveller*, Oct. 28, 1856.

63. *Daily Evening Traveller*, Sept. 1 and 3, 1856; Ely to Lawrence, Oct. 16 and 27, 1856, Lawrence Papers. Ely placed a distant third in his district, a disappointment somewhat mitigated by the trouncing of William Appleton in his house race. The latter result spurred one unreconstructed Whig to comment, "You must have got to a pitch of political frenzy at home unknown since the days of the French Revolution!" See G. Shaw to Franklin Dexter, Nov. 20, 1856, Franklin Dexter Papers, MHS.

64. Ezra Farnsworth to Lawrence, Oct. 30, 1856, Lawrence Papers; Benjamin Wade to Schouler, March 1, 1856, Schouler Papers. Lawrence took a contrary position, arguing that the contest was between Fillmore and Buchanan and that unless all opposition to Buchanan united behind Fillmore, the Democrat would win. See Lawrence to Gardner, Oct. 22, 1856, Letterbooks, Lawrence Papers.

65. Everett to Fillmore, July 16, 1856, Letterbooks, Everett Papers; Adams to S. M. Gates, Sept. 9, 1856, Letterbooks, Adams Family Papers.

66. Hale, *Report on the Massachusetts Legislature, 1856*; Gienapp, *Origins of the Republican Party*, 414, 419–20.

67. Gienapp, "Nativism and the Creation of the Republican Majority," 546, 557, n. 46, 558 n. 47.

68. Ibid., 542, 545–47; Thomas J. Gould to Banks, Dec. 1, 1855; J. P. Gould to Banks, Dec. 4, 1855, Banks Papers; J. Z. Goodrich to Adams, March 6, 1857, Adams Family Papers.

69. Gienapp, *Origins of the Republican Party*, 418–48.

Chapter Seven

1. Gienapp, *Origins of the Republican Party*, 439; *Boston Daily Advertiser*, Dec. 8, 1856; *Boston Daily Bee*, Dec. 15, 1856.

2. *Boston Journal*, Jan. 7, 1857. The modified platform dropped the twenty-one year residency requirement from the neutralization plank, leaving it without a specific time limit. For the complete platform, see the *Boston Daily Bee*, Jan. 7, 1857.

3. *Boston Morning Journal*, Jan. 3, 1857.

4. Henry J. Gardner, "Inaugural Address of 1857," Mass., *Acts and Resolves, 1857* (Boston, 1857), 707; *Boston Daily Advertiser*, Jan. 10, 1857; *Gazette* (Dedham), June 20, 1857.

5. Gardner, "Inaugural Address of 1857," 707.

6. Ibid., 708–9.

7. Ibid., 710.

8. Ibid., 711.

9. Adams, Diary, Nov. 20, 1856, Adams Family Papers; *Daily Evening Traveller*, Jan. 9, 1857.

10. Edward L. Pierce to Sumner, May 10, 1857, Sumner Papers.

11. T. Davis to Dwight Foster, Oct. 24, 1856, George Frisbee Hoar Papers, MHS; Henry Wilson to E. L. Pierce, March 12 and April 23, 1857, Edward L. Pierce Papers; *City Advertiser* (Charlestown), Oct. 29, 1856; *Bunker Hill Aurora*, March 28, 1857; *Boston Daily Bee*, April 2, 1857. The Know-Nothings claimed that they had a clear understanding with the Republicans whereby American legislators would support Sumner's bid for reelection in exchange for Republican backing for the constitutional amendments. See the *Boston Daily Bee*, March 26, 1857, and the *Boston Morning Journal*, March 26, 1857.

12. *Letter of Edward L. Pierce of Chicago Containing Important Statistics in Regard to the Foreign Vote* (Boston, 1857), 15; Adams to Sumner, May 5, 1857, Letterbooks, Adams Family Papers; Mass., *Senate Doc. No. 109* (1857), 2; *Boston Daily Advertiser*, April 29, 1857; Pierce to Sumner, May 10, 1857, Sumner Papers.

13. Wilson to Pierce, April 23, 1857, Pierce Papers; *Boston Daily Advertiser*, June 1, 1857.

14. *Boston Daily Advertiser*, April 14, 1857; *City Advertiser* (Charlestown), Sept. 12, 1857.

15. William S. Robinson to G. F. Hoar, Dec. 7, 1856, George F. Hoar Papers; Gienapp, *Origins of the Republican Party*, 418–22.

16. Adams to Sumner, May 5, 1857, Sumner Papers.

17. Gardner to A. A. Lawrence, April 20, 1857; A. A. Lawrence to Judge Conway, Jan. 22, 1857, Letterbooks, Lawrence Papers; Mass., *Acts and Resolves, 1857*, 759–65; *Boston Daily Bee*, May 30, 1857.

18. Mass., *Acts and Resolves, 1857*, 785; *Boston Morning Journal*, May 19, 26, 28, and 29, 1857; *Boston Daily Advertiser*, May 29 and Aug. 29, 1857; *Gazette* (Dedham), Sept. 19, 1857; Richards, *Samuel Gridley Howe* 2:455–60.

19. *Boston Daily Bee*, June 1, 1857; Pierce to Sumner, May 10, 1857, Sumner Papers; Adams to Sumner, June 26, 1857, Letterbooks, Adams Family Papers.

20. *Boston Daily Bee*, June 6, 1857. As late as April 29, the *Bee* had been urging the American party to cut itself adrift from the Republicans because of the latter's opposition to the fourteen-year amendment. The newspaper's sudden about-face stemmed in part from *Bee* publisher and erstwhile Gardner ally Samuel Bradbury's wish to be on the winning side, but the General Court's repeal of the *Bee's* lucrative contract as the official state organ, which Bradbury blamed on Gardner, no doubt also influenced the decision. See the *Boston Daily Advertiser*, Feb. 9, 1857; *Boston Daily Bee*, April 29, 1857; Mass., *Acts and Resolves, 1857* 666.

21. Adams to Sumner, June 26, 1857, Letterbooks, Adams Family Papers.

22. *Boston Daily Advertiser*, June 17, 1857; *Worcester Palladium*, March 25, 1857; *Boston Daily Bee*, June 17, 1857.

23. *Boston Morning Journal*, June 20, 1857; *Boston Daily Advertiser*, June 20, 1857.

24. *Boston Daily Advertiser,* June 17, 1857; *Worcester Palladium,* June 24, 1857; *Gazette* (Dedham), Nov. 14, 1857.

25. Adams to Sumner, June 26, 1857, Letterbooks, Adams Family Papers.

26. *Boston Daily Advertiser,* June 12, 1857.

27. Adams to Sumner, June 26, 1857, Letterbooks, Adams Family Papers; Bean, "Party Transformation in Massachusetts," 359–60.

28. Bird to Sumner, June 8, 1857, Sumner Papers; Francis W. Bird, *Review of Gov. Banks' Veto of the Revised Code on Account of Its Authorizing the Enrolment of Colored Citizens in the Militia* (Boston, 1860), 11.

29. Bird to Sumner, June 8, 1857, Sumner Papers; *Boston Morning Journal,* June 20 and 24, 1857.

30. *Boston Morning Journal,* June 20, 1857. Wilson's boast that the Republicans could have easily defeated Gardner in 1856 rings hollow. As William Gienapp notes, if the Republicans had been certain of victory in a face-off with the Know-Nothings, they would have mounted a challenge. See Gienapp, *Origins of the Republican Party,* 387.

31. Wilson to Sumner, Jan. 19, 1857, Sumner Papers.

32. *Boston Daily Advertiser,* June 25, 1857.

33. Ibid.; *Boston Morning Journal,* June 24, 1857; Adams to Sumner, June 29, 1857, Letterbooks, Adams Family Papers.

34. *Boston Morning Journal,* June 24 and 25, 1857; *Boston Daily Bee,* June 25, 1857; *Boston Daily Advertiser,* June 25, 1857; *Gazette* (Dedham), June 27, 1857; Adams to Sumner, June 26, 1857, Letterbooks, Adams Family Papers. The nomination of Banks further illustrates the inability of the Bird Club to influence Republican policy and underscores the sensitivity of Republican decision makers to the appeal of nativism. For a contrary view, see Baum, *Civil War Party System,* 3–4, 6–7, 48–49.

35. *Boston Daily Bee,* July 16, 1857; *Boston Morning Journal,* July 18, 1857.

36. *Boston Daily Advertiser,* Aug. 29, 1857; *Boston Morning Journal,* Aug. 29, 1857; *Boston Daily Bee,* Aug. 29 and 31, 1857; Harrington, *Banks,* 45–46.

37. *Boston Daily Bee,* Aug. 29, 1857.

38. Ibid., Sept. 3, 1857.

39. *Boston Daily Advertiser,* Aug. 29 and Sept. 1, 1857; *Boston Daily Bee,* Sept. 3 and 11, 1857; Lawrence to Moses Cobb, July 8, 1857, Letterbooks, Lawrence Papers; Bird to Sumner, June 8, 1857, Sumner Papers.

40. *Boston Daily Advertiser,* Sept. 11, 1857; *Boston Daily Bee,* Sept. 11 and Oct. 3 and 8, 1857; *Boston Morning Journal,* Sept. 11 and Oct. 9, 1857.

41. *Boston Daily Advertiser,* Aug. 29 and Sept. 11, 1857; *Bunker Hill Aurora,* Sept. 12, 1857.

42. *Boston Morning Journal,* Sept. 11, 1857; *Boston Daily Bee,* Sept. 12, 1857.

43. *Boston Daily Advertiser,* Sept. 11, 1857.

44. Ibid.; *Gazette* (Dedham), Sept. 19, 1857; *Boston Daily Bee,* Sept. 24 and 30, 1857.

45. Boutwell, *Reminiscences* 1:107; Robinson, *"Warrington" Pen-Portraits,* 437–38; Fred H. Harrington, "Nathaniel Prentiss Banks—A Study in Anti-Slavery Politics," *New England Quarterly* 9 (December 1936): 627.

46. Harrington, "Nathaniel Prentiss Banks," 638–39.

47. Erastus Hopkins to Adams, Aug. 19, 1857, Adams Family Papers;

Boston Daily Advertiser, Oct. 16, 1857; *Boston Daily Bee*, Oct. 16, 1857; Robinson, *"Warrington" Pen-Portraits*, 87, 220; Bean, "Party Transformation in Massachusetts," 360. The spat between the Bird Club and the patrician Free-Soilers was over tactics, not principles. Charles Francis Adams, for example, when asked by a Native American if he considered antislavery principles paramount to the issue of "Americanism," replied that he could not "summon the shadow of an apprehension" with regard to an alleged foreign influence. To peddle the idea that a tiny minority of ill-educated foreigners is going to rule the native-born through the process of free elections, he explained, is "the greatest insult that can be offered to the energy and intelligence of the American people." See Adams to J. Orton, Feb. 20, 1855, Letterbooks, Adams Family Papers.

48. Robinson, *"Warrington" Pen-Portraits*, 418; Adams to Hopkins, Aug. 20 and 26, 1857, Letterbooks, Adams Family Papers.

49. Adams to Sumner, Oct. 5, 1857, Letterbooks, Adams Family Papers.

50. *Bunker Hill Aurora*, Oct. 3, 1857; *Boston Daily Advertiser*, Oct. 16, 1857; F. E. Parker to R. H. Dana, Jr., Aug. 24, 1857, R. H. Dana, Jr., Papers; A. J. Clough to Banks, Oct. 23, 1857, Banks Papers; Everett, Diary, Feb. 3, 1856, Everett Papers. Dale Baum, in making the case that tensions over slavery fueled the rise of the Republican party, minimizes the importance of nativism and anti-Catholicism in the party's development. See Baum, *Civil War Party System*, 26–27. Banks's replacing the pure Republicans on his ticket with Know-Nothing converts was but one of a whole series of events, ranging from Gardner's near win at the first Republican convention to the overwhelming Republican vote for the Know-Nothing governor in 1856, that are inconsistent with the assertion that ethnocultural tensions did not play major part in the formation of the Republican majority. See Gienapp, *Origins of the Republican Party*, 219–20, n. 93, 420, n. 27.

51. *Boston Daily Advertiser*, Sept. 9, 1857; Robinson, *"Warrington" Pen-Portraits*, 438. George F. Clark, *History of Temperance Reform in Massachusetts, 1813–1883* (Boston, 1888), 89.

52. *Boston Daily Bee*, Oct. 30 and 31, 1857. Garner's stock-in-trade was his strategic dispensation of patronage plums. Not all of his appointments proved felicitous, however. In 1855, he had named A. B. Ely to a two-year term on the board of directors of the Western Railroad. See Mass., *Senate Journal, 1855*. Gardner's siding with Fremont against Fillmore in 1856, however, led to an irrevocable breach between the governor and the Native American ideologue.

53. Everett to Fillmore, Dec. 16, 1854, Letterbooks; Everett, Diary, Nov. 15, 1854, Feb. 3, 1856, and Nov. 3, 1857, Everett Papers.

54. *Daily Herald*, (Newburyport); *Boston Daily Advertiser*, Oct. 17 and 29, 1857; *Bunker Hill Aurora*, Oct. 17, 1857; Harrington, *Banks*, 43–44.

55. *Daily Herald*, (Newburyport), Oct. 27, 1857; *Boston Daily Advertiser*, Oct. 15 and 21, and Nov. 23, 1857.

56. *Boston Daily Advertiser*, May 1, 1857; *Salem Gazette*, May 1, 1857; *Worcester Palladium*, Oct. 28, 1857.

57. *Worcester Palladium*, May 20, June 10, July 1, and Oct. 28, 1857; *Gazette* (Dedham), June 27, 1857; *Bunker Hill Aurora*, Sept. 26, 1857; Hale, *Report on the Massachusetts Legislature, 1856*, 39.

58. *Boston Daily Advertiser*, Sept. 15, 1857.

59. Ibid., May 1, 1857; *Salem Gazette*, May 1, 1857.

60. Joseph G. Rayback, "The American Workingman and the Antislavery Crusade," *Journal of Economic History* 3 (Nov. 1943): 61–62.

61. Robinson, *"Warrington" Pen-Portraits*, 408–9, 435; *Boston Daily Advertiser*, Oct. 21, 1857.

62. Congdon, *Reminiscences*, 147–48.

63. R. B. Hubbard to Banks, Oct. 7, 1857, Banks Papers.

64. Robinson, *"Warrington" Pen-Portraits*, 225; *Boston Daily Advertiser*, Nov. 5, 1857; *Salem Gazette*, Nov. 6, 1857.

65. Haynes, "Local History of Knownothingism," 84–87, 90, 93; Morse Papers, Sept. 12, 1855; Baum, *Civil War Party System*, 35–41; Baum, "Know-Nothingism and the Republican Majority in Massachusetts," 969–70; Gienapp, *Origins of the Republican Party*, 222.

66. Robinson, *"Warrington" Pen-Portraits*, 25–26.

67. Ibid., 302.

68. *Gazette* (Dedham), Nov. 14, 1857; *Salem Gazette*, Sept. 17, 1858; Winthrop, Jr., *Memoir of Robert C. Winthrop*, 207.

69. Adams to Goodrich, Nov. 5, 1858; Adams to Sumner, Nov. 28, 1858, Letterbooks, Adams Family Papers.

70. Harrington, *Banks*, 42–46; Richards, *Samuel Gridley Howe* 2:474; James Schouler, "The Massachusetts Convention of 1853," *Proceedings of the Massachusetts Historical Society* 38 (Nov. 1903): 5; Roe, "Governors of Massachusetts," 545.

71. Gienapp, "Nativism and the Creation of a Republican Majority," 557–59; Baum, *Civil War Party System*, 41.

72. *Gazette* (Dedham), Nov. 14, 1857; Bird, *Review of Gov. Banks' Veto*, 11.

73. *Gazette* (Dedham), Oct. 24, 1857; *Boston Daily Advertiser*, Oct. 20, 21, and 26 and Nov. 2, 1857; Harrington, *Banks*, 44.

74. Silbey, *Partisan Imperative*, chap. 8; Formisano, *Transformation of Political Culture*, 340; Gienapp, *Origins of the Republican Party*, 419–23.

75. From a speech by the Hon. Henry W. Davis of Maryland delivered in the U.S. House of Representatives, Jan. 6, 1857, and quoted in Cooper and Fenton, *American Politics*, 115–16.

76. *Boston Morning Journal*, June 5, 1857; *Boston Daily Advertiser*, June 12, 1857.

77. Holt, "Politics of Impatience," 320.

78. Gienapp, *Origins of the Republican Party*, 214–23; Baum, "Know-Nothingism and the Republican Majority," 970; Baum, *Civil War Party System*, 41.

79. Baum, "Know-Nothingism and the Republican Majority," 969–972.

80. Bean, "Party Transformation in Massachusetts," 365; John W. Foster to Banks, Dec. 8, 1857, Banks Papers; William S. Robinson, *Scrapbook* 3:93, Boston Public Library.

81. Gienapp, *Origins of the Republican Party*, 367, 445–46; Silbey, *Partisan Imperative*, 134–36, 164.

82. J. R. Pole, "Suffrage and Representation in Massachusetts: A Statistical Note," *Willian and Mary Quarterly* 14 (Oct. 1957): 590–92. For example, while turnouts in Massachusetts were plunging in the late 1850s, those in nearby New York were soaring. See Silbey, *Partisan Imperative*, 157.

83. Gienapp, *Origins of the Republican Party*, 356, 372.

Epilogue

1. Mass., *House Journal*, 1855, 1738.

2. Proponents of the traditional interpretation that party transformation in

antebellum America stemmed from sectional divisions over slavery include Foner, *Free Soil, Free Labor, Free Men* and Richard Sewell, *Ballots for Freedom: Antislavery Politics in the United States* (New York, 1970).

3. Among the leading members of the ethnocultural school are Lee Benson, *The Concept of Jacksonian Democracy: New York as a Test Case* (Princeton, 1961); Ronald P. Formisano, *The Birth of Mass Political Parties: Michigan, 1827–1861* (Princeton, 1971); Michael F. Holt, *Forging a Majority: The Formation of the Republican Party in Pittsburgh, 1848–1860* (New Haven, 1969); Paul Kleppner, *The Third Electoral System, 1853–1892: Parties, Voters, and Political Cultures* (Chapel Hill, N.C., 1979); and Silbey, *Partisan Imperative.*

4. Historians who have argued the case for economic determinism include Vernon L. Parrington, *Main Currents in American Thought*, 3 vols. (New York, 1927–30); Arthur M. Schlesinger, Jr., *The Age of Jackson* (Boston, 1945).

5. Dawley, *Industrial Revolution in Lynn*; Prude, *Industrial Order*; Wilentz, *Chants Democratic.*

6. In addition to V. O. Key, Jr., "A Theory of Critical Election," *Journal of Politics* 17 (1955): 3–18, see Burham, *Critical Elections*; Jerome M. Clubb, William H. Flanigan, and Nancy Zingale, *Partisan Realignment: Voters, Parties, and Government in American History* (Beverly Hills, Calif., 1980); and Sundquist, *Dynamics of the Party System.*

7. The above summary of the major historical schools of interpretation for party transformation in the 1850s is by no means complete. The most exhaustive examination of historiographical debate is Richard L. McCormick's *The Party Period and Public Policy: American Politics from the Age of Jackson to the Progressive Era* (New York, 1986), which contains an incisive synopsis and analysis of each school and a discussion of the major historical works contributing to each.

8. Everett to Fillmore, Dec. 16, 1854, Letterbooks, Everett Papers.

9. Congdon, *Reminiscences*, 144.

10. Richard Hofstadter, *The Age of Reform* (New York, 1955), 19–20; Formisano, *Transformation of Political Culture*, 341–43.

11. Prescott to George Bancroft, Nov. 18, 1854, George Bancroft Papers, MHS.

12. Everett to Caleb Cushing, Oct. 11, 1855, Letterbooks, Everett Papers; Congdon, *Reminiscences*, 150.

13. Hoar, *Autobiography* 1:196.

Index